WITH NAPOLEON IN RUSSIA

ARMAND DE CAULAINCOURT, DUKE OF VICENZA
1773-1827

Portrait by Gérard

From the collection of Mme. la Comtesse Gérard de Moustier

WITH NAPOLEON IN RUSSIA

The Memoirs of
General de Caulaincourt, Duke of Vicenza

FROM THE ORIGINAL MEM-
OIRS AS EDITED BY JEAN
HANOTEAU. ABRIDGED, EDITED,
AND WITH AN INTRODUC-
TION BY GEORGE LIBAIRE

WILLIAM MORROW AND COMPANY
NEW YORK

WITH NAPOLEON IN RUSSIA

CONTENTS

ILLUSTRATIONS

A Map of the Emperor's Route to Moscow
and the Retreat, with a sketch of the
crossing of the Beresina, faces page 400.

WITH NAPOLEON IN RUSSIA

INTRODUCTION

At all times in his career, though more particularly at the last, Napoleon I was a man of letters. He liked to believe that historical studies had given him the first clear vision of his destiny. Whether or not he was frank in this opinion, one thing is sure: Napoleon, who felt that he owed so much to professional historians, has done more than any of them to promote the reading of history for its own sake.

For us the record of his life has the appeal of every great story that ends: "If only . . ." The recital of Waterloo alone has given rise to countless speculations about what might have been, "if only"; and Waterloo is but the epilogue to the drama of *La Gloire*. No matter how often we read the tale of Napoleon's life, we find ourselves carrying into it the thought that perhaps this time there will be a different ending. In short, the life of Napoleon is a tragedy in the proper sense, making the heart beat faster, moving us to pity and terror—as well it may.

The Russian campaign of 1812 was the crisis of the Napoleonic tragedy. In that campaign nothing failed like success. "I beat the Russians every time," said the Emperor; "but that doesn't get me anywhere." There was to be an end, however; and nowhere, unless in Tolstoi's *War and Peace*, is the coming of that end accounted for so clearly as it is in the Memoirs of Armand de Caulaincourt, first Duke of Vicenza.

These Memoirs are the findings of a professional soldier, sitting in judgment upon the foremost soldier of fortune the world has known. But they are something more than that. They are the observations of a man of the Old Régime, whose lot had been cast in with the new Empire. The soldier who wrote them was a statesman as well—a diplomatist of the school of Talleyrand, but without any of that strange creature's womanish ways. He was also—and one often feels the lack of this quality in memorialists who were near Napoleon—an administrator of sufficient skill to comprehend the Emperor's plans, and to do justice to the recording of them. And finally, he was a man with physical energy enough to match, and on occasion to outdo, the Emperor's own.

For reasons that will be stated in due order, these commentaries, though written more than a century ago, were first published in 1933; and none of them has ever appeared before in English.

Armand-Augustin-Louis, Marquis de Caulaincourt in his own right, was born at Caulaincourt, near Saint-Quentin in Picardy, December 9, 1773, and died in Paris at the age of fifty-four, February 19, 1827. He was thus four years younger than Napoleon, whom he outlived by six.

The feudal tenure of Armand's family to the lands of Caulaincourt can be traced back to 1370 at least. He himself was the grandson and son of generals, and, with his younger brother Auguste, he was to complete the list of four Generals Caulaincourt in three successive generations. Tradition bound him, then, to the profession of arms; and his personal virtues were those of his caste, whose duty it was to improve their lands in peacetime and to be sparing of their men in time of war. This latter attribute, this concern for winning campaigns less by killing the enemy than by keeping his own men alive, was what chiefly distinguished the professional soldier from the soldier of fortune, howsoever talented. It was largely through the exercise of this concern, which with Caulaincourt was instinctive, that he was to retain Napoleon's esteem without ever enjoying his favour.

At fourteen, Armand Caulaincourt passed from the hands of his tutor into the ranks of the Royal cuirassiers. Eighteen months later, when the events of 1789 had converted his regiment into the Seventh Cavalry, Caulaincourt was brevetted second-lieutenant. His father, Lieutenant-General Gabriel-Louis de Caulaincourt, had subscribed to the ideas of the Revolution—an example that was followed by the rest of his family, none of whom emigrated. Pleading ill-health, Gabriel-Louis resigned from the army in the face of the uncertainties of 1792, and afterwards went into hiding. His elder son weathered the storm in garrison-duty with the National Guard, and later by serving under Kléber and Hoche in the Vendée. While on the way to join his regiment there in 'ninety-three, Armand was denounced as an aristocrat and thrown into prison. Fortunately the gaoler's wife was a woman whose poverty Caulaincourt's mother had once relieved. Armand made his escape, disguised in the gaoler's own clothes; and so the Western Army of the Republic missed losing a sub-lieutenant to the zeal of the Republican tribunal.

It would be needless here to give in detail the account of Caulaincourt's next few years. Suffice it to say that Hoche recommended his promotion which, however, was yet further delayed; that he was employed on two minor diplomatic errands which brought him to the notice of Talleyrand; and that when, under the Directory, promotion did come to him, it was not in Italy or Egypt but in the armies along the Rhine. Consequently, his promotion to colonel kept him engaged in a sector where the glamour of Bonaparte's first exploits was little felt and less appreciated. But even there, and especially by Caulaincourt, were felt the cross-currents of dissatisfaction that gave leeway to the Strong Man. Jourdan had fallen back before the Archduke Charles. The Directors, having pillaged the Treasury, were taxing the last private fortunes out of existence. The Duke of Enghien was in Paris, openly intriguing for the

Bourbons' return. As the century was closing with peace nowhere in sight, Armand wrote in a letter home:

"The time has passed for this ridiculous love of royalty.
Experience makes everyone think that the government offering
protection is the government to be preferred. Everyone is attached to his native land when it offers him security and defence. Unhappily, private passions ever take the place of true
love of country; the schemer displaces the honest man. From
that proceed these grievous disturbances which are wrecking
the public credit and destroying confidence. . . . As for our
armies, their courage is what it was, but no man is more than
human when his adversary is as brave as himself. . . . In a
word, Mother, let our legislators give security to our families—
let our parents look to them as to parents of their own—and
we shall be victorious again; but may peace be the reward of
our success. . . . Officers and men are at least what they were
before: they want nothing but leaders worthy of them."

One wonders what had become of Barras's censorship.

With the Consulate, Jourdan's place on the Rhine was taken
by Moreau. Peace followed shortly after the appointment of
that great strategist, so soon to be exiled; and Colonel Caulaincourt returned to Paris. Immediately, on his commander's
recommendation, he found himself entrusted with a diplomatic
mission to St. Petersburg. He went there to deliver a letter from
the First Consul to the Tsar Alexander I. The process required
six months. When he left Russia, Caulaincourt was given a
present from the Tsar—a box with Alexander's portrait on the
cover, studded with diamonds. As long as he lived, Armand
was to think of Alexander in terms of that likeness.

In August, 1802, Caulaincourt was named eighth aide-de-
camp to the First Consul. The number of Napoleon's personal
aides had been fixed at seven, but already the Consular entourage was taking on an Imperial tone. Caulaincourt was
added to the staff to give it a flavour of the great days at Ver-

sailles, where much of his childhood had been spent, and also
to show that the new order would care for the interests of men
of the Old Régime. The job was no sinecure, however. Napoleon's aides followed him wherever he went—a task that was
something of a career in itself—and at any moment the aide
in special attendance was likely to be saddled with whatever
remote or difficult commission there happened to turn up. After
a year of it, and on the eve of his promotion to brigadier,
Armand wrote to his aunt: "We don't travel, . . . we race—
and not merely from one spot to another but from one handsome
action to the next."

Caulaincourt was twenty-nine, a veteran who had seen fifteen
years' service, had made thirteen campaigns and had been twice
wounded. His advancement had not been rapid, as careers went
in those days.

The young aide-de-camp soon discovered that the pursuit of
Glory might lead to actions far from handsome. He found out,
too, that in the court of a dictator the Master's conduct must be
viewed as exceptional, not as a criterion. The learning of these
two lessons left Caulaincourt still wishful to protect, as he
worded it, "the interests of the Emperor's peculiar Glory"; but
by the time he had learnt them no other course was open to him.

The Enghien affair, and the part he was compelled to take
in it, was a nightmare to him for the rest of his life and plagued
his descendants as far down as 1890. Even to this day Frenchmen breathe faster when that affair is mentioned—perhaps
because it was one of the few instances of individual terrorism
that Napoleon appears to have allowed himself.

Henri de Bourbon, Duke of Enghien, was seized by French
dragoons at Ettenheim, in Baden, at five in the morning of
March 15, 1804. His kidnapping—or "extradition," as it was
called—was explained on the ground that he had been engaged
in a widespread plot to murder the First Consul. He was smug-

gled across the French border, held at Strasbourg until just after midnight of March 17, and then sent under guard to Paris, presumedly for safe-keeping. There he was turned over to a military tribunal, convicted of treason, and executed in the moat at Vincennes at three in the morning of the twenty-first. Caulaincourt, meanwhile, had been in command of a similar raiding expedition into Baden. He arrested a number of suspected émigrés there, but never saw the Duke of Enghien. However, the order to send the Duke to Paris was relayed through Caulaincourt's hands. Bourbon partisans made the most of that fact. They accused Caulaincourt of treachery to his class, of deliberate complicity in the Duke's death, and even of having been present at the execution. As Mme. de Rémusat put it: "Public opinion was roused against M. de Caulaincourt; in certain quarters, it let the Master off easily to crush the aide-de-camp."

Actually, Caulaincourt was sent to Baden because he was aide-de-camp on duty when the second expedition was projected. He did not return to Paris until the evening after the shooting at Vincennes. He first heard of it from Josephine when he reported at Malmaison; and he wept openly with chagrin at finding how he had been used. It is said that for a moment he was at the point of taking his own life. From that time on he treated Napoleon with what the diplomats call "distinguished courtesy," and always made it a point, moreover, to tax the great man frankly with what he thought were the motives behind each avowal of policy.

For his part, Napoleon seems not to have regretted Caulaincourt's exposure to the assault of Bourbon propagandists. Again according to Mme. de Rémusat, Josephine took her husband to task for having added to the scandal of the Enghien affair by letting a former aristocrat be involved in it. "And what of that?" he answered. "If Caulaincourt is compromised, there's no great harm; he will only serve me the better on that account."

That summer Napoleon became Emperor of the French, and

on July 10 Caulaincourt was appointed Grand Ecuyer. The Master of Horse was lodged by the Crown, received the first orders of the day, pulled out the Emperor's chair for him at meals, had charge of all Imperial equipages, despatch riders and orderly officers. He saw to all journeys of the Household, and to the administration of headquarters in time of war, when also he rode into battle with the Emperor, prepared to surrender his horse to him in case of need. Thus Caulaincourt was organizer of the transportation service and planner of the schedules that made possible those sudden and disconcerting appearances of Napoleon where he was least expected to be. Thus also he viewed the great battles of Ulm and Austerlitz, Jena, Eylau, Friedland and afterwards Borodino, from his post at the Emperor's left hand. Incidentally, he supervised the Imperial stud-farm at Saint-Cloud, where were trained those famous chargers Coquet, Turcoman, Courtois, Emir and the forty-odd others, of which Napoleon often exhausted three or more in a day—as he did even at Borodino, when he is supposed to have been ill.

In 1805 Caulaincourt was raised to general of division. And in that year he learnt the second of the two lessons mentioned above. Napoleon was laying plans for the divorce. The procedure would cause as much scandal of that kind as a parvenu dynast could afford to have in his Court. Consequently, when Caulaincourt fell in love with Adrienne de Canisy, one of Josephine's ladies-in-waiting, a married woman whose husband had left her, he discovered that the affair was hopeless. The Emperor would not hear of Mme. de Canisy's divorcing a husband who was her own uncle, with whom she had been forced into marriage at thirteen in order to keep the family properties united. It seems likely that the great man's opposition to Caulaincourt's affair added not a little to the Grand Ecuyer's resolution to pursue it. Until then his successes with women had been noteworthy, even in that society of inveterate amorists.

But after 1805 he was devoted to Mme. de Canisy alone. Not until 1814, however, in the last days before Elba, when all was lost, when he had nothing else to give, and when Caulaincourt almost alone of the glittering troupe had not betrayed him, would Napoleon consent to the marriage.

Characteristically, it was through this affair that Talleyrand attempted, and with some measure of success, to shape the political opinions of the Grand Ecuyer. Talleyrand represented himself as Mme. de Canisy's friend. He let it be understood that he was using his influence with the Emperor to further the match. There was of course nothing that he could really do; but he could enlist the outspoken Caulaincourt's support against his own rivals for office. More than that, he could help to keep Caulaincourt in a state of mind which would make the young diplomat eager to get through with any embassy the Emperor might send him on. In his eagerness to be called home, Caulaincourt would then oppose Napoleon's grandiose foreign policy. Instead, he would advocate Talleyrand's pet doctrine of the Balance of Power, with no French intervention north of the Rhine. These terms, as Talleyrand foresaw, were the worst that France could be made to accept in case the Emperor fell. He wished to be on record as having advocated them all along. To Caulaincourt, on the other hand, this moderate foreign policy seemed the best way to protect the Emperor's interests—if it could be followed before circumstances made its pursuit unavoidable. Caulaincourt therefore tried to curb Napoleon, in the heyday of *La Gloire,* by advocating the course that was to destroy him when it was pursued too late. Why that counsel of moderation was bound to fail, these Memoirs show clearly enough. But Talleyrand stood to win no matter how the cat jumped.

Such, then, were the forces at work in Caulaincourt's mind in the summer of 1807, when the Tsar Alexander and the

Emperor Napoleon met on the raft at Tilsit and agreed to share the world between them. The scene is familiar: the old drawing in black-and-white has shown us the lords of East and West, advancing on tiptoe as though they were walking on eggs, hats off and arms outstretched, to embrace each other. It would seem that for once, though briefly, Napoleon was genuinely impressed by a man other than the one his mirror showed him. It is small wonder that five years earlier the youthful Caulaincourt had been dazzled, too.

The November after Tilsit, Caulaincourt was sent as ambassador extraordinary to St. Petersburg. Alexander was still in his early phase of liberal indecision, the lone and lofty Romantic at the head of a vast folk to whom the Age of Reason was coming late. He professed to see in Napoleon his elder brother in Romance, the man whom Reason, speaking with the voice of an enlightened people, had made her chosen instrument. Between them, they would break England's unreasonable monopoly of world trade, bring peace and plenty to the Continent—and meanwhile, if Russia should find occasion to seize Constantinople, on what grounds could the favourite child of Reason object? Napoleon's enthusiasm, on the contrary, was already cooling. Not until St. Helena, perhaps, would he speak of the Tsar as "a Greek of the decadent régime"; but already he was prepared to say: "It would be difficult to have more intelligence than the Emperor Alexander, yet I find a piece missing there, somewhere—and I can't discover what."

Here plainly was a balancing of power more precarious than any that a Talleyrand could imagine. Caulaincourt wrote his misgivings home to the Emperor as freely as he would have spoken them face to face. The prospect frightened him, even as he was charmed anew by Alexander's fine familiarity. He had gone to Russia against his will, and the Tsar's personal friendship was what chiefly reconciled him to remaining there. He was able, however, to live in the grand style, since it was part of his mission to impress the Muscovites by doing so. He hired the best chef in Russia and gave dinners with four hundred covers; and he compelled the Austrian ambassador to let him have precedence, on the ground that the Imperial title of the Hapsburgs was newer than Napoleon's. He had been given two hundred and fifty thousand francs to establish himself with; his salary was eight hundred thousand francs. And in March, 1808, he was decreed the title of Duke of Vicenza. Napoleon's selection of that title for him seems to have been quite arbitrary. Unlike those given to many of the marshals—titles which Caulaincourt, as a man of the older nobility, often used when the Emperor forgot them—his title had no reference to his military career.[1] It was of the sort given to officers of administration, who shared Italian and Peninsular honours amongst them, seemingly, at random. Thus Cambacérès drew Parma, and Fouché—shades of Horace Walpole!—was made Duke of Otranto.

The exaltations of Tilsit were followed, in the autumn of 1808, by the anticlimax of Erfurt. After that conference the two monarchs parted full of mutual distrust. Napoleon was growing impatient with his brother Alexander's dilatory nature —and besides, his brother had shown himself unwilling to see French and Russian troops co-operate unless he could have a share in the high command. This was unthinkable to the man who had said: "I go accompanied by the god of Fortune and of War." The Continental System was not working well, either; England was far from starvation; and Alexander was beginning to complain because Napoleon winked at French violations of the blockade, yet insisted that Russian ports be closed tighter than ever. Ironically, it now fell to Caulaincourt to try to patch up the alliance by arranging a marriage between Napoleon and one of the Tsar's sisters. Nothing came of it; but the ambas-

---

[1] Biographical notes on the chief titled persons of the narrative will be found on page 403.

sador managed the negotiations with such address that his master was spared an embarrassing rebuff.

After the summer of 1809 Napoleon never wrote to Caulaincourt except formally, through official channels. This was a strong hint for the ambassador to reply only in kind. Talleyrand had slipped from power, to be replaced later by the Duke of Bassano, Maret—that statesman who provoked a contemporary to remark that there was only one man in France stupider than Maret, and that was the Duke of Bassano. At the close of 1810 Mme. de Canisy was deprived of her Court duties and forbidden to enter Paris. Caulaincourt demanded his recall. He had long wished to leave St. Petersburg, where the Tsar, though affable as ever, would no longer discuss affairs with him. But by that time Napoleon could not replace an ambassador of Caulaincourt's known opinions until he was ready to make an open declaration of French policy. Instead, he continued to keep his representative in the dark.

In February, 1811, however, the Emperor felt that the time had come to declare himself. He then wrote to Alexander that the Duke of Vicenza was being called home because of his "poor state of health." Caulaincourt, safe, sound and decorated with the Grand Cross of St. Andrew, arrived at Paris on June 5. His place at St. Petersburg had been taken by General Lauriston, the artillery expert. And so it went, in a fashion that can only be left for the Memoirs to relate.

In 1821 Caulaincourt drew his will, stipulating that a considerable sum be put aside to finance the writing of a history of his life and times. He was living in complete retirement, broken in health and without access to the Bourbon Court. In the years after the return from Russia, he had twice served Napoleon as Minister for Foreign Affairs. Alone, he had negotiated at Châtillon, trying to save the Emperor's crown for him. He had been Napoleon's informal ambassador from Fon-

tainebleau to the victorious leaders in Paris; and it was to him
that the fallen Emperor had clung after taking poison. He had
gone to meet the returning exile, had served in the ministry
during the Hundred Days, and thus had closed public life to
himself forever. Now, with his wife and two sons, he spent
the winters on his estate, which Alexander, playing the generous
conqueror, had prevented the Prussians from selling off at auction after Waterloo. In summer he went to Plombières to seek
relief from his malady, which in time proved to be cancer of
the stomach.

No memorialist had to be found for him, however. During
the 1820's several of his associates in the Russian campaign
published their memoirs; and it appeared that nearly all of
them, but notably Gourgaud and Fain, had written under the
inspiration of Maret, Duke of Bassano. This was more than
Caulaincourt could stand. He felt in better health, he found
himself being misrepresented—and there, in his elaborate files,
were copious notes of what he and the Emperor had said and
done in the days of *La Gloire*. Without change or suppression,
he had jotted it all down as soon as the great man's study-door
had slammed to, or beside bivouac fires outside the Imperial
tent, or while the Emperor napped and the sleepless Grand
Ecuyer kept watch during the long flight home from Poland.
He would put his own notes in order, link them up just as they
stood, and let posterity judge, simply on the evidence thus presented, between him and Maret.

Caulaincourt's method was happily chosen. To-day the dis-
tinctions between him and the Duke of Bassano are a matter for
formal scholarship. But what Caulaincourt has left us is the
report of one of those advisers, useful, fascinated, yet without
servility, such as the Strong Man sometimes keeps by him. At
the crisis of Napoleon's career, when there could have been no
possibility of clairvoyance after the fact, Caulaincourt spoke
at the Emperor's elbow like the voice of history. The sounder

his advice, the more readily it was disregarded; and in preserving Napoleon's replies, Caulaincourt has given us the self-portrait of the man who was dictator *par excellence*.

How, then, have these Memoirs gone so long unpublished? In large part, they were withheld for the very reason that led the first Duke of Vicenza to compile them. There had been an alliance between his descendants and the Duke of Bassano's family. Moreover, sentiment about the Enghien affair, and therefore about the Grand Ecuyer's part in it, lay outside the realm of reason. Publication would but have reawakened unhappy echoes. And it may be assumed, too, that the laws of libel were a factor to be reckoned with. The working of libel laws is as unaccountable in France as it is elsewhere; and for a long while an enterprising advocate might have done wonders with some of Napoleon's remarks. The large number of First Empire commentaries that did not appear until the 1880's is evidence enough to support this surmise.

An edition of the Memoirs was being projected when the World War put a stop to it. The Germans were at Saint-Quentin. The original manuscript was walled up for safe-keeping in the conservatory of the Caulaincourt château. In 1917, for some strategic reason or other, the château was mined by the invaders and totally destroyed. Nothing was left but a few standing columns and a rubbish-heap.

It was not until some years after the War that another edition was begun. Necessarily, this had to be prepared from a document of less certain authenticity than the original—a copyist's work, which had been preserved in Paris. Only in August, 1933, when the edition had gone to press, did the original draft come to light. Disordered, water-stained and enclosed in a battered tin chest, it had survived the bombing. When the ruins had been sorted over, the chest was left for worthless in a heap of tile and other such fragments. There it was discovered by M. Beloborodoff, the architect who had undertaken to rebuild the château. The original, with its revisions in Caulaincourt's own hand, was thereupon put in order and compared with the copy in press. The differences were trifling, and there was time to note them in an appendix.

Caulaincourt was still working on the Memoirs when his last illness overtook him. As he left them, they form two independent parts. One deals with his embassy and the Russian campaign, as hereafter presented, and the other covers the events from the spring of 1813 through Napoleon's first abdication. The present volume has been prepared from the work of M. Jean Hanoteau, whose admirable French edition of the entire manuscript has put all confirmed students of the period, and the American editor in particular, in his debt. M. Hanoteau has been drawn upon freely for notes to elucidate the text, and for the materials of this essay. The text has been divided into sections and chapters as the nature of it suggested. Some slight transpositions have been made to preserve chronology; and the material has been cut only to avoid repetition or the recital of events in which Caulaincourt had no part.

George Libaire

PART I

PREPARATION

CHAPTER I

AMBASSADOR'S RETURN

THE events in Europe leading up to 1812 had so great an influence on those which followed later, by placing the balance of Europe's destinies into the hands of Russia, that I have felt it would be valuable to preserve the notes which I made regarding various circumstances of those days. In writing them my sole motive was to keep an account of my life, my impressions, and my conduct. Since then I have come to regard them as indispensable material for the completion of the official part of my correspondence as ambassador, and even, it may well be, for the history of that great epoch.

My aim will be fulfilled if my notes help also to formulate opinion on the character and the political views of the Emperor Napoleon.

My notes were made everywhere, at my desk and in camp, every day and at all times of day; they are the work of every moment. I have touched up nothing and disguised nothing, because although there were moments when the man showed himself, it was the demigod whom one recognized most often. More than once the thought occurred to me that this journal, written under the very eyes of the Emperor, might fall into his hands; but that reflection did not check my pen. This fact is an answer to those who have claimed that men could neither think nor speak nor write under his reign, and that the truth made him an irreconcilable enemy. No doubt the truth chilled his good will, but his strong and lofty character raised him above all criticisms made in good faith. I was confident that,

3

as my notes were only the exact record of what I had said to him, they would seem to him injurious only if I published them as an attack on his policy and his fame.

If these pages should some day be read and severity imputed to me, I hope that allowance will be made for the happenings under the influence of which they were penned.

The Emperor was at Saint-Cloud. By eleven o'clock I was there. [June 5, 1811.] His Majesty received me coldly, and at once began heatedly to enumerate his imaginary grievances against the Tsar Alexander, but without reproaching me personally. He spoke of the ukase prohibiting foreign imports,[1] and of the admission of neutral and American ships into Russian ports, which, he said, was an infringement of the Continental System. He went on to say that the Tsar was treacherous, that he was arming to make war on France. The Emperor repeated all the fantastic stories which, to please him, were fabricated in Danzig, in the Duchy of Warsaw, and even in the north of Germany—stories the accuracy of which had been disproved time and again, sometimes by means of investigations carried out on the spot, sometimes even by the march of events.

"Admit frankly," said the Emperor Napoleon, "that it is Alexander who wants to make war on me."

"No, Sire," I replied once again; "I would stake my life on his not firing the first shot or being the first to cross his frontiers."

"We're agreed, then," the Emperor went on; "because I have no intention of going into Russia, nor any wish for a war or the re-establishment of Poland."

[1] The ukase of December 31, 1810, which prohibited the entry of foreign merchandise and silks, was intended to remedy the falling rate of exchange brought about by the constant drain of capital abroad to pay for imported goods, Russia being unable to export anything herself. It was also intended to encourage the development of home industries.—Caulaincourt's note.

"Then, Sire, you ought to explain your intentions, so that everyone may know why Your Majesty's troops are concentrated in Danzig and the north of Prussia."

The Emperor made no answer to this. He spoke of the Russian nobles who, in the event of a war, would fear for their palaces, and, after a good battle, would force the Tsar Alexander to conclude a peace.

"Your Majesty is mistaken," I replied, and repeated to the Emperor words used by the Tsar which had greatly impressed me in the course of certain private conversations I had with him after the arrival of M. Lauriston,[2] when my position no longer had any political significance; words which were merely a more emphatic expression of what he had led me to understand some time before. They impressed me so much that I noted them down on returning home, and quote them here with the certainty that, to the best of my knowledge, my recollection of them was substantially correct:

"If the Emperor Napoleon makes war on me," the Tsar Alexander said to me, "it is possible, even probable, that we shall be defeated, assuming that we fight. But that will not mean that he can dictate a peace. The Spaniards have often been defeated; and they are not beaten, nor have they submitted. But they are not so far away from Paris as we are, and have neither our climate nor our resources to help them. We shall take no risks. We have plenty of room; and our standing army is well organized, which means, as the Emperor Napoleon has admitted, that we need never accept a dictated peace, whatever reverses we may suffer. What is more, in such circumstances the victor is forced to accept the terms of the vanquished. The Emperor Napoleon made a remark to this effect to Tchernychev[3] in Vienna after the battle of Wagram.

[2] Caulaincourt's successor as French Ambassador to St. Petersburg.

[3] The Emperor Alexander's aide-de-camp. He was present at the battle of Wagram, and stood beside Napoleon, who decorated him with the Legion of Honour.

He would not have made peace then if Austria had not kept an army intact. Results have to keep pace with his thoughts, because, being often absent from France, he is always anxious to return there. This is the teaching of a Master. I shall not be the first to draw my sword, but I shall be the last to sheathe it. The Spaniards have proved that lack of perseverance has been the undoing of all the States on which your master has made war. The Emperor Napoleon's remark to Tchernychev, in the latest war with Austria, shows clearly enough that the Austrians could have obtained better terms if they had been more persevering. People don't know how to suffer. If the fighting went against me, I should retire to Kamtchatka rather than cede provinces and sign, in my capital, treaties that were really only truces. Your Frenchman is brave; but long privations and a bad climate wear him down and discourage him. Our climate, our winter, will fight on our side. With you, marvels only take place where the Emperor is in personal attendance; and he cannot be everywhere, he cannot be absent from Paris year after year."

The Emperor listened to me with the closest attention, even with some astonishment. He appeared to be greatly preoccupied, and kept silent for a while. I thought I had made a deep impression on him, since his face, his whole bearing, which hitherto had manifested only an extreme severity, became open and friendly. He seemed to wish to encourage me to go on, not only by looks but by the questions he put. He spoke of society in Russia, of the army, of the administration, and even referred to the Tsar Alexander without manifesting his usual ill-humour at mention of this name. In fact, the Emperor gave every indication at this moment of being kindly disposed towards me, and referred appreciatively to the manner in which I had served him. I assured him that he was mistaken about the Tsar Alexander and about Russia; that it was of the utmost importance not to base his conclusions about that country on what certain persons told him, or about the army on what he had seen at Friedland; that, having been threatened for a year, it had been possible for the Russians to take account of all eventualities, particularly to take account of the possibility of our enjoying immediate successes.

After listening to me attentively, the Emperor began enumerating the troops and general resources at his disposal. When he reverted to this theme I realized that all hope of peace was at an end, since it was enumerations of this kind which, more than anything, intoxicated him. Indeed he ended by telling me that one good battle would knock the bottom out of my friend Alexander's fine resolutions, not to mention his sand fortifications, alluding to the defence works which were being thrown up along the banks of the Dwina and at Riga.

He spoke of the situation in Spain, and complained irritably of his generals there and the setbacks they had suffered, expressing his opinion that this vexatious state of affairs was due to the incompetence of the King, his brother [Joseph of Spain], and of the French generals, and announcing his determination to make an end of it. He tried to persuade me that he could do this whenever he was so minded, but that the English would then attack elsewhere, perhaps even in France. Thus, he concluded, it was just as well—perhaps a positive advantage—for them to be in Portugal. Then he returned to the Tsar Alexander.

"He is fickle and feeble," he said once again.

"He is obstinate," I replied. "His conciliatory nature makes him give way easily when he does not feel the issues at stake to be particularly important; but nonetheless he draws a line beyond which he will not be pushed."

"He has the Greek character—he is untrustworthy," the Emperor repeated yet again.

"I would not suggest," I said, "that he has always spoken everything that was in his mind; but whatever he has deigned to say to me has proved correct, and whatever promises he has made to Your Majesty through me he has kept."

"Alexander is ambitious. There is some hidden purpose which he hopes to achieve through war. He wants war, I tell you. Otherwise, why should he refuse every arrangement I put forward? He has some secret purpose. Can't you see through him? No, he has larger motives than Poland and Oldenburg."

"These motives, and the fact that your army is at Danzig, are in themselves enough to explain the line he has taken; though naturally, like every government in Europe, he is uneasy about the change Your Majesty has made in your policy since Tilsit, and, more particularly, since the Peace of Vienna."

"What has all that to do with Alexander? It does not affect him. Have I not told him to take Finland, Wallachia and Moldavia? Have I not suggested that he should partition Turkey? Did I not give him three hundred millions for the Austrian war?"

"Yes, Sire; but you would not expect such enticements to blind him to the fact that Your Majesty has since then marked out a quite new policy, whose execution begins in Poland— that is, in Russian territory."

"Like him, you are simply dreaming! Once more—I do not want to go to war with him; but he must fulfil the commitments which he has undertaken, and enforce an embargo on English trade. What has he to fear from changes in my policy? What do such changes matter to a country like Russia, away at the back of beyond?"

"On that point he has never explained himself to me."

"I don't prevent him from extending his dominions in Asia, or even in Turkey, if he wants to, so long as he does not touch Constantinople. He is vexed that I should hold Holland. That galls him because he needs foreign loans."

"The reunion of the Hanseatic towns, the establishment of

the Grand Duchy of Frankfort, which means that Your Majesty intends to keep Italy; the giving of Hanover to Westphalia— all these changes, made in times of peace and simply announced by decree, alienate England and put obstacles in the way of making peace with her. Therefore they conflict with Russia's best interests. Even so, it will not be on that account that she goes to war."

"And must I be dictated to by the English and by my brother [Louis of Holland?] just to please Alexander? Rumi- antsof[4] knows quite well that before taking these steps I did everything in my power to induce England to make peace. Labouchère has been to London several times, even on behalf of the Dutch. Am I to allow the north of Germany to be flooded with English goods?"

"Had one merely threatened to put those measures in force, that would have been good policy. The execution of those measures, however, plus the movement of whole armies to- wards the north—instead of a few battalions to put pressure on the customs officers—has aroused apprehension."

"You see no further than Alexander; and he is merely frightened. It is these very policies to which you object that are taking all the heart out of the English, and will force them to make peace."

This conversation continued for some time longer. The Emperor jumped from one question to another, and, at long intervals, returned to the same questions, no doubt to see if I kept to the same answers. To judge from his air of preoccu- pation, and from the long silences which broke up our five hours of conversation, it looked as if he were giving more serious consideration to the matters under discussion than per- haps he had ever given them before. After one of these long silences, he said, "It is the Austrian marriage which has set us

[4] The Russian Foreign Minister.

at variance. The Tsar Alexander was angry because I did not marry his sister."

I took the liberty of reminding the Emperor that, as I had formerly reported to him, Russia was not at all eager for such a marriage; that, although the Emperor had not been able to refuse outright to lend himself to the project, he would never have given way on the question of religion; that in any case there would have been a year's delay, even if the Tsar had been able to obtain his mother's consent; in short, that he had not committed himself in regard to the matter, and that Russia was rather pleased than otherwise to learn of the unexpected Austrian marriage having taken place,[5] notwithstanding our somewhat unceremonious manner of going back on the proposals of our own making—proposals which, happily, had not been accepted, but which, had they been accepted, would have made my position decidedly embarrassing.

"I have forgotten the details of the affair," the Emperor replied; "but Russia was certainly angry about our rapprochement with Austria."

I pointed out that in fact, as everyone had realized at the time, and as was proved by conversations with the Emperor and Count Rumiantsof when the first overtures in regard to this matter were made, the immediate reaction in Petersburg was an agreeable sense of relief at the removal of a very delicate question between the French and Russian governments, and a still more delicate question between the Tsar and his mother and family.

The Emperor Napoleon again repeated that he desired neither war nor the re-establishment of Poland, but that an understanding in the matter of neutral shipping and other differences was essential.

[5] "Everyone's very satisfied here; the master and the rest of them."— Caulaincourt to Talleyrand, St. Petersburg, February 25, 1810.

"If Your Majesty really desires an understanding, it will not be hard to bring one about," I said.

"Are you sure about that?" the Emperor asked.

"Quite sure," was my reply. "But reasonable proposals must be put forward."

"What proposals?" the Emperor said, and urged me to enumerate them.

"Your Majesty knows as well as I do, and has known for long enough, the causes of the present estrangement; and you know better than I do what you are prepared to do to remedy it."

"But what? What does he want me to do?"

"In regard to trade between the two countries, an arrangement should be made on a basis of reciprocal benefits, and a similar arrangement for merchant shipping in general. The admission of neutral ships into Russian ports should be countenanced, as long as we go on selling licences and allowing licenced vessels into French ports. The Prince of Oldenburg should be provided for in such a way that he is not, as at Erfurt, entirely dependent on you. An arrangement should be made about Danzig, another about Prussia, and so on. . . ."

When the Emperor saw that I was touching on political matters the discussion of which would force him to commit himself probably more than he wished to, he said that M. Lauriston had been made responsible for the carrying out of this policy—that I ought to take a holiday.

I begged His Majesty to let me say one thing more.

"Go on," the Emperor said.

"It is for you, Sire, to decide whether there is to be peace or war. May I beseech Your Majesty, when you make your choice between the certain good of the one and the hazards of the other, to take full account of your own welfare and of the welfare of France."

"You speak like a Russian," replied the Emperor.

"On the contrary, like a good Frenchman—like one of Your Majesty's most faithful servants."

"I repeat, I do not want war; but I cannot prevent the Poles from wanting me and expecting me. Davout and Rapp report that the Lithuanians are furious with the Russians; and that they are constantly sending delegates to them to urge us on, press us to make up our minds."

"You are being misled, Sire," was my reply.

I explained to the Emperor that, of the governments which had partitioned Poland, the Russian government was by its nature best suited to the Polish nobility; that they had been well treated by the Tsar Paul, and even better treated by Alexander; that I had met many land-owners from Polish Russia, and had found that, while of course they regretted their lost national independence, they had little stomach for a new venture to recover it which might not, even if it succeeded, involve Poland's being reinstated as an independent power; that the example of the Duchy of Warsaw, whose situation, from their point of view, was far from satisfactory, had not turned them in our favour so much as His Majesty thought; that the rivalries persisting between the great Polish families, no less than the natural instability of the Polish character, would always hinder their common action. I added that the Emperor ought not to shut his eyes to the fact that it was only too well understood in Europe nowadays that, when he concerned himself with the affairs of a country, it was to serve his own rather than its interests.

"You think so, do you?"

"Yes, Sire," I replied.

"You don't believe in spoiling me," he said jokingly. "It's time to go to dinner," he added, and withdrew.

Thus ended a conversation which had lasted for five hours and left me with no hope that peace would be maintained in Europe.

Later, I saw the Duke of Bassano [6] once more. He assured me, as the Emperor had done, that there was no question of wanting war; that Petersburg's fears were groundless, and that the Emperor was not prepared now to reverse any of the measures he had thought it necessary to take.

Henceforth I had small hope of seeing the Emperor change his policy; nevertheless I did not allow myself to be discouraged. The situation in Spain, bad though it was, might precipitate events which would induce a different political outlook. For two months past the tendency had been to carry on less agitation amongst the Poles, and to restrain the activities of generals and secret agents in Germany. The Emperor's views remained, I think, the same; but the probability is that the course of events in Spain, and a realization of the probable consequences of his prospective policy and his vast undertaking, made him somewhat indecisive. Ostensibly, the government's attitude was less aggressive, its object being to make the adoption of a pacific policy possible if developments made such a policy necessary, or if its wisdom became so apparent that the party favouring it triumphed. Meanwhile, military preparations were completed; and no real steps were taken to prevent the outbreak of war.

After my interview with the Emperor, it was some considerable time before we had any private conversation. My position was uncertain. In public he treated me well enough. I did not cease my protests against the exile of Mme. de C—.[7]

[6] Hugues-Bernard Maret, created Duke of Bassano by Napoleon. Minister for Foreign Affairs, 1811.

[7] Adrienne-Hervé-Louise de Carbonnel de Canisy, 1785-1876. Appointed lady-in-waiting to Josephine, 1805, and later to Marie Louise. Deserted by her husband, to whom she had been married at thirteen, she now wished to divorce him and marry Caulaincourt. But Napoleon, who feared that further divorces at Court would add scandal to his own, had refused consent; and so Mme. de Canisy had been in exile since the close of 1810.

Though I worried him with letters and petitions, the Emperor avoided speaking to me personally about the matter. At last, however, he granted me an audience and promised that she should be recalled, but without definitely authorizing it. I continued with my campaign, until, having been told by Duroc at my request that unless he kept this promise I should ask to be retired, His Majesty once more promised to allow Mme. de C— to return, and even obligingly said that she should resume her duties at the Court, which was more than I had ventured to ask for. But next day it was clear that the Emperor had tacitly put a price on this mark of his favour, because, when I refused his request to tell Prince Kurakin[8] that in my opinion the Emperor had no intention of re-establishing Poland nor any wish to see it re-established, and that he stood by the alliance and was arming only because Russia had mobilized, his promise to recall Mme. de C— remained unfulfilled, despite the fact that His Majesty had twice invited me to dine with him, and for eight days treated me in such a way as to suggest that he held me in great favour. During this time he had several long conversations with me at Saint-Cloud, and once, after dinner, at Bagatelle. In each case the conversation was about Russia.

The Emperor continued to assure me that he had no desire for war, and really had small regard for the Poles. "A trivial people," he said, "and a State difficult to shape to any useful purpose. If the king I give them does not happen to suit, everything will go badly. And it is difficult to make a good choice. My family does not back me up. They are all insanely ambitious, ruinously extravagant, and devoid of talent." For the rest, the remarks about Russian affairs in the course of my first audience with the Emperor on arriving in Paris were more or less repeated.

The Emperor's real desire was for me to persuade Prince

[8] Russian Ambassador to France from 1808 to 1812.

Kurakin that there had been a mutual misunderstanding; that both sides had become irritated without knowing exactly why; that he had no intention of attacking Russia, and only stood out for the upholding of the Continental System so far as it was directed against England, and that therefore a consideration of ways and means of upholding it, and an adjustment of existing differences, were necessary. But when I approached fundamentals, and began to discuss in detail the mutual concessions whereby this object might be realized, the Emperor changed the subject. Since it was clear enough that he had not really altered his plans, but had, at the most, merely postponed their execution, and that all he wanted of me was that I should allay Russia's suspicions so that he might gain time, I avoided becoming his intermediary, and begged the Emperor to entrust M. Lauriston with any communications he might wish to make to the Russian government. This suggestion greatly displeased him, and brought our conversation to a summary conclusion.

Henceforth the Emperor, besides persecuting my friends, inflicted on me every sort of vexation which he could inflict on a State official, even to the extent of withholding payments to which I was entitled. He let slip no occasion to make me feel the weight of his displeasure, and replied to my complaints about my financial claims by pleading ignorance of the matter. My renewed solicitation to the Emperor in regard to Mme. de C—'s exile met with no success, no matter whether I broached it verbally, or by letter, or through the mediation of Duroc. Finally, I again raised the question of my retirement with the Grand Marshal.

"Less than ever is this the moment to take such a step," he said to me. "You will lose your friends and ruin yourself. Have patience, and things will straighten out. Just now the Emperor is annoyed with you; but he holds you in esteem; he

is even fond of you. He takes a great interest in Mme. de
C—. Things will straighten out, I tell you, if you do not lose
your head and put yourself in the wrong. It is absurd of you
to take the Russian business so much to heart. We can do
nothing about it. Since you cannot hope to change the Emperor's plans, why irritate him? He has his point of view; he
is aiming at some objective of which we know nothing. You
can be certain that his policy is more farseeing than ours. In
short, I strongly advise you as a friend to postpone your plans
for retirement."

He continued in this strain for a long time. But discussing
the same topic a few days later, the Emperor gave him reason
to hope for a definite change in the near future. Duroc, who
brought me this good news, again made me promise to be
patient, and pointed out that as a soldier I could not leave the
service before peace was concluded. He repeated that the
Emperor would come round in time; that he was bitter, but
always spoke of me with esteem.

Realizing that I was achieving nothing by this means, I
addressed myself officially to the Minister of Police, the Duke
of Rovigo, who broached the question frankly with the Emperor,
pointing out that there was no reason for continuing an act of
severity which was making a bad impression, even from the
political point of view. But he obtained no satisfaction on this
occasion.

It was at this period, I think, that the Emperor summoned
one of his ministers [9] to Saint-Cloud. After a few minutes of
general business conversation, he said to him: "Let us go for
a stroll." When they reached a place on the terrace whence it
was possible to see anyone approaching, and where no one

[9] Identifiable as Lacuée Cessac, head of the ordnance department since
January 3, 1810.

could overhear them, he went on, "There is something I want you to do of which I have not spoken to a soul—not even to any of my ministers. In any case it has nothing to do with them. I have decided on a great expedition. I shall need horses and transport on a large scale. The men I shall get easily enough; but the difficulty is to prepare transport facilities. I shall need an immense amount of transport because I shall be starting from the Niemen, and I intend to operate over large distances and in different directions. This is why I need your help, and secrecy."

The minister remarked that the project would involve considerable expenditure; that he would carry out his part with despatch and all possible discretion; but that he could not prevent people talking when they saw waggons being assembled, and so on and so forth.

The Emperor, replying sharply to his first remark, said:

"Come to the Tuileries the next time I go there. I'll show you four hundred millions in gold.[10] Do not let the question of expense check you. We'll meet any outlay that will be needful."

Continuing the talk, the Emperor elaborated his policy, which was based on the necessity of crushing England by crushing the only Continental power still strong enough to join forces with her against him. He spoke of the usefulness of isolating the Russians from European affairs, and of establishing in Central Europe a state which should act as a barrier against invasions from the North, adding that the moment was opportune; that later there would be no time for such an expedition; and that it was essential to strike this last blow, in order to achieve a general settlement and years of peace and of prosperity for us and our children after all these years of glory, but of weariness and discomfort as well.

[10] Actually there was at this time about three hundred and eighty millions in the cellars of the Tuileries.—Caulaincourt's note.

One evening at a Court function [Tuileries, August 15, 1811] the Emperor came up to Prince Kurakin near the throne. He had a long conversation with him, and spoke so loudly that those about His Majesty felt it their duty to retire somewhat. At the same moment I was chatting with someone in the embrasure of a window. The Emperor was standing with his face towards me, at the left of the throne. All the despatches of the time have reported this conversation. The Emperor Napoleon complained that the Tsar Alexander wished to attack him; that he was no longer in the alliance, since he admitted pretended neutrals [to his ports]; that Russia was the scene of vast movements of troops. At the end of this conversation, which lasted for half an hour, the Emperor exclaimed loudly enough for me to hear him from where I was standing:

"According to Monsieur de Caulaincourt the Tsar Alexander wishes to attack me."

The Emperor was so excited and spoke with such warmth, and his words came out with such rapidity, that Prince Kurakin, standing with his mouth open to reply, could not get a word in. Although they had withdrawn some distance, the bystanders were all ears, especially those members of the diplomatic corps who happened to be in the room.

"M. de Caulaincourt," the Emperor went on, "has turned Russian. The Tsar's beguilements have won him over."

Leaving Prince Kurakin, the Emperor took a few steps towards the middle of the room, seeking to read in the bystanders' eyes what impression he had made. Noticing me in the window—for I had certainly not escaped his attention—the Emperor came up to me and remarked peevishly:

"You have turned Russian, haven't you?"

"I am a very good Frenchman, Sire," I answered steadily; "and time will prove that I have told Your Majesty the truth, as a faithful servant should."

Seeing that I was taking the matter seriously, the Emperor then pretended that he had been joking.

"I know well enough that you are an honest man," he said; "but the Tsar Alexander's cajoleries have turned your head. In fact you have become a Russian," he added, with a smile.

He then turned away and began to speak to other persons.

Next day, having failed to obtain a private audience with the Emperor, I made so formal a declaration to Duroc, for him to pass on to His Majesty, of my wish to retire from the Court— and at the same time I expressed myself so forcibly to the Minister of Police—that within twenty-four hours Mme. de C— [11] had been granted permission to return from exile.

On this point I must render the Duke of Rovigo the justice that many others beside myself owe him. He spoke frankly to the Emperor about this act of severity—as he did, indeed, about many similar affairs, seeking to delay action or even to bring about a reversal of his decision—without fearing the harsh and disagreeable consequences that he might bring on himself. Undoubtedly Savary told the Emperor the truth more than any other Minister of Police ventured to do.

I had spoken to Duroc with the tone of a man who has made up his mind, and he came to see me on the following morning. He told me that the Emperor had not meant to say anything distasteful to me: he had merely said to Prince Kurakin what he had subsequently said to me, in order that the Tsar Alexander should know that I remained his friend; he valued me highly, but I ought to consider his susceptibilities more in some ways, and not fall out with him as I did when he discussed policy with me; it was easier to lead him by giving way on certain points than by running directly counter to his views. He told me that I worried myself needlessly with matters which actually did not concern me, and by so doing harmed myself and my friends without benefit to policy or person; it

[11] Mme. de Canisy was permitted to return to Paris in August, 1811.

was foolish to sacrifice oneself for high matters which one
could in no way change, or when one had not armies to set up
in opposition. It was a vain self-sacrifice. I tried unavailingly
to explain my feelings to him. He joked about what I called
doing my duty. He let me see, however, that at heart he agreed
with me, but that it would be a waste of his time and devotion
even to hope to persuade the Emperor to other political views.

The journey to Boulogne, along the coast and down through
Holland, which followed the Emperor's round of visits to
various palaces, put an end for a while—by taking us away
from Paris—to the host of petty annoyances that plagued my
life. But there was no alteration in the Emperor's acerbity
towards me, even when the almost superhuman achievments of
my department [12] occasionally drew his involuntary though
grudging praise during these astonishing journeys and im-
promptu excursions.

The maze of details connected with these journeys had rendered me indispensable to the Emperor. [September 19–November 11, 1811.] Too just not to appreciate my usefulness,
he was nevertheless brusque in his relations with me. Once
back in Paris the Emperor seemed in no disposition to treat me
better.

Engaged in a matter that touched my honour, in that it concerned my country, and my self-esteem, in that I had no mind
to be the agent of a policy of which I disapproved, I was in

[12] In peacetime Caulaincourt, as Master of Horse, was responsible in
particular for the planning and conduct of all Imperial journeys. He also
had charge of all couriers and despatch riders, and he commanded the
corps of orderly officers. Those were but a few of his duties which, in
time of war, were greatly extended. He was then responsible for moving
and provisioning the Imperial headquarters. His travelling carriage preceded the Emperor's; on horse he was on the Emperor's left hand and
accompanied him into battle; and his quarters were always as close as
possible to the Imperial lodging, so that he could receive the first and last
orders of the day.

an embarrassing position; but my silence in public on all these questions was my salvation.

Bowing to the unjust severity of a sovereign, who can never give way to a subject, I refrained from my complaints regarding things that affected me personally; but I appealed direct to the Emperor, or through Duroc and the Duke of Rovigo, against the injustice dealt out to my friends, who were entirely ignorant of my political views. My silence in public and my restraint were noticed by the Emperor. According to what Duroc told me, he approved of my conduct; yet not for one moment did he modify his own.

During the winter there were many festivities, full-dress balls and masked balls. At the state ball [February 6, 1812] I was the only high official not included in the grand quadrille with the Empress and the Princesses. I was likewise passed over, or rather I was the only high official not invited, to supper at the Empress's table. So far as the supper was concerned I took this rebuff lightly, for it was possible to consider invitations to that as a personal matter; but as the quadrille concerned one of the prerogatives of my position and was much commented upon, I considered it my duty to lodge a complaint. The Emperor sent me word that the omission of my name had been a mistake; but I learned from Duroc, to whom he had dictated the list, that it had been intentional.

Duroc even warned me, with that obliging friendliness which characterized him, not to mention for the moment the return of my friends to Court, adding that he did not know what I had done or said, but that the Emperor was more incensed against me than ever. He observed that I spoke too warmly against Polish affairs; that when the Emperor discussed business with me I appeared to be putting him in the wrong, and that this irritated him. He was doubtless alluding to two conversations the Emperor had had with me; one at the château of Loo, during our journey to Holland, and the other just two days before, in Paris. I will confine myself to but a brief summary of them, for with the exception of a few phrases which I will record, the conversations were on the same lines, and in almost the same terms, as what I have already reported.

"This journey," said the Emperor, "together with the measures I am going to take against English commerce, will prove to the Tsar Alexander that I remain staunch to the System of the alliance, and am more concerned with the internal prosperity of the Empire than with the warlike schemes attributed to me."

"In the meantime, the troops Your Majesty has assembled here are proceeding northwards. That does not seem to accord with the maintenance of peace."

"The Poles are calling me, but I am not thinking of the restoration of Poland; and although it would politic and even in the interests of civilization, I am not planning it. That would be too great an undertaking, on account of Austria."

"And yet, Sire, that's the only compensation I can see for sacrificing the Russian alliance."

"I have no wish to sacrifice it. I am only occupying North Germany in order to strengthen the Continental System, and really shut out England in a strict quarantine from the rest of Europe. To do this I must be strong everywhere. My brother Alexander is obstinate; he sees these measures as veiling some project of attack. He is wrong. Lauriston is constantly telling him so; but when a man is afraid he sees double, and at St. Petersburg they can see nothing but divisions on the march, armies standing in readiness, Poland in arms. It is I who might take offence, for the Russians have moved up the divisions which they had previously brought from Asia."

After making many observations to prove to the Emperor that he could not deceive St. Petersburg regarding his real projects, I added that no political interest could justify a war that would take him eight hundred leagues from Paris whilst he had Spain and all the resources of England against him.

"It is because England is in Spain, and obliged to stay there, that I am not uneasy about her. You don't understand politics. You are just like the Russians; you can see nothing but threats, nothing but war, whereas this is just a disposition of forces necessary to make England sue for terms before six months have passed—if only Rumiantsof does not lose his head."

The Emperor closed these conversations by a show of something more than impatience.

But returning to Duroc: he made me promise to see no more of Talleyrand, who, he told me, had been out of favour for some time with the Emperor for more reasons than one: notably on account of the reflections he had permitted himself to make regarding the war in Spain, notwithstanding the fact that he had been among the first to urge the Emperor to seize that throne. Duroc added that we did not know the Emperor's wider projects nor his political views; he centred everything on the need of forcing England to make peace so that Europe might finally enjoy lasting tranquillity. All Duroc's reflections were made in a spirit of kindness and concern for myself.

CHAPTER II

ON THE EVE: 1812

THE winter wore on. Negotiations had already started with Austria for an offensive and defensive alliance to be imposed on Prussia. In all directions greater exertions than ever were being made to further the arrangements and dispositions for the Emperor's great undertaking. We were approaching the dénouement of the events for which the projected interview at Dresden was the intended prelude. In the meantime Paris and the Court were busy with parties and entertainments.

Towards the end of winter and in the spring I had two further lengthy conversations with the Emperor, one of which took place very shortly after this interview with Duroc. They turned on political questions. In the first, the Emperor tried once again to persuade me that he no longer contemplated the restoration of Poland, and had no wish whatever to go to war with Russia; in a word, that he only wanted to force England to abandon her groundless pretensions and make peace, and to accomplish this it was essential that Russia should effectively close her ports to English commerce; whereas for a year past she had been admitting English goods under the American flag.

To this I objected that we ourselves had been admitting those same goods under licences—only of course such goods and licences were taxed double-rate.

"Possibly so," answered the Emperor, laughing. "I cannot go back on that, because of my maritime towns. Alexander has only to do the same himself. I would rather that Russia

24

and its treasury should reap the profit than that it should go
to so-called neutrals."

He then returned to his old idea, that by impounding all
neutral goods the Emperor Alexander would be doing immense
good, and so on.

"You may be sure," he said, "that I have no intention of
sacrificing such great interests for a speculative re-establishment of Poland."

"Undoubtedly Your Majesty would not make war on Russia
solely for the sake of Poland," I answered; "but rather that
you should have no rival in Europe, and see there none but
vassals."

I added that this occupied him much more than his Continental System, which could have been put rigorously into force
from Archangel to Danzig as soon as the Emperor had frankly
imposed upon himself those privations and sacrifices which he
wished to demand from others. Finally, I urged, he would
not have gathered such forces in the North, to the detriment of
the Spanish campaign, nor would he have spent so much money
in all sorts of preparations, if he had not been resolved to put
them to some use, either for a political end or to satisfy his
fondest passion.

"What passion is that?" asked the Emperor, laughing.

"War, Sire."

He tweaked my ear, with weak protests that it was not so.
He then gave me free leave to say whatever I desired, and
accepted with the utmost good humour everything I said. Whenever I touched a sore spot he pinched my ear again, giving me
a gentle tap on the nape of my neck—especially when I
seemed to him to be going rather far.

I told him that his desire was, if not for universal monarchy, at least for a supremacy which should be more than
primus inter pares, and should place him in the position of
demanding from others sacrifices which he would not be called

upon to make himself; and this without allowing them the right of complaint or even of comment. This could only appear of momentary advantage to France; it had already resulted, and in time to come would result yet more, in provoking hostile opinion—ill-feeling and jealousy which sooner or later were bound to end tragically for us, as a situation of this kind could not be forced upon the nations in the present century. He laughed heartily at what he called my philanthropy, and at my remarks about *primus inter pares*. He was in the best of humours, laughing very readily; he took no offence. He had the air of saying, "You're quite right; you've guessed correctly; but don't say anything about it. . . ."

The harder the Emperor found it to persuade me, the more art and persistence he put forth to attain that end. His calculated wiles, and the language he used, would have made anyone believe that I was one of the powers whom he was so much concerned to win over.

I have often observed in him that care and persistence, and am far from flattering myself that I was the occasion of it. He acted so towards all whom he wished to persuade, and he was always wanting to persuade someone.

I enter into all these details because they delineate his character; that is my sole purpose. I will even add that his persistence arose, I think, from the habit that he had but too firmly contracted, whether by reason of his power or on account of the real superiority of his genius and the ascendancy that it gave him, of either communicating his conviction to others or of imposing it upon them. Certain it is that to the success which he was accustomed to obtain thus must be attributed his predilection for interviews with sovereigns, and his habit of dealing in any particularly delicate and important matters directly with the ministers and ambassadors of foreign powers. When he so wished, there could be a power of persuasion and fascination in his voice, his expression, his very manner, giving him an advantage over his interlocutor as great as the superiority and flexibility of his mind.

Never was there a man more fascinating when he chose to be; to withstand him one had to realize, as I did, the political errors which lay concealed beneath this art. However prepared for him I might be—even when on my guard—he was often for a moment on the point of winning me to his opinion; and I only broke the spell because, like all curt and obstinate people, I remained on my own ground, maintaining only my own ideas and not heeding those of the Emperor. To avoid being carried away by the geniality which he often assumed when wishing to inspire confidence—to withstand the forceful arguments and reasoning of the Emperor, often specious but always clever and full of apt comparisons as useful to illustrate his own ideas as to conceal the end he wished to attain—one had to behave as if one did not understand what he was saying, and to repeat diligently to oneself in advance: "This is just; this is right; this only is in the interest of France, and therefore in the true interests of the Emperor."

It was necessary to confine one's attention to the question as it appeared to oneself, and not to stray beyond the circle thus traced; above all not to follow the Emperor in his digressions, for he never failed to shift the centre of argument when he encountered opposition. Woe to him who admitted a single modification, for the adroit interlocutor led from concession to concession to the end he had in view, casting up a previous concession against you if you defended yourself, and assuming that it consequently implied the point you refused to concede. No woman was ever more artful than he in making you want, or agree to, his own desire, when he thought it was to his interest to persuade, or merely wanted to do so. These reflections call to my mind what he once said on a similar occasion, which explains better than any other phrase could have done the price he was ready to pay for success.

"When I need anyone," he said, "I don't make too fine a point about it; I would kiss his ——."

Once he had an idea implanted in his head, the Emperor was carried away by his own illusion. He cherished it, caressed it, became obsessed with it; one might say he exuded it from all his pores. By what means, then, did he strive to convey this illusion to others? If he sought to fascinate you, you could be sure he had already fascinated himself. Never have a man's reason and judgment been more misguided, more led astray, more the victim of his imagination and passion than the reason and judgment of the Emperor on certain questions. He spared neither pain, care nor trouble to arrive at his end, and this applied as much to little things as to great. He was, one might say, totally given over to his object. He always applied all his means, all his faculties, all his attention to the action or discussion of the moment. He put passion into everything. Hence the enormous advantage he had over his adversaries; for few people are absolutely engrossed by the moment's thought or action.

I hope I may be pardoned these reflections. I return to my conversation with the Emperor.

The Emperor's endeavours to prove to me that all his wars were for political purposes, that his only aim was peace with England, that all his projects were conformable to this and aimed at that goal, induced me to touch once more on the great political questions relative to the project of war which I attributed to him on behalf of Poland. I said that I understood as well as he did, and that I had written to him to that effect when he might have had Poland's restoration in mind, that if it was to form a great buffer state in the centre of Europe, Poland was not in herself sufficient; it would be necessary to fashion that power on a proper scale, with boundaries, a political position, and an organization which would ensure general respect. I added that I understood perfectly well the utility of such a power, and that in consequence I considered any means admissible which would lead to that end, if he had had no other wars on his hands. This arrangement, I continued, could not but be agreeable to the ideas of England and Austria, according to my views; the Tsar Alexander, although he could not publicly agree to this project on account of his Polish provinces, was a man who could appreciate the wise political scope of such an arrangement; interest and honour would prevent him from giving up his portion of Poland without a struggle; but this war, fought at some other time, and with the acquiescence of Europe, would soon be over; and if it were waged for that purpose, it must be made clear that such was its purpose, so that Europe would regard it only as a fight for security.

It would be essential to make an authentic and positive declaration of his views and principles, and of the end he had in mind—to make Austria disinterested, moreover, by restoring her outlets to the sea—in short to refashion the States of Europe with reasonable boundaries. I added that it was essential to take a firm and definite attitude with regard to Prussia, and to come to an understanding with the great powers that the buffer state should be ruled by a dynasty neither French, Russian nor Austrian: in fine, that this state should be entirely independent in respect of its organization as well as its dynasty; and it seemed to me that a question of this importance, and an arrangement of this nature, would induce England to make peace more than would the Continental System, as offering a tranquil future to all cabinets, and so setting an example of moderation, even of sacrifice.

This step, I told him, would conciliate general feeling towards him; this great political move ought to be made openly; and if this really was his object, it seemed to me so sweeping, so noble, so well calculated to immortalize his reign, that he ought to proclaim it, announcing his intentions to the world at large, and leaving nothing vague or likely to cast doubts on his good faith in carrying them out. All the mysterious ways of our existing political system, I continued, all the pinpricks that were given, ostensibly to make one's adversary explain his intentions, but really to force him into a corner and make him the aggressor, would then become out-of-date and useless; that in such an event I should esteem myself happy to be the agent, the verbal go-between for such a project; and I was prepared to be the intermediary at St. Petersburg, however little the cabinet there might relish the message I took them.

I concluded by saying that such a purpose, worthy as it was of the Emperor's genius, was the only thing which could make the Polish war intelligible to me. Otherwise it seemed quite unreasonable; for a war in Russia, without a previous declaration of the freedom of Poland, without the loyal aid of Austria previously recompensed for the loss of Galicia by the cession of Illyria, without the secret assent of England, would be a very risky enterprise, presenting nothing but difficulties without any real advantage to compensate for them. A hundred Russians slain beyond the Oder did not appear to me sufficient compensation for the death of a single Frenchman slain on the same field of battle.

The Emperor listened to me with attention, but with occasional flashes of impatience. I paused often, hoping that he would answer me, and that in touching on various details of this great question he would come to the point. He answered only on the general lines of his previous remarks, adding ironically to his old refrain, "Austria ought to be delighted to hear what you say. In creating a kingdom for the King of Prussia, Alexander's friend, I should rouse too much laughter among the English. Don't you see that this would be playing their game?"

"I have not mentioned the King of Prussia," I answered. "The King of Saxony, or any other monarch, might rule this state. Who knows, in the arrangements for intervention, whether the powers would not consent to have on the throne some prince of the Confederation or some other person agreeable to Your Majesty?"

Although my observations appeared to be little to the Emperor's taste, yet I reflected that I had already said too much to stop at that point, and that the Emperor would do well to realize that no one was hoodwinked by our policy. So I added:

"If Your Majesty does not act on these lines, I ought to say frankly that everyone in Europe, as in France, will see that the war in Russia or Poland, for which you are preparing, is not in order to create a buffer state, as Your Majesty would have us believe, but for some purpose for which that is merely the pretext."

The Emperor seemed a little provoked and said, as he invariably did when a matter was broached that displeased him: "I am not asking your advice."

Nevertheless he led the conversation round to the topic of Russia. He went into each question in detail, spoke of every grievance as though he were going over each step with his cabinet and seeking to explain himself and win agreement.

As the Emperor still seemed anxious that I should see Prince Kurakin, I told him that I would not be a party to deceiving anyone, least of all the Tsar, by taking a step that would amount to trickery, for I had no longer any authority to speak of affairs. All these preparations would be a misfortune for France and a matter for regret and embarrassment to the Emperor himself, and I had no wish to give myself cause for reproach for having contributed to it. The Emperor turned his back on me, saying drily that I understood nothing about policy, and thereupon left me.

I continued to live in retirement, maintaining the utmost reserve. I saw no Russians, and even avoided meeting Prince

Kurakin. More than a month had passed without my seeing any of them, when the Emperor had another conversation with me, shortly before his departure. Once again he returned to his supposed grievances. This time his conversation seemed to show what was really in his mind. The Emperor could no longer make pretences about his plans for departure, but he still tried to persuade me that he neither wished to establish Poland nor to have any kind of war, but hoped that everything would be cleared up and arranged without coming to blows.

We used the same arguments on each side and talked from the same premises. I further urged all my beliefs as to the inconveniences, not to say the dangers, of such a distant expedition which would keep him away from France so long. I spoke of how he was continually being reproached for running such risks, for gambling with such splendid and mighty destinies, when he could exercise a great and powerful influence from his desk in the Tuileries. I mentioned the effect in France of risks forced on the youth of the nation—risks no longer, as afore-time, confined exclusively to the lower orders of society. I represented to him how he had already been condemned in this connection for the war in Spain, and the danger of going far away before its termination.

I told him that he should strike first in Spain, if he persisted in his desire for this unfortunate war with Russia. I described the country to him, the climate, the advantage the enemy would have in allowing him to advance and wear himself out by marching without the chance to fight. I reminded him of the words of the Tsar which I had already reported. I also re-called to him the privations and discontent of the troops during his last campaign in Poland. To all my arguments his reply was that *I had turned Russian, and that I understood nothing of great affairs.*

"But if I understand nothing, Sire," I retorted with a smile, "why does Your Majesty do me the honour of discussing policy with me? I can do nothing in this matter except through love of my country and attachment to your person. Such noble sentiments cannot lead me into error and keep me in error so long. Your Majesty is not so gracious towards those who are not of your opinion that you can imagine it is amusing to contradict you; indeed, such a course, so far as my friends and myself are concerned, has not been so successful as to encourage me to continue it. It must therefore be a matter of conscience and conviction. Your Majesty is carried away by false reports. You are confused and deluded as to the dangers of the course you are taking. You think you are pushing forward to a great and politic objective, and I am convinced that you are mistaken."

The Emperor replied with warmth that it was the Tsar of Russia who desired war; M. Lauriston had informed him that all the Russian armies were on the march, even those from the Turkish frontier; the soft words of the Emperor Alexander had befogged me. He said that he had known of Russia's hostile intentions only when he sent another ambassador, who informed him by every courier that the English were trading openly in St. Petersburg, and that there had even been an attempt to rob M. Longuerue, the aide-de-camp, of the despatches which M. Lauriston had forwarded to him.

The Emperor was doubtless unaware that I had seen young M. Longuerue and knew all about his adventure.

This young officer, travelling as a courier in a heavy barouche which was making slow progress through the sand, had quarrelled with a Russian courier whose light *kibitk* overtook him. The Frenchman thought he had the same right in Russia as in France to stop the Russian from passing him; the other, staunch in his rights as a government courier, and with his lighter equipage, urged his postilion forward, easily overtaking and passing M. Longuerue's carriage, which was half stuck in the mud. In a fury, M. Longuerue fired his pistols at the Russian, who paid as little heed to the other's shots as to his threats. At Riga the governor intervened, pointed out to the Frenchman the irregularity of his conduct, and, out of regard for his position as a bearer of government despatches, let the impetuous young man proceed. But the governor reported the matter to his Court, and M. Lauriston was so incensed at the conduct of his aide-de-camp that he dismissed him. This is what the Emperor cited to me as an attack against one of his couriers for the purpose of robbing him of his despatches.

During this conversation with the Emperor, I noticed that he was more thoughtful than usual. Some of my reflections seemed to have impressed him more than he was willing to show. The arrival of the Duke of Bassano, who was announced as bringing despatches from Vienna, interrupted this conversation, which I felt that the Emperor wished to prolong. He dismissed me, and doubtless resumed in another conversation the irresistible course of fatality which was drawing him forward.

By this time the Emperor had already taken his decision. Austria had practically consented to become his ally, and Prussia had had no alternative but to lay up a rod for her own back.

Some days after my last conversation with the Emperor he had sent off a portion of the Household. Horses and carriages were already on the way to Dresden, ostensibly for the interview with the Emperor of Austria.

The Emperor left Paris on May 9.

It is said that we went to Dresden by way of Bamberg to avoid the German princelings. The truth is that the Emperor wanted to avoid Weimar.[1] He kept on saying, and the Court repeated it after him, that he did not want war. Rumours were purposely spread of an interview with the Tsar Alexander, and attempts were made to find confirmation of these rumours in the

[1] The Grand Duke of Weimar was the Tsar's brother-in-law.

mission of M. Narbonne, who was sent to that sovereign's
court.

Dresden was reached on May 16.

The Emperor and all those attached to the ministry were at
pains to tinge our conduct, views and actions with moderation,
in order to keep appearances on our side, and so impress
Austria. To this end particular care was taken to appear conciliatory and moderate; efforts were also made to lull into a
false sense of security those whom it was desired to attack.

The Emperor had travelled with the Empress. For six weeks
the whole countryside had been working to repair the roads we
had to follow. The King and Queen of Saxony had preceded
Their Majesties to Plauen. There was a torchlight procession
at our entrance into Dresden, where the Austrian Court arrived
two days later. Since politics was none of my business, I did
not gather enough certain knowledge of what passed at that
interview to enable me to relate it in detail.

The Emperor set things in motion to circumvent M. Metternich—and especially to see that there should be echoes about
his moderation and his anxiety to obtain, through M. Narbonne, the explanations which the Tsar of Russia had refused
to Austria, so as to effect a general conciliation without recourse
to hostilities. For the first, and perhaps for the last time, the
Emperor spoke very well of M. Metternich.

Russia had indeed betrayed a certain arrogance in not entering into explanations with the Viennese cabinet, which would
gladly have listened to them. If this conduct showed a certain
dignity it also showed clumsiness; for it strengthened our cause
in the public view, and thus played into our hands.

M. Narbonne, who had been sent to Wilna to the Tsar
Alexander, arrived back at Dresden. The Emperor instructed
him to see M. Metternich and tell the Emperor of Austria what
he wished to be known about his mission.

The Emperor, who thought that the part he had taken in the

marriage of the Archduchess Marie Louise, his reputation as a man of intelligence, and his relations with Prince Schwarzenburg, would render M. Narbonne particularly agreeable to the Austrian Court, had chosen him expressly for this mission, thinking that whatever he said would have all the more effect on the mind of the Imperial father-in-law.

M. Narbonne came to see me and told me what the Tsar had said to him, what he had observed, and what he had loyally reported to the Emperor Napoleon, who had instructed him to repeat it in part to the Emperor of Austria and M. Metternich.

I note, more or less, M. Narbonne's exact words, for I wrote them down at the time; and this conversation having been repeated to me several times by him, I have been able to verify the accuracy of my notes.

The Tsar Alexander had welcomed him cordially. He had been welcomed by everyone; their general bearing was appropriate to the occasion, dignified but not boastful. He attended two reviews. The troops appeared to be a fine body of men. M. Rumiantsof was not there at the time of his arrival. From the outset the Tsar had spoken to him frankly:

"I shall not be the first to draw the sword. I have no wish to be saddled, in the eyes of Europe, with the responsibility of the blood that will be shed in this war. For eighteen months I have been threatened. The French army is three hundred leagues from its own country and actually on my frontiers, whereas I am on my own territory. Vital points on my frontiers are being fortified and armed; arms are being sent up; the Poles are being incited; an outcry is being raised that I harbour neutrals and admit Americans, while all the time the Emperor is selling licences in France, admitting vessels that are being used to carry freight from England. The Emperor is swelling his fiscal receipts and ruining some of his unfortunate subjects. From the start, I have declared that I have no intention of doing this. I cannot take money from the pockets of my subjects to put into my own.

"The Emperor Napoleon and his agents declare that I favour England and do not carry out the measures of the Continental System. If this were true, would sixty or eighty ships have been seized as contraband? Do you imagine that the English have not been knocking at my door in every way they could? Had I wished, I could have had ten English agents for every one that I have had; but I have not so much as listened to them. Three hundred thousand French troops are ready to cross my frontier, though I am still in the alliance and faithful to all the engagements I have made. When I change, I will do so openly. Ask Caulaincourt what I said to him when the Emperor Napoleon deviated from the alliance, and what I told him on his departure. Caulaincourt is a man of honour, and not a man to be imposed upon. As I was then, so I am to-day, whatever the Emperor Napoleon may have done to break our friendly relations.

"He is raising Austria, Prussia, all Europe in arms against Russia; yet I am still in the alliance, so firmly has my reason forbidden me to believe that he would wish to sacrifice real advantages to the hazards of this war. I am under no illusions. I render too much justice to his military talents not to have calculated all the risks than an appeal to arms may involve for us, but, having done all I could to preserve peace honourably and uphold a political system which might lead to universal peace, I will do nothing to besmirch the honour of the nation over which I rule. The Russian nation is not one to shrink from danger. All the bayonets in Europe waiting at my frontiers will not make me speak otherwise.

"My patience and moderation come not from weakness, but from the duty of a sovereign to heed no feelings of resentment—to envisage nothing but the peace and welfare of his people in questions of such far-reaching importance, and when he can hope to avert a struggle which must cost them so many sacrifices. Can the Emperor Napoleon, in all good faith, demand explanations when, in a time of total peace, he invades the north of Germany, when he fails to observe the engagements of the alliance and carry out the principles of his Continental System? Is it not he who should explain his motives?"

The Tsar, moreover, told him that at the moment of speaking he was under no engagement contrary to the alliance; that he was strong in the rights and justice of his cause; and that he would defend himself if attacked. He concluded by spreading out a map of Russia and pointing to the farthest limits of the country.

"If the Emperor Napoleon is determined on war," he said, "and if Fortune does not smile on our just cause, he will have to go to the end of the earth to find peace."

He then said once again that he would not fire the first shot, but also that he would sheathe the sword last.

M. Narbonne further told me that during his stay at Wilna the Tsar Alexander had always spoken to him in this sense, unaffectedly and without ill-feeling, not even showing any bitterness towards the Emperor Napoleon personally; he had also spoken of myself with great esteem and kindness. M. Narbonne seemed quite content with all that the sovereign had said, and was convinced of the truth of his arguments. He added that the Emperor Napoleon seemed to be impressed by the report made to him, though he kept on complaining of the Tsar's falseness, and constantly returned to his chapter of grievances against him.

The King of Prussia and the Crown Prince, whom the Emperor had wished to meet in Dresden for the purpose of some kind of public reconciliation which would guarantee the satisfactory and free co-operation of Prussia, arrived in Dresden [May 26]. Some thought that the Emperor would not treat the

King well, for he did not like him and always observed, when speaking of him, "He is merely a drill sergeant, a blockhead." But the Emperor made his good-humour wait on his interest; and at the moment it was very much to his interest to persuade the King that he was admitting him freely into the political scheme of France, and had no hidden motives of hostility. The King and the Crown Prince went away delighted with the welcome they had received.

The Emperor left Dresden on May 29; the Empress was at Prague, where she had gone to pass a short time with the Austrian Court. The Emperor stayed from June 7 to 10 at Danzig. That was the great army depôt, the place where everything had been organized and prepared during the last two years, and to which the Emperor devoted the greatest attention; for it was the strong point which had to supply all his needs.

The King of Naples, who had not received permission to repair to Dresden, ostensibly out of regard for the Emperor of Austria, was waiting there for the Emperor Napoleon. On the score that his father-in-law always had Italy much at heart, the Emperor pretended that he did not wish to mar the Emperor Francis's pleasure at seeing his daughter again by the sight of a sovereign who would only recall painful memories. The truth is that that was a very convenient pretext. The Emperor remarked, in confidence, that he did not want Murat to establish relations with the Austrians, with whom too many ties already existed between the Queen and Metternich. "Murat's head will be turned if the Emperor of Austria treats him well, and he will be certain to talk all sorts of nonsense. . . ."

The Emperor Napleon's first words to General Rapp, Governor of Danzig, were:

"What are your merchants doing with all their money? War is going to start. Now I will look after that myself."

In the course of a conversation after dinner he remarked to Rapp, the King of Naples and several other persons that the Prussians and even the Austrians would make common cause with us; that Alexander did not expect this, and would be greatly embarrassed, although he had wanted the war. He added that if Alexander really did not want war he could still avert it; but that the situation would be clarified in a few days. It could easily be seen that this talk was designed to be repeated by all the political echoes. The Emperor's real wishes were expressed in the remarks, uttered in the presence of myself and several other persons, when he first saw Rapp.

That evening and the next morning the Emperor complained much to me of the King of Naples, who, he said, was no longer a Frenchman and had forgotten what he owed to his country and his benefactor. On his side, the King complained to Berthier, Duroc and myself that the Emperor had made him merely a viceroy, an instrument for squeezing money out of his subjects, and so on.

The Emperor welcomed the King quite cordially in public; but taking him aside, undoubtedly to forestall his complaints, he began by scolding and being angry with him. He expostulated with him for his ingratitude, and, at the close of the conversation, he showed both vexation and sentiment—"both necessary in dealing with this Neapolitan Pantaloon," he told me. "He has a good heart, and at bottom he likes me better than his lazzarone. When he sees me he is mine; but away from me, he sides, like all spineless men, with anyone who flatters or makes up to him. If he had come to Dresden his vanity and self-interest would have led him into countless follies in trying to manage the Austrians. His wife is ambitious, and has stuffed his head with foolishness. He wants to have the whole of Italy; that is his dream, and that is what prevents him from wanting the crown of Poland.

"I would put Jerome on the throne and make a splendid kingdom for him; but he would have to do something for it, for the Poles love true glory. Jerome cares for nothing but pageantry, women, plays and fêtes. My brothers do not back me up. Their only princely quality is their foolish vanity; they lack talent and energy. I have to govern for them. Without me they would ruin the poor Westphalians to enrich their favourites and mistresses, to give fêtes and build palaces. My brothers think of nothing but themselves, yet I set them a good example. I am the King of the people, for I spend nothing except on encouraging the arts and leaving memories that shall be glorious and useful to the nation. It can never be said that I endow favourites and mistresses. I give rewards only for services rendered to the country—nothing else."

Headquarters and the staff were moved to Thorn, whence everything was sent on to Insterburg, along with the Guard, on the morning after arrival. The Emperor joined headquarters at Insterburg and followed its movement in the direction of Kovno, passing by Gumbinnen, Stalluppöhnen, Wilkowischki and a forest road, leaving Mariampol on the right. The troops marching along the road were superb, and received the Emperor with real enthusiasm. The men of the First Corps [Davout's] were noticeable for their fine bearing and general smartness. Coming from excellent quarters, fresh from the hands of a commander who had drilled them long and well, they could rival the Guard. All this mass of youth was full of ardour and good health. In their knapsacks the men of this corps carried rations for a fortnight.

PART II

ADVANCE

CHAPTER III

FIRST BLOOD

THE Emperor came up with the Prince of Eckmühl's head-quarters at a spot two miles and a half from the Niemen and from Kowno. Day was breaking [June 23, 1812]. He immediately made a reconnaissance of the river banks and the whole terrain. He did not return till evening, when he spent two hours dictating orders. He then took horse again and made a reconnaissance by moonlight, nearer the bank, to decide on a place for the crossing. The whole lot of us were left some way behind, so as not to draw the attention of any Russian scouts who might be on the farther side. The Emperor went up and down the bank, accompanied by General Haxo of the Engineers. Even that morning he had been obliged to wear a Polish soldier's cloak, in order to attract less attention.

When the reconnaissance was finished he rejoined his staff officers, and once more examined the different points to be occupied by the troops. As he galloped through the wheat, a hare started out between the legs of the Emperor's horse—Friedland—and made him swerve slightly. The Emperor, whose seat was poor, rolled to the ground but got up so quickly that he was on his feet before I could reach him to give him a hand. He mounted again without saying a word. The ground was very soft and he was only slightly bruised on the hip. It struck me then that here was a bad omen; nor was I the only one to think so, for the Prince of Neuchâtel instantly seized my hand and said:

45

"We should do better not to cross the Niemen. That fall is a bad sign."

The Emperor, who at first had kept a complete silence, though his private thoughts were doubtless no more cheerful than our own, presently began to joke with the Prince of Neuchâtel and myself about his fall; but his bad temper and forebodings were obvious despite his efforts at concealment. In other circumstances he would have complained about the charger which had caused this foolish accident, and would not have spared the Master of Horse. Now, however, he affected the utmost serenity, and did all he could to dispel the misgivings which he sensed that everyone must have felt—for men are superstitious despite themselves, in such serious moments and on the eve of such great events.

Talk about his fall was general: some of the headquarters staff observed that the Romans, who believed in portents, would not have undertaken the crossing of the Niemen. During the whole of that day the Emperor, usually so cheerful and active when his troops were carrying out extensive operations, was very serious and preoccupied.

There was no news from the other side of the river; communications had been interrupted for some days.

The only sign of life on the opposite bank was an occasional Cossack patrol. During the day the Emperor inspected his troops and continued to reconnoitre the neighbourhood. The corps on our right knew no more than we did of the enemy's movements. They had no news whatever of the Russians. Everyone was complaining that no spies came back, a fact which put the Emperor in bad humour. We only heard from Mariampol that a Jew, coming from the interior, reported that the Russian army was in retreat, and that we were faced only by Cossacks. The Emperor believed that the Russians were massing about Troki for the defence of Wilna.

The Emperor sent for me after dinner and asked what had

caused him to be thrown; he said he was scarcely hurt but had got up so quickly that probably in the darkness no one would have noticed the accident. He asked if it was being talked about at headquarters. He then renewed several inquiries about Russia, the mode of life of the inhabitants, the resources offered by the towns and villages, the state of the roads. He asked if the peasants had any energy, if they were the sort of people to arm themselves and form bands like the Spaniards, and finally if I thought that the army had retreated and thus delivered Wilna to him without giving battle. He seemed to be very anxious that this should be so, but he argued to convince me that the Russian army could not have retreated from Mariampol, as had been reported, and thus given up the capital of Lithuania [Wilna]—and in consequence the whole of Russian Poland—without fighting, if only not to dishonour itself in the eyes of the Poles. He urged me to give him my opinion of this retreat.

I answered that I did not anticipate any pitched battles; that I thought, as I had always told him, that the terrain was so ample that they might yield a great deal, if only to lead him a long distance from his base and oblige him to divide his forces.

"Then I have got Poland," answered the Emperor briskly. "And in the eyes of the Poles Alexander has the undying shame of having lost it without fighting. To give me Wilna is to lose Poland."

He dwelt at some length on this point, on the deployment of his forces and their rapid movement; and he drew the conclusion that it was impossible for the Russians to save their stores and artillery. He even believed that some of them would be destroyed through their inability to escape the speed of his movements. He counted and reckoned up the hours it would take him to reach Wilna, and plied me with questions as if I had done the journey—as if it were only a question of travelling there in a post-chaise.

"In less than two months' time," the Emperor said to me, "Russia will be suing for peace. The great landowners will be terrified, some of them ruined. The Tsar Alexander will be in a very awkward position, for at heart the Russians care nothing for the Poles, certainly not enough to face ruin for their sakes."

To avoid being contradicted, the Emperor delivered a rapid fire of questions and of the answers that he wished to hear, preserving meanwhile the appearance of urging me to reply, and continually asking me—without giving me the chance to get in a word—whether I did not think as he did.

When he had done speaking, my silence angered him. He wanted a response that would strengthen his preconceptions. . . .

The Niemen was crossed by Morand's division during the night [June 23-24, 1812]. The others followed; the pontoon detachments had been brought down ahead of time within reach of the stream. This operation was carried out in a few hours without the slightest difficulty, and without any opposition, even from the Cossacks, small numbers of whom were on the farther bank and who only replied to our shots when our troops entered the first village on the other side, some distance from the river.

The Emperor crossed during the morning, as soon as the First Division was established; and he seemed greatly astonished to learn that the Russian army, which had been at Wilna, had retreated three days previously. Several reports had to be made, and various people who had come from there had to be brought to him, before he would believe the news. He followed the movements of the advance-guard for more than two leagues, hurried the whole army forward, and questioned all the countryfolk whom he could find, but obtained no positive news; Poles were sent out in all directions to gather information.

The Emperor returned to Kowno, visited the town and its environs, and was occupied until nightfall in hastening the crossing of the Wilia, which was undertaken by some swimmers, and by erecting a bridge for the passage of an army corps which was to operate on the other side of that river.

It was M. Guéheneuc who led a couple of hundred determined swimmers across the river. He turned back from his regiment of light infantry and leaped fully clothed into the stream to save a lancer who was being carried away by the current. The Emperor considered that this deed, praiseworthy enough in a civilian, was not appropriate to a colonel at the head of his regiment in the face of the enemy. He told him so.

The Emperor spent the night at a Russian convent a quarter of a league from Kowno. There he stayed until the twenty-sixth to work out his plans, speed up the passage of the Niemen, and accelerate the movement of the troops in every direction. He learned that the Russian army was in full retreat; but that as it covered too extended a front, the left, under Bagration, was so far away that it would have difficulty in keeping communication with the centre.

"I will take a hand in it," said the Emperor, "if the Russians will not fight before Wilna."

The Emperor would gladly have given wings to the entire army. On the twenty-seventh he slept at Owzianiskai, and on the twenty-eighth arrived at Wilna at nine o'clock in the morning. This rapid movement without stores exhausted and destroyed all the resources and houses which lay on the way. The vanguard lived quite well, but the rest of the army was dying of hunger. Exhaustion, added to want and the piercing cold rains at night, killed off ten thousand horses. Many

of the Young Guard died on the road of fatigue, cold and
hunger. The leaders wanted these young men to rival the veterans who had survived so many toils, perils and privations;
and the youth of the army was thus the victim of misplaced
zeal.

The Prince of Eckmühl, who supported the advance-guard
of the King of Naples, had announced that Lieutenant-General
Balachof, chief aide-de-camp to the Tsar, had arrived at his
headquarters with a letter for the Emperor. The Prince was
ordered to invent some pretext to detain him. It was not until
two or three days after his arrival that he was given leave
to come to Wilna. Our advance-guard had had a lively engagement some leagues from the city, and another quite close
to it. Our cavalry had not come off best, and M. Ségur,
captain of light cavalry, had been taken prisoner.

The Emperor had definite information of the retreating
movement of the enemy. He was amazed that they had yielded
Wilna without a struggle, and had taken their decision in time
to escape him.

It was truly heart-breaking for him to have to give up all
hope of a great battle before Wilna. . . . He flattered himself that the Prince of Eckmühl would be more fortunate in
his movements against Bagration, and that the corps which
were to march on the Dwina would get into touch with the left
flank of the Russians.[1] His first question to any officer coming
to headquarters from the various army corps was, "How

[1] At the opening of the campaign the Russian forces on the Niemen
were composed of three armies. The First Army of the West, commanded
by Barclay, had its right wing (Wittgenstein) on the Baltic, its left wing
(Doctorov) in the environs of Grodno, its headquarters at Wilna. The
Second Army of the West, under Bagration, was extended from Grodno
to the Muchaviec, with headquarters at Wolkowysk. The Army of the
Reserve, under Tormasov, was extended beyond the Wolhynian marshes,
with headquarters at Luck. Opposite these forces the French army was
divided into two parts. One part, composed of the corps of Davout,
Oudinot, Ney, Eugène, Saint-Cyr, the Guard (Mortier) and Murat's cav-

many prisoners have been taken?" He was anxious for trophies, so as to encourage the Poles; and no one sent him any.

The Duke of Bassano and Prince Sapiéha undertook to organize the country and raise the Poles in arms; but the inhabitants seemed little disposed to respond to the appeals made to their patriotism. The pillage and the irregularities of all kinds in which the army had indulged had put the whole countryside to flight. In the towns the more respectable people kept within doors. Whatever the zeal of those Poles who had come with the army, the Emperor had to send for any of the responsible persons of Wilna whom he might require; for not a soul presented himself or offered his services.

The Emperor decided to summon M. Balachof to Wilna. The way in which His Majesty spoke of M. Balachof's mission made it seem a veritable trophy presented to the Poles, for he interpreted it as a proof of the Russian government's embarrassment, and a source of encouragement. I only learned of his arrival from the Prince of Neuchâtel, who told me what he knew of this mission, from which we augured nothing likely to favour peace. The Emperor Napoleon said:

"My brother Alexander, who showed himself so haughty with Narbonne, already wants a settlement. He is afraid. My manœuvres have disconcerted the Russians; before a month is over they will be on their knees to me."

M. Balachof brought a letter from the Tsar Alexander, and also instructions in keeping with its contents, to demand the

alry, was under the direct orders of the Emperor. The other, composed of the corps of Poniatowski, Reynier, Vandamme and the cavalry under Latour-Maubourg, was commanded by Jerome. The left wing, under Macdonald, was at Tilsit with orders to operate against Riga; the right wing, under Schwarzenberg, was on the Bug. After the twenty-sixth the First Russian army beat a retreat from Wilna on to Drissa. The Second Russian army got into motion on the twenty-ninth and retreated from Wolkowysk to Nikoliaev. As soon as they had cleared the Niemen Napoleon sent Oudinot and Ney in pursuit of Barclay, and Davout in the direction of Minsk to separate Bagration from Barclay.—Clausewitz, *La Campagne de 1812 en Russie*, Paris, 1900, 37 et seq.

reasons for this invasion in peacetime and without any declaration of war. He was also to propose, in the absence of any
known grievance caused by misunderstanding between the two
States, to exchange explanations and to avoid war if the Emperor Napoleon would retire to his positions behind the Niemen, pending negotiations.

It seemed, to the few who were initiated into the secret of
this proposal, that the rapidity of our movements had from
the outset disconcerted and upset the military dispositions of
the Russians; and that now, embarrassed and doubtful whether
he could rally Bagration's corps in front of the Dwina, the
Tsar Alexander was trying to delay our advance by any kind
of palaver whatsoever. I am repeating what I heard said, for
at the time I had no personal knowledge of the matter. I do
know, however, that in the presence of the Prince of Neuchâtel,
the Duke of Istria, myself and, I think, Duroc, the Emperor
Napoleon said in a loud voice:

"Alexander is laughing at me. Does he imagine that I have
come to Wilna to discuss trade treaties? I have come to finish
off, once and for all, the Colossus of Northern Barbarism.
The sword is drawn. They must be thrust back into their
snow and ice, so that for a quarter of a century at least they
will not be able to interfere with civilized Europe.

"Even in the days of Catherine," he went on, "the Russians
counted for little or nothing in the politics of Europe. It was
the partition of Poland which gave them contact with civilization. The time has come when Poland, in her turn, must drive
them home again. Do the battles of Austerlitz, of Friedland,
or the Peace of Tilsit give ground for the claims of my brother
Alexander? We must seize this chance to cure the Russians
of their curiosity about what goes on in Germany. I consent
to their admitting the English to Archangel, but the Baltic
should be closed to them. Why did not Alexander explain

himself to Narbonne or to Lauriston, who was at Petersburg and whom he would not receive at Wilna?

"Up to the very last, Rumiantsof has refused to believe in the possibility of war. He has persuaded Alexander that our movements were merely threats—that the maintenance of the alliance was too much in my own interest for me to be determined on war. He thought that he fathomed me; that he was more subtle than I am diplomatic. Now that the Tsar sees it is a serious matter, and that his army has been cut in two, he is afraid and wants to come to terms; but I will sign the peace at Moscow. . . . Since Erfurt Alexander has become too haughty. The acquisition of Finland has turned his head. If he must have victories, let him defeat the Persians, but don't let him meddle in the affairs of Europe. Civilization rejects these people of the North; Europe must settle its own affairs without them."

M. Balachof was well received by the Emperor, who invited him to dinner [July 1], together with the Prince of Neuchâtel, the Duke of Istria, and myself. I was more than astounded at this compliment, but it could not have been paid me on my own account, the Emperor having long since accustomed me not to expect any favours which he could possibly refrain from granting to those in his entourage.

The Emperor treated M. Balachof perfectly and spoke freely to him. In the conversation after dinner His Majesty remarked, apostrophizing me:

"The Tsar Alexander treats ambassadors handsomely. He imagines that he can conduct diplomacy with blandishments. He made a Russian out of Caulaincourt."

It was the customary reproach. Since he could not harm me in the eyes of my countrymen, who knew me well enough to discount this kind of reproach as I did myself, I paid no heed to it. But when it was repeated with the obvious intention of commending me to the good graces of the Emperor

Alexander, the words grated on me, and I could not refrain from answering the Emperor with some warmth:

"It is doubtless because my freedom of speech has too successfully proved to Your Majesty that I am a very good Frenchman that you can pretend to doubt it. The marks of kindness with which the Tsar Alexander so often honoured me were in reality addressed to Your Majesty. As your faithful servant, Sire, I shall never forget them."

The Emperor, observing my irritation, changed the subject, and shortly afterwards dismissed M. Balachof.

M. Balachof having left the Emperor's presence, His Majesty said to me jokingly that I was wrong to be incensed at his remarks about my having turned Russian; it was only a trick on his part to prove to the Tsar that I had not forgotten his tokens of goodwill.

"You torment yourself," added the Emperor, "by considering the harm I shall do your friend. His armies dare not await us; they will no more save the honour of his arms than they will that of his cabinet. Before two months are out the Russian nobility will force Alexander to sue me for peace."

To his usual grievances he added many other matters to prove to the Prince of Neuchâtel, the Duke of Istria, Duroc, and (I think) one or two of his aides-de-camp who were present, that I opposed this war and condemned his System.

So outraged was I at the reproach, "You are a Russian," that I could not contain myself. I answered the Emperor that I was a better Frenchman than those who extolled this war; that I had always told him the truth when others, in the hope of pleasing him, merely told him tales to excite his feelings. I added that, knowing the respect I owed to my sovereign, I took his pleasantries in good part when only my countrymen were present, for I already possessed their esteem; but that it was an outrage to doubt my fidelity and patriotism before a foreigner. Since the Emperor had published the fact, I said,

I was proud to be against this war—to have done all I could
to prevent it—and I even felt honoured at the discomfort and
vexation which my attitude had brought me. I concluded by
saying that, having for a long time seen that my services were
no longer acceptable to him, I begged permission to retire;
but as I could not honourably go into private life while the
war lasted, I begged him to give me a command in Spain and
permission to start on the morrow.

The Emperor answered me very quietly:

"Who is doubting your fidelity? I know well enough that
you are an honest man. I was only joking. You are too
touchy; you know perfectly well that I hold you in esteem.
Just now you are talking at random. I shall not reply to
what you are saying."

I was, I confess, so beside myself that, far from growing
calmer, I was on the verge of saying the most unbecoming
things to the Emperor.

The Duke of Istria pulled one tail of my coat, the Prince
of Neuchâtel the other, and between them they drew me aside
and begged me to retort no more. The Emperor—who kept
his patience and spoke, I am bound to admit, with the same
kindness—seeing that I was beyond listening to reason, retired to his study and left me to those gentlemen, who tried
vainly to lead me away and calm me. I had lost my head
completely. At last I reached my quarters, firmly resolved
to go. I did not retire to bed until I had put all my affairs
in order and left everything arranged for my departure.

Very early the next morning I asked Duroc to take over
my duties and receive the Emperor's orders. In vain did he
remonstrate with me. A little later the Prince of Neuchâtel
and Duroc came in succession from the Emperor, who, not
seeing me in the bedchamber at his rising, charged them to
tell me that he did not want to hear any more about my going.
But I persisted in my desire to be gone. Not seeing me when

he mounted his horse, the Emperor sent for me twice; but I was not to be found. I wished to avoid the embarrassment of answering people with whom it was unfitting that I should enter into explanations of my refusal to attend His Majesty.

Seeing that I did not appear, the Emperor, having taken some turns about the town and stopped by the bridge, gave orders that I should be found and told that his orders were for me to come speak with him. I could not refuse obedience, and I joined him whilst he was inspecting the outworks in front of Wilna.

As soon as I presented myself he pinched my ear.

"Are you mad to want to leave me?" he said. "I esteem you, as you know, and have no desire to hurt your feelings."

Whereupon he galloped off, pulled up soon afterwards, and began to speak of many other matters. Neither Duroc nor I could come to any other decision or say anything else, except that it was impossible to leave him.

The Diet of Warsaw, which met on June 24 as a general Confederation, had called the Poles to arms and summoned them to desert the standards of the oppressors whom they were serving. It sent a deputation to Wilna to lay its wishes and desires before the Emperor, and also to stir up the Lithuanians. The Emperor's reply to their address [July 11, 1812] treated Galicia as no part of Poland, and was so evasive that it chilled and dissatisfied the most zealous.

The Emperor showed incredible activity during his stay at Wilna. Twenty-four hours did not give him a long enough day. Aides-de-camp, orderly officers, staff officers, were constantly on the roads. He waited with growing impatience for reports from the corps on the march. His first words to all who arrived were invariably, "How many prisoners have been taken?"

The Emperor's plans were taking shape, and late at night

on July 16 he left Wilna to join his Guard at Swenziany. There the Emperor received despatches from the King of Naples giving details of a check to his cavalry. At the same time the King announced the evacuation by the Russians of the entrenched camp at Drissa, and the general retreat of the Russian army, which had abandoned all its positions and the works upon which it had been labouring for two years. This was inevitable, for Bagration would have been cut off from Barclay and the Southern provinces if he had not hastened to take this step. The Emperor had long predicted it, and it augured well; the news went to his head, and at the same time kindled the enthusiasm of those who were coldest towards the Polish Cause, as it was called at headquarters.

His Majesty at once decided to go to Gloubokoje, and the Guard was immediately despatched towards that place. The Emperor spent twelve hours at Swenziany to dictate orders, and marched the whole of that night in the hope that, by the rapidity of this movement, he could make contact with the Russian army. In the morning he arrived at Gloubokoje, a fine monastery in a very fertile stretch of country. This astounding march from Wilna to Gloubokoje proved that horses well ridden can cover a surprising distance, for the mounted chargers and the animals laden with heavy packs left Wilna at six o'clock in the morning, reached Swenziany at eight o'clock in the evening, and by noon of the following day were at Gloubokoje, having thus covered forty-eight leagues. The saddle-horses made the journey of thirty-four leagues from Swenziany to Gloubokoje in eighteen hours without one falling sick.

The King of Naples, who commanded the advance-guard, was on the Dwina. Various cavalry skirmishes with mixed success had followed that ill-performed reconnaissance which had cost us General Saint-Geniès and many officers. The Russian army, having concealed its line of retreat, was able to effect it without being harassed; but the Marshal-Prince of Eckmühl, by his rapid march on Mohilew, had cut off the retreat of Prince Bagration, who engaged in a lively battle with the advance-guard at Salta-Nowka in a vain attempt to reopen his communications.

Having failed to do this, after futile efforts in which he lost from four to five thousand men, he decided to attempt a new détour to get into touch with the main army, but was not able to rejoin it until they reached Smolensk. This affair was very costly in men, principally to the Russians—though very few prisoners were taken.

It was ascertained at the same time that the Tsar Alexander had left Polotsk on July 18, and his army some days previously; also that he had gone on to Moscow to call the nation to arms.[2] It was thought that he had left the army in order to escape the responsibility of subsequent military reverses— since its earlier movements had been unfortunate, in that the forces had been separated and obliged to evacuate the great entrenched camp at Drissa, which was looked upon in Russia as an invincible barrier if held by sufficient troops. Everything seemed to indicate that the corps were far from being up to strength, as was supposed, and as they might easily have been if, as the Emperor said, the Russian chiefs and commissariat had not put a quarter of the army into their own pockets.

It was also learned that a ukase had been issued for calling to the colours one man in every hundred, as well as two proclamations by the Tsar Alexander, one to the Russian nation and the other to the people of the city of Moscow, which could leave no manner of doubt as to the desire to make the war a national one. Printed notices, signed by Barclay and tossed to our outposts, proved that he was not even scrupulous

[2] Alexander I, who held no actual command himself, left for Moscow on July 14 at the instance of his generals, who were apprehensive of his incapacity.—Cf. K. Waliszewski, *Le Regne d'Alexandre I*, II, 59.

as to the means he would employ, for the French and Germans were asked to desert their standards and settle in Russia.

The Emperor appeared amazed at this.

"My brother Alexander stops at nothing," he said. "If I liked, I could promise his peasants freedom. He has been deceived as to the strength of his army, he does not know how to employ it and he does not want to make peace; he is not consistent. A man who is not the strongest should be the most politic; and his policy should be to make an end."

The Emperor was overjoyed when he learned of the evacuation of the camp at Drissa which the Russians had taken two years to fortify. Alexander's departure thence seemed to him a great achievement. He rightly attributed it to his own rapid movements, which had prevented the joining up of the various corps of the whole army, and had obliged it to evacuate the camp without a battle in order to seek a rallying-point further away. Now, he said, he could choose between Moscow and Petersburg, if Russia did not sue for peace.

By rapid manœuvres he hoped to force the Russian army to give battle as he desired, or else to demoralize and undermine them by continual retreat without fighting. He added that Bagration's corps would not join the main army, that it would be captured, or anyhow be partially destroyed, and that this would cause a great sensation in Russia, as that general was one of Suvarof's old comrades in arms. The Emperor had quickly decided to move against Witepsk, in the hope of forcing the Russian army to fight in defence of that town and await Bagration, whom the Prince of Eckmühl continued to press so closely.

His Majesty left Gloubokoje on the twenty-first, and slept at Kamen on the twenty-third. The hussars of the Russian Guard suffered severely in an affair with our advance-guard near Beschenkowitschi [July 25]. It was on reaching that small town that the Emperor noticed what we had already observed for days past—that all the inhabitants had fled, leaving their houses absolutely deserted, and that everything went to prove that this migration was in accordance with a definite plan carried out under orders recently issued by the government.

From Beschenkowitschi to beyond Witepsk we were always in bivouac or under canvas.

The Emperor was so anxious for a battle that he drove the army forward with all his energy and all the brilliance of his genius. The battle of Ostrowno [July 26], after Beschenkowitschi, was quite costly but sufficiently advantageous. It was nevertheless only a rear-guard action in which the enemy really obtained the result he desired, for he hindered our movement, forced us to make fresh dispositions, and in consequence delayed us several hours.

The army again began to advance, and on the morrow we found ourselves in presence of the enemy, who was occupying the heights crowning a great plateau in front of Witepsk. The Emperor was on horseback before daybreak [July 27], and the reconnaissances pushed as far as the Lutchiesa River found a strong body of enemy cavalry in position. Our infantry arrived. Two regiments had already crossed the bridge but were waiting on a plateau, a little in advance and to the right, until the artillery and the remainder of the cavalry should join them. The enemy deployed considerable masses of cavalry, which bore down on the weak regiments of light troops that composed our advance-guard, who were formed in two lines, to the left of the road and in front of the gully. Our cavalry regiments reached them, but could not form up quickly enough to make headway against the masses of men already engaged with our advance-guard, over which the enemy gained at the outset an easy success.

During this time a company of light infantry, detached from

our left to support the small force of our cavalry, proved
what the resolution of this admirable branch of infantry can
do, even when it is cut off.   Placed along the stream and in
some bushes and houses in front of the gully, these brave
fellows were surrounded by a cloud of cavalry against which
they fired at will in support of our feeble squadrons.   They
kept up a continuous fire, and emptied many saddles among
the enemy, doing such damage that by degrees they forced
him off the flank of our squadrons, which would have been seriously threatened from the onset of the attack had it not been
for this valuable help.

Several times we saw five or six of these light infantrymen
assemble some fifty paces from the enemy squadrons, when
a knot of horsemen was bearing down on them, and stand back
to back, holding their fire and waiting till they had them at
point-blank range.   They even took some prisoners.   This
company played a great part in the events of the day.   The
Emperor said to several of them, who brought him prisoners
and asked for the cross: "You are all brave lads, and you all
deserve it."

The day was spent in manœuvring, bombarding, and minor
attacks to test and adjust our respective positions in preparation for the great battle for which the Emperor and the
majority of the French were hoping on the morrow.   The Emperor was cheerful and already beaming with pride, so confident
was he of measuring his strength with the enemy and obtaining
a result that should give some colour to his expedition, already
too far-flung.   He spent the day in the saddle, reconnoitred the
terrain in every direction, even at a considerable distance, and
returned to his tent very late, having actually seen and checked
everything for himself.

It is impossible to give any idea of the general disappointment—especially the Emperor's disappointment—when at day-

break [July 28] the certainty was borne in upon us that the Russian army had vanished and abandoned Witepsk. Not a soul was to be found, not even a peasant, who could indicate the direction taken by the enemy [Barclay], for he had not passed through the town.

For some hours we had to act like huntsmen and follow up in every direction the track he had taken. What was the use? What route had his masses of men and artillery followed? No one knew, and for some hours no one could know, for there were signs of them on all sides.

Moreover, the Emperor at first only sent out his advance-guards. He passed rapidly through the streets and outside the town, and then rejoined his Guard, which, like the rest of the troops, was already on the march along the road to Smolensk. The troops were constantly harassed. Many of the horses were unable to stand up through the charges the vanguard made; and so their riders were lost. The Emperor bivouacked at Lochesna with the Guard, and remained there through part of the following day [July 29], waiting for news.

But there were no inhabitants to be found, no prisoners to be taken, not a single straggler to be picked up. There were no spies. We were in the heart of inhabited Russia and yet, if I may be permitted the comparison, we were like a vessel without a compass in the midst of a vast ocean, knowing nothing of what was happening around us. At last it was learned from two peasants who were caught that the Russian army was far ahead of us, and that it had been on the move for four days.

For more than an hour the Emperor remained undecided.

"Perhaps the Russians want to give battle at Smolensk," he said. "Bagration has not yet joined up with them; we must attack them."

CHAPTER IV

SMOLENSK

AT last he decided to give the army a much-needed rest. Part of the cavalry was already worn out, the artillery and infantry were exhausted, the roads were covered with stragglers who destroyed and wasted everything. It was essential to organize our rear and await the result of the operations undertaken by the corps that had remained on the Dwina. The certainty that the Russian army was going to escape him, and that he would not, for some time, obtain the battle he desired so keenly, cast the Emperor into deep gloom. Eventually [July 29] he resigned himself to the necessity of returning to Witepsk.

As I have said, our cavalry and artillery had already suffered severely. A very large number of horses had died. Many were lagging behind, wasting away, wandering at the rear; others followed their corps, to whom they were but a useless embarrassment.

The King of Naples was better able to appreciate these troubles than anyone, and he told the rest of us about them when he chatted with us. He even ventured to make some remarks to this effect to the Emperor, but His Majesty did not care for reflections that ran counter to his projects, and lent a deaf ear. He changed the subject; and the King of Naples, who above all wished to please him—and who flattered his own vanity at the same time, by so doing—kept to himself the wise reflections which he had voiced to us alone. He soon forgot them entirely. Always at the forefront of the skir-

mishers, and eager to thrust his ostrich-plumes and fantastic
uniform beneath the very noses of the Cossacks, he succeeded
in ruining the cavalry, ended by causing the loss of the army,
and brought France and the Emperor to the brink of an abyss.

One day, however, General Belliard, chief-of-staff to the
King of Naples, observed in his presence to the Emperor, who
was questioning him:

"Your Majesty must be told the truth. The cavalry is rapidly disappearing; the marches are too long and exhausting,
and when a charge is ordered you can see willing fellows who
are forced to stay behind because their horses can't be put
to the gallop."

The Emperor paid no attention to these prudent observations. He wanted to reach his prey; and in his view it was
evidently worth paying any price to attain that object, for he
sacrificed everything to gain it.

While these events befell with the Grand Army, the King
of Westphalia was detached for the support of the Prince of
Eckmühl's corps. Jerome had let his troops pillage the Duchy
of Warsaw—of which he flattered himself he was the ruler—
and had driven that loyal country into discontent. Like a
good many other people, he imagined that Poland had been
awarded to him—this Poland which the Emperor wished to
revive and make into a buffer state. Accordingly, the King
of Westphalia thought it beneath his dignity to serve under
the victor of Auerstädt and Eckmühl; so he left the army [July
16] and returned to Cassel with his Guard.

Such was the support given to the Emperor in sore straits
by the brothers whom he had made kings. According to the
Emperor, the King was the cause of the Prince of Eckmühl's
failure to carry out his operations successfully, for he enabled
Bagration to escape, and thus brought about the initial failure
of the campaign.

The Emperor had left the Prince of Eckmühl only a portion of his corps. As soon as the Emperor understood the Russian movements, and saw that Bagration's corps had been separated from the main army, he threw the Prince against Bagration's army corps with the few troops left to him (a division and a half), but at the same time informed him that he was putting the King of Westphalia and his corps at his disposal.

The Prince, realizing the importance of the operation the Emperor had entrusted to him, pressed forward, knowing that Bagration had long and difficult defiles to traverse between extensive marshes; and he resolved to forestall the Russian at the end of these defiles, even if only with the head of his column. He accordingly informed the King of his intended movement. However, not only did the King give a cold reception to the officer who handed him the orders, but he even permitted himself to pass unsuitable comments about them, and, as I have said, took himself off with his Guard.

As he had planned, the Prince fell on the convoys and parks that preceded Bagration's march, captured a considerable part of them, took some prisoners, and continued his movement without encumbering himself with his captures, so as to be in position before the Russians could debouch.

Not being in sufficient force, after the King's departure, to give battle in open country, he took up his position before Mohilew [July 20], towards which town Bagration was heading; for the King of Westphalia's disobedience had saved him by facilitating his change of route.

Knowing that he had only to deal with the weak corps hurriedly mustered by the Prince, and that no one was pressing him, Bagration had the insolence to send an aide-de-camp to the Prince of Eckmühl to say that for some days he had been deceived by the Prince's activity, but that now he knew there was only the head of a column to oppose him; and to avoid a useless engagement he informed him that he intended to sleep the following night in Mohilew. Instead of replying to this boastful impertinence, the Prince strengthened his position as best he could. At the outset of the engagement success was evenly divided; but, though attacked with vigour, the Prince defended himself bravely [Salta-Nowka, July 23], eventually put four or five thousand of Bagration's men out of action, and forced him to retire and change his direction during the night.

When it is considered what an effect on subsequent events the destruction of Bagration's corps might have had, and the result that might have been obtained at the outset of the campaign by this first manœuvre of the Emperor and the masterly strategy of the Prince, it is impossible not to feel pity at the sight of that great captain betrayed by his own relations, before being betrayed in the end by Fortune.

On his return to Witepsk [July 29], the Emperor's first care was for provisions and hospitals. I was given the duty of visiting them, distributing money to the wounded, consoling and encouraging them. Never was there a situation more deplorable, or a spectacle more heart-rending for those who could think, and who had not been dazzled by the false glamour of Glory and ambition.

With the exception of the chiefs, the indifference of the administrative officers was complete. The innumerable waggons, the enormous quantity of supplies of all sorts that had been collected at such expense during the course of two years, had vanished through theft and loss, or through lack of means to bring them up. They were scattered along the roads. The rapidity of the forced marches, the shortage of harness and spare parts, the dearth of provisions, the want of care, all had helped to kill the horses. This campaign at express speed from the Niemen to Wilna, and from Wilna to Witepsk, had, without any real result, already cost the army two lost battles and deprived it of absolutely essential provisions and supplies.

To ensure that no indiscreet word should be uttered, the Emperor had consulted no one. Consequently our waggons and all our transport, built for metalled roads and to accomplish ordinary distances, were in no way suitable for the roads of the country we had to traverse. The first sand we came across overwhelmed the horses; for the loads, instead of being cut down in proportion to the weight of the vehicle and the distance to be covered, had been increased in the notion that the daily consumption would sufficiently lessen them. But in working out this scheme of daily consumption the Emperor had not taken into account the distance that would have to be covered before the point was reached when this consumption would begin.

The men, lacking everything to supply their own needs, were little inclined to pay any heed to their horses, and watched them perish without regrets, for their death meant the breakdown of the service on which the men were employed, and thus the end to their personal privations. There you have the secret and cause of our earlier disasters and of our final reverse.

Disorder reigned everywhere; in the town, as in the country around, everyone was in want. The Guard was no better provisioned than the other corps, and thence arose indiscipline and all its attendant evils. The Emperor was angry, and took the corps commanders and administrators to task with something more than severity; but this did no good in the face of the continued failure to bring up rations.

From a spirit of inexplicable and unpardonable meanness the provisioning of the ambulances had been inadequate. Even the personnel was too scanty. Never had carelessness been carried to greater extremes by the underlings of the administration: never had the courage of unfortunate men been more abused. The army surgeons and the administrative chiefs, as praiseworthy for their zeal as for their talents, were in despair at the state in which they found the hospitals. In vain did they endeavour to make up, by their care and attention, for whatever was lacking. We had got only as far as Witepsk, we had not fought a battle, and there was not even any lint!

The Emperor was extremely preoccupied and, though such behaviour was by no means usual with him, was often in such surly humour that he was careless in the expressions he used towards those who displeased him. He was greatly struck by the departure of the townsfolk and the flight of the country people. This method of retreat opened his eyes, maybe, to the possible consequences of this war, and to the distance it might take him from France; but the thousand-and-one things that ought to have opened his eyes to his position vanished before the slightest incident which might revive his hopes. A captured Russian officer brought to headquarters raised his spirits. He assured the Emperor that battle was certain to be given before Witepsk, that it had only been put off because a letter had been received on the twenty-seventh from Prince Bagration, containing news that he would not be able to join the army until they reached Smolensk. The Emperor flattered himself that as soon as the Russian army had joined up with Bagration it would make an attack. Full of hope, he immediately recovered his good temper.

The King of Naples, who, like the Emperor, had constantly been nibbling at the Russians, while doing ten or twelve leagues a day, and whose hopes for a success on the morrow had hindered him from calculating his daily losses, realized his weakness as soon as he was in position. He saw with apprehension the decreasing strength of his regiments, most of which were reduced to less than half their numbers. Forage and stores of all sorts were lacking, for his forces were always in close

order and on the alert. Arrangements had not been made for
rationing the men during the first few days, and the Cossacks
were already hindering them from bringing up stores. The
horses were not shod, the harness was in a deplorable state.
The forges, like all the rest of the material, had been left in
the rear. *The greater number of them, indeed, had been abandoned and lost.* There were no nails, no smiths—and no supplies of iron suitable for making nails.

For some days the men were turned to grinding corn, and
the ovens built by the Emperor's orders were put into service.
He strove to infuse everyone with his own activity, but everything proceeded listlessly. No amount of reasoning, not even
the experiences he had met with since the Niemen, nothing
could enlighten him as to the fatality looming ahead. If the
Emperor occasionally saw the situation and the consequences
of this war in their true light, if for a moment he spoke of it
dispassionately, the next instant his conversation took an entirely different turn. He was obsessed once more by his old
illusions and returned to his gigantic projects. The most insignificant skirmish, the arrival of reinforcements, the appearance of some ammunition waggons, a report from the King of
Naples, a few cries of *"Vive l'Empereur!"* at a parade, and
above all the letters from Wilna,[1] were enough to turn his head
once more.

The Prince of Neuchâtel was snapped at all day long, and
overwhelmed with distasteful business in return for his freedom of speech, his inconceivable activity, his unflagging devotion. As a matter of fact, a number of things went wrong:
the staff foresaw nothing. But on the other hand, as the Emperor wanted to do everything himself and give every order,
no one, not even the chief-of-staff, dared to assume the most
trifling responsibility. The administration, deprived, as we
have seen, of the means of execution and transport, was quite

[1] The Duke of Bassano, Minister for Foreign Affairs, was at Wilna.

unable to produce the results demanded by the Emperor, or to carry out orders which he gave without troubling himself as to how they should be executed.

The Prince of Neuchâtel was not any more discouraged than myself or the rest of us. We made it a point to seize every opportunity of enlightening His Majesty about the real state of affairs—to allay that spirit of excitement which tended to drive us forward, trusting in luck alone. Never was the truth so dinned into the ear of a sovereign—though, alas, to no effect. But it is only fair to say that, if the Emperor was far from welcoming the truth because it ran counter to his wishes, he did not reject it violently. At bottom he was not even unduly aggravated with those who had the courage to tell it, perhaps because he attached no value to it.

Those who had access to the Emperor were worried as much over the state of irritation engendered in him by the annoyances of the campaign as they were by the intoxication arising from his illusions—which last were encouraged by the very small number of persons who still shared them. The detractors of this great epoch may say what they like; never was sovereign surrounded by more capable men, men who were honest before all else and not mere courtiers, however strong the admiration and attachment which they professed for the Great Man. In spite of the varying shades of character and habits of each of them, wherever the Emperor cared to probe he was sure to find, if he wanted it, a sterling and even disagreeable truth rather than mere flattery.[2] Whether because there had been

[2] It is interesting to compare this passage with what Ségur says: "Each of these ministers and generals, in whatsoever concerned his own department, did not conceal the truth from the Emperor. If he then grew angry, Duroc, without yielding, wrapped himself up in a cloak of impassiveness; Lobau became rude; Berthier groaned and went away with tears in his eyes; as for Caulaincourt and Daru, one pale and the other flushed with anger, they vehemently repelled the Emperor's denials, the first with impetuous doggedness and the other with cold and dry firmness."—Ségur, *Histoire et Mémoires*, IV, 93.

a surfeit of Glory, or because common sense had taught us to distrust its glamour, the fact remains that no one was intoxicated with it. We remained moderate, and good Frenchmen above all.

It must be credited to the honour of the Emperor that his principles, his impartiality, the staunchness of his confidence which kept the spirit of intrigue at arm's length, had all contributed to the birth and growth of these noble sentiments. The master's well-known dislike of any change [among his entourage] gave everyone a sense of security which proved greatly to the advantage of truth. His strength of will had united all opinions and checked all private ambitions. France and the Emperor were blended in a glory which had become common to both. He had subjugated all minds and, without their knowing it, had bent the wills of all men to co-operate in the accomplishment of his own.

Who has not been carried away by the ascendancy of that superior genius, by the pre-eminently sovereign qualities, by his good-nature which was that of a private man in his own intimate circle? Who has not admired in him the great captain, the legislator, the restorer of social order—the man, in short, to whom the country owed its internal prosperity and the end of civil war? The Revolution checked; religion re-established; our laws, our administration, our industry increased a hundredfold; the prosperous state of our finances— was not all this a constant proof to us of our debt to the Emperor, and of what we could still hope for from him? If some persons, however, perceived the dangers of a collapse, when such continual success and glory were likely to delude the good sense of the majority, their foresight only applied to the particular situation in which they found themselves.

The Emperor had changed the national character. The French had become serious; their bearing was grave; the great questions of the day preoccupied all minds; petty interests were subordinated; the general sentiment was, one may say, patriotic; one would have blushed to show any other. The men who surrounded the Emperor prided themselves on not flattering him. Some even paraded the need of telling him the truth at the risk of displeasing him. It was the spirit of the time.

This reflection cannot have escaped those who had eyes. Opposition, as the Emperor noticed, did not cause the zeal or devotion of anyone to relax. He paid little attention to it and attributed it in general to narrow views, and to the fact that few people were capable of grasping his great projects in their entirety. It is certain that this opposition, if I may judge from my own case, arose solely from the wish to protect the interests of the Emperor's peculiar Glory. What personal sentiment or interest could have held sway amid such a unanimous concert of devotion? Who could then foresee what has since happened?

I can assert that no one was moved except by the interests of France and the need of preserving the prodigies of the Emperor's Glory. Only this twofold interest could be opposed to the inordinate ambitions of that Glory, all the dangers of which a secret instinct seemed now to be revealing. This enthusiasm of the Emperor—this ambition that induced him to run such hazards so far from France—certainly grew more noticeable to everyone as soon as the trend of events began to breed doubt of its success. Moreover, everyone condemned it in him, privately. But Peace, always rejected by England and forever represented by the Emperor as the motive of all his enterprises, justified him in the eyes of a nation over which, for some time to come, power and imagination would still hold more influence, and even more dominion, than reason and experience.

Only ten days had elapsed after our arrival at Witepsk before it became necessary to send ten or twelve leagues for fodder. The inhabitants who had not fled were everywhere in arms; consequently it was impossible to find any means of transport. Horses already in need of rest were further enfeebled by having to go in search of food, and were exposed, together with the men, to the danger of being caught by the Cossacks or slaughtered by the peasants, as frequently happened.

Having no further hopes that the enemy might attack him, as he had made himself believe when he knew that Prince Bagration had joined up with the main army [August 4], and on the other hand being unable to give his own army the rest it needed so long as the enemy was in force so close at hand, the Emperor decided on the tenth to follow him; he announced his intention of moving his right across the Dnieper at Rossasna, while the Russians, with the same object in view, would be carrying out the same movement in order to attack us on the right bank of that river.[3] The Emperor left Witepsk on the twelfth at eleven o'clock in the evening. On the morning of the thirteenth he was at Rossasna on the left bank of the Dnieper; the Guard arrived during the day. A very weak garrison had been left at Witepsk with the sick and wounded.

The Emperor planned to fight a big battle and drive back the enemy so that he should be able to rest his army and organize the country for winter-quarters, while his corps on the Dwina should act with the same end in view. He was still fixed in his original purpose. He desired to reorganize everything so as to be in a position to march on the capitals when the spring campaign opened, if the measures he hoped to take— and the consequent embarrassment of the Russian government —did not induce the Petersburg cabinet to make peace during

[3] The Russians had actually decided to take the offensive, in three columns, on August 7. They gave up this plan on the eighth.

the winter, or even before. The Emperor counted on this outcome more eagerly than ever; for he was already tired of the
war and, as he said, would not raise difficulties in the matter
of peace conditions.

The next morning [August 14] he was in the saddle at daybreak. When night fell the Emperor returned to the Guard's
bivouac near Liadouï. The information obtained from some
wounded prisoners put an end to all the Emperor's uncertainties and confirmed his knowledge of a movement by Barclay
de Tolly on the right bank, which he had been led to suspect
since midday by the report of a reconnaissance. All corps were
ordered to press their march on Smolensk. The Emperor set
out with the Guard before daybreak, hoping to reach the place
in advance of the Russian army, in front of which we had
unknowingly defiled in going to Rossasna by way of Babino-
witschi.

Very early in the morning of the fifteenth he galloped off
to the advance-guard, at the gates of Smolensk. Having in-
vested the town closely, he quickly reconnoitred the environs.
The enemy appeared in force, our troops came up, and the
day was passed in bombardments and minor attacks to
straighten his positions and get as near the town as possible.

On the morrow the investment was made yet closer; a ceme-
tery and several houses which commanded the plateau on which
the town is built were destroyed. That evening the Emperor
brought some guns into position to bombard the bridge, which
could be seen plainly enough to observe troops defiling across
it, some entering the town, others marching out.

A little later it was seen that these were Barclay's last corps
arriving, and that part of the garrison had been relieved by
them. What was the reason for this change? Did it foreshadow
yet another retreat? The Emperor was puzzled, and at once
became annoyed at the idea of having to march on and move
yet further from his base, so as to come up with this army

which he could have forced into giving battle had he attacked forty-eight hours earlier.

He asked me what I thought of these movements of troops. He tried to make me say that the Russians would hold and fight a battle, which was what he wanted. He was like a man in need of consolation. I thought, on the contrary, that since the Russians no longer held the initiative and were therefore unable to choose their ground, they would prefer to retire; and I said so very plainly.

"If that is so," answered the Emperor, in the tones of a man who had suddenly reached a decision, "by abandoning Smolensk, which is one of their Holy Cities, the Russian generals are dishonouring their arms in the eyes of their own people. That will put me in a strong position. We will drive them a little farther back, for our own comfort. I will dig myself in. We will rest the troops; the country will shape up around this pivot—and we'll see how Alexander likes that. I shall turn my attention to the corps on the Dwina, which are doing nothing; my army will be more formidable and my position more menacing to the Russians than as if I had won two battles. I will establish my headquarters at Witepsk. I will raise Poland in arms, and later on I will choose, if necessary, between Moscow and Petersburg."

Delighted to find the Emperor embued with such good and sound ideas, I applauded his resolution; he seemed to me sublime, great, far-seeing, as in the day of his most splendid victory. I told him that this plan would really lead to peace, for it would strengthen him step by step as he advanced, and would deter him from running too great risks. The Russian plan of campaign proved that they wished to draw him into the interior of the country, lead him further from his base, and shut him up amid the ice. It was imperative not to play their game, I added.

His Majesty seemed to approve my reflections highly, and

to have made up his mind at last. I hastened to report my conversation to the Prince of Neuchâtel, so that he should do his utmost to hold the Emperor to his wise resolutions; but the Prince seemed to be doubtful whether they would survive the taking of Smolensk. Alas, how right he was! In my joy at what I heard, I too had let illusions run away with me.

On the seventeenth the Russians were compelled to evacuate all their positions outside the walls. The Emperor brought up the siege batteries and placed thirty pieces to break down the bridge, which was plainly visible now that we were close to the town. This battery so harassed the enemy that his columns defiled across it at the double. They were clearly in full retreat. Wishing to launch an assault, the Emperor, some engineer officers, and some of the staff decided to reconnoitre the enceinte, but they had no scaling ladder. Finally, the reports which he received made the Emperor decide to abandon that project. Towards evening the enemy's retreating movements were unmistakable. The town had been on fire since morning, and the flames, fed by the enemy themselves, showed no sign of abating.

During the night the conflagration grew worse. It was a fearful sight—the cruel prelude to what we were to behold at Moscow. Unable to sleep, I walked about (it was two o'clock in the morning), reflecting mournfully on the consequences that must ensue from this war if the Emperor did not hold to the good intentions he had shown on the previous day. These scenes of horror and devastation inspired in me, I believe, a presentiment of those of which I was later to be the unhappy witness. My conversation with the Emperor continually came to my mind, and consoled me a little; but the Prince of Neuchâtel's observations were no less insistent, and past experience inclined me all too strongly to share his opinion and his apprehensions.

The night was cold. I drew near to a fire burning before the Emperor's tent, on the side facing the town, and was growing drowsy as I sat before it, when His Majesty came up with the Prince of Neuchâtel and the Duke of Istria. They gazed at the flaming town. It lit up the whole horizon, already studded with the sparkle of our own bivouac fires.

"An eruption of Vesuvius!" shouted the Emperor, clapping me on the shoulder and waking me from my stupor. "Isn't that a fine sight, *Monsieur le Grand Ecuyer?*"

"Horrible, Sire!"

"Bah!" he said. "Gentlemen, remember the words of a Roman Emperor: 'A dead enemy always smells sweet!' "

We were all taken aback. For my own part, I at once recalled what the Prince of Neuchâtel had said; and this and the Emperor's remark long haunted my inmost thoughts. I looked at the Prince—and we exchanged glances, as men who understand each other without speaking. . . .

At four o'clock in the morning [August 18] some marauders, who had been on the watch, made their way into the town through old gaps that the enemy had not so much as repaired; and at five o'clock the Emperor learned that the place was evacuated. He gave orders that the troops should not enter except in formation; but the men had already got in by several loopholes which they had opened and scaled. The Emperor mounted his horse, reconnoitred the enceinte on the east, and entered the town by an old breach in the wall. He went all round the city at once, and eventually stationed himself at the bridge, where he spent the day hastening its repair.

The buildings in the public square and the finest houses in the town had been but little damaged. The arsenal was intact, though not much of anything was left in it. Every quarter of the town had suffered; the inhabitants had fled with the army, the only people left being some old folk of the lowest classes, a priest and an artisan. They told us all they knew about what had happened in the town, but could give no information concerning the army, not even what its losses had been. The Emperor seemed well satisfied, even triumphant.

"Before a month is out," he said, "we shall be in Moscow; in six weeks we shall have peace."

Marshal Ney had made all preparations for crossing the Dnieper a league from the town, in order to follow up the Russians, whose rear-guard only was in sight; pursuing the enemy [August 19], he found them in position at Valutina. General Borrelli, who was attached to the staff of the King of Naples, came to inform the Emperor of this.

He refused to believe that they would offer any resistance, or that anyhow there was more than a rear-guard in position; but successive reports convinced him that it was a more considerable corps. He proceeded thither himself and immediately sent several officers to the Duke of Abrantès and even the Prince of Neuchâtel, with orders to advance and engage the Russians, without letting a single man escape. In the meantime Marshal Ney had attacked and overthrown the enemy with his usual boldness; but a grenadier division, sent to reinforce the rear-guard, held the position despite a fresh attack by Gudin's division. This general, one of the most distinguished in the army, was mortally wounded at the start of the action, and lived but a short while. He died esteemed by the whole army and mourned by all who knew him. This occurrence did not hinder the troops from taking the first position. But the enemy were successively reinforced, and the Duke of Abrantès, who was to have outflanked him and turned his left, did not come up in time; [4] so the Russians held the crest of

---

[4] Junot, ill and discouraged after crossing the Dnieper at Prouditchevo, had been seized with a fit of indecision from which Gourgaud, sent to him by the Emperor, was unable to rouse him.—Cf. Gourgaud, *Napoléon et la Grande Armée en Russie*, Paris, 1825, 172.

their position until nightfall. When the Emperor reached a point which gave him a view over the whole countryside, he again sent orders to the Duke of Abrantès to act with vigour.

"Barclay is mad," he said. "That rear-guard is ours, even if Junot only marches here at ease."

The Emperor learned of the end of the affair before he reached Valutina, and returned to Smolensk highly incensed with the Duke of Abrantès, who had not acted with the vigour he had shown on previous occasions. The Prince of Neuchâtel and the Dukes of Istria and Elchingen reproached him for not having marched up fast enough; for his part, the Duke of Abrantès, whose corps was composed of foreign troops, contended that, since he was obliged to march in close order so as to run no risks, his movement had been delayed by obstacles which forced him to bear to the right.

From what the Prince of Neuchâtel and the King of Naples said, no such obstacles existed. I remember the different reports that were made to the Emperor. At the sound of gunfire the King of Naples went in person to the Duke of Abrantès, whose corps was in front of his own. Seeing how useful, and indeed how glorious a diversion he could make, the King pressed him to hasten his movements.

"You are annoyed at not being a marshal," he said. "Here is a fine chance! Take it! You are sure of winning your baton."

While waiting for his cavalry to come up, the King placed himself at the head of the Württembergers who formed the Duke's advance-guard, with the object of beginning and pressing on the advance, at the same time making the Duke promise to support him. When the King put this cavalry to the charge, they would have distinguished themselves and driven back the Russians, but the Duke of Abrantès's corps did not follow up, and the King was obliged to slacken his movement for fear of being cut off; he had to wait for his own troops, who, still at some distance, were moving up at the trot. The Emperor's anger can readily be imagined, when he received several reports of what had taken place.

"Junot has let the Russians escape," he said bitterly. "He is losing the campaign for me."

At that instant he followed up this reproach with the severest strictures and threats; but as usual the memory of good services in the past outweighed the faults of the moment, and his discontent had no sequel.

The Emperor busied himself with making Smolensk what he called his pivot—a safe stronghold for his communications, in the event of his being reluctantly forced to push on further. He worked night and day in attending to all the administrative details, notably for provisions and the requirements of the hospitals.

He had ordered several reconnaissances of the fortress and the environs. General Chasseloup [of the engineers] having come to him with an account of what had been done, the Emperor remarked jokingly, "Wouldn't you like to make another Alexandria of the place and eat up another fifty millions of money? Russia is not worth that."

General Chasseloup was proposing nothing of the sort; he only wanted to erect some outworks in order to form a point of defence on the Dnieper. The next day [August 20] the Emperor stopped all the work in hand, appearing to have no wish to go beyond Smolensk.

This retreat of the Russians, without any possibility of saying where they would halt, the increasing certainty that they themselves had set fire to Smolensk, and this war of mutual destruction with no result beyond the gaining of ground,—all these circumstances gave food for serious thought to the Emperor, and confirmed his desire to go no further and to do his best to bring about negotiations. The following details can leave no doubt of his intentions, which he openly explained to the Princes of Neuchâtel and Eckmühl.

After his arrival at Smolensk the Emperor enquired whether there was any slightly wounded officer or any man of some standing in the place. The only person they could find was a Russian officer, who had come, I believe, with a flag of truce, and for some reason or another had been detained. The Emperor interviewed him and, after a few insignificant questions, asked him if there was going to be a battle. He added that honour required the Russians not to yield their country without giving battle—without even once measuring strength with us. Thereafter it would be easy to make peace, as between two champions reconciled after a duel. The war, he said, was only a matter of politics. He wished for nothing better than that the Tsar Alexander should feel as little resentment as he did.

The Emperor added later that he was going to send this officer back to his own army, on condition that he would repeat to the Tsar what he was going to tell him: namely, that he, the Emperor Napoleon, wished for peace; that he had wanted nothing better than to reach an understanding before war had broken out.

The officer promised to convey these messages, but at the same time observed that he did not think peace possible so long as the French were on Russian soil.

CHAPTER V

BORODINO

THE Russian army marched in good order, without undue haste, like men intent on abandoning nothing and prepared in case of necessity to stand their ground. The King of Naples believed that their good marching order showed their intention of giving battle. He even had the idea—it is not known why—that Barclay de Tolly had taken up his position behind the Ouja, and that he was establishing entrenchments in front of Dorogobouje in preparation for this battle.

The King thought this might be the battle for which the Emperor had expressed so many hopes, and that if we gained it the army could be ensured of a long rest in billets without being forced to leave its base too far behind. Our numerical superiority and our habit of success justified us in believing that we should gain a victory. The King of Naples poured forth his dreams and hopes to the Emperor. I call them dreams, for Miloradovitch's reinforcements had not come up, and the Russians were in no position to give battle.

But these hopes were too sanguine, and accorded too well with the Emperor's own views, not to sweep him off his feet. He left Smolensk in all haste [one A.M., August 25]. The Guard moved ahead in echelon to support the King of Naples if necessary, and was ordered to press forward; and once again the Emperor was running a blind risk, to some degree against his will. Reaching Dorogobouje on the twenty-fifth, he stayed there through the twenty-sixth.

Once more the gauntlet was flung down, and the Emperor

was not the man to turn back. The sight of his troops and all
the warlike bustle exalted him. As soon as he found himself
amidst these elements, the wise thoughts he had entertained in
Smolensk yielded to the enticements of Glory. It was said that
we should overtake the enemy forces on the morrow; they were
hard-pressed; they could not always escape, at the rate they
were being driven. It was useless to expect real rest until a
battle had been fought; otherwise we should be kept constantly
anxious. In short, as many good reasons were found for pushing forward as had been discovered, forty-eight hours earlier,
for staying at Smolensk; and once again we set off in pursuit
of the glory, or rather the fatality, which relentlessly prevented
the Emperor from holding to his good intentions and wiser
projects.

The news of a success obtained by Prince Schwarzenberg
[Austrian] over the Russians revived the Emperor's hopes.

"This gives colour to the alliance," he said. "That gunshot
will re-echo in Petersburg, in my brother Alexander's throne-
room. It is a good example for the Prussians. Maybe it will
put them on their mettle."

He asked me if Prince Schwarzenberg was well-known at
Petersburg, and whether his connections were with the most
exalted personages of the Court. He granted him a second
sum of five hundred thousand francs on account of secret ex-
penses, and instructed the Prince of Neuchâtel to send him the
bond.

Several corps received bread at Dorogobouje—an unusual
occurrence.

Confirmation was had there of details about the Tsar's arrival
at Moscow on July 24, of which we had known little and had
not even heard until after our arrival in Smolensk. We learned
that he had convoked the nobility and townsfolk; that he had
not concealed the true condition of the State, and had asked
the various governments for aid. Moscow had offered eighty

thousand men, and the others in proportion. Little Russia had
given him eighteen thousand Cossacks; and private individuals
had supplied battalions, squadrons, and companies all fully
equipped. To give this armament a national and religious
character, Archbishop Platow had offered the Tsar the miracle-
working ikon of St. Sergius, which His Majesty in turn had
given to the Moscow Militia. In short, a crusade was being
preached against the French.

From Dorogobouje the army marched almost in line, the
King's cavalry, the Guard, the First Corps and Marshal Ney's
corps on the road, the Poles on the right, the Viceroy [Prince
Eugène] on the left. We found ourselves on the highest plateau
in Russia, the watershed from which the Volga flows into the
Caspian Sea, the Dnieper into the Black Sea, and the Dwina
into the Baltic. Since crossing the Dnieper the troops and the
artillery had become exhausted by the sand; but Barclay's
supposed readiness to give battle made us hold to what sem-
blance we could of mass formation.

Some believed that the burning of the cities and market-
towns which we entered was due as much to the disorders of
our vanguard as to the Cossack rear-guard, who cared little for
Russia. I confess that at first I shared this opinion, not com-
prehending what object the Russians could have in destroying
all their public buildings of a non-military character, and even
private houses, which could not, after all, be of great service to
us. Several persons spoke to the Emperor about these fires. He
ordered my brother [1] to take a strong detachment of the Guard
[August 29] near Wiasma and press the enemy so closely as
to enter the town on the heels of their rear-guard, thus finding

---

[1] Auguste-Jean-Gabriel de Caulaincourt, younger brother of the Duke
of Vicenza. Born September 15, 1777—killed September 7, 1812, at
Borodino. General-officer of the Imperial cavalry since 1808: now aide-
de-camp to the Emperor. Auguste Caulaincourt was promoted general
of division in 1809, after he had distinguished himself during the crossing

out at first hand what really happened and whether the Russians actually started any fires. The Emperor instructed my brother to keep order in the town, and not let a single straggler remain there.

These orders were obeyed to the letter. The enemy rearguard was in position, but evacuated the town after a hot engagement. My brother entered Wiasma in hot haste with some sharpshooters. The town was already on fire in several places. He saw Cossacks set light to inflammable material, some of which he discovered in various quarters where fire broke out later, before the last Cossacks had to flee. He set our troops to subdue the fire; everyone worked his hardest and some houses were saved, together with supplies of grain, flour and brandy. At first everything was saved from pillage, but that did not last long.

It was ascertained, from particulars supplied by some of the inhabitants who had stayed in their houses, that complete arrangements had been made by a detachment of Cossack rearguard long before our arrival, and that the place had been set on fire as soon as we came in sight. Everyone was taken aback, the Emperor as well as his men—though he affected to turn this novel method of warfare into matter for ridicule. He often spoke to us jokingly about what he called "*A people who burn their houses to prevent our sleeping in them for a night.*"

In spite of these fires, after leaving Dorogobouje those who were first on the spot found plenty of food, brandy, and even wine. The horrible spectacle of this dreadful destruction was therefore less staggering to men who found something to put into their stomachs—not to mention their knapsacks and canteens. There had been such desperate want and privation, such

of the Tagus at Arzobispo. He had been invalided early the next year, but was recalled to active service in the Russian campaign. Since July 7, 1812, he had been commandant of the Imperial general headquarters; and it was said (cf. p. 140) that the Emperor was grooming him to relieve Murat in command of cavalry.

exhaustion, and Russia had appeared at first such a forbidding country, that for most men the belly had become the sole barometer of feeling, belief and judgment.

In Poland everything had been lacking; at Witepsk, by dint of infinite pain and care, we had fared meagrely; at Smolensk, by searching the countryside, we had found standing crops, grain, flour, cattle, and even forage, but no brandy or wine. After Dorogobouje all was in flames, but the shops and cellars were well stocked, even to the point of luxury. The houses were soon found to contain hiding-places where abundance of everything was discovered. The soldiers pillaged; nor could this be stopped, since there was no issue of rations, nor, as we were marching without transports and living from hand to mouth, could there be any such distribution.

Most of the men fared well, even very well. It was the officers alone who sometimes suffered privation, for they did not enter houses until after the ransacking, and so could not share in the plunder. Thus the general or senior officer would be eating a piece of black bread at some soldier's camp-fire where fowls were roasting alongside sheep, where ham was sizzling among hundreds of eggs. The luxury, frequency and size of the houses—all signs showed that a great capital was near. Once again the soldiers became indefatigable.

The King of Naples, who was in command of the advance-guard, often covered ten or a dozen leagues a day. The men were in the saddle from three o'clock in the morning until ten at night. As the sun never sank beneath the horizon, the Emperor forgot that the day contained no more than four-and-twenty hours.

The roads were littered with dead horses, but every day and every moment the Emperor flattered himself that he was about to make contact with the enemy. He needed prisoners at any price; they were the only source of information about the

Russian army, for spies had become useless from the moment we crossed on to Russian soil. The prospect of Siberia or the knout cooled the zeal of the cleverest and most intrepid spy; besides, it was extremely difficult to penetrate into the country and even more so into the army. The only information received was by way of Wilna; nothing came to us direct.

By the end of the day our horses were so weary that a mere skirmish would cost us several brave fellows, their horses not being able to stand the pace. When our squadrons were recalled we saw troopers on foot, in the midst of the fray, dragging their horses by the bridle, and others obliged to abandon them altogether and escape on foot.

The Prince of Neuchâtel, Counts Durosnel and Lobau, and some other brave men in the Emperor's entourage, were continually presenting him with a picture of what was going on, and urging him to husband what resources he had left, if, as he said, he desired to meet the enemy in battle or to push forward to Moscow. The Emperor listened to us; but, since he always hoped to have on the morrow what escaped him that day, he was led on and on despite himself, and was forced to cover a dozen leagues when he had intended to make only five.

While we were following the Russian army, powerless to obtain the least information about it, great changes were taking place in its formation. General Kutusof, who had been summoned to the command in deference to the opinion of the nobles, joined it at Tsarewo, between Ghjat and Wiasma, on the twenty-ninth, without the Emperor Napoleon being aware of the fact. We were threatening the capital city; the Holy City was burnt down and occupied by the French; we were at the gates of Ghjat; and the Tsar, who had sent M. Balachof to Wilna, now vouchsafed no answer to overtures.

At last, about two leagues in front of Ghjat, the advance-guard captured a Cossack whose horse had been killed, and shortly afterwards a negro who called himself the Hetman

Platow's cook.[2] This latter fellow was taken as he was leaving a village where he had been pillaging. The King of Naples sent them both to the Emperor, who plied them with questions. Their replies struck me as so pointed that I made rather full notes.

The negro gave us particulars of the mode of life of his general, upon whom he always waited at table. He thus heard the conversation that went on, and was able to recount the rivalries of some of the generals, who were jealous of one another; but he knew nothing of the army's marching movements. He kept on asking to whom he was talking—before whom he had been brought—and at the same time making the most comical grimaces and contortions. He and the Cossack had to be told again and again that it was the Emperor himself who was interrogating them. Neither would believe that it could be the Emperor Napoleon marching with the vanguard and so near their Cossack friends; for they could not believe that the Tsar would be so near the enemy.

"Platow sometimes comes to the vanguard," said the negro, "but he does not march with them like this; nor does he stay with them. As for the Russian generals, they never go with the Cossacks, nor even with the Russian troops. If the Russians were to be in the van with the Cossacks, the French would not be at the gates of Ghjat, for there are many more Russians and Cossacks than there are French, and the Cossacks are not afraid of the French."

When told once again that it was the Emperor he was speaking to, he bowed, prostrated himself several times, and then began to dance, sing, and make every imaginable contortion. This negro had assured the King of Naples, who had no

[2] Count Matthew Ivanovitch Platow, general of cavalry and ataman of the Don Cossacks. Thiers, who was acquainted with this incident, confused the Cossack and the negro and combined them into a single person, whom he made "a Cossack, gunner in Platow's corps."—Thiers, XIV, 288.

THE EMPEROR NAPOLEON

Sketched from life by Girodet in 1812 at Saint-Cloud

Property of the Museum of Chateauroux

guide, that he knew the entire countryside, so His Majesty ordered the man to be sent back to him; and this was done.

The Emperor then had the Cossack brought before him. He had been kept to one side while the negro was being questioned; he was a man between thirty and thirty-six years of age, dark, five feet tall, with quick eyes, an open and intelligent face and a serious air; and he was apparently much distressed at finding himself a prisoner. He was especially troubled at having lost his horse, his money, and what he called his little package—that is to say the effects he had taken or stolen, which he carried on his saddle and used for padding out his seat. The Emperor told me to give him some gold pieces and lend him a horse from the stables; this consoled him, and his confidence was soon restored; he then talked as much as was wanted.

Attached to the rear-guard, he had seen nothing of the main army since Smolensk; it had suffered greatly in what he called the battle, that is to say at Smolensk. It would fight another battle in front of Moscow. The Russians complained bitterly of Barclay, who, they said, had prevented them from fighting at Wilna or Smolensk by shutting them up in the town. Kutusof had reached the army to replace Barclay two days previously. The Cossack had not seen him, but a young staff-officer had come on the previous day to speak to the Cossack officer and had disclosed this news, adding that the nobles had forced the Tsar to make this change, and that it was warmly welcomed by the army.

This news, which seemed highly probable to the Emperor, afforded him the greatest pleasure, and he repeated it to everyone. Barclay's temporizing nature was wearing him out. This retreat, in which nothing was abandoned despite the inconceivable activity of the pursuers, gave no hopes of obtaining from such an adversary the result he so much desired.

("This plan of theirs," the Emperor would sometimes remark, "will give me Moscow. But a good battle would finish the war sooner and lead us to peace—and that is how we are bound to finish it, anyway.")

On learning of Kutusof's arrival, he immediately observed with an air of satisfaction that the Russian general could not have come for the purpose of continuing the retreat. He would certainly give battle; he would as certainly lose it, and deliver Moscow to us, for he was too near the capital to save it. Thanks were due to the Tsar for having made this change at such a moment, which could not have been more propitious. The Emperor commended Marshal Kutusof on the score of his intelligence, but spoke of his ineptitude at Austerlitz and of his manœuvres there and in Turkey, adding that, with the finest army the Russians had ever had on the Danube, he had not been able to make peace at the gates of Constantinople, or to seize Wallachia. With an enfeebled and demoralized army he would certainly not prevent the French from reaching Moscow.

Kutusof would have to give battle in order to please the nobles, and in a fortnight the Tsar would have neither a capital nor an army. True, this army would have had the honour of not yielding the ancient capital without a struggle, and this was probably the Tsar's intention in making this change in the command, as he could then make peace without incurring the reproaches and censure of the high nobles who had chosen Kutusof, and upon whom, in consequence, could be imputed the effects of any reverses they might encounter. Undoubtedly, this had been his motive in yielding to his nobles.

The Emperor continued to question the Cossack, whose answers were all given with spirit, and showed a degree of intelligence remarkable in a common soldier.

"If Alexander's Russian soldiers, especially his generals, were like the Cossacks, you and your Frenchmen would not be in Russia," he told the Emperor. "If Napoleon had had Cossacks in his army he would have been Emperor of China long

ago. It is the Cossacks who do all the fighting; it is always
their turn. While the Russians sleep the Cossacks keep watch.
The Cossacks will defend Moscow because of Alexander, who
is a good prince, though his ministers and generals are deceiving him. His generals only fight when they have to; they
have given up Smolensk the Holy and that is a bad sign. If
Moscow is taken and the French enter the Cossack country,
Russia is lost. Cossacks are good soldiers; they will do their
duty to the very last, and then they will side with Napoleon.

"Napoleon is a great general; Alexander is a good Tsar. If
he liked, Alexander would be the best general in Russia. Russian generals are too fond of their ease; they sleep too much;
they must have cushions and every comfort; they only think of
themselves, not of their soldiers' needs. The French fight well,
but they do not keep a good look-out. They like to pillage;
they slip away from their units to hunt through houses, and
the Cossacks profit by this and capture large numbers every
day, and recover their booty from them. Had it not been for
the Cossacks the French would have been in Moscow, in Petersburg, even in Kazan. It is the Cossacks who hold them up
every day.

"The Cossacks like the King of Naples, who makes a fine
show, for he is a brave fellow and always the first to come
under fire. Word has gone round that he is not to be killed, but
they do want to take him prisoner."

We found Ghjat [September 1] partly burned and still
smoking. They had been caught at work sooner than at
Wiasma. Attempts were made to stop the fire. The Emperor
made an extended reconnaissance in front of the city and all
round it; he visited the hospital, which lay at the town gate
and had not been burned. He speeded up the rebuilding of
the bridges and the crossing of the troops. He did not return
until very late. The time had come at last for the battle he so

ardently desired. He went over with relish all he had heard, adding the following reflections: "The new general cannot continue this plan of retreat, which is condemned by national opinion. He has been summoned to command the army on condition that he fights; therefore, the system of warfare pursued hitherto must be changed."

These considerations decided the Emperor to prepare likewise for action. He spent the second and third at Ghjat in order to collect his troops and give the cavalry and artillery a little rest.

Feeling it needful to bring some order among the convoys that were blocking the roads, and thus give the artillery a chance of getting to the front in time for the battle which he deemed imminent, the Emperor ordered the burning of all vehicles that were jammed in front of the convoys. "I will even have my own carriage burned," he said to me next day, "if it is out of its proper place."

While proceeding on horseback, the Emperor came across a number of carriages that were being driven out of column, alongside an artillery train. He made the chasseurs of his bodyguard stop them, leaped from his horse, and ordered the leading one to be burned. There were objections; and M. Narbonne [whose carriage it was] pointed out that this might leave some officer stranded, should he lose his leg on the morrow.

"It will lose me a lot more than that if I have no artillery tomorrow," answered the Emperor.

Straw and wood had to be fetched to start the fire. While this was going on he had the calèche dismantled, and a light van following it was consigned to the same fate. As soon as the fire was lit the Emperor galloped off, and the drivers, I think, salvaged their somewhat singed vehicles.

"I wish it had been your carriage," said the Emperor to the

Prince of Neuchâtel. "That would create more effect; and you deserve to lose it—I'm always running into it."

"Behind Your Majesty's carriage," answered the Prince.

"That is Caulaincourt's fault," rejoined the Emperor. "Anyhow, I have promised him I'll burn it if I come upon it. Do not be put out at my threat, for I will show no more mercy to my own carriage than to anyone else's. I am commander-in-chief, and I must set an example." [3]

On the fourth, headquarters were in bivouac near Prokofewo, and on the fifth near Borodino. The Emperor stayed only a moment in his tent, which was pitched, as usual, in the middle of the Guards' square, but set off at once towards the attack which our right was making against two redoubts supporting the enemy's left.

This attack was carried out with such vigour that we were masters of the forts in less than an hour. The troops were ordered to remain in position and the infantry in square. This was a wise act of foresight on the part of the Emperor, because half-an-hour after dusk, and long after the action had taken place, Russian cuirassiers supported by infantry charged on our squares with great vigour, making for the redoubts, which they hoped to force us to evacuate and allow them to occupy during the confusion of a night attack.

The first square, taken unawares, lost its artillery and some men; the others, put on their guard by the firing, held firm, and the Russian cuirassiers, badly mauled by our guns and musket-fire and ill-supported in their attack, were obliged to retire and leave us these redoubts, which were the key of their position. Our troops even gained a little ground when they

[3] It is to be observed that Caulaincourt makes no mention of Napoleon's violent rating of Berthier, which took place at Ghjat, and as a result of which the chief-of-staff ceased to take his meals with the Emperor until they reached Mojaisk. This is related in several contemporary memoirs, notably by Denniée, *Itinéraire*, 62.

pursued them in the dark, and we established ourselves at the edge of a wood which it was of the utmost importance for the enemy to retain, if only to delay our attack and afford a post from which to observe our movements.

During the night the Emperor went through our encampment, inspected the captured redoubts, rode several times up and down the line to judge with his own eyes as to the enemy positions and their strength at each point. At the same time he visited his troops, as was his custom on the eve of battle.

At daybreak [September 6] the Emperor went once more to the principal redoubt; and under cover of the wood, the whole of which had been occupied during the night, he and the Prince of Neuchâtel and I approached very close to the enemy position. His Majesty then traversed the whole extent of the line, more particularly the centre and the left, which he reconnoitred as far as the outposts. He returned once again to the centre accompanied by the King of Naples, so that he could explain all his dispositions on the spot.

He then visited the extreme right, which was under the command of Prince Poniatowski, who had fought a brilliant engagement at the head of his Poles on the previous day and had gained much ground. The resistance of the Russians at this point was not what it ought to have been, nor what it had been elsewhere. The Emperor hesitated whether he should make a large movement on his right to turn the enemy position and partly avoid his redoubts, or whether he should simply take advantage of the two redoubts he had captured and engage their centre from the front and flank by launching an attack with our right. He was apprehensive lest the first of these plans, which would have threatened the enemy from the rear, would decide the Russians to make another retreat, especially as the loss of the redoubts which had been captured the previous day had greatly weakened their position. These considerations determined him to adopt the latter plan.

Seeing the enemy at ease in their positions, the Emperor decided to let the army rest during that day. This would also give him an opportunity of bringing into line the artillery reserves, and whatever had got slightly to the rear. He also thought—and this last consideration determined him—that the enemy, who had come at nightfall to retake the redoubts essential to the support of their left, would make some efforts during the day to recapture that position, or at least make some efforts to recover the ground gained by the Poles. If they did this, the Emperor hoped for an engagement which would produce exceedingly advantageous results for himself; but the day was spent on both sides in observing one another, except on the part of the Poles, who gained a little more ground, thus allowing us a very advantageous deployment on the enemy's flank for the morrow's attack.

Seeing that the Russians had not stirred, the Emperor came to the conclusion that they had constructed new fieldworks to replace those they had lost the previous day. About three o'clock it was even thought that they were retiring, and the Emperor, who was constantly watching them, was on the point of launching an attack; but upon a closer inspection from places which permitted the movements of the Russians to be better understood, it was ascertained that they were in their same positions. That evening the Emperor returned to his tent.

M. Bausset [Prefect of the Palace] had arrived during the afternoon. He brought letters from the Empress, whom he had accompanied as far as Prague on the way from Dresden, and he was also the bearer of a fine portrait of the King of Rome, by Gérard. The Emperor found this portrait hung in his tent when he returned from reconnoitring the enemy posts. The aide-de-camp of the Duke of Ragusa had arrived at the same time with reports of the bad state of affairs in Spain. The courier from Paris had brought the Emperor advance news of this some days previously. But Russian matters were too serious at the moment for him to pay much attention to the Duke of Ragusa's reverses in the Peninsula.

"The English have their hands full there. They cannot leave Spain and go to make trouble for me in France and Germany. That is all that matters," he said to me next day.

On the seventh, before daybreak, the Emperor was at the redoubt by our right, and, together with the Prince of Eckmühl, Berthier, and myself, went to the edge of the wood in front. As soon as daylight came, the Emperor's order of the day was read to the troops. It was brief but forcible, like all those written by himself on great occasions.[4]

The Poles, the King of Naples with his cavalry, who were on the left, and the Prince of Eckmühl's troops, were in motion before daybreak. Their attack was impetuous, and the defence stubborn. Prince Bagration, facing them, resisted vigorously and tenaciously, but our troops were so full of enthusiasm that nothing could stop them. General Compans, who was wounded in these first attacks, was replaced by General Rapp, who shared a like fate at the head of the same brave fellows. Generals who were killed or wounded were replaced without the least sensation being caused, without the action being in the least delayed, even when the Prince of Eckmühl himself was hit.

Marshal Ney overwhelmed and broke up the advance corps of the centre with his usual boldness. At seven o'clock there

[4] *Correspondance*, 19182.

> At the Imperial camp on the heights of Borodino.
> September 7, 1812, two o'clock in the morning.

Soldiers!—this is the battle that you have longed for. Victory now depends on you: it must be ours. It will bring us abundance, good winter-quarters and a quick return home.

Do as you did at Austerlitz, at Friedland, at Witepsk, at Smolensk; and may your conduct to-day be spoken of with pride by all generations to come. May it be said of you: *He was at that great battle beneath the walls of Moscow!*

was at this point a cannonade and a roar of musket-fire such as has not often been heard. In the meanwhile, the King of Naples backed up with his cavalry the impetuous attack of the infantry on the right, and of the Prince of Eckmühl's corps; and the two remaining fieldworks on the Russian left were taken.

At eight o'clock the Emperor was informed that Montbrun, general of division and commanding the First Cavalry Corps, composed of three divisions, had been killed. He recalled my brother, whom he had sent to the attack on the right, and who came up a moment later to announce the taking of the two redoubts and the subsequent successes.

"Go and take command of the First Cavalry Corps," the Emperor said to him. "Do as you did at Arzobispo."

The Prince of Neuchâtel drew him up a written order to show to the generals of division. My brother seized my hand, saying, "With things this hot, I don't suppose I shall see you again. We shall win, or I shall get myself killed."

His chronic sufferings often made him desire death; did they now conjure up in him this mournful presentiment? Or was it possibly the heat of the action? I do not know, but I could not rid my mind of this ominous farewell until an even more fatal event occurred to confirm the foreboding which had overtaken me.

Supported by part of the Viceroy's corps, Marshal Ney was backing up the right, and by ten o'clock the enemy had lost all the ground in front of the Great Redoubt at their centre. They had consequently lost the position on the left and the village that supported their centre [Borodino]; but their reserves were coming up. For a moment success hovered between the two sides towards our right, and we even had to draw in our advance-troops to the main body while falling back on the captured redoubts.

A formidable array of guns spat forth death in every direction; the Russian infantry made fresh efforts to regain their lost ground. The Great Redoubt belched out a veritable hell on our centre. In vain did Marshal Ney and the Viceroy combine their forces to attack it; they were repulsed. Returning to the attack a second time, they were no more fortunate, and Ney even lost a little ground. A section of the Guard, who had followed by echelons the movement of the corps which united the centre to the right, took up a position from which, if necessary, they could support this corps if the momentary forced retirement should become more serious. But our artillery checked the dash of the enemy, who for a long time stood firm under the fire of a devastating bombardment. Finally they were forced to yield the ground which we had previously taken from them.

All this time the Emperor was watching the movements at the centre; he had stationed himself opposite the last redoubt we had taken, and he gave a general order to halt for the moment and hold the positions we occupied, so as to give the artillery time, he said, to demolish those masses of infantry which stood motionless. It was then nearly eleven o'clock. Shortly before this, Lieutenant-General Likatcheff and some fifteen prisoners taken in the redoubt were brought to him. The officer in charge of them told the Emperor that they had put up a gallant defence. The Emperor received the general well. Seeing that his prisoner was without a sword, he expressed regret that he had been disarmed.

"I respect the courage of the unfortunate too much, sir," he said, "not to give myself the pleasure of returning his arms to a brave man."

With that he handed the general his sword, and asked him some questions. He then gave orders that the other prisoners should be questioned, taken care of, and treated, as the general had been, with the utmost respect.

This capture gave the Emperor great pleasure; but it seemed

inconceivable to him that so few prisoners had been taken, when these redoubts had been captured in such a rush and entirely surrounded by the King of Naples's cavalry. He complained bitterly and asked a great number of questions about it, not concealing the fact that he had desired and hoped for other results.

"We shall win the battle," he said. "The Russians will be crushed, but it will not be conclusive if I do not take prisoners."

He showed signs of anxiety. Between noon and one o'clock the Emperor ordered the Viceroy to resume the offensive and support the left of Marshal Ney, who was already supporting General Junot. The right, reinforced by the Young Guard, likewise had orders to push forward. The enemy, smashed by the guns and pressed simultaneously on all points, massed their troops and held firm despite the ravages made in their ranks by the guns. The Emperor then climbed into the redoubt to follow with his own eyes and direct the general movement he had ordered all along the line.

Our troops redoubled their efforts without gaining ground. The fire increased to greater intensity; we were at grips at all points. It was at this moment that my brother, having put in motion two of his divisions supported by two battalions of infantry, placed himself at the head of the Fifth Cuirassiers to lead the troops under his command on the Great Redoubt and thus ensure the success of this attack, already attempted in vain several times. He drove out the enemy, and from that moment the battle was won, as the Emperor himself said, for the Russians at once began a general retreat.

I think it was about three o'clock when an aide-de-camp arrived in hot haste to tell the Emperor that the Great Redoubt had been taken by my brother and that the enemy was retiring at all points. An instant later M. Wolbert, my unfortunate brother's aide-de-camp, who had not quitted his side, brought the Emperor the details of this affair, and told him that my brother had been killed by a bullet below the heart, just as he was coming out of the Redoubt to pursue the enemy who had rallied at some distance and were advancing to retake it. I was at the Emperor's side when this report was brought.[5] I need not attempt to describe my feelings.

"He has died as a brave man should," said the Emperor, "and that is in deciding the battle. France loses one of her best officers."

His Majesty immediately set off at a gallop in front of the cavalry, to join the King of Naples and make such dispositions as he considered necessary to assure and follow up this success. Marshal Ney and the Viceroy had supported the decisive movement of General Caulaincourt. The enemy's counterattack on the Great Redoubt was in vain, and the Russians were forced to retreat along the whole of their front.

One redoubt still remained to them, as well as a little fieldwork that commanded the Moscow road; and it seemed as though they wished to hold them. A thin wood covered their march and concealed their movements from us at this point. The Emperor flattered himself that the Russians were going to hasten their retreat, and he reckoned on hurling his cavalry on them in an attempt to break them. The Young Guard and

[5] Writing of these events, Ségur says: "Messengers were hastened to inform the Emperor of this victory and this loss. The Master of Horse, brother of the unfortunate general, heard the news. At first he was overcome, but he soon steeled himself in face of this misfortune and, save for the tears that rolled silently down his cheeks, he appeared impassive. The Emperor said, 'You have heard the news; would you like to retire?' He accompanied these words with an exclamation of sympathy. But at that moment we were advancing against the enemy. The Master of Horse made no reply; he did not retire, he merely lifted his hat slightly as a token of his gratitude and refusal."—Ségur, *Histoire de Napoléon et de la Grande Armée*, Paris, 1925, I, 401. Castellane (*Journal*, I, 150) confirms Ségur's account: "His brother, the Duke of Vicenza, learned the news in a cruel manner. He was at the Emperor's side; and an aide-de-camp came up sobbing, to announce the death of his general. The Emperor turned round and said to the Duke of Vicenza, 'You have heard the sad news; go to my tent.' The Master of Horse remained in the saddle."

the Poles were already on the march towards these outworks which the Russians held. In order to make out their movements the Emperor went with the sharpshooters. Bullets whistled around him; but he had made his escort stay behind. Seeing me at his side, the Emperor told me to go back.

"It is over," he said. "Go and wait for me at headquarters."

I thanked him but remained with him. The Emperor was certainly running a great risk, as the fusillade became so lively that the King of Naples and several generals hurried up to urge him to retire.

The Emperor then went in front of the columns that were coming up. The Old Guard followed them; the carabineers and the cavalry marched in echelon. The Emperor seemed determined to carry these last Russian fieldworks, but the Prince of Neuchâtel and the King of Naples pointed out to him that the troops were marching thither without any commander; that nearly all the divisions in the army had likewise been deprived of their commanding officers through death or wounds; that the regiments of cavalry and infantry were, as he could see, greatly reduced in strength. They added that it was growing late; and that though the enemy were certainly retreating, they were doing so in good order and showing an inclination to dispute every inch of the ground tenaciously, whatever the havoc wrought in their ranks by our guns.

They also urged that the only chance of success was to use the Old Guard for the attack, and that in the existing circumstances success at such a price would really be a check—while failure would be a reverse that would counterbalance the entire success of the battle. Finally they urged him not to engage the only corps in the whole army which remained intact and ought to be kept so for future occasions.[6] The Emperor hesi-

---

[6] It would be superfluous to emphasize the importance of Caulaincourt's testimony on the subject of the intervention and opinion of Berthier and Murat. The Emperor's hesitation at this juncture surprised all observers,

tated; he went forward once more to observe for himself the enemy's movements.

Meanwhile the King of Naples and the Prince of Neuchâtel had, in different directions, reached the walls of these redoubts. They rejoined the Emperor, whom they assured that the Russians were in position and far from retreating—that several corps were massing, with the look of men determined to retreat no longer. All the successive reports represented our losses as very considerable. The Emperor came to a decision. He suspended the order for an attack and contented himself with sending up supports for the corps still engaged, in case the enemy should be planning a counter-attack. This was unlikely, for their own losses were also immense.

Nightfall put an end to the fighting. Both sides were so weary that in several places firing ceased without orders having been given. At night the Emperor established his headquarters at the spot where he had taken up his stand at the beginning of the battle, on this side of the redoubts.

Never had a battle cost so many generals and officers.[7] Success was hardly won, and the fire was so murderous that generals, like their subordinate officers, had to pay in person for victory. We did all we could for the wounded whilst the battle was raging and during the night that followed, but most of the houses in the vicinity of the battlefield had been burned during the day, and in consequence many casualty stations passed the night without shelter.

There were very few prisoners. The Russians showed the

but historians have attributed it either to the state of Napoleon's health, or to the impression created in his mind by the hecatomb of the battlefield. *It is clear that Berthier and Murat themselves judged it useless and dangerous to order the intervention of the Guard,* which was the only corps left intact to enable the Emperor to consolidate his victory.

[7] "The returns I compiled from reports sent to the major-general by the chiefs-of-staff of the different army corps . . . showed forty-nine general officers killed and wounded."—Denniée, *Itinéraire*, 80,

utmost tenacity; their fieldworks, and the ground they were forced to yield, were given up without disorder. Their ranks did not break; pounded by the artillery, sabred by the cavalry, forced back at the bayonet-point by our infantry, their somewhat immobile masses met death bravely, and only gave way slowly before the fury of our attacks. Several times the Emperor repeated that it was quite inexplicable to him that redoubts and positions so audaciously captured and so doggedly defended should yield us so few prisoners. Several times he asked, of the officers who came with reports of our successes, where the prisoners were who ought to have been captured. He even sent orderlies to the various positions to make sure that more had not been taken. These successes, yielding neither prisoners nor trophies, made him discontented. Several times he said to the Prince of Neuchâtel and me:

"These Russians let themselves be killed like automatons; they are not taken alive. This does not help us at all. These citadels should be demolished with cannon."

That night the enemy began their retreat in plain view. Orders were given for the army to follow their movements. At dawn on the following day [September 8] there were only Cossacks in sight, and they were five miles away from the battlefield. The enemy had taken with them the great part of their wounded; and we had only the few prisoners I have mentioned, twelve guns from the Redoubt captured by my unfortunate brother, and three or four other pieces taken in the line by our troops during their first attack.

From early morning the Emperor was out in all parts of the battlefield, supervising with the utmost care the collection and removal of the wounded, Russian as well as French. Never was a battlefield so thickly strewn with dead. In the village round which the attack had centred, the Russian dead lay in heaps. On the plateau behind it the ground was covered with the corpses of Litowski's and Ismaelowski's Guards, slaughtered

by our guns. The Emperor carefully examined every portion
of this battlefield, the positions of each corps, the movements
they had made, the difficulties they had had to overcome. At
each point he demanded minute details of everything that had
happened, dealt out praise and encouragement, and was greeted
by his troops with all their wonted enthusiasm.

The Emperor took stock in detail of all the works thrown up
by the Russians. I cannot describe my feelings as I passed
over the ground which had been dyed by my brother's blood.
If the eulogies and the justice rendered by an entire army to
the memory of a brave man could have consoled me, I ought
to have had peace in my heart. . . .

After completing his reconnaissance, the Emperor galloped
off to the advance-guard. According to reports which he had
received that morning from the King of Naples, there were none
but Cossacks to be seen. A very small number of stragglers
were rounded up; the enemy had not abandoned so much as a
cart. The King counted on passing Mojaisk, and made the Emperor agree to establish headquarters there that evening; but
when he arrived before the town he found it strongly held by
enemy infantry and a large body of cavalry. A late start had
been made, and the day was declining. Not being able to
reconnoitre the position, we were obliged to come to a halt.
The Emperor established himself in the village in front of
Mojaisk; the enemy evacuated the town during the night, and
our troops entered it the next day at dawn.

The Emperor went into the town towards noon. He was
very much preoccupied, for affairs in Spain were weighing him
down just when those in Russia, despite this victorious battle,
were far from satisfactory. The state of the various corps
which he had seen was deplorable. All were sadly reduced
in strength. His victory had cost him dear. When he had
come to a halt on the previous evening, he had felt convinced
that this bloody battle, fought with an enemy who had aban-

doned nothing in their retreat, would have no result beyond allowing him to gain further ground. The prospect of entering Moscow still enticed him, however; but even that success would be inconclusive so long as the Russian army remained unbroken. Everyone noticed that the Emperor was very thoughtful and worried, although he frequently repeated:

"Peace lies in Moscow. When the great nobles of Russia see us masters of the capital, they will think twice about fighting on. If I liberated the serfs it would smash all those great fortunes. The battle will open the eyes of my brother Alexander, and the capture of Moscow will open the eyes of his nobles."

PART III
MOSCOW

CHAPTER VI

THE FIRE

MOJAISK was nothing but a vast hospital. Generals, officers, privates, all arrived there seeking the help which none could give.

The army continued its movement until September 11. Marshal Ney, in command of the advance-guard, was five leagues from Mojaisk along the road to Moscow, and the King of Naples a little further on. This retreat resulted in only a few prisoners. The Emperor had halted to give the troops some rest, and to carry out the reorganization necessary in case there should be a second battle.

On the thirteenth, when the whole army was again on the move, the Emperor halted all the columns. Our cavalry were so exhausted that they could not push their reconnaissance to any distance, and at the moment we knew so little of the enemy's movements that, doubtful as to the direction taken by Kutusof, of whom there was no news, the Emperor judged it advisable to pause. He had not received any reports from Prince Poniatowski on our right, and was for a moment uneasy about him, since he felt that the Russians might have taken advantage of our rest to fall upon us from that side and threaten our flank and rear in the hope of stopping, or at least delaying, our entry into Moscow until they had received replies from Petersburg. The Emperor still inferred that the enemy desired to propose a settlement whilst offering battle too.

Officers were sent out one after another in all directions. The King of Naples was ordered to make a strong reconnais-

sance along the Kaluga road.   At last the Emperor was reassured, and the army resumed its march.   He was delighted
to learn that the enemy, encumbered with wounded and baggage, were taking the Moscow road, where, according to various reports, outworks had been thrown up in preparation for a
second battle. . . .   The Prince of Neuchâtel told me that the
Emperor was amazed at the King of Naples's receiving no proposal from the enemy, who, notwithstanding their reinforcement by the militia and recruits, had done nothing to put themselves in an attitude of defence.   From that he inferred, and
he repeated it more than once, that the Russian army had lost
far more heavily at Borodino than had been supposed, and
that it would be in no position to continue the campaign that
year.   Since the battle the Emperor had spoken to scarcely one
of his entourage; he seemed to be in continual anxiety.

At ten o'clock in the morning of the fourteenth the Emperor
was on the heights overlooking Moscow, called the Sparrow
Hills, when he received a note from the King of Naples informing him that the enemy had evacuated the city and that a
Russian staff officer had been sent with a flag of truce to ask
for a suspension of hostilities while the troops were crossing
the city.   The Emperor agreed to this, but ordered the King to
follow the Russians step by step—to force them as far away
as possible, once they were outside the barriers.   He likewise
enjoined him not to enter the city, but to go round it if he
could.   He instructed the King to send him as soon as might be
a deputation of the city authorities, who were to meet him at
the city gate.

Shortly afterwards he ordered General Durosnel, whom he
had appointed governor, to enter the city with as many picked
gendarmes as he could muster, establish order there, and take
possession of the public buildings. He urged him particularly
to maintain order, to guard the Kremlin, and to keep him supplied with information.   The general was especially enjoined

to hasten the deputation of city authorities which the King of
Naples was to collect. This, the Emperor said, would give the
inhabitants of the town the best possible guarantee for their
tranquillity.

Not imagining for a moment that this deputation would fail
to appear, or that he would receive no news—a natural omission, considering the distance to be covered—the Emperor
reached the barrier of the moat at noon and dismounted there.
He grew impatient. He sent out fresh officers every minute,
and kept calling for a deputation or some citizens of note. At
last, one after the other, reports came from the King and General Durosnel. Far from having found any of the civic authorities, they had not discovered so much as a single prominent
inhabitant. All had fled. Moscow was a deserted city, where
one came across none but a few wretches of the lowest class.

Step by step the King of Naples followed the retreat of the
enemy's rear-guard,[1] and the Russian officer in command could
not speak highly enough of his courage, though he protested
against His Majesty's temerity. "Such is our admiration of
you," he said, "that our Cossacks have passed word round that
no one is to fire a shot at so brave a Prince. However, one of
these days," he added, "you will meet with misfortune." He
urged the King to be sparing of courage so fine as his. A
certain amount of time was gained in the exchange of such
compliments, and they were dispensed all the more lavishly as
the King seemed to welcome them. Wishing to make some gift
to so courteous a foe, His Majesty asked his staff if one of them
could not lend him some piece of jewellery. M. Gourgaud, the
orderly officer who was attending him in order to carry out the
Emperor's scheme of liaison, offered his repeater which the
King hastened to present to the Cossack officer.

While waiting for information the Emperor had spent his

[1] Murat entered Moscow at midnight, September 14, 1812.

time in reconnoitring, in various directions, the hills which commanded Moscow on that side. When he returned to the gate of the city he ordered me to write to the Archchancellor in Paris and to the Duke of Bassano at Wilna, informing them that we were at Moscow, and dating my letter from that city. He placed pickets to prevent any soldier from entering the place, but there were so many gaps in the walls that this precaution was of little avail. In the town itself a few shots were exchanged with armed peasants, stragglers from the Russian army and Cossacks who were met with everywhere.

As was the case in most of the private palaces, nothing had been disturbed in the Kremlin; even the clocks were still going, as though the rightful owners were in occupation. A few Russian stragglers caused some disorder; men were constantly being caught, but the gendarmes at M. Durosnel's disposal were quite insufficient to cope with them, so he confined his attention to the Kremlin and the Orphanage, which he kept intact. He asked the Emperor for more troops, informing him that all the houses were full of stragglers and deserters, and that, in view of the great size of the city, he must not think of making an entrance until a number of the houses had been searched and a proper system of patrols established in every quarter. The Emperor instructed him to apply to the Duke of Treviso, whose corps was to occupy the town. But the Duke's forces were greatly reduced in strength, and, as he did not see the need of scattering his men so soon, and at nightfall besides, he sent only a meagre and insufficient number to Durosnel.

As I have already remarked, the well-to-do inhabitants had fled; all the authorities had left the place, which was entirely deserted. There was no possibility, even, of getting together any kind of administrative service. No one remained but a few *outchitets* (French tutors), a few foreign shopkeepers, the servants in some of the hotels, and for the rest, people of the lowest classes of society.

It would be difficult to describe the impression made on the Emperor by this news. Never have I seen him so deeply impressed. He was already greatly disturbed and impatient at having had to wait for two hours at the city gate; and this report undoubtedly plunged him into the gravest reflections. His face, normally so impassive, showed instantly and unmistakably the mark of his bitter disappointment.

Count Durosnel had kept sending information to the Emperor as fast as he gathered it, and this completely confirmed what had already come through. M. Rostopchin, the Governor of Moscow, had not left the city until eleven o'clock that same morning, after having sent off the officials, the whole administrative staff and the population. A very small number of householders and some thousand or so of people of the lowest classes had stayed behind, simply because they did not belong to overlords, and because their ignorance prevented them from knowing where to go. Most of the houses were as deserted as the streets. The Governor had kept from the inhabitants any news of the loss of the battle, and had not even said anything about the projected evacuation of the town until the last moment. Only a small portion of the archives and valuables could be taken away. Some arms remained in the arsenal and a few soldiers and militia were hidden in the houses; these men were armed and the militia were little better than savages. Durosnel accordingly urged the Emperor once again not to enter the city yet, especially as the difficulty of making oneself understood and even of finding guides or obtaining intelligent information involved the waste of considerable time. He stayed near the bridge all night, his headquarters being established in a mean tavern built of wood at the entrance to the suburb.

The King of Naples, who was in pursuit of the enemy, sent word to the Emperor that numerous stragglers were being caught, that they all said the army was being disbanded, that the Cossacks openly declared they would fight no more, and that the army was heading for Kazan. He confirmed what had been learned in the city; that Kutusof had kept silence as to the loss of the battle and the retreat on Moscow until the previous day, and that the authorities and inhabitants of the city had taken to flight that same evening, and even on the day of our arrival. He told us that the Governor, Rostopchin, had not heard of the loss of the battle until forty-eight hours before our entry into Moscow; that up to that moment Marshal Kutusof had talked of nothing but success, of his skilful manœuvring and the damage he had done to the French. The King of Naples confidently expected to seize part of the enemy convoys, and felt certain of being able to break up their rear-guard, so completely disheartened did he believe the Russians to be. He repeated these particulars in all his despatches, and likewise insisted that the Cossacks were demoralized and were on the point of quitting the Russian army.

All these details delighted the Emperor and restored his cheerfulness. He had not received any proposals at the gates of Moscow, but the actual state of the Russian army, its discouragement, the discontent of the Cossacks, the impression certain to be caused in Petersburg by the news of the occupation of the second capital of Russia, all the happenings which Kutusof had doubtless concealed from the Tsar just as he had kept them from Rostopchin,—all these things, said the Emperor, must surely lead to peace proposals. He made no comment on Kutusof's march on Kazan.

About eleven o'clock in the evening news came that the Bazaar was on fire. The Duke of Treviso and Count Durosnel went to the spot, but in the darkness it was impossible to cope with this conflagration, for there was nothing at hand and no one knew where to find pumps and hoses. The inhabitants and soldiers pillaged such shops as they had time to enter.

During the night there were two small outbreaks of fire in the suburbs also, at some distance from that where the Emperor was quartered; but they were attributed to carelessness in lighting camp fires, and orders were given to redouble vigilance. These accidents having no immediate sequel, little importance was attached to them. The Guard was ordered to furnish sentry-posts for the various points. The Duke of Treviso and M. Durosnel, who were constantly in the saddle, did all they could to ensure the tranquillity of the vast city.

Finding himself without sufficient means to maintain order, Durosnel came in person to report to the Emperor in the morning, and suggested that the command of the city should be entrusted to the Duke of Treviso. Mortier's troops [the Young Guard] were occupying the place, and he could therefore take the situation in hand. The Emperor approved this proposal; and Count Durosnel himself delivered to the Duke the order to assume responsibility for the government of Moscow.

The Emperor went to the Kremlin at noon [September 15]. A gloomy silence reigned throughout the deserted city. During the whole of our long progress we met not a single person. The army took up its positions round the town, and some corps were billeted in the barracks. At three o'clock the Emperor mounted his horse, made a tour of the Kremlin and the Orphanage, went to see the two principal bridges, and then returned to the Kremlin, where he had installed himself in the apartments of Tsar Alexander.

Various reports said that Kutusof and Rostopchin had met to discuss affairs on the day before the evacuation. Rostopchin was said to have proposed the destruction of the city, but Kutusof had been opposed to this step, and had been so indignant at the suggestion and at the other measures desired by the Governor that he had gone away in a rage. From other details it seemed that these two personages, who disliked each other, rarely met; that Kutusof had left Rostopchin as ignorant as he had left the Tsar up to the very last moment: for in Moscow as in Petersburg a *Te Deum* had been sung for the supposed victory of the Russian arms. We heard that the first convoy of wounded arrived on the twelfth [from Borodino]; that on the thirteenth rumours of a defeat began to spread, though they were discounted; that even on that and the following day some of the city militia were sent out to join the main army. In short, even persons in authority were totally in the dark as to what had happened until the day before our entry.

Much of the information we received was contradictory, and proved that those who had left the city had not confided their intentions to those who remained, even at the very last. An aged French actress repeated so often a conversation she was supposed to have had with a certain General Borozdine, that the Emperor expressed a wish to see her. According to the general—or according to this actress—disaffection towards the Tsar and the popular dislike of this war over Poland had reached such extreme lengths that the Russian nobility, threatened with the loss of their property and the greater part of their fortunes, were anxious for peace at any price and would force the Emperor Alexander to come to terms. Kutusof had deceived the court at Petersburg even as he had deceived the public and the Governor of Moscow. Everyone imagined that he had been victorious. The precipitate evacuation of the city would ruin the Russian nobility and force the government to sue for peace. The nobles were enraged with Kutusof and Rostopchin for having lulled them into a false sense of security.

At eight o'clock in the evening flames broke out in one of the suburbs. Assistance was sent, without more attention being paid to the matter, for it was still attributed to the carelessness of the troops.

The Emperor retired early; everyone was fatigued and as anxious to rest as he was. At half-past ten my valet, an energetic fellow who had been in my service during my embassy to Petersburg, woke me up with the news that for three-quarters of an hour the city had been in flames. I had only to open my eyes to realize that this was so, for the fire was giving off so much light that it was bright enough to read in the middle of my room. I sprang from bed and sent by valet to wake the Grand Marshal [Duroc], while I dressed. As the fire was spreading in the quarters farthest away from the Kremlin, we decided to send word to Mortier, to put the Guard under arms, and to let the Emperor sleep a little longer, as he had been extremely tired during the past few days.

I mounted my horse hurriedly to go and see what was happening, to gather what assistance I could muster, and to make sure that everyone connected with my own department, scattered throughout the city as they were, were running no unnecessary hazards. A stiff wind was blowing from the north, from the direction of the two points of conflagration that we could see, and was driving the flames towards the centre, which made the blaze extraordinarily powerful: About half-past twelve [September 16] a third fire broke out a little to the west, and shortly afterwards a fourth, in another quarter—in each case in the direction of the wind, which had veered slightly towards the west. About four o'clock in the morning the conflagration was so widespread that we judged it necessary to wake the Emperor, who at once sent more officers to find out how things really stood and discover whence these fires could be starting.

The troops were under arms; the few remaining inhabitants were fleeing their houses and gathering in the churches; there was nothing to be heard but lamentation. Search had been made for the fire-engines since the previous day, but some of them had been taken away and the rest put out of action. From different houses officers and soldiers brought *boutechnicks* (policemen on point duty) and *moujiks,* who had been taken in the act of setting fire to inflammable material which had been laid in houses for the purpose of burning them down. The Poles reported that they had already caught some incendiaries and shot them; and they added, moreover, that from these men and from other inhabitants they had extracted the information that orders had been given by the Governor of the city and the police that the whole city should be burned during the night. These reports seemed incredible. The arrested men were put under guard, and fresh search and increased watchfulness were enforced. Pickets had already been sent to those quarters of the town which were not already in flames; and the further particulars which continued to arrive confirmed our gravest suspicions.

The Emperor was deeply concerned. Towards half-past nine he left the courtyard of the Kremlin on foot, just when two more incendiaries, caught in the act, were being brought in. They were in police uniform. When interrogated in the presence of the Emperor they repeated their declarations: their commanding officer had ordered them to burn everything. Houses had been designated to this end. In the different quarters everything had been prepared for starting the fire—in accordance with orders from Governor Rostopchin, so they had been told. The police officers had spread their men in small detachments in various quarters, and the order to carry out their instructions had been given in the evening of the previous day and confirmed by one of their officers on the following morning. They were reluctant to tell the name of this official, but one of them did so at last: he was a mere underling. They could not or would not indicate where he was at the moment, nor how he might be found. Their replies were translated to the Emperor in the presence of his suite. Many other depositions confirmed unmistakably what they

said. All the incendiaries were kept under observation; some
were brought to judgment and eight or ten executed.

The conflagration continued to spread from the borders of
the boroughs where it had started. It had already reached
the houses around the Kremlin. The wind, which had veered
slightly to the west, fanned the flames to a terrifying extent
and carried enormous sparks to a distance, where they fell
like a fiery deluge hundreds of yards away, setting fire to
more houses and preventing the most intrepid from remaining
in the neighbourhood with safety. The air was so hot, and
the pine-wood sparks were so numerous, that the beams supporting the iron plates which formed the roof of the arsenal
all caught fire. The roof of the Kremlin kitchen was only
saved by men being placed there with brooms and buckets to
gather up the glowing fragments and moisten the beams. Only
by superhuman efforts was the fire in the arsenal extinguished.
The Emperor was there himself; his presence inspired the
Guard to every exertion.[2]

I hastened to the Court stables, where some of the Emperor's
horses were stabled and the coronation coaches of the Tsar
were kept. The utmost zeal, and, I may add, the greatest
courage on the part of the coachmen and grooms, were necessary to save the place; they clambered on to the roof and
knocked off the cinders that fell there, whilst others worked
two fire-engines which I had had put in order during the night.
(They had been totally dismantled.) I may say without exaggeration that we were working beneath a vault of fire. With
these men's help I was able to save the beautiful Galitzin Palace and the two adjoining houses, which were already in flames.
The Emperor's men were ably assisted by Prince Galitzin's

[2] "The gunners and soldiers of the Guard, apprehensive at seeing Napoleon expose himself to such great danger, only added to it by their eagerness. General Lariboisière begged the Emperor to go away, pointing out
to him that his presence was making the gunners lose their heads."—
Fain, *Manuscrit de 1812*, II, 91.

servants, who displayed the utmost devotion to their master's interests. Everyone did his best to further the measures we took to check this devouring torrent of flame, but the air was charged with fire; we breathed nothing but smoke, and the stoutest lungs felt the strain after a time. The bridge to the south of the Kremlin was so heated by the fire and the sparks falling on it that it kept bursting into flames, although the Guard, and the sappers in particular, made it a point of honour to preserve it. I stayed with some generals of the Guard and aides-de-camp of the Emperor, and we were forced to lend a hand and remain in the midst of this deluge of fire in order to spur on these half-roasted men. It was impossible to stand more than a moment in one spot; the fur on the grenadiers' caps was singed.

The fire made such progress that the whole of the northern and the greater part of the western quarter, by which we had entered, was burned, together with the splendid playhouse and all the larger buildings. One drew breath in a sea of fire— and the westerly wind continued to blow. The flames spread continuously; it was impossible to predict where or when they would stop, as there was no means of staying them. The conflagration passed beyond the Kremlin; it seemed that the river would surely save all the district lying to the east.

About four o'clock in the afternoon, while the fire was still raging, the Emperor began to think that this great catastrophe might be connected with some movement of the enemy, even though frequent reports from the King of Naples assured him that the Russians were still retreating along the Kazan road. The Emperor therefore gave orders to leave the city, and forbade anything to be left within its walls.

Headquarters were established at the Petrowskoïe Palace, on the Petersburg road, a country mansion where the Tsars were accustomed to take up residence before making their solemn entries into Moscow for their coronations. It was im-

possible to proceed thither by the direct road on account of
the fire and the wind; one had to cross the western part of
the town as best one could, through ruins, cinders, flames
even, if one wanted to reach the outskirts. Night had already
fallen when we got there; and we spent the following day in
the palace. Meanwhile the fire continued with renewed violence, but a part of the quarter between the Kremlin and
Petrowskoïe, where headquarters and the Guard were billeted,
was saved. The Emperor was deep in thought; he spoke to
no one.

The existence of inflammable fuses, all made in the same
fashion and placed in different public and private buildings,
is a fact of which I, as well as many others, had personal evidence. I saw these fuses on the spot, and several were taken
to the Emperor. They were also found in the quarter by
which he entered the city, and even in the Imperial bedroom
in the Kremlin. M. Durosnel, the Duke of Treviso, Count
Dumas, and many others observed them on their entrance, but
paid no further attention, for they were far from thinking
that the Governor and the government had any ambition, as
the Emperor said, to go down to posterity as a modern Eros-
tratus.

The examination of the police rank-and-file, and further
admissions by the police officer who was caught on the day
we entered the city, all proved that the fire had been prepared
and executed by order of Count Rostopchin. This police officer, whom Baron Lelorgne had discovered in the city while
looking for the deputation His Majesty had expected, was a
simpleton who knew all that was afoot and was very candid
in all his avowals, as was proved by many reports. He supplied details about the preparation for that fire which left no
further doubt as to the Governor's orders, and in time shed
the fullest light on the matter. Of the various incendiaries
who were brought to judgment some were executed and others

left in prison, hapless victims of their obedience to their superiors and the orders of a madman, as the Emperor said.

Baron Lelorgne's police officer—from whom at first, for lack of a better, he had drawn a thousand bits of information—was so terrified at the outset that he appeared to be slightly deranged. Such at least was the impression left by his statements. His revelations seemed to be the delusions of a demented man, and at the time no heed was paid to them. This unfortunate fellow kicked his heels for some time in the custody of the guard where he was left when he was no longer needed. After the outbreak of the fire his first statements were recalled. It was also remembered that when he had seen the first small fire break out, which was attributed to some camp fires having been lit too near the wooden houses of the quarter, he had announced that before long there would be many other outbreaks; and when the main conflagration started he exclaimed that the whole city would be burned, orders having been issued to that effect. In fact, all that we had imputed to a disordered mind actually came to pass; so he was questioned anew.

To what he had already told us he now added, in confirmation of what several other incendiaries had informed us, that on the day before Governor Rostopchin's departure several police officers were summoned to a particular locality which he designated (other depositions confirmed this), where they received orders to prepare for burning the city; that they had been instructed to be ready to carry out this order as soon as the signal was given; and that subsequently, after every meeting, the chiefs of police named a new rendezvous where their subordinates were to make their reports. On the appointed day each senior officer had received the order at a time decided on by the Governor and had transmitted it to the subordinates in his district, for them to carry out. The fire-engines had been taken away by the firemen, and those that they had not been able to harness up had been deliberately made unfit for action and hidden away.

Before entering Moscow, the Emperor had intended not to take up his residence in the city. The fire, and the consequent destruction of part of the supplies, seemed likely to make him follow this first impulse. In fact everything was ready for a withdrawal, and for a time the Prince of Neuchâtel imagined that this would be carried out. But the successive reports from the King of Naples as to the breakdown of the Russian army, and despatches in which he drew pictures of the results which he hoped for and promised because of it, soon made the Emperor modify these arrangements.

The King always saw the Russian army in flight along the Kazan road, the men deserting, disbanding in troops, the Cossacks ready to leave the army, some even disposed to make common cause with the victorious French. The Cossack chieftains overwhelmed the King of Naples with continual flattery, and he never ceased to give them tokens of his munificence. The vanguard had no need to fight; the Cossack officers took instructions from the King as to the direction in which he wished to march, and where he desired to establish his headquarters. From the moment his outposts arrived they were practically taken care of, to see that nothing went amiss. Out-and-out blandishments were resorted to, to gratify the King, and those marks of deference delighted him greatly.

Accordingly the Emperor put small faith in his despatches; those marks of deference looked suspicious to him. He saw that the King was being made a fool of, and he told him to distrust Kutusof's pretended march on Kazan. The Emperor could not fathom this movement of the enemy. This affectation of regard for the King—these exaggerated accounts of the enemy's breakdown and the discontent of the Cossacks—

appeared to him as proofs of underhand work. Although such circumstances—if true—would have delighted him, he saw them for what they were: blinds to deceive the King as to what was really afoot, or baits to draw him into some trap.

On September 18 the Emperor returned to the Kremlin. His departure from Moscow had been the signal for outbreaks of the gravest disorder. Such houses as had been saved from the fire were pillaged. Such unfortunate inhabitants as had remained were ill-treated. Shops and wine-cellars were forced open; and thence flowed every excess, every crime that can result from the drunkenness of soldiers who have got out of their superiors' control. The city rabble, taking advantage of this disorder, began pillaging, too, and led the troops to the cellars and vaults and anywhere else that they thought might have been used to conceal property, in the hope of sharing the pillage. Those army corps not actually in the city sent in detachments to secure their portion of the victuals and booty. The result of this systematic search can be guessed. All kinds of supplies were found, and plenty of wine and brandy. The grain and fodder warehouses along the quays had escaped the fire. The army horses had been so short of provender between Smolensk and Ghjat, and from the battle until we reached Moscow, that everyone hastened to forage for them and got enough hay, during the two days of the fifteenth and sixteenth, to last several months. Part of these provisions were consumed in the houses as they were found; and it was thanks to the surplus that we were able to live in abundance until our departure from the city, and even to keep the men and horses alive during part of the retreat.[3]

As soon as he returned to Moscow the Emperor began to busy himself with clearing the French army, in the eyes of Petersburg, from the odium of having caused the fire, which

[3] Larrey (*Chirurgie Militaire*, IV) estimates that the provisions found in Moscow would have been sufficient to feed the whole army for six months.

they had done their utmost to extinguish and from which self-interest alone was sufficient to exonerate them.

He instructed M. Lelorgne to find some Russian to whom all the details of the affair could be confided and who would relay what he was told to the proper quarters. M. Toutolmine, head of the Orphanage, had stayed courageously, like a good father, at the head of that establishment, although most of the foundlings had been evacuated; and he seemed eminently suited to fill the part. His position as head of one of the dowager Empress's institutions would lend authority to his report in the eyes both of the upper and lower classes in Petersburg. He appeared before Napoleon, and M. Lelorgne undertook the duties of interpreter.

The Russian was profuse in his gratitude for the help and protection accorded to his establishment. The Emperor assured him that he had undertaken this war from purely political motives and from no spirit of animosity. Peace was his primary aim, as he had explained on more than one occasion. He added that he had been forced to come to Moscow in spite of himself; that he had done everything at Moscow, as elsewhere, to protect property and to suppress the incendiarism started by the Russians themselves.

As soon as M. Toutolmine's letters were ready he was given a passport and every other facility to enable one of his employees to act as courier to Petersburg.

With the exception of the King of Naples's corps, the entire army was in the town or quartered close at hand. Fugitives from the fire had sought shelter in churches, cemeteries, or wherever they felt secure from annoyance by the troops. The churches, which for the most part stood in the clear on public squares, had offered also greater security from the ravages of the flames. Many of these unfortunate refugees had made their way out to Petrowskoïe. We did what we could for them. I housed some two dozen of them in the Galitzin mansion, and among the number was M. Zagriaski, Master of Horse to the Tsar, who had hoped, by remaining in Moscow, to save his house, the object of his lifelong care. There was also a major-general, German by birth, who had gone into retirement in Moscow after long service with the Empress Catherine. These unhappy men had lost everything; nothing remained to them but the greatcoats which they wore.

Our return to Moscow was no less gloomy than our departure. I cannot relate all that I had suffered since the death of my brother. The sense of these recent events was the last straw; the horror of all that was going on around us added to my grief at his loss. True, one cannot nurse one's personal troubles exclusively in the midst of so many public disasters—but one is only the more wretched on that account. I was overwhelmed. Happy are they who never saw that dire spectacle, that picture of destruction!

A greater portion of the city was reduced to ashes; the northern district, nearest the Kremlin, had been saved by the wind shifting to the west; some isolated districts to windward had not suffered at all. The splendid mansions all round the city had escaped the plans for their destruction; only that of M. Rostopchin, the Governor, had been burned to the ground by its proprietor. He had posted up a notice of his intention, unquestionably very patriotic in his eyes, on the signpost that marked the road into his estate at Wornzowo, a short distance from Moscow. This notice was brought to the Emperor, who turned the whole thing to ridicule. He joked a lot about it and sent it to Paris, where doubtless it produced, as it had in the army, an impression quite contrary to what His Majesty expected. It had a profound effect on every thinking man, and won the Governor more admirers than critics—though only, of course, for the patriotism he had shown in sacrificing his house. This is how the notice was worded:

For eight years I have improved this land, and I have lived happily here in the bosom of my family. To the number of one thousand seven hundred and twenty the dwellers on my estate are leaving it at your approach, while, for my part, I am setting fire to my mansion rather than let it be sullied by your presence. Frenchmen!—in Moscow I have abandoned to you my two residences, with furniture worth half-a-million roubles. Here you will find only ashes.

CHAPTER VII

INDECISION

SOME days after his return to the Kremlin, the Emperor announced openly that he had resolved to take up his winter-quarters at Moscow, which, even in its present state, would furnish him with better accommodations and more supplies than any other place. He therefore put the Kremlin and the monasteries and convents round the city into a state of defence, and ordered several reconnaissances in the neighbourhood with an eye to establishing a plan of defence for the winter.

The Emperor took many other measures in anticipation. He announced that he was ordering fresh levies of men in France and Poland; that he was preparing the organization of the Polish Cossacks, "for which orders have already been issued," he said. Reserves had instructions to join us, and all the reinforcing detachments, which had been echeloned in their advance, were detailed to safeguard our rear, protect convoys, and keep open communications.

The post-houses were fortified; the courier service which I had organized at the start of the campaign was given special attention. The despatch-case for the Emperor and his headquarters arrived regularly every day from Paris in fifteen—often fourteen—days. The Emperor was always impatient for the arrival of his courier; he noticed the delay of a few hours, and even grew anxious, though this service had never suffered any breakdown. The Paris portfolio, the packets from Warsaw and Wilna, were the thermometer of the Emperor's good

128

or bad humour. It was the same with all of us, for everyone's happiness depended on the news from France.

Small consignments of wine and other objects arrived. Officers, surgeons and administrative officials also came to join the army. The reports from officers in command of the principal points in our lines of communication were reassuring. It was as easy to travel from Paris to Moscow as from Paris to Marseilles. Yet everyone was loath to resign himself to passing the winter so far from France, whither all eyes and thoughts continually turned. We had been spoiled by the Emperor's previous campaigns, when peace had always been bought with a few months' toil. Except in the Prussian and Polish campaigns, winters had always been spent in France; and recollections of Osterode and Güttstadt, of the snows of Pultusk and Pratznitz [campaign of 1806-7], brought only sombre reflections.

Some, myself among the first, doubted whether the Emperor really intended to pass the winter at Moscow. The immense distance between ourselves and Poland would give the enemy too many opportunities of harassing us; and there seemed a thousand other considerations against carrying out this plan. On the other hand, the Emperor busied himself with so many precautions, discussed them in such positive terms, and seemed to regard them as so essential to the success of his enterprise if peace were not secured before the winter, that the most incredulous among us ended by believing that he intended to go through with his plans. At that time even the Grand Marshal and the Prince of Neuchâtel seemed convinced that we should remain in Moscow. Everyone laid plans accordingly, and collected furniture and anything else abandoned in the city that might be useful for consolidating his domestic arrangements. Wood and forage were collected; in short, everyone acted as though he would certainly have to pass in Moscow the eight months that must elapse before spring.

For my part, I must confess that in the Emperor's glibness in talking of this plan, as well as in the measures he took for carrying it out, I saw only the desire to give a turn to public opinion, to ensure the collection of provisions, and, above all, to support the overtures he had made. Nobody knew of these overtures. M. Toutolmine had kept the secret as faithfully as M. Lelorgne, who had been entrusted with a second attempt. But the Emperor let fall a few words to the Prince of Neuchâtel as to the nature of his proposals.

As he later admitted, the Emperor felt certain that his overtures, made partly to emphasize the fact that the French had had no hand in the burning of Moscow and had done all in their power to check its ravages, and partly to prove his readiness to enter into an agreement, would elicit a reply and even proposals for peace. The burning of Moscow had roused serious reflections in his mind, though he did his utmost to banish from his thoughts the consequences implicit in such action on the part of the Russians, and the scant hope that the Russian government was disposed to make peace. He was always eager to believe in his Star, and that Russia, wearied of war, would seize any occasion to bring the struggle to an end.

I think, indeed, that the Emperor Napoleon would have been very amenable in the matter of conditions at that moment, for to make peace was the only way out of his predicament. He made his advances as if actuated by generosity, under the impression that he was outwitting Petersburg as regards his true motives. He tried to make believe that the fear of his proving too exigent had prevented proposals reaching him. In this way he hoped to extricate himself from the embarassing situation in which he had placed himself. It was in this hope of an imminent peace that he prolonged his unfortunate sojourn at Moscow.

The splendid weather and the mild temperature that continued so late that year helped to mislead him. Perhaps it had also been his intention to make his winter-quarters in Russia before his rear should be threatened and attacked. In that case, as he said, Moscow was by its name a political position, and by the number and nature of its still extant buildings and resources a military position preferable to any other, if he remained in Russia.

In his intimate circle the Emperor conversed, acted, and issued orders all on the presumption that he was going to stay in Moscow, so that even those most closely in his confidence entertained no doubt on the matter for some time.

Such was our situation ten or twelve days after our arrival, and everybody believed that we were staying in Moscow up to the very moment when our artillery convoys were attacked and our couriers delayed.

At last, seeing the season so advanced and still no preparation made for our departure, I, too, doubted whether Moscow would be evacuated voluntarily. To me it seemed impossible that the Emperor should even think of a retreat when the frost set in, especially as no measures had been taken to cross the ice—although some idea of what a Russian winter meant could have been gleaned from what had happened at Osterode and in Poland. And besides, the memory of 1807 furnished an idea of the Emperor's tenacity of purpose.

Every day some discovery was made of shops and cellars where stuffs, cloths, and furs were concealed; and everyone purchased what he thought necessary for the winter. This precaution proved to be the salvation of those who took it.

I paid the wages of all those employed in my department and issued orders that all their greatcoats should be lined with fur, or at least provided with fur collars if they could not buy large enough pelts. I also gave orders that fur hats and gloves should be made. On my arrival, too, I organized a number of workshops for adding to the means of transport of biscuits and fodder. I had a large stock of horseshoes made up sharp for travel on ice. In a word, I took every possible precaution against such difficulties as might be encountered in winter operations; and to these measures I owed the satisfaction of being able to transport my sick and my vehicles in safety as far as Wilna.

As soon as he returned to Moscow the Emperor gave orders for parades to be held in the court of the Kremlin. A cookhouse service had been organized and great activity expended on building ovens. The defensive works were pushed forward vigorously, and a portion of the Prince of Eckmühl's corps was quartered in the city. The immense fields of vegetables, especially cabbages, surrounding the town were carefully cut; numerous stacks of hay were also brought in, and the potato fields within a radius of two or three leagues were cleared. The transport waggons were in constant use. I organized a body of men to run a mill for the Emperor's Household, as flour was beginning to be scarce. I had a large supply of biscuits baked, and a considerable number of sledges constructed. In short, I had everything in readiness for either a prolonged sojourn in the city or an immediate departure.

The hospitals were well organized; I established one for the Household in a wing of the Kremlin. A great number of unfortunate fellows, who were already enfeebled by excessive fatigue, had been attacked by nervous fevers.

The overtures for peace which M. Toutolmine had forwarded to Petersburg were considered there as proof of the state of embarrassment in which the Russians already suspected we were. While the proposals were under discussion, the Emperor busied himself, as I have said, with all his wonted activity; night and day were one to him. Paris and France were the object of all his thoughts, and couriers were constantly setting off with decrees and decisions dated from Moscow.

Accustomed as he was to dictate peace on his arrival at

the palaces of the sovereigns whose capitals he had conquered, he was amazed by the silence of his adversary. The more this silence testified to the enthusiasm of the Tsar and the exasperation of his people, the more the Emperor Napoleon was convinced that peace could only be made at Moscow. His moderation ought to conciliate everyone; he had cleared himself of blame for the fire; he had even done all in his power to arrest the disaster. "It is difficult to see," he said, "any special motive for animosity that should prevent us coming to an understanding. Having reached the ancient capital of Russia, it would seem a political defeat to leave it without having signed the preliminaries for peace, no matter how advantageous another position would be from a military point of view. Europe is watching, and would regard [our waiting for] a sure success in the spring as sure proof of a reverse to-day. That might entail grave consequences."

The Emperor was from that time prepared to evacuate Russia and content himself with enforcing some measures against English commerce to save the honour of his arms. He hoped to win over the Emperor Alexander afresh by giving him, as though it were a voluntary sacrifice which he could not have expected, an arrangement that would justify the Tsar personally in the eyes of his people. Imbued with this idea, and dismissing from his mind the importunate memory of the steps already taken, Napoleon determined to write directly to the Tsar, and M. Lelorgne was ordered to search the hospitals, or amongst the Russian prisoners, for some senior officer who might be sent to Petersburg. He found the brother of a Russian diplomatic agent in Germany.

The Emperor repeated to him exactly what he had said to M. Toutolmine. He put forward the same views on reconciliation and peace; but this officer respectfully expressed his doubts as to the possibility of coming to an understanding so long as the French remained in Moscow. The Emperor paid little heed to his observations at the time, but sent the officer away with his letter, still deluding himself that the silence of the Petersburg cabinet was caused only by their belief that he would demand too much. He thought that they would eagerly seize the opportunity of profiting by his avowed moderation. It was this fatal belief, this unfortunate hope, that made him stay on in Moscow and brave a winter that exacted a greater toll than any plague could have done.

This move was at the time known only to the Prince of Neuchâtel, M. Lelorgne and myself, and remained secret for a long while, as the Emperor desired.

I return now to the King of Naples, who had confidently followed up the Russian army along the Kazan road. He came to pass a night at Moscow, saw the Emperor, and next day returned to the advance-guard.

While the King was in Moscow the Viceroy, the Princes of Neuchâtel and Eckmühl, and His Majesty happened to be all four with the Emperor; the Emperor raised the question whether it would not be sound policy to march at once on Petersburg. According to the King the Russians were in full flight, in a state of complete disorder and discouragement, while the Cossacks were ready to leave the army at any moment. Did the Emperor really believe in the possibility of such an expedition? Did he imagine he would have time to carry it out before the hard frosts set in? Did he think the army in a fit state to carry it out? From what he said previously and afterwards to the Prince of Neuchâtel, it was clear to me that he never really entertained this project, impracticable in view of the state of our artillery and cavalry, while Kutusof was so close to us with a well-organized army and numerous cavalry.

The Viceroy and the marshals were less deluded than the

King regarding the supposed disorder of the Russians. They dwelt on our army's need of rest, and on the necessity of ensuring, as soon as possible, good winter-quarters for its reorganization.

The Emperor would have liked to give a turn to the opinion held by the army, to distract it from its losses by persuading it that it was still fit for any undertaking. He would have liked to disperse the echoes from Petersburg which lingered in Moscow, and was anxious to know what was in the minds of the intelligent men in the army. There was no further question of this project and we stayed in Moscow.

The Russians diverted the King with talk, paralyzed his activity by their solicitous attentions, and the advance-guard, wholly occupied in the exchange of compliments, made scarcely any progress from day to day. This was all the more to the taste of our troops, who regretted every step that took them further from the Moscow cellars and all the good things that were being enjoyed by those who remained in the city. Thanks to their nearness to the capital, they were still able to participate every day in these things, for it was possible to send in daily messengers to procure provisions.

Reluctant to place himself at too great a distance, and doubtless not realizing the importance of the Emperor's orders,[1] the King acted in a leisurely way and made but slight daily advances, merely changing his position from one place to another. (I am repeating what I heard at the time from the Emperor.) To justify his slowness the King repeated that he was humouring the Cossacks, who no longer wished to fight against us; that he might have attacked them, though they would not fire on our troops; in short, that they were no longer defending themselves, but were actually on the point of leaving the Russian army. He added, moreover, that he found

[1] Napoleon ordered Murat to proceed from the Riazan road to the Toula road and to advance until he had obtained some news of Kutusof.

the peasants very discontented, and many of them already talking of gaining their freedom.

The Prince of Neuchâtel showed me two of these letters;
the Emperor let me see three of four more, all containing the
same details, and asked me what I thought.

"I think they are fooling the King of Naples," I said.

The Emperor and the Prince thought likewise.

Seeing the uselessness of his repeated orders to the King
that he should push the enemy vigorously and send reconnaissances to find out where Kutusof was and unmask his movements, the Emperor formed a corps for the Duke of Istria,
composed of Davout's infantry and the cavalry of the Guard,
to which he joined La Houssaye's division.

The King of Naples, who finally had recognized his error,
began to carry out the movement on Kaluga ordered by the
Emperor. Up to this time he had kept in constant touch with
the Cossacks. Having given them his watch and his jewels,
he would even have given them the shirt off his back, had he not
discovered that the good Cossacks were playing with him and
keeping him on the Kazan road while the Russian army,
masked by their manœuvres, had been on the Kaluga road
for five days. They had made their march at night, lit up by
the flames of the burning capital.

By September 23 our convoys were already somewhat disturbed; the pourparlers between our advance-guard and the
Cossacks were still being carried on; and the Emperor was
so displeased that he forbade their continuance. The purport
of these conversations was repeated in Moscow and came back
to the Emperor; and the matter seemed so grave that he gave
it his particular attention. He was especially suspicious of
what was talked about with regard to General Sébastiani's
corps.

"These communications," said the Emperor, "are made for no
other purpose than to alarm the army about its remoteness

from France, and the climate, and the winter. I know it is being said that this is an unjust war, that it is impolitic, and my attack on the Russians an act of iniquity. My soldiers are being told of the peaceful aims of the Tsar, of his moderation and his liking for the French. By their smooth speeches the Russians are trying to turn our brave fellows into traitors, to paralyze the courage of stouthearted men, and to gain partisans for their cause. Murat is the dupe of men far more astute than himself. . . . I will have the first man who speaks with the enemy shot, even if he be a general."

Indeed, orders were promulgated absolutely forbidding any intercourse with the enemy *sous peine de mort;* and to spare the susceptibilities of the King of Naples this order was addressed to General Sébastiani.

Matters had reached such a point that a sort of tacit armistice was in operation with the advance-guard, and the enemy profited by this to lull our suspicions and send parties to Smolensk, where they burned fifteen of our ammunition waggons which they were unable to carry away. These parties delayed the couriers, made the rear posts of the army uneasy, and caused the Emperor one of the greatest annoyances he suffered during the whole of the campaign. This mania for fraternizing with the enemy spread now to the troops under the command of the Duke of Istria. The Emperor was so vexed that he even disapproved of two flags of truce having been received and forbade the Duke to admit any more, ordering him to have any further letters from the enemy accepted at the outposts and handed back, in order to avoid any personal conversations.

"All this talk under flags of truce," he said to Berthier in my hearing, "does good only to those who began it. It invariably turns out to our disadvantage."

He ordered Berthier to send this message to Marshal Bessières.

Almost every day the Emperor rode out to visit the different quarters of the city, and inspected the surrounding convents, whose high walls gave them the appearance of small citadels. He worked all day and part of the night. France was administered, Germany and Poland felt the impulse of his mind, just as if he had been at the Tuileries. Every day couriers brought despatches and went off with orders to France and Europe. This courier service had become so regular that despatches arrived every day about two o'clock.

After dinner the Emperor received the marshals, the Viceroy, and such generals of division as could leave their commands for a brief period. Three or four times a week he had some of them in to dine with the marshals. In the conversations that followed the meals the Emperor steered the opinion of those present in the direction he desired, and indicated the political angle he wished handed on to the army.

The Emperor would have liked to put some prominent Russian at the head of the municipal administration, if only in the interest of the wretched inhabitants who were left. Search was made for such a man, but M. Toutolmine was the only person suitable, and he was too badly needed at the head of the Orphanage to accept other functions.

As it was long since the Emperor had discussed matters with me, and as the Prince of Neuchâtel at the outset had but a very imperfect knowledge of the negotiations which the Emperor had tried to open up, I only got to know of them later. Having invariably found my opinion opposed to his own, the Emperor was so frequently out of humour with me that I did not venture to see even M. Toutolmine. As to M. Zagriaski and the other Russians whom I had taken under my protection during the catastrophe, I had to request the Grand Marshal to make my action known to the Emperor lest it should be misinterpreted. In any case, they were all old men, and people of such insignificance that they had long since ceased to be connected with the government. The Emperor wished to employ them in the administration of the city, and later hinted that he would like to see them; but they refused to undertake any function, and declined the honour the Emperor wished to do them—for the very just reason that they had no clothes to wear. It is impossible to conceive the state of their destitution.

I never left my own quarters except to accompany the Emperor on horseback. I read much and had no lack of books, although the Galitzin residence where I had established myself and my staff, with the carriages, had been completely ransacked during the night we had gone to Petrowskoie. In the Kremlin I occupied two small rooms opening on the southern terrace. With the exception of the state apartments nothing was furnished, and we were obliged to buy furniture salvaged from burning houses or from abandoned joiners' shops. In this way I bought, for a few napoleons, portraits of the entire Imperial family of Russia which the troops were using as screens in their bivouacs.

The weather was so fine and the temperature so mild that even the natives were amazed. It seemed as if even the seasons were conspiring to deceive the Emperor.[2] Every day His Majesty remarked very pointedly, when I was present, that the autumn at Moscow was finer and even warmer than at Fontainebleau. He rode horseback every day, and I do not think he once went out without ironically comparing the weather and the temperature with that of France, or without adding, as he hummed one of the old airs to which he adapted catch-phrases or apt verses: "A traveller lies with the greatest of ease"— *A beau mentir qui vient de loin.* Then, for fear that this allusion was not sufficiently pointed, he would sometimes add, remarking on the bright sunshine, "So this is the terrible Rus-

[2] "Magnificent weather; the inhabitants say: 'God must be with you, it is usually much colder.'"—Castellane, *Journal,* I, October 8.

sian winter that Monsieur de Caulaincourt frightens the children with."

We had been three weeks in Moscow, and since the battle the Emperor had not mentioned to me the loss of my brother, although he had been most honourably mentioned in the bulletin.

"What can I do for your brother's aides-de-camp?" were his first words about a loss which had been very painful to me. "They must be fine officers, for their general was a splendid man. He would have gone far."

I answered His Majesty that, when he would permit me, I would present several proposals for promotion and reward for them, and for all the officers of my brother's staff, as well as his orderly officers, for whom nothing had been done.

"Let me have it to-day," was the Emperor's reply.[3] His silence about my brother arose solely from his irritation with me, for he spoke well of him to the Prince of Neuchâtel and to Duroc.

On the evening of the battle he had said to the Prince of Neuchâtel, speaking of my brother:

"He was my best cavalry officer. He had a quick eye, and he was brave. By the end of the campaign he would have replaced Murat."

The Emperor granted all the promotions I suggested to him, particularly those for my brother's aides; but he never spoke another word to me about him.

All the reports that reached the Emperor were grave; everything was done to make him sense the difficulty of his position. But the greater the difficulties the more determined he

[3] To make this passage clear I ought to observe that the orderly officers, all the aides-de-camp of generals on the Emperor's staff, interpeters, and all generals or officers attached by the Emperor to his headquarters, were under the orders of the Master of Horse.—Caulaincourt's note.

was to overcome them. . . . For the most part the corps had
reserves of supplies, but the services which a proper administration ought to supply were gravely menaced, there being
neither soldiers nor transports to bring them up. The Emperor had thought that here, as in other campaigns, he would
meet with concerns which for gold, or preferably paper, would
deliver what was required; but where there was no proper
administration there could be no contractors. Undaunted by
difficulties, and, as usual, always seeking to evade what he
could not surmount, he thought it would be practicable to make
use of the most destitute refugees, for he imagined that the
Cossacks who were harassing our own lines of supply would
take pity on their compatriots, and thus supply their needs and
part of what we ourselves wanted. He therefore ordered the
formation of a Russian company to go out into the villages to
purchase food; but no one dared to volunteer for it, although
they were promised payment in ready cash, for they knew
perfectly well that the Cossacks would treat the inhabitants
of Moscow no better than they treated its garrison.

On October 2 or 3 the Emperor, who had not discussed
affairs with me for a long time, asked me whether I thought
that the Tsar would be disposed to make peace if overtures
were made to him. He did not tell me of those which he had
already attempted. I answered frankly that it seemed to me
that the sacrifice of Moscow argued a disposition far from
pacific; that the more the season advanced the greater were
the chances in favour of Russia; in a word, that it was scarcely
probable that the Tsar would have set fire to his capital with
the object of signing a peace among the ruins.

"Would you go to Petersburg?" the Emperor asked me.
"You will see the Tsar Alexander. I shall entrust you with
a letter, and you will make peace."

I answered that it would be useless to send me on such a
mission, as I should not be received. Assuming a jocular and

kindly air, the Emperor told me that I did not know what I
was saying; for the Tsar would be all the more eager to profit
by the opportunity given him to enter into negotiations, inas-
much as his nobles, already ruined by the war and the burning of Moscow, were anxious for peace. He was certain of
it. "That fire," he added, "was the sort of folly of which a
madman might boast when he kindled the flame, but which
he would repent next day. The Tsar Alexander sees quite
well that his generals are incapable—that the best of troops
can do nothing under such leadership."

He continued to press me with arguments to convince me
of what he said, and to induce me to accept this mission.

In vain did I repeat all the objections I have mentioned
above. The Emperor replied that I was mistaken. He had
just heard from Petersburg that they were packing up in the
utmost hurry; that the most valuable effects had already been
sent into the interior and even to England. The Tsar was
labouring under no further illusions, for he saw his army
diminished and disheartened while the French army was all
ready to march on Petersburg. The season was still favourable, added His Majesty; and by such a march the Russian
Empire would be lost, for a defeat would gravely embarrass
the Tsar. He would therefore seize with eagerness any overture made by us, as it would furnish him with an honourable
way of getting out of the unfortunate position in which he was
placed.

Finding that he was unable to shake my resolution, the Emperor added that, beginning with myself, everyone who had
been in Russia had told him fairy-tales about the climate.
He then insisted anew on his proposals. The Emperor thought
that perhaps my distaste came only from such embarrassment
as I might feel about going, at a moment when Russia was
being thus ravaged, to Petersburg where I had been so well
treated; and he said:

"Very well!   Just to Marshal Kutusof's headquarters."

I replied that either attempt would be equally unsuccessful, and added that I recalled what the Tsar Alexander had said to me on another occasion, and that I knew his character and was refusing this mission because I was certain he would never sign a peace in his capital.   As this overture of ours, I concluded, could achieve nothing, it was advisable not to make it.

The Emperor turned on his heel abruptly, saying:

"Very well, I shall send Lauriston.   He shall have the honour of making peace and saving your friend Alexander's crown for him."

Shortly afterwards, indeed, the Emperor entrusted M. Lauriston with this mission.

Lauriston presented himself at the Russian field headquarters on the fourth and fifth, and was handsomely received. Kutusof had refused to let him proceed; but it seemed to him that everyone was anxious to put an end to this struggle, of which the Russians appeared even more weary than we were. It was said that a reply would shortly be received from Petersburg; and this delighted the Emperor, who hoped and desired a suspension of hostilities while terms were being made.   He supposed that, as was customary in similar circumstances, there would be nothing to do but settle the lines each side was to preserve while the negotiations were going forward.[4]

From what the Prince of Neuchâtel and Duroc told me, the Emperor attributed the silence of the Russians regarding the overtures made at Smolensk and since our arrival in Moscow to the conviction, held by them since the return of Balachof from Wilna, that His Majesty would consider no arrangement that did not have the restoration of Poland on some scale

[4] In his interview with Lauriston, Kutusof refused any kind of armistice; but he had agreed that the advance-posts should cease fire.   Kutusof reserved his freedom of action, however, in the two extreme wings, thus leaving the field free to the raids of Cossacks.

as its basis. The Emperor began to think, however, that the course of events and the burning of the countryside had turned their heads, and that the destruction of Moscow had, for the time being at least, carried them away with enthusiasm. He even doubted whether they would receive his plenipotentiary; and on the night before Lauriston's departure he wrote to the King of Naples telling him to announce to the Russians that one of the Imperial aides-de-camp was being sent, and to make sure in advance that he would be received.

At heart he still flattered himself that negotiations would be opened; at least he said so, and he must be believed, since he stayed at Moscow in spite of his overtures remaining un-answered—and although the lapse of time since his first endeavours, and his reason itself, must have cried aloud that Alexander had no wish to treat. None the less, he stubbornly set to work on fresh approaches.

Like everyone else, the Emperor must have realized that the repeated messages, indicative of his embarrassment, might only confirm the enemy in their hostile intentions—yet he went on sending them. For a man of such fine political sense, of such careful calculation, how blind must have been his faith, his confidence in his Star! What blindness or feebleness he must have attributed to his foes! With his eagle eye and his pre-eminent judgment, how could he have entertained illusions on such a point? I leave these reflections to observers of human nature; for such opposites in so great a character—this tendency of the heart to believe what it most desires even in face of all improbabilities—would be a great reproach in a man of the Emperor's exalted judgment, were not this strange contradiction a part of our nature, and were not this hope a man's last consolation in adversity.

(The King of Naples, despite all orders to the contrary, continued to treat with the enemy. . . . The Cossacks were accustomed to notice him on account of his singular uniform, and, seeing him the bravest man in the midst of his gallant skirmishers, they always refrained from shooting in his direction. Their officers came to compliment him, assuring him, as before, that so highly did they admire his bravery that they were resolved never to fire on him but to content themselves with making him prisoner. One day, however, a Cossack who had evidently been imperfectly coached in this new system of advance-guard politics, fired a pistol almost point-blank at him while His Majesty was chattering and strolling about. Happily he was not hit. Instantly an officer came up to offer excuses and to assure His Majesty that this disloyal enemy would be punished. One good resulted from this incident. The King lost something of his confidence, and was less inclined to believe in the pacific dispositions of these gentry.)

Both the Prince of Neuchâtel and the Duke of Friuli repeated to me what I am about to recount as proof that the Emperor, who was detained at Moscow by his hopes of concluding a peace, had no illusions as to his position, although he tried to impose them upon many other people, especially myself. He admitted from the very outset, to those persons whom he honoured with his more intimate confidence, that Moscow was a bad situation, and that he could remain there only long enough to reorganize; that the Austrians and Prussians, the allies entrusted with the defence of our rear, would become our most dangerous enemies if we met with the slightest reverse.

However clearsighted he may have been on this point, his enthusiasm was such, and so eager was he to nurture the illusions and hopes raised in his own mind, that he cherished the hope of receiving a reply from the Tsar, or at least negotiations for an armistice with Kutusof, which should lead to further results. It might almost be said that he was carried away by the very difficulty of his situation and blinded as

to his perils, so that every development combined to close his
eyes and push him further into the path of danger.

The Prince of Neuchâtel had received, together with a despatch from Prince Schwarzenberg, a letter which gave him
food for thought no less serious than it did Daru, Duroc
and myself, to whom he showed it. Prince Schwarzenberg's
loyalty and honourable sentiments lent especial value to this
letter. Here is the tenor of it: "The position is already embarrassing, the situation may become graver; anyhow, whatever happens, I assure you [Berthier] of my personal regard
and of the value I place and shall always place on my relations with you."

Discussing this letter with Berthier, the Emperor said:

"This gives warning of defection at the first opportunity.
It may even have started already. The Austrians and Prussians are enemies behind our backs. The die is cast. . . ."

He paused, thought a moment, and added:

"*Du destin qui fait tout, telle est la loi suprême.*"

Berthier urged the instant necessity of pursuing his original
plan as soon as possible, which was to leave Moscow and move
back towards Poland, as this would circumvent all their malice
and double the strength of our forces.

"You are anxious to go to Grosbois and see Madame Visconti," [5] was the Emperor's reply to him.

Seeing that he had hurt him, the Emperor added:

"This letter is sentimental nonsense. Schwarzenberg is making up to you because he prefers shooting your pheasants at
Grosbois, or his own in Bohemia, to being worried every
morning by Tormasov. Maret, however, is very pleased with
him. He knows all that is going on. All is well at Vienna,
and even the Prussians are fighting perfectly. If there were

[5] The beautiful Josephine Carcano, wife of François Visconti, was
Berthier's mistress; and the château of Grosbois, near Boissy Saint-Léger,
was Berthier's estate. His hunting parties were famous.

anything to all this, Maret has every means of information at hand and would know about it. He is satisfied—he tells me that all is well; and we will wait at Moscow for Alexander's reply, for he is much more embarrassed than I am—with his Senate and the Kutusof they have forced upon him."

CHAPTER VIII

NO TRUCE

WHILE headquarters were dreaming dreams of negotiations and peace, the Cossacks were harrying our foragers daily and seizing prisoners almost at the very gates of the city. They also appeared between Mojaisk and Moscow. A few isolated men were chased and captured; one courier was delayed fifteen hours, and this worried the Emperor extremely. Every quarter of an hour he sent to ask me, and the chief-of-staff, too, whether we had learned anything of the cause of this delay. I profited by the occasion to renew the demand I had been making ever since our arrival for an escort for the courier, even if only a couple of men; but to establish this at all the relays would have entailed a considerable detachment of troops, and the cavalry was already greatly reduced in strength. So the Emperor thought to dismiss the matter by saying that it was an unnecessary precaution—that the road was perfectly safe.

Three days later the postilion driving the courier to Paris was shot at beyond Mojaisk, and was chased for five miles. Thereupon the Emperor lost no time in sending out the detachments I had asked for. As I have said, the slightest delay in his communications with Paris irritated and disquieted the Emperor, though the enemy could have obtained no real advantage by seizing the despatches, as all important papers were in cipher. But it was disagreeable to him to see his communications with France threatened, nor did he wish the news to be known there, or in Europe, that the enemy was at our backs.

The Emperor became very preoccupied, and undoubtedly began to consider inwardly the inconveniences of the situation which he had hitherto sought to conceal. Neither his losses in battle nor the state of his cavalry had perturbed him so much as the appearance of a few Cossacks on our rear. During his conversations while he took his walk, or at the reception after dinner where his marshals and generals were invited along with the principal personages of the Household, the Emperor always talked of the fine weather, of how the winter could be spent in Moscow. . . . The Emperor likewise openly announced his intention of marching against Kutusof to drive him further away and thus give the army some repose. He talked of the news he had received from the Duke of Bassano, of the considerable levies that were to be made in Poland, and the expected arrival of six thousand Cossacks from that country.

It was at this time that the Emperor instituted means for the evacuation of generals and wounded officers unable to rejoin their units at once. To these were added men of the rank and file who had lost limbs, as well as cadres of non-commissioned officers, taken from all the regiments, who were to organize the new corps that were being trained in France. Everyone was required to supply horses and carriages, the Emperor himself setting an example. The ambulance administration no longer existed save on paper: Lieutenant-General Nansouty, himself wounded, was placed in command of this convoy [October 10], which crossed the Niemen before the extreme cold set in, and luckily reached France in safety. In preparation for this evacuation, the Emperor required from the intendant-general [Dumas] a report as to the time it would take to reach the Niemen, and was much upset at the estimated number of days [fifty], either because he did not like to think he was so far from his point of departure, or because he thought that others, making the same calculation for themselves, would be discouraged. He questioned the accuracy of the calculation and grew very angry, as if Count Dumas could have shortened the distance.

The overtures made to Petersburg remained unanswered, and the Cossacks continued to harry the fringes of Moscow. They had even penetrated the suburbs, and seized men and horses who were out foraging. Strong escorts of cavalry and infantry were required for their protection.

Although he dropped no hint as to plans for a retreat, not even to the Prince of Neuchâtel, I think it was at this juncture that the Emperor decided to evacuate Moscow and retire to Witepsk, there to take up the line he had formerly wished to hold and to place his troops in winter-quarters. But although he had resolved to do this, he unfortunately continued to delay the execution of his plans, however much he realized the urgency of the matter, because he liked above all else to imagine that what he desired would be successful. He could not admit to himself that Fortune, which had so often smiled upon him, had quite abandoned his cause just when he required miracles of her.

A new convoy of artillery had been attacked and several ammunition waggons captured near the manor of Wezianino, where the Emperor had slept before entering Moscow. Anyone could see, in these preliminaries, signs of a new system of warfare designed to isolate us. It would have been impossible to devise a plan that could have given the Emperor more trouble or have affected his interests more severely. We discussed it with him—the Prince of Neuchâtel, the Viceroy and myself.

Matters seemed to me to be taking so serious a turn that I felt it my duty to throw off the reserve which I had so long imposed upon myself. I requested an audience with the Emperor. As I saw him daily and always accompanied him wherever he went, he seemed astonished at my formal request, and, granting it immediately, commented:

"Well, what is so urgent?   Anything out of the ordinary?"

My observations on the dangers of a protracted sojourn at Moscow, and of the winter, if we marched during the cold, were received most graciously, though at the moment they evoked no reply or hint which could give me any indication of his intentions.

"Caulaincourt is already half-frozen," he said to Duroc and the Prince of Neuchâtel, when telling them what I had done.

The Prince and the Viceroy had themselves pointed out to the Emperor all the inconveniences and even dangers that would arise from a more prolonged stay in Moscow. The carelessness and negligence of our troops in looking after themselves added to the misfortunes of our situation, and I have no doubt that the Emperor saw and thought as we did. But the difficulty of getting out of his embarrassing position gave fresh food to his hopes of entering into negotiations, and held him virtually a prisoner in the Kremlin.

About September 24, the Mojaisk road being entirely cut off by a corps of Russian dragoons and Cossacks, the Emperor sent some squadrons of chasseurs and dragoons of the Guard, and they had several skirmishes with the Russian cavalry. Our dragoons, having pushed a successful charge too far, were surrounded by superior forces and obliged to yield. Major Marthod, a few officers, some dragoons and part of two squadrons were taken prisoners. Although the utmost bravery had been shown, this slight reverse suffered by a corps of the Guard irritated the Emperor as much as the loss of a battle would have done. But it must be remembered that at the time this incident impressed everyone more than had the loss of fifty general officers at Borodino.

Also other points on the Smolensk road were taken over by

enemy parties; with the result that all certain communication with France was cut off. Wilna, Warsaw, Mayence, Paris were no longer in daily receipt of their orders from the Sovereign of the *Grand Empire*. In Moscow the Emperor waited in vain for despatches from his ministers, reports from his governors, news from Europe. From the expression on our faces one might have thought that the possibility of such an interruption had never entered anyone's head. It was all right to have to fight in order to get a crust of bread, to risk being taken prisoner for the sake of a truss of hay, to run the chance of being frozen to death by staying in Russia; everyone was familiar with such possibilities—or rather probabilities; but the idea that an expected letter from France might not arrive was a quite different matter. General Saint-Sulpice was sent with a second body of mounted Guard, and re-established our communications.

At the end of this month so rashly passed in Moscow, the French army was composed of an active force of ninety-five thousand men. Of the five hundred guns that the army still possessed more than half might have been limbered up.

Come what might, the Emperor was desirous of sending to Paris some trophies of his sojourn in Moscow, and so he made enquiries as to what should be sent to France as tokens of the success of his arms. He visited every part of the Kremlin himself, as well as the church of Ivan Veliki and the other church alongside it.

The Poles had always mentioned the church of Ivan Veliki as being the object of the Russians' devotion, and even superstition. The iron cross surmounting the belfry, the Emperor was told, was venerated by all the Orthodox. As far as I can recollect, a Russian proclamation that had been shown to the Emperor, or some report that he had received, spoke of the cross of Ivan Veliki as one of the sacred objects in the hands of the enemy, the recovery of which should be the first aim of all the faithful. This fixed the Emperor's determination: he gave orders that it should be taken down. The difficulty was to do this, as no workmen could be found to climb to such a height.

The Prince of Neuchâtel, like everyone else, was reluctant to deprive an already ruined city of part of the sole monument left intact within its walls. The Emperor repeated his order, and specially charged the sappers of the Guard with the execution of it. From that moment there could be no more talk of difficulties; but the cross, partly dismounted, was not so much taken down as dropped to the ground. To this iron cross were added various objects which were believed to be used at the coronations of the Tsars, and two old cannon asked for by the Poles, as having formerly been taken from them by the Russians. But the cannon remained in position, for, as not one horse was left in the whole country to replace our own losses, and we had not enough to harness to our artillery, we could not spare any for taking away trophies. So the Poles had to content themselves with some old standards which the Russians had formerly captured from them and had left in the arsenal.

On Lauriston's return the Emperor had spoken to me of his mission; and on this occasion he discussed matters in a friendly tone to which I was unaccustomed.

"The Emperor Alexander is stubborn," he said. "He will regret it. Never again will he be able to obtain such good terms as I would have made now. He has done himself no end of harm by burning his towns and his capital—what more could *I* have asked of him? It would not have cost him that much to confiscate English shipping. If the Poles do not rise *en masse* to defend themselves against the Russians, France has sacrificed enough for them so that I can close out and make peace, at the same time looking after their particular interests.

"I am going to attack Kutusof. If I beat him, as is probable, the Tsar runs grave risks. He can stop it to-day by a word. Who can tell what will happen in the forthcoming campaign? I have money, and more men than I need. I am about to get six thousand Cossacks; in the next campaign I shall have fifteen thousand. I have learned much from this war; my army is getting to know the country and the troops confronting them. These are incalculable advantages.

"If I make my winter-quarters here and at Kaluga, even at Smolensk or at Witepsk, Russia will be lost. Having offered here, as at Osterode,[1] all the concessions that I can be expected to make, I shall have no choice but to pursue the interests of my System, to pursue the great political aim which I have set for myself. If the Tsar would only use his intelligence, he would realize that he could go a long way with a man of my character. Now I will have nothing more to do with him because he won't reply to any of my overtures. You were right," added the Emperor, "when you did not accept that mission; you would have made them see when they were well off."

I answered him, as on other occasions, that I should have met with no better hearing than M. Lauriston . . . that all these fine phrases might merely be a sort of game to foster our hopes of a speedy settlement: in other words, to lull the Emperor into a false sense of security while he was in Moscow, since at Petersburg they realized their advantages and our difficulties.

At the words *lull* and *difficulties* the Emperor gave a start.

"What do you call our difficulties?" he asked, with an air of irritation.

"The winter, Sire," I answered, "is a big difficulty, to begin with; the lack of stores, of horses for your artillery, of trans-

[1] February 21 to March 31, 1807. An allusion to the offers of alliance made to Russia before the Friedland campaign.

port for your sick and wounded, the poor clothing for your soldiers. Every man must have a sheepskin, stout fur-lined gloves, a cap with ear-tabs, warm boot-socks, heavy boots to keep his feet from getting frost-bitten. You lack all this. Not a single calkin has been forged to rough-shoe the horses; how are they going to draw the guns? There is no end to what I could tell Your Majesty on this subject. Then there are your communications; the weather is still fine, but what will it be in a month, in a fortnight, perhaps in even less?"

The Emperor listened. I perceived that it was with impatience, but at least he let me speak. This time, it seemed to me, what I implied with thoughts of retreat in my mind irritated him no less than my words *lull* and *difficulties*. He was above all upset at having been found out.

"So you think I am leaving Moscow?" he demanded.

"Yes, Sire."

"That is not certain. Nowhere shall I be better off than in Moscow."

The hardships of winter, the total lack of all precautions against cold, and so forth, did not enter into his calculations.

"You do not know the French," he said to me. "They will get all they need; one thing will take the place of another. . . . The extreme rigours of winter do not come on in twenty-four hours. Although we are less acclimatized than the Russians, we are fundamentally more robust. We have not had autumn yet; we shall have plenty of fine days before winter sets in."

"Do not trust to that, Sire," I answered. "Winter will come like a bombshell—and you cannot be too apprehensive, considering the present state of the army."

This conversation shows all too clearly the Emperor's hopes, desires, and wishes; it would be superfluous to add further details. In the event of not meeting with the success he anticipated in his attack on Kutusof, the Emperor considered himself in a fit state to keep the field, and imagined that the temperature would allow him to do so for some time yet. He intended to make no movement without having previously beaten Kutusof; but should he decide to retire on Witepsk he wanted at the same time to arrange everything in Moscow, so that if necessary the winter could be passed there, and so that he could retain the means of keeping the place if he decided to hold that line. In the event of a withdrawal, he considered that he would have time and the means to withdraw the Moscow garrison when he wished to do so.

Such was the reasoning upon which the Emperor based his conduct and his prolonged stay in Moscow, waiting for a reply which never came and could not come.

Since October 3 our troops had been ordered to concentrate, and on the fifteenth or sixteenth the Emperor seemed inclined to evacuate Moscow and move his headquarters to Witepsk, keeping Smolensk as an advanced post or, perhaps, as headquarters if he did not deem it necessary to establish himself at Witepsk to be nearer the Dwina. He complained more bitterly than ever that the King of Naples was losing his cavalry. On the evening of the fourteenth he had ordered him to make ready for a possible attack on Kutusof, and relying on details the King had supplied as to the state of the cavalry, daily losses, and the difficulty of finding provisions, had authorized him to take up his position at Woronovo for the time being, as he would there be covered by infantry. But the tacit armistice which had existed for some days made the King decide to stay where he was.

Meanwhile the Emperor once again sent Lauriston to Russian headquarters to propose an armistice, and to ascertain whether any reply had come from Petersburg. The King of Naples was instructed to forward Lauriston's despatches as rapidly as possible, for the Emperor awaited them with all the more impatience because he realized that the season was passing. The Prince of Neuchâtel wrote in this sense to Kutusof on the sixteenth, urging him to make war in such a way as to keep the country in hand rather than devastate it. He proposed certain measures to this end. On the twenty-first (after his success at Woronovo), Marshal Kutusof replied: "A people that has not seen an enemy on its soil for three centuries is unable to make the distinction which frequent occupations and familiarity with the customs of modern warfare have established in civilized nations."

The Emperor considered this a worthy reply, and after reading it, observed:

"These people have no wish to treat for terms. Kutusof is courteous because he wants to finish the war, but Alexander has no such desire. He is pig-headed."

The King of Naples had already proposed this armistice desired by the Russian generals, and only refused by them because the Tsar had not authorized it. It was on this occasion that the Tsar remarked, on receiving the despatches and proposals from headquarters:

"Now is the moment when my campaign opens."

Some days later (after the affair of Woronovo) it was learned from the Russians that the Tsar had expressly forbidden the marshal and his generals to consent to any armistice or cessation of hostilities. Lauriston came back on the seventeenth, while Kutusof was preparing for the next day the surprise which was to disillusion everyone so cruelly.

At this time, while searching for food and wine, some soldiers discovered cellars in which a prodigious quantity of furs had been concealed, and all who could afford it bought them. The bearskins were too costly for junior officers, but I purchased one for a few napoleons.

By October 18 everything was ready to move on Kaluga on the twentieth. The Emperor had decided to leave part of his Household at Moscow and had given me orders to that effect. At one in the afternoon, as he was holding a review of Ney's corps after parade, he received news of the King of Naples's defeat at Winkovo. The Emperor decided on the spot to hasten his own movements and advanced everything by a day. The entire Household and all his carriages were ordered to start, and even as many of the sick as could be moved. The Emperor's first words to the Prince of Neuchâtel and to those to whom he issued orders in person were:

"We must wipe out the effects of this surprise. It must not be said in France that a check like this has forced us to retire. What folly of the King! No one takes proper care. This up-sets all our plans; it spoils everything. The honour of our arms must be re-established on the battlefield. We will see if the Russians carry matters off there as they did in this sur-prise. Anyhow, it looks as if the King has done them some damage, for they dare not follow him. In any event, we must march to his help and avenge him."

The King had lost several pieces of artillery, a number of excellent and gallant officers had been killed, others captured and many wounded. He lost also a number of his prisoners, and the greater part of his own carriages and those of his army corps.

The King had carried out his retreat in good order and with-out annoyance from the Russians, of whom only a few corps had crossed the Tchernitchnia. Kutusof had only intended this skirmish to be an affair between out-posts, a snatched ad-vantage. He contented himself with this small success and did not trouble to risk the advantage he had gained. Unwill-ing to run the hazards of a battle, he halted, resumed his posi-tion on the Nara, and left only Platow, supported by some regular troops, to pursue the King of Naples. With soldiers of different calibre, serving under a different chief, few of our men would have escaped. Prodigies of valour were performed.

The Emperor blamed the King, and especially General Sébastiani who had suffered the surprise, for not having sent out-posts or continual patrols into the small wood that dominated the position at General Sébastiani's right; for it was from this position that the Russians, more alert and active than ourselves on this occasion, were able, as the Emperor said, to observe all Sébastiani's movements, even to what went on in his own quarters.

The Emperor was all the more displeased that he should have to blame his generals for having been taken by surprise, because this same place had been attacked by the Cossacks early in October and from the same wood; this, he considered, should not have escaped the notice of those in command. The Emperor did not fail to reproach himself for having stayed in Moscow without inspecting this position.

"It means that I must see everything with my own eyes," he said. "I cannot rely upon the King. He trusts in his own bravery; he leaves things to his generals and they are careless. The King performs prodigies of valour. Without his presence of mind and courage everything would have been lost, and he himself jeopardized—had the Russians been better led."

If this surprise attack was proof of our lack of watchfulness, the way we fought, although far fewer in numbers, must have shown the Russians that fatigue and privations had by no means diminished our courage. The entire success of the enemy was attributed to the Cossacks, whose activities engaged only too much of our attention. Our men were doubtless very brave, but they were careless and lacking in vigilance, which arose as much from their character as from lack of order and discipline.

This was frequently the subject of serious reflection on the part of the Prince of Neuchâtel and other generals about the Emperor. There were too many young officers in the corps. Dashing courage was valued above all else; method, foresight, and even a love of discipline were underestimated. At all his reviews the Emperor made everything of audacity, courage and luck.

Those who organized, trained the men at the bases, and kept things going, obtained no recognition if they were no longer with the Grand Army or had not taken part in such-and-such a battle. No commanding officer was ever brought to book for the losses occasioned by his negligence, his lack of order and discipline, even if two thirds of his force had been wasted from these causes. If he led a gallant charge at the head of the hundred men left him on the day of battle, he obtained whatever he desired—and nothing was given to the brave lieutenant-colonel who, after fighting his twenty campaigns, was back in the depôt organizing and drilling the detachments that were to reinforce the Army. He was forgotten, because he had had no chance of contributing any brilliant deeds to the successful affair of the moment.

Far be it from me to say that the Emperor did not reward the old soldiers. There are too many instances to prove, on the contrary, that they were the objects of his solicitude when they remained with the army or were invalided out; but let them remain in the depôts even in the interests of the service, and they could obtain no promotion until they returned to the fighting line.

Undoubtedly this system had the advantage of making all officers anxious to get back to the front, but it was really detrimental to the service and to the best officers as well; for the depôts were only given to the most capable men. Any honest investigator who would compare the conditions of his corps at the beginning of the campaign with its state at the end, seeking the causes of loss and wastage, would certainly find that it was not the enemy's guns which had done the most damage to our cavalry. The fine state in which some corps were maintained to the very last moment, compared to the disorder and destruction suffered by others that had seen no longer service, proves that our greatest foe was lack of discipline; and the disorders that followed in its train originated in the negligence of the commanding officers.

For his headquarters the Emperor had altogether seven hundred and fifteen saddle and draught horses in Russia to draw the waggons loaded with provisions of all kinds as well as a great outfit of tents. As his headquarters were always the last to arrive, and that invariably in a place already laid waste because the whole army had already passed by, it was necessary to carry everything with us or seek what we needed from a distance. (It must also be observed that the general service of supply did not furnish in all a thousand pounds of bread, a hundred trusses of hay, nor a particle of oats to the Emperor's Household throughout the campaign.) I have, therefore, had experience of what can be done by method and care in supplementing the provender both in kind and quantity. All persons attached to headquarters were in the same plight, but as none had more than a few horses it was much easier for them to find and provide fodder. It is also an admitted fact that the mounts of the Emperor and his suite made much longer and faster rides than other horses. Yet on reaching Wilna on December 8, during the retreat, only eighty horses had been lost out of the seven hundred and fifteen with which we had started the campaign.

I enter into these particulars in order to answer in advance all the fables that have been told, and that will yet be told, as to the effects of the cold, the lack of provisions, and so forth. During the retreat horses fell and lay by the roadside chiefly because they were not properly shod to keep their footing on ice, and once down, and vainly having attempted to rise, they ended by lying where they fell, and were cut up for food before they were even dead. With proper shoeing and the exercise of a little care, the greater number would certainly have been saved.

Before leaving the subject of Moscow it is essential that I should say something about its administration. The Duke of Treviso had been charged with the government of the city; and M. de Lesseps, formerly consul-general at Petersburg, had been placed at the head of the administration. This estimable gentleman was on his way back to Paris with his wife and eight children when a courier caught him up as he was disembarking at Danzig, and handed him imperative orders to proceed at once to Imperial headquarters, then at the gates of Moscow. Despite his urgent request to be excused from all duties, after a week the Emperor appointed him intendant. This excellent man did all he could. Like a true governor, he put a stop to many evils, among them the issue of forged papers, the loss of many billions by pillage, and the destruction of such archives as had been saved from the fire.

It was the honourable and worthy Lesseps who raised more opposition than anyone else to the proclamation for the liberation of the serfs; it was he who collected, sheltered, nourished, and in fact saved, quite a number of unfortunate men, women and children, whose houses had been burned and who were wandering like ghosts amid the ruins of the capital. On this occasion he showed that he had not forgotten the thirty years' hospitality he had met with in Russia. I was an eye-witness of this estimable man's efforts; he often confided in me his disappointments and all the sorrow that so much distressed him. It is only right that I should render justice to the honourable sentiments that have been his invariable guide.

The Emperor had had prepared a proclamation to give the serfs their freedom. This was early in October. Some dregs of the lowest classes of society, and a few firebrands (German artisans who made themselves the mouthpiece for these people and egged them on), had raised an outcry and demanded that this should be done. These same men had persuaded the Emperor to begin the proclamation by announcing that hopes of freedom were germinating in every peasant's head; that, thereafter, instead of finding himself surrounded by enemies, the Emperor would have millions of auxiliaries. Yet was not this measure radically opposed to his acknowledged principles? He felt, and some time later observed to me, that the prejudice and fanaticism excited against us in the minds of the populace would prove a great obstacle, for some time at least, and that consequently he would have to bear all the odium of that measure without reaping any of the benefits.

The disorder and pillage which inevitably followed our forced marches had caused the initial damage and alienated the peasants. The fires that had been so skilfully started, for which the peasants blamed the French; the different language; the crusade preached against us by the Russian clergy—all had combined to make that superstitious folk regard us as barbarians who had come to overturn their altars, steal their goods, ravish their women and children, lead them into captivity. And so they fled from us as from wild beasts.

It would have taken time to re-establish our relations with the inhabitants. You have to confer before you can agree. As matters stood, there was no one to confer with. The Russian government had been wise to send away the inhabitants before the French arrived. In those grave circumstances— now it can be said—the Russians lacked neither talent nor forethought. This being the case a proclamation which, apart from anything else, was not in accordance with the Emperor's views, could have served no purpose; for it would have had no effect, and would have imparted to the war a revolutionary character which would have been highly unseemly in a monarch who, with reason, prided himself on having restored social order to Europe. So the preparation of this proclamation was merely a threat; it deceived nobody who really knew the Emperor.

It was one of those countless gestures he made to see if a threat would produce any effect. He wished, if possible, to intimidate. It was some of that avenging thunder of his—that heat-lightning which never struck. He left nothing untried to bring about the negotiations he desired, but this proclamation was not a device that entered into his political scheme, although he spoke as if it were a definite project.

One day the Emperor even said to me:

"Like you, Lesseps is against emancipation. Yet there are some, who know as much about the Russians as you, who think differently. You're opposed to it because it would not be playing fair with your friend Alexander. But those fires were not fair either. They would fully justify reprisals. Otherwise, I think exactly as you do about this emancipation. It is impossible to tell where such a measure would lead. Up to the present, except that Alexander has burned his towns to prevent us from occupying them, we have played the game with each other. There have been no offensive proclamations, no insults. He is wrong not to come to terms now that our duel is over. We should soon be in agreement and remain the best of friends."

PART IV
RETREAT

CHAPTER IX

SAUVE-QUI-PEUT

THE Emperor and the Guard did not leave Moscow until about noon on October 19. Then, since the successive reports of the King of Naples confirmed the retreat of the enemy, the Emperor took his whole establishment with him. Numbers of refugees followed the army. On the road we met many of the wounded from Woronovo, the full details of which encounter the Emperor learned only now, when he was already on the march. We slept at the manor house of Troitskoie where we stayed during the whole of the twentieth to rally our forces, for many men and transports had again fallen behind.

It was here that the Emperor finally decided to abandon Moscow. He was forced to this decision by the losses incurred at Woronovo, the reports about the state of our cavalry, and the realization that the Russians would not come to terms. He was still determined, however, to attack Kutusof; and to that end he speeded up his advance. It was his intention, if his success were such as he hoped, to push beyond Kaluga and destroy the ordnance establishment at Toula, which was the most important in all Russia. In any case, he was resolved to direct his forces upon Smolensk, which he wished to make his principal outpost. The Duke of Treviso was ordered to evacuate Moscow on the twenty-third if he did not in the meantime receive other orders. He was to make ready, also, for blowing up the Kremlin and the barracks.

Several detachments of Cossacks appeared on our flank, but did not venture to cross our line of march. I had arranged, by sending out detachments, that the couriers from Paris should come direct to us from the second relay station before Moscow. The Cossacks, however, controlled that point and delayed the couriers, so that none reached us for three days. As usual, this worried and annoyed the Emperor more than I can express. On the second day he said to me:

"I see it will be absolutely essential to be in closer touch with my reserves. It will be useless to drive off Kutusof and force him to evacuate Kaluga and his entrenchments: the Cossacks will keep interrupting my communications so long as I haven't my Poles."

The weather was bad [October 21-22] and the ground so sodden with rain that we had great difficulty in making Borowsk in two marches across country. The draught horses were finished. The cold nights were too much for them; and already we were beginning to abandon ammunition-cases and transports. It was on the evening of the previous day that the Prince of Neuchâtel told me how for the first time the Emperor, in discussing the army, its movements, and the possible issues, had made no reference to his former project: the scheme of holding Moscow while we occupied the "fertile province of Kaluga," as the Emperor called it. This province must have been the apparent rather than the real object of our expedition. . . . The Emperor was more than ever set upon driving Kutusof from his position and forcing him to an engagement, not wishing it to be thought that the unfortunate skirmish at Winkovo had compelled him to retire. At no matter what cost, there must be some incident in the bulletin to balance the defeat of the King of Naples and prevent Kutusof from flattering himself that our retreat was the immediate consequence of it.

The belated couriers arrived, but only to inform us that a body of Cossacks, together with a great number of peasants armed and organized as a militia, were cutting off our communications beyond Ghjat; and that the range of their activities

A PAGE OF THE CAULAINCOURT MANUSCRIPT

appeared to be spreading. A month earlier I had directed the officer in command of each relay post to make a note of what was going on in his district on the covering sheet of the despatches, where the time of arrival and departure were always entered. These reports from the road I passed to the Emperor daily, and he used to read them before anything else. At this time they indicated movements of peasants and the presence of Cossacks at every stage; and they made a great impression on the Emperor, who said to me, as early as the twenty-first:

"We shall be without news from France; but the worst of it is that France will have no news of us."

He instructed me to advise anyone writing home to write with great discretion, since any letter might be intercepted.

The Emperor reached Borowsk on the twenty-third. In spite of the very bad weather, in the afternoon he reconnoitred the neighbourhood of the town and the banks of the river [Protva] for a good distance out. But it was not until the morning of the twenty-fourth that he went forward to within a quarter of a league of Malo-Jaroslawetz, where Delzons's division had been fighting since daybreak against Doctorov's corps.

While waiting for the arrival of the Viceroy, Delzons accomplished marvels. The Viceroy hurried to his support as soon as he knew how much superior were the forces by which he was engaged; but Delzons was killed in the midst of his men. General Guilleminot took his place and renewed the engagement. Like the experienced soldier he was, he occupied and fortified a church and two houses which flanked our defence and which prevented the Russians, although they were greatly superior in numbers, from passing beyond those points in their different attacks. These fortifications gave the leading division of the Fourth Army Corps time to come up and relieve him. At the same time Kutusof's advance-guard came up with Doctorov; and the fresh troops put in on both sides not only made the engagement brisker but turned it into a battle.

The Emperor, who arrived by eleven o'clock, ordered the Prince of Eckmühl to quicken his march and move to the right of Prince Eugène, whom the Guard were also ordered to support. The First Army Corps went into the line about two o'clock. We could see perfectly the movements of the Russians, and expected that Kutusof would take full advantage of this very strong position [1] to block our advance and himself take the offensive; but the Fourth Army Corps proved sufficient. Davout was hardly engaged. We had at least four thousand men put out of action, and a remarkable number of Russians were killed.

That night and the following day, together with the Emperor, I went over the battle-ground most carefully. We blamed Kutusof for sacrificing a good number of men, only to be beaten in the end and fail of his object—for since he defended his position, he must have intended to hold it at least till nightfall. The truth is that Kutusof, having learnt of the Emperor's movements only on the twenty-third, was taken by surprise. The successive bodies of troops which arrived later to support Doctorov were only put into action to cover the retreat of his army upon Juchnow, for he was unwilling to run the risks of a pitched battle. The general opinion was that Kutusof might have better defended his position. For our part, we had to leave it in the hands of a small rear-guard.

Some Cossacks appeared that evening on the right of Ghorodnia, where headquarters had been established [in a weaver's hut]. They were thought to be a party that had lost their way and would blunder into our outposts. We paid less

[1] "Malo-Jaroslawetz stands on heights at the foot of which the river Luja runs through a marshy bed. The French, coming from Moscow, had to cross the river, then climb the heights, and maintain themselves in Malo-Jaroslawetz. The Russians, marching on the other side of the river, had merely to enter the town."—Thiers, XIV, 476.

attention to them than we might have done, because about noon in the same district, but on the left of the road, we had chased off some new Cossacks wearing crosses on their caps. They were mounted troops founded on the model of the Don Cossacks, and named after the provinces that provided them.

Two army corps were drawn up beyond the town; but the roads were so broken up that only one section of the artillery had been able, and that with difficulty, to reach their position. The Emperor moved back to spend the night [October 24-25] in a hut near the bridge at Ghorodnia, a small hamlet one league from Malo-Jaroslawetz. Nearly all of us camped in the open. The Viceroy's success had got us nowhere. We held the field, but Kutusof had given us the slip. Our situation was therefore unchanged; and the army was not in a position to pursue the enemy.

The Emperor spent the night in receiving reports, issuing orders, and, on this occasion, discussing his difficulties with the Prince of Neuchâtel. He sent for me several times, and also for Duroc and the Duke of Istria, and discussed matters with us, but without reaching any decision. Should he follow Kutusof, who, having abandoned an impregnable position, had probably eluded us? And what route should he take to Smolensk if he did not find the enemy drawn up beyond Malo-Jaroslawetz? He had to make up his mind; and the course that drew the Emperor away from his enemy, whose measure he so much wanted to take, was always the one that came hardest to him.

An hour before daybreak the Emperor sent for me again. We were alone. He looked very preoccupied and seemed anxious to relieve himself of the thoughts that oppressed him.

"This is a bad business," he said. "I beat the Russians every time, but that doesn't get me anywhere."

After a quarter hour of silent pacing back and forth in his little hut, the Emperor went on:

"I'm going to find out for myself whether the enemy are drawing up for battle, or whether they are retreating, as everything suggests. That devil Kutusof will never make a fight of it! Fetch the horses—let's be off!"

As he spoke he picked up his hat to go. The Duke of Istria and the Prince of Neuchâtel, who luckily happened to enter just as the Emperor was starting out, joined me in trying to persuade him to wait until dawn. They reminded him that it was very dark—that he would reach the outposts before it was light enough to see—and that, as the Guard had taken up their positions by night, no one was certain where the corps lay.

The Emperor, however, was still resolved to go until one of the Viceroy's aides-de-camp arrived to announce that, though nothing could be seen of the enemy but the fires of the Cossacks, some peasants and soldiers had just been taken who confirmed the news of their retreat. These particulars made the Emperor decide to wait; but a half hour later his impatience drove him to start.

Dawn was hardly showing, and three-quarters of a mile from headquarters we found ourselves face to face with some Cossacks belonging to a troop of which the greater part, who were ahead of us, had set upon an artillery park where they heard some guns moving. They had carried off several pieces. It was still so dark that we were warned only by their shouts, and were almost upon them before we could see them. It was so unexpected to find them inside the lines where our Guard were bivouacked that (I must admit) we paid little heed to the first shouts. It was only when the shouting increased and closed in around the Emperor that General Rapp (who was ahead of him with Lauriston, Lobau, and Durosnel, the orderly officers on duty, and the advance-guard of the picket) came back to the Emperor and said:

"Halt, Sire! The Cossacks!"

"Take the chasseurs of the picket," he answered, "and go forward."

The chasseurs, only ten or twelve of whom had so far joined us, were already moving forward unbidden to join the advance-guard. The light was still so poor that nothing could be seen more than twenty-five yards away. Only the clash of arms and the shouts of the men fighting indicated the direction of the skirmish, or even that we were at grips with the enemy. M. Emmanuel Lecouteulx, the Prince of Neuchâtel's aide-de-camp on duty, had a sabre run clean through his chest by a trooper of the Guard who mistook him for a Russian.[2]

The Emperor was left alone with the Prince of Neuchâtel and myself. All three of us held our swords drawn. As the fighting was very near and shifting closer towards him, the Emperor decided to move off several yards, on to the crest of the rise, so as to see better. At this moment the remaining chasseurs of the picket caught up with us; and the squadrons in attendance, to whom the Emperor had not given time to mount horse before he set out, came up immediately after. Guided by the shouts of those already engaged, the first two squadrons to arrive charged and broke up the foremost Cossacks. The two other squadrons, who were close behind, headed by the Duke of Istria, came up in time to support the first two, who were hard pressed and surrounded by a swarm of the enemy. By this time daylight was near enough to light up the scene. The plain and the road were alive with Cossacks. The Guard recaptured the guns and the few artillerymen in

[2] Denniée (*Itineraire*, III) is probably more exact when he says: "It was in this skirmish that Emmanuel Lecouteulx, aide-de-camp to the Prince of Neuchâtel, armed himself with a lance snatched from one of the Cossacks: whereupon a mounted grenadier of the Guard, deceived by his appearance, pursued him in turn and wounded him with a sword-thrust. By a miracle, the blade went under his collar-bone without damage to the artery." Lecouteulx lived until 1844.

the enemy's hands, and forced the Cossacks to recross the river; but we were left with many wounded.

It is clear that if the Emperor had set out, as he had wished, before dawn, he would have found himself in the midst of this swarm of Cossacks with only his picket and the eight generals and officers who accompanied him. If the Cossacks, who came face to face with us and at one moment surrounded us, had shown more courage and fallen upon our route silently, instead of shouting and wrangling at the side of the road, we should have been carried off before the squadron could rescue us. No doubt we should have sold our lives as dearly as one can by hitting out blindly with a light sword in the dark, but the Emperor would certainly have been either killed or captured. No one would even have known where to look for him, in a wide plain dotted all over with clumps of trees under cover of which the Cossacks had been able to hide within musket-shot of the road and the Guard.

If these details had not the testimony of the army and of so many trustworthy men to confirm them, they might be called in question. And how, indeed, can anyone believe that a man of such foresight, a sovereign, and the greatest commander of all time, could have been in danger of capture five hundred yards from his headquarters?—on a high road, the route of march of the whole army, and among the bivouacs of a considerable guard both of cavalry and infantry? Is it credible that a thousand men could have lain in ambush and passed the night within the range of three or four musket-shots from our headquarters without being discovered? But this is all explained and proved by the following particulars, which I have summarized with care as being illustrative of the Emperor's habits.

We had very few light-armed troops left. They had not been spared, and were sorely harassed; and since they had been sent that same day to other points, this section of our position was poorly covered. In general our men fought well but kept a poor look-out. In no other army can the duties of reconnaissance have been so neglected. At nightfall they set up a few sentry-posts hither and yon, so as to have time to mount before the enemy might arrive; but they seldom took the trouble to cover rear or flank.

The Emperor only selected his headquarters at the last moment. Two considerations had led him to form this habit: first, a measure of wise prudence; and second—he admitted this himself—the advantage of having the whole of his entourage at his call until the very end of the day, thus keeping everyone on the alert.

He used sometimes to say to me: "If you make everything difficult, the really hard things seem less so."

Officers and men sometimes suffered from these practices, no doubt. But that did not trouble the Emperor, who looked only to the main result and, being in the midst of his army and of a considerable guard, gave little thought to the organization of detail. Ever intent on taking the offensive, he failed to notice the trouble the Cossacks gave, now that the odds were against us.

The Guard had been in advance throughout that day, and so were obliged to fall back later on in order to take up position. Not having bivouacked until after dark, they did not themselves know where they were, or what was the lie of the land, but must have thought themselves still in the midst of the army. They put out no patrols. They felt secure in the belief that the rest of the troops were covering headquarters from a distance, and did not trouble even to make contact with them. In fact, the Guard and the headquarters took no account of anything that went on outside their own area. One battalion of the Guard was bivouacked barely three hundred yards from the spot, on the same side of the road, where the

Cossacks had spent the night, and whence they came upon the Emperor.

By night or by day, the Emperor would mount his horse without warning: he even took pleasure in going out all of a sudden and throwing everyone off the scent. His saddle-horses were divided into troops. Each troop consisted of two horses for himself, one for the Master of Horse, and as many as were necessary for the other officers on duty with the Emperor. Throughout the whole twenty-four hours there was always one troop of horses saddled and bridled. Every officer had also to have a horse bridled; and the picket on duty, which consisted of an officer and twenty light horse, was always saddled and bridled. The squadrons in attendance provided and relieved the picket. On the other campaigns there was one squadron in attendance, but on the Russian there were four—half light cavalry and half grenadiers and dragoons. The picket never left the Emperor. The squadrons followed in echelon formation, and saddled only when the Emperor called for his horses. As he did so in haste and without warning, he always set out with only two or three other persons. The remainder caught up.

After Moscow, and indeed after Smolensk, the same squadrons remained in attendance for two or three days running: men and horses both were worn out. The Emperor usually returned to his quarters very late, after nightfall. The squadrons in attendance bivouacked as best they could, hurriedly and in the dark. When the Emperor mounted his horse in the field he usually set out at the gallop, if only for two or three hundred yards. However keen and alert they were, therefore, it was difficult for a troop to be actually alongside him from the very start. This explains how the Emperor came to be almost alone at one moment on the day of this scuffle.

The Prince of Neuchâtel and I were always close behind the Emperor's horse. The general-in-command of the Guard who was then on duty [3] rode at our side; but during the Russian campaign the generals of the Guard all had other commands, and the Master of Horse then fulfilled their duties by right. When mounted, we rode in the following order: an advance-guard of four light horse, three orderly officers, two or four aides-de-camp—this group eighty paces forward; the Emperor; behind him the Master of Horse, the Guard's officer of the day, the chief-of-staff; behind these several aides, if the Emperor so commanded, and six staff-officers from the Emperor's staff, two other aides-de-camp, and two officers attached to the chief-of-staff; then the officer and chasseurs constituting the picket; and then, five hundred paces behind, the squadrons in attendance. If we were riding easily, they followed. If the Emperor galloped, they trotted. These details show how small was the Emperor's escort, and how far he was from surrounding himself with a whole host of men, as some have asserted. . . .

The Emperor wavered for some time [October 25]. The fight at Malo-Jaroslawetz was, in his opinion, not enough to counterbalance the defeat of the King of Naples. Moreover, at the moment he wished to put himself in the right about that morning's escapade. It was only after long insistence on our part—and after he had weighed the probability that Kutusof, if he would not stand and fight in an excellent position such as Malo-Jaroslawetz, was not at all likely to join battle twenty leagues further on—that we were able to persuade the Emperor, in this unofficial sort of council, to take the road to Borowsk. There part of the troops, the greater part of the artillery, and all the carriages were already stationed. In view of the state of the horses, this last was a weighty consideration.

Did the Emperor wish it to seem that he was yielding only

[3] The Guard had four generals-in-command: Gouvion Saint-Cyr (cuirassiers), Eugène (chasseurs), Baraguey d'Hilliers (dragoons), and Junot (hussars).

to the convictions of others? Or did he really believe that he might yet break the Russian army and at last turn the whole campaign to his advantage before he decided on his winter quarters? I cannot say. But it is certain that the same question had been urgently presented to him during the night by some of the same people, and that he had resisted every conceivable argument brought forward to persuade him. He merely postponed his decision until he could see for himself whether the enemy had really escaped him. It was for this reason that he had wished to set out before dawn.

He came back to Ghorodnia, and from there sent out his orders. Next day the army marched towards Borowsk, where the staff slept on the night of the twenty-sixth. A few inhabitants had returned to the town. It might be thought that when he left Moscow the Emperor had somehow anticipated the course of events, for he had ordered various precautionary measures against the Cossacks. But, as we have seen, they were unavailing. Nobody was used to keeping good guard, and all were too much disheartened and too exhausted to change their ways.

Every man's first thought on arrival was to find food for himself and his horses; and this could only be done by going off the main road, and so risking capture by Cossacks or murder by peasants. The marches were too hard, and the cavalry too few and exhausted, for adequate detachments to be sent out on reconnaissance or to cover our flanks. We made light, as far as was possible, of the risks run by the Emperor in the scuffle with the Cossacks, but within forty-eight hours the whole army knew the story; and the impression made was regrettable. This incident should have served as a warning to everyone, proving as it did our want of vigilance; but the lesson passed unnoted. At the same time it reflected no credit on the daring or courage of the Cossacks, who allowed themselves to be driven off, and yielded their gains to two or three hundred horsemen.

They are certainly the finest light troops in the world for

guarding an army, scouting the countryside, or carrying out skirmishing sallies; but whenever we faced up to them, and marched against them boldly in a solid body, they never offered resistance, even when they outnumbered us by two to one. Attempt to attack them singly, or charge them in scattered formation, and one is lost. They return to pursue as quickly as they withdraw from attack. Being better horsemen, and mounted on more responsive horses than ours, they can escape us when necessary or pursue us when it suits them. They spare their horses: they may sometimes race them, or set them to long and exacting rides, but they generally spare them the futile running to-and-fro by which we wear out our own.

On the twenty-seventh the Emperor passed the night at Wereia, to give the artillery and other horse-drawn equipment time to take the lead. Having started very early, he reached the town during the morning, passed straight through, and did not halt until he was half-a-league beyond, on the road to Mojaisk, at the top of a rise overlooking the country round. There he stayed to watch the troops and convoys pass; and there they brought him Lieutenant-General the Count of Wintzingerode,[4] aide-de-camp to the Tsar. He had commanded a body of light troops stationed on the road to Tver in order to cover Petersburg and keep watch on Moscow, where he was taken prisoner.

As divergent accounts of this affair have been told since the war, I shall give here the particulars I noted down, from the reports made to the Emperor, at the time it took place. Having probably learnt that the French army had gone, M. Wintzingerode, who was near Moscow, went into the suburbs and entered into talk with some of the inhabitants. Several slight attacks

[4] Ferdinand Charles Frederic Guillaume de Wintzingerode, born at Allendorf, near Göttingen in Württemberg, on February 15, 1770, died at Wiesbaden on June 17, 1818. He had been one of the authors of the Coalition of 1809.

by the Cossacks or by armed peasants had forced the Duke of
Treviso to draw in his small forces so as not to expose them to
danger in that large city. Our troops being concentrated round
the Kremlin, M. Wintzingerode came disguised into the town
as far as our outposts; and he entertained the hope of carrying
out some military operation which should force the Duke of
Treviso to evacuate, or else of achieving the same result by
suborning our soldiers; which the inhabitants thought would
be easy, as they believed the men to be discontented. Our
troops were guarding only the Kremlin and our line of communications to Mojaisk, which led also to the army. M. Wintzingerode, wearing a civilian top-coat over his uniform, got into
conversation with the soldiers at our furthest outpost. He was
accompanied by several of the townspeople who also spoke
French, and, following his example or instructions, these men
talked informally to the soldiers about what was going on—
the set-backs we had experienced, the privations ahead of us,
the useless dangers we were running, the goodness and generosity of the Tsar Alexander, his kindness toward foreigners, his
liking for soldiers, the uselessness of fighting now that the Emperor Napoleon was in retreat, how advantageous it would be
to lay down arms and live in peace until the end of the war in
a country so ready to welcome them, and so forth.

Some of the soldiers, taking him for a mere townsman, let
him run on without paying much heed to him or his talk. A
more perspicacious hussar, having heard some of his final remarks, kept him under observation. Shocked by his suggestions, he arrested him and took him to the guard-room. From
there, in spite of his protests and objections, he was taken before the officer in charge of the city. When he was recognized
as a Russian officer, he vainly tried to plead that he had come
to parley. The story would not hold water. He was kept under
arrest and taken to the Duke of Treviso, who treated him with
consideration, but as a prisoner of war, being unable to accept

the pretence by which M. Wintzingerode wished to extricate himself; for he had come secretly, in disguise, in an attempt to suborn our soldiers, and had not been announced by a trumpeter as an emissary.

M. Narishkin, son of the Grand Chamberlain and aide-de-camp to M. Wintzingerode, waited at a distance with a few Cossacks. Not seeing his commander return, he enquired of the townsmen what had happened, and they reported that he had been taken under arrest. Then, without giving notice, without sounding any bugle or calling an officer or sergeant to a parley, Narishkin went over to the French outpost and simply gave himself up, holding it a point of honour not to abandon his chief. This filial devotion on the part of an officer commanding a troop of men excited some surprise. The young man was sent to the marshal under guard.

The Emperor, to whom the capture of these officers was reported, ordered them to be brought to him. They arrived just as we did at the spot on the road where the Emperor chose to dismount. M. Wintzingerode was brought to the Emperor by himself; and the Emperor reproached him for serving with the Russians when he was born in Germany, the subject of a country either ruled by France or allied with her. He added that, M. Wintzingerode being one of his subjects, he would have him tried by a court-martial, which would also charge him with espionage; and that he would be shot as a traitor to his country. The more M. Wintzingerode tried to justify himself, the more angry the Emperor became. He reproached him with having been for a long time in the pay of the English, with having taken part in all the plots against him and against France, with trying to suborn the soldiers at Moscow, urging them to desert, and advising them to commit acts of cowardice, in the name of a sovereign who would have despised them for it. M. Wintzingerode replied that he was not born in a country belonging to France; furthermore, that he had not been in his own country since childhood, and that he had been in the Russian service for many years on account of his attachment and gratitude to the Tsar Alexander, who had befriended him.

Then, attempting to put a different colour on his actions at Moscow, for which the Emperor justly rebuked him, he went on to say that he parleyed to avoid useless bloodshed, and above all to avoid further misfortune for the town: that since the French were going to evacuate it, he limited himself to the suggestion that they should do so without fighting—a suggestion to their common advantage—and so forth.

The Emperor, more and more annoyed, was raising his voice to the point where the picket could hear him. From the first his personal officers had withdrawn a little. Everyone was on pins and needles. Glancing at each other, we could see in every eye the distress caused by this painful scene between a sovereign ruler and a captured officer—for of course what Wintzingerode had done at Moscow was not worth a second thought. I kept on talking to the Duke of Piacenza [then Charles Lebrun], who, like myself, commented very unhappily on the scene that was taking place. The Prince of Neuchâtel was even more uncomfortable, as he had remained close to the Emperor. We could see this in his expression, and his remarks confirmed it when, on some pretext, he was able to move away and join us. The Emperor called for guardsmen to remove M. Wintzingerode. When no one passed on this order, he called again in such loud tones for guardsmen that the two attached to the picket came forward. The Emperor then repeated to the prisoner some of the charges he had already made against him, and added that he deserved to be shot as a traitor. At this word M. Wintzingerode, who had been listening with eyes on the ground, stood erect, raised his head, and, looking straight at the Emperor and at those standing nearest to him, said loudly:

"As whatever you please, Sire—but not as a traitor."

And he walked away by himself, ahead of the guards, who kept their distance.

The King of Naples, who had joined the Emperor a few moments before, tried in vain to calm him, as did also the Prince of Neuchâtel. He was walking to and fro with hurried, nervous steps, summoning now one of us, now another, to vent his anger. He met only with silence. I have never seen him so angry. The poor Prince of Neuchâtel was beside himself. He came to talk with me, and sent one of his aides-de-camp to instruct the guards that they were to treat the prisoner with consideration.[5] He directed his own officers to supply him with anything he required. Meanwhile, to various people, the Emperor was telling all over again the tale of his grudges, both old and new, against this general. Some dated from earlier, even, than the war-before-last against Austria. The Prince of Neuchâtel, like myself, had never seen the Emperor so completely lose control of himself.

A little way off we could see a fine large house. The Emperor, whose nervous irritability had not passed off, sent two squadrons to sack and fire it, adding: "Since these barbarians like to burn their towns, we must help them."

The order was all too well obeyed. It was the only time I ever heard him give such an order; as a rule, indeed, he tried to prevent destruction which would damage only private interests or ruin private citizens. He returned to Wereia before nightfall. Not one inhabitant remained.

I called for the Prince of Neuchâtel as we had agreed, and together we went to the King of Naples to make him undertake to speak to the Emperor about M. Wintzingerode. We had obtained information from him about his family and the exact date when he had left Germany; and the Prince of Neuchâtel

[5] The Emperor's violence "was disapproved; no one took any notice of it, but on the contrary everyone hastened to wait upon the captive general to reassure and condole with him."—Ségur, *Histoire de Napoléon*, II, 145.

had already taken an opportunity, on the way back, of explaining to the Emperor that M. Wintzingerode was not one of his subjects. I was easy about the outcome of this affair in proportion to the Emperor's annoyance; for princes, like other men, have a conscience which bids them right the wrongs they have done. But as the hours seem long to prisoners, we were impatient to obtain the decision, which we could foresee, but which alone could remove all anxiety.

The Emperor sent to me to enquire if I had news of the courier. This order seemed to me to promise well, for it was much earlier than he could possibly arrive. The Emperor, although considerably calmed down, still needed to vent his spleen. I listened, and agreed that M. Wintzingerode's behaviour at Moscow had been irregular; that he had made himself liable to trial and judgment by the corps which had taken him; but I concluded by saying that the Emperor could not have sent for him and spoken to him himself merely in order to show him a pointless severity—for the Emperor, I said, had used his prisoner so sternly in words that no further punishment was needed. I added that severity would now look like personal vengeance, and an act of malice against the Tsar Alexander, whose aide-de-camp the prisoner was; and that rulers had no need, after so many cannon-balls had been fired, to come to grips with each other in person.

The Emperor began to laugh, and pulled my ear affectionately, as was his habit when he sought to tease people. He said:

"You're right; but this Wintzingerode is a bad character—a schemer. Is it proper for a man of his rank to go about suborning soldiers?—to lower himself to play the spy, the pimp?—to allow himself to use his sovereign's name to incite soldiers to cowardice and mutiny? I shall send him to France. . . . I would rather they had taken a Russian: these foreigners in the service of the highest bidder are poor booty. . . . So it's for Alexander's sake that you take an interest in him? Well, well, we won't hurt him."

The Emperor gave me a little tap on the cheek, his signal mark of affection. From the first I had seen that he only wanted an excuse to go back on his words.

I did not wait for dismissal to go off with such good news; but the Emperor called me back and instructed me to persuade M. Narishkin to dine with us. He added that he would send him back to the Russian outposts in a few days, but that I was not to mention it.

"As to M. Wintzingerode," the Emperor said to me jokingly, "you don't take so much interest in him because he isn't a Russian."

Then he began again the tale of all his faults:

"He is a secret agent of the London government. He was a spy in Vienna, a spy in Petersburg. He is a framer of intrigues wherever he goes, and doesn't deserve the least consideration—certainly not, on any grounds, the post of aide-de-camp to the Tsar Alexander, for close personal duties of that kind belong only to born subjects, honourable men against whom there is no political scandal."

In this conversation with the Emperor I brought in, as we had agreed with the Prince of Neuchâtel, the plea that in the interest of French prisoners some consideration should be shown this man.

"That will not be the reason," replied the Emperor sharply, "for my showing him mercy; his behaviour has put him outside ordinary rights. It is because I never really wanted to do him any harm; and though the Emperor Alexander is at fault in making such a man his aide-de-camp, I will not be likewise at fault in ill-using a man who is particularly close to him. I shall send him to France, with a good escort, to prevent him from intriguing throughout Europe with three or four other firebrands of his sort."

The Emperor, in dismissing me, told me again not to mention as yet his good intentions toward M. Wintzingerode. I confined myself to telling the Prince of Neuchâtel that he could be easy about the fate of his prisoner, and he went with the King of Naples to dine in the Emperor's quarters, intending to obtain a definite decision in this matter. A moment later the Emperor sent for me again, just as we were having dinner, and questioned me about the family and mode of life of young Narishkin. He directed me to tell Narishkin, as though it were from myself, that he wanted peace; that it rested with the Tsar to make an honourable one; . . . that his position was very favourable, and enabled him to offer good terms to the Tsar Alexander, because it was clear that no military reverse compelled him to it; that the moment was no less favourable to Russia, as the movement of the French army, being in some sort a retreat, counterbalanced the constant advantages our troops had obtained, and put both governments in a position to negotiate with honour; . . . that the Emperor would possibly send him, Narishkin, back to the outposts because he knew that his family were particularly close to the Tsar and he did not wish the Tsar to remain any longer in anxiety about Narishkin's safety. . . .

I went back to M. Narishkin, who had dined with us; I reassured him as to his general's fate, and carried out all the Emperor's instructions.

Meanwhile the King of Naples and the Prince of Neuchâtel talked to the Emperor with their usual amiability. M. Wintzingerode was regarded as a prisoner and sent to France—and M. Narishkin with him. I gave M. Narishkin some money and, after overtaking our carriages on the following day, sent him an overcoat, as he had only his uniform. My body-servant found them marching with the head of our column, which they followed as far as Ghjat. Thence they were started off to Paris with an officer and a guardsman as escort. Chance served them

well, for they were set free by M. Tchernychev [and a troop
of Cossacks], who fell in with them beyond Borissow.

The Duke of Treviso had evacuated Moscow on the twenty-
third, after blowing up the Kremlin and the barracks in accordance with the orders he had received. On the twenty-seventh
he was at Mojaisk. From there, for several days, they had
been sending back the wounded by the scanty means of transport they had been able to get together. Some consignments
of rice had arrived there, and the Duke of Abrantès had established depôts which supplied the needs of the first arrivals.

The following day, the twenty-eighth, we passed within sight
of Mojaisk but did not enter it. On his way by, the Emperor
halted beside the road to obtain some account of the evacuation
and of the distribution of supplies that he had ordered for
the wounded.[6] He himself took part in placing many of them
in his own carriages, and in any that passed. In spite of all
warnings that this would inevitably mean death, the unfortunate
men who had left the field hospital to drag themselves along
the road were placed, by his orders, wherever they could hang
on—on the covers of waggons, and even in the forage-carts, or
in the back of vehicles already crowded with the sick and
wounded from Malo-Jaroslawetz. And in due course they were
the victims of the Emperor's good intentions, who had thought
to remove them from any danger they might run through the
barbarity of the Russian peasants. Those who did not die of

[6] When they left the sick-ward they were given provisions for two days.
This was a quite insufficient supply, since those to whom the wounded were
given in charge, having for the most part no provisions themselves, could
not come to their help. Moreover, a considerable number, hurrying to get
away and reach those fatal transports in which they thought they saw their
salvation, and already greatly inconvenienced by being outside the town,
did not take these rations. They soon regretted them; for though on the
first and second day some of them moved men to pity, they were not long
in learning that hunger makes those who suffer it insensible to all humane
feeling.—Caulaincourt's note.

exhaustion, through the discomforts of their position, either fell victims to the cold nights or died of hunger. The wounded of the Guard, and those who were in the Emperor's carriages, were nourished and cared for . . . but of the rest, since all the other carriages were lost, not a score of them reached Wilna. Men in the best of health could not have endured this mode of travel, and could not have held on to the vehicles in the positions in which most of them were placed. So one can imagine the state of these unhappy men when they had covered a league or two. They had to endure jolting, fatigue, and cold all at once.

The carriages, drawn by tired and underfed horses, were travelling fourteen and fifteen hours of the twenty-four. They kept to the road, and found no place that afforded them any supplies. During the halts the drivers went aside from the road with some of their horses in search of food and fodder, however poor, in the deserted villages and encampments. Being uncertain as to what they would have to-morrow, they kept whatever they found carefully to themselves. Often they had not even time to start a fire. Never was there a sadder fate, a more wretched or hopeless position. Inevitable death seemed to beset us on all sides. The surgeons and doctors, with neither food nor physic nor bandages, and having for the most part not even bread for themselves, were forced to shun the hapless sick or wounded, to whom they could no longer be of any service.

As far as Orcha we had to cross a veritable desert. The country on either hand of our route had been marched over, eaten out, and left bare, by the army and by the detachments that joined us. The plight of the carriages can be imagined. Having left Moscow with us, already full of refugees, women, and children, they had had to take up the men wounded at Winkovo and Malo-Jaroslawetz; and to these, as I have said, were added also the wounded at Mojaisk. They were put on the top-seats of the carts, on the fore-carriage, behind on the trunks, on the seats, in the fodder-carts. They were even put on the hoods of the waggons, when there was no room underneath. One can imagine the spectacle our convoys presented. At the least jolt those who were most insecurely placed fell off; the drivers took no care. The driver following, if he were not distracted or in a stupor, would not be minding his horses; or even, for fear of stopping and losing his place in the line, he would drive pitilessly on over the body of the wretch who had fallen. Nor did the other vehicles coming behind pay any heed.

My eyes never saw a sight so horrible as the march of our army forty-eight hours after Mojaisk. Every heart was closed to pity by the fear of starving, of losing the overladen vehicles, of seeing the horses die, already exhausted by toil and starvation. I still shudder when I say that I have seen men deliberately drive their horses at speed over rough ground, so as to get rid of the unfortunates with whom they were over-weighted; and although they knew that hoofs would mutilate them or wheels crush them, they would yet smile triumphantly when a jolt freed them of one of those wretches. Every man thought of himself, and of himself alone. Every man felt that his life depended on the preservation of his little vehicle with its few provisions, and would have sacrificed twenty lives to spare the poor hacks that drew this last treasure. Each heartened himself with the thought that in front of him he would find foodstuffs; but except in some large towns, such as Smolensk, which had a few stores, they found nothing. The horses were fed on rotting corn and straw from old encampments, except when they were driven off from the road for at least a league's distance, at the risk of capture and massacre.

On the twenty-eighth the headquarters staff halted at Ouspenskoje [a ruined manor house between Mojaisk and Borodino]. At two in the morning the Emperor sent for me. He was in bed. He told me to see that the door was well closed, and come and sit close to the bed; this was not his habit. He then spoke to me about the situation in general, and about the state of the army, whose extreme disorganization he still did not or would not admit. He ended by bidding me speak to him frankly, and tell him what I myself thought. I did not have to be pressed, but gave the Emperor my opinion in full on the consequences that would ensue from the disorganization of the army, and especially on the miseries that would be caused by the severe cold. I reminded him of the reply which the Tsar Alexander was reported to have made when he received, through Lauriston, the proposals of peace sent from Moscow: "My campaign is just beginning." I told him that he must take this reply literally: the further the season advanced, the more everything would favour the Russians and, above all, the Cossacks.

"Your prophet Alexander has been mistaken more than once," he said; but there was no lightness in the tone of his reply.

The Emperor did not seem convinced of the truth of my forecast. He flattered himself that the superior intelligence of our troops would enable them somehow to safeguard themselves against the cold—that they would take the same precautions as the Russians, or even improve on them. He did not question that the army would establish its winter-quarters at Orcha or Witepsk. He would not yet admit that he might be forced to retire behind the Beresina. . . . The arrival of the Polish Cossacks, of whom he still expected to find fifteen hundred or two thousand in a few days, ought, it seemed to him, entirely to change the situation and the state of our affairs; for they would guard the army and give our soldiers time to rest and feed themselves. Since Malo-Jaroslawetz these wretches had lived on horseflesh and a little mouldy flour paste. And this latter nourishment was had only by those who had gone on marauding expeditions; for the rest, they lived on grilled horseflesh alone. Horses that fell in their tracks were carved up while still alive.[7]

After an hour's conversation about the army, about Russia, Poland, the prosperous state of France, and the means of making good his losses, the Emperor reached the main question, about which he had sent for me, and to which he had led up with this introduction. He told me it was possible—it was even probable—that he would go to Paris as soon as he had established the army in some definite position. He asked what I thought of this proposal: whether it would make a bad impression on the troops; whether it would not be the best way of reorganizing the army, and thus of holding Europe with a firm hand and keeping everything quiet; and whether, finally, I foresaw any difficulties about crossing Prussia without an escort.

He added that in a week's time the Russian army would be in no better state to give battle than his own. They too needed rest and reorganization; it froze as hard for the Russians as

[7] In another connection, Caulaincourt wrote of these scenes:

". . . Bad luck for the horse that fell! It was pounced on at once, and its driver could seldom protect it. The first-comers attacked the rump. The more expert cut open the flank and took the best morsel, the liver, which was of course the tenderest. While all this went on, no one ever thought to knock the poor beast in the head; everyone was too anxious to get back on the march.

"The most fortunate stragglers made gruel, if that name can be given to dirty flour—more often it was bran—that was swept up from the dust of granaries and mixed with water. Lucky for those who had saved any kind of utensil to cook it in. Such men went pot in hand, and treasured their skillets more carefully than their cash. But since we had to laugh despite our misery, the wretches who marched with skillets were called the pastry-cooks; and even those who were starving joked at the expense of the clever fellows who had saved the means of keeping alive. If you were one of the pastry-cooks, and came up to a fire to cook your gruel, men who had no pot queued up behind you to get the loan of yours. Anyone who found some potatoes was the object of universal envy. Once we were in Poland the big estates offered a plentiful supply, but they were remote and widely scattered, and none wished to stray so far off the road. Master and servant, colonel and private—all alike lacked everything."

for us. Moreover, the way in which Kutusof was following
us without embarking on any major operation proved that he
lacked the necessary strength. We had travelled so slowly, he
said, and with so many stops, that it should have been easy
for him to get ahead of us; Kutusof must know we were marching in column of route; yet we heard nothing of him. He said
further that we should find a fresh and well-organized army
at Smolensk, and another on the Beresina. . . .

I told the Emperor that, since our plight seemed to me more
precarious than he could see or believe, I felt no hesitation
about the remedy. There was but one: that he should date his
orders of the day, like his decrees, from the Palace of the
Tuileries.

I told him that I would not be restrained by minor considerations, such as what might be said or thought in the army, when
the question really was what might be attempted in Europe. I
added that what he had thought of doing was the one thing
which could be really useful, the one thing which a faithful
servant could advise. He had no need to hesitate: he needed
only to choose his moment carefully. As to the danger of
crossing Prussia, it could be avoided by travelling under another name. Since nobody would know of the journey in advance, the possible dangers could be classed with the thousand
risks to which one is exposed every day.

I tried to open the Emperor's eyes to the real state of the
army, pointing out that the evils of its disorganization were all
the more difficult to check because discouragement on the part
of certain leaders was one of its causes. They were indeed letting their units break up entirely, and would do nothing to
keep the soldiers in hand, lest they should have to give battle
with the men, too few in number, whose loyalty had made them
stay with the colours. I told the Emperor what impression I
thought would be made, not only in France but in Europe, by
the news of his retreat, and, even more, by the news of those

disasters in which he was still reluctant to believe; and I drew the conclusion that his return was necessary to offset this.

The Emperor, in the end, seemed less sceptical about my forebodings. He thought that only his presence [at Paris] could adequately hasten the mustering of all the forces needful to give us an army in three months. He ended by asking if I did not think that overtures to the Tsar Alexander, now that the Russian provinces would be evacuated, might not lead to peace.

"No more than at Moscow," I replied. "The news of our retreat will have made everyone exultant."

It was half-past five when the Emperor dismissed me. He told me to think over what he had said, and that he would discuss it with me again after he had talked to the Prince of Neuchâtel.

CHAPTER X

HUNGER

O N the next day, October 29, we were at Ghjat. The cold was already intense. The despatches, which were now more frequent as we were going to meet them, had again been interrupted; since the previous day enemy parties had appeared on our line of communications. The latest despatches from Paris were dated in September. At Borowsk we had begun to feel the cold. Only the surface of the ground was frozen. The weather was fine, and the nights were quite endurable in the open if one had a fire. Here at Ghjat the winter was already more noticeable. Since leaving Wereia, I had taken to travelling on foot. I made the daily marches of the army and found it beneficial, for I did not suffer from the cold and felt no indisposition during our long retreat.

At Ghjat we found the remnant of a consignment sent from France for the Emperor's household in the charge of two footmen. Part of the consignment had been pillaged by the Cossacks. Having no means of transport for these supplies, we distributed them all round, and there was abundance at headquarters. Clos-Vougeot and Chambertin were the common drink. We stored up strength and a sense of well-being against the days of real privation just ahead of us. Everyone still had a few provisions. There was a small ration of biscuit. The men endured the long marches well, in spite of the cold nights and several bad patches of ground which a brief thaw had made very rough going. It was otherwise with the horses. All but the strongest died. The reserve horses were harnessed up; and

194

as there were no longer enough of them, we were already beginning to abandon some of the vehicles.

So far the Cossacks following our rear-guard gave very
little trouble. The state of the cavalry and the speed of our
march prevented us from sending out scouting parties—hence
we had no news of the enemy. However, as there were no
Cossacks alongside our route, the raiding parties from the head
of the column went out and returned, seeing only a few peasants who fled at our approach. This easy foraging had one
great disadvantage, in that the sense of security thus created
increased the number of stragglers. Since there was no food
without raids, everyone wanted to raid. The raiders and stragglers of the rear-guard were not so fortunate. The enemy captured a good number of them every day. Satisfied no doubt
with this accomplishment, they seldom ventured within range
of our muskets.

On the thirtieth, we made Weliczewo our headquarters for the
night. This fine manor, however, had not a single rafter left,
and we had difficulty in collecting enough material from the
wreckage to patch up one room for the Emperor and one for
the chief-of-staff. The billiard-table was the only piece of
furniture still intact. Here we received the delayed despatches.

On the following day, the thirty-first, the headquarters and
the Guard were stationed at Wiasma, where we stayed through
the first of November. The Emperor did not even make a guess
at Kutusof's march; and Kutusof left us very quiet. The
weather was fine. The Emperor repeated more than once that
the Russian autumn was like the autumns at Fontainebleau;
and judging what the weather would be like in ten days' or a
fortnight's time by what it was on that particular day, he said
to the Prince of Neuchâtel that this was just the weather one
had at Fontainebleau around St. Hubert's day, and that the
stories people told about the Russian winter would only scare
children.

On the second we halted at Samlowo; on the third at Slawkowo, where we had the first snow. It was the general opinion
that the security of our flanks during the preceding few days—
the enemy having barely kept up with our rear-guard—was
only a ruse to foster confidence and to bring about, somewhere
near Borodino, another skirmish on the lines of Woronovo.
But Kutusof's weak pursuit was actually due, as we afterwards
discovered, to his uncertainty regarding our movements. He
did not know definitely until the twenty-seventh that our march
against him had been only the prelude to a retreat. On the
twenty-eighth he directed Miloradovitch, to whom he attached
a strong body of infantry and cavalry, to attack us and cut off
our rearward divisions before we reached Wiasma.

The Emperor learned of this attack on the third, at Slawkowo.
He learnt that the Viceroy, Prince Poniatowski, and Elchingen
had had to support Eckmühl . . . who commanded the rear-
guard, and whose progress was slowed up and hindered by the
large number of stragglers whom hunger and sickness already
had separated from their units. He was still a good distance
from Wiasma when the Russian infantry appeared. Not having a strong force, the marshal had to hasten his march. Meanwhile Marshal Ney was encamped before Wiasma. The Viceroy and Prince Poniatowski had known since the previous day
that the enemy was closing in on the Prince of Eckmühl, and
had consequently slackened their advance. They also took up
their position before Wiasma in order to await him.

The Cossacks swarmed over the countryside, and constantly
cut off communications between our corps, however close they
were to each other. The fight went to our advantage, once we
were in battle order; but it was unfortunate that the Emperor,
not expecting this renewed activity on the part of Kutusof, and
thinking that the Russian general would try to get ahead of us
rather than harass us, was at Slawkowo on that day—and the
Guard with him. As nobody held supreme command, there

was no unity in the dispositions made. Our men fought bravely for six hours, but solely on the defensive. The enemy were thus made to pay dearly for their daring attempt, and lost a great number of men; and for this they achieved nothing except that they inflicted severe damage on the First Corps, in which some disorder was shown when it passed ahead of the Viceroy's army. This disorder was still greater at the crossing of the bridge [over the Wiasma].

Until then—as long, that is, as it had to withstand alone the attacks of the enemy—the First Corps had maintained its honour and reputation, although it was fiercely attacked and its formation broken by the artillery. This momentary disorder was conspicuous because it was the first time that these gallant infantry broke their ranks and compelled their dogged commander to give ground. I have related these painful details because from this incident must be dated our disorganization and misfortunes. The First Corps, which on taking the field was the largest and finest, a rival to the Guard, was thenceforward the hardest hit; and the evil spread. Poniatowski, the Viceroy, and Ney all fought as in the days of our success.

The Emperor had to give the command of the rear-guard to Marshal Ney, whose energy and courage increased with his dangers and difficulties. The Emperor busied himself drawing up a body of instructions on the manner in which the retreat should be conducted. This, he thought, would put right all the troubles of which we complained, arising from the attacks of the Cossacks. He likened them to the Arabs, and directed that we should march, as in Egypt, with the baggage in the centre, a half-battalion at the front and the rear, and battalions in file on the flanks. In this way we should be able to direct our fire, in case of need, on all sides, like a square. The units could march, he said, at a short distance from each other, with artillery between them. He talked a great deal about these dispositions, which he regarded as a sure safeguard for the army, flattering himself that he would be able to take up a position at Smolensk.

The danger, however, was not in the attacks of the Cossacks, which our soldiers, when in platoons, never feared and had always repulsed when they were so minded. The danger lay in hunger, in the lack of provisions, and in the absence of any organized service of supply, which led to the disorganization of all the units—an inevitable consequence of the speed of the march and the devastation over this line of country. It would have been necessary to limit the march to three or four leagues a day, measured along the route, in order to cover as much ground again in collecting food on our flanks. In this way the soldiers would have followed the flag, and would nearly all have been saved. The enemy, however, would have gained the lead, or else overtaken us and attacked us from all quarters: and to obviate this danger, it was held, the other disadvantages had to be endured.

The Emperor, thinking that this attack by the Russians was a general movement of their whole army, decided to halt. By massing his troops near Slawkowo he hoped to have a good opportunity of falling unexpectedly upon the enemy, who thought they were only following up a rear-guard, and so of making them regret their rash pursuit. But, in consequence of the disorder of the First Corps, Ney made so discouraging a report on the events of the day before that any man but the Emperor would have abandoned this idea of a surprise attack. Ney announced that he was occupying the narrow passage of a wood behind Wiasma, but that, on account of the withdrawal of the First and Fourth Corps, he would have to continue his retreating movement before dawn in order not to risk the loss of his troops. He added that the behaviour of the First Corps on the previous day had set a bad example to all the troops, and had had a dangerous effect on them.

This report, however, which arrived in the middle of the

morning, did not change the Emperor's dispositions. He still believed that all the Russian army was massed together, and that a lively and sudden attack on this cumbersome body of troops would have a glorious result. He stayed at Slawkowo, hoping for a thorough revenge, throughout the fourth. The enemy, however, attempted nothing. Ney's discouraging reports followed one upon another; and so did the arrival of the various corps, who threw each other into confusion. On the fifth the Emperor had to resume his march. Junot led off, followed by the Young Guard and the Second and Fourth Cavalry; then the Old Guard, Poniatowski, Eugène, and Davout, whose corps was disintegrated. Ney conducted the rear-guard with a vigour worthy of his courage, and infused his own energy into all around him.

On the fifth, we spent the night at Dorogobouje. The despatches continued to arrive regularly. The weather, which had been milder for thirty-six hours before, became suddenly colder. There was no news of the enemy. Was Kutusof following behind? Or was he ahead of us? This uncertainty added further to the Emperor's difficulties and anxieties. On the sixth, headquarters were at Mikhaïlewska. It was a day of bad news. The Emperor was first much concerned about the details he had learned of the retreat of his troops on the Dwina, which occurred just when he most needed their success. Then he was greatly perturbed by the first news he received of Malet's conspiracy.

Malet, a former general, who was held prisoner in a private asylum, had formed the scheme of starting a republican revolution by means of a forged decree of the Senate and an engineered rumour of the Emperor's death. On the evening of October 22 Malet escaped; and he gained such influence over certain public officials and over the troops of the Paris garrison that he succeeded in paralyzing the government from midnight until nine in the morning. During this time he placed the Minister [Savary, Duke of Rovigo] and the Prefect of Police [Pasquier] under arrest, and seriously wounded General Hulin, Commandant of Paris.

This conspiracy was foredoomed to failure; at the same time that the Emperor learned of it he learned also that all the conspirators had been arrested and brought to trial. Nevertheless the daring of the attempt, carried out at the very seat of government, made a remarkable impression on him. He was not reassured as to its consequences, nor convinced that the government held all the guilty parties and all the threads of the affair in their hands, until three or four more despatches had come in. There were no private letters of that date, and so we knew of the affair only from the Emperor, who spoke of it as insignificant, the action of a madman. On that particular day he discussed it intimately with none but the Prince of Neuchâtel; and in that discussion he did not spare the Minister of Police. He was of the opinion that this incident, a lunatic's undertaking, had few if any ramifications.

Malet had put his scheme into action on the night of October 22-23 by forging orders to the Prefect of Police, the troops, and the warders of the gaols where the men were held whom he made his tools—Generals Lahorie and Guidal. According to the minister, these men, who were themselves deceived by the conspiracy at first, went to the barracks; and the Prefect of the Seine [Frochot] was foolish enough to prepare a council chamber for the new government. Colonels Soulier and Rabbe and a few other officers had been imposed upon in their turn, and had brought out their troops, thus making it possible to arrest the Minister and the Prefect of Police. The former had been taken in his bed . . . while . . . Malet went to the quarters of the Commandant, General Hulin, who offered resistance and had his jaw shattered by a pistol-shot. However, Colonel Laborde and certain other officers, recovering from their first surprise and seeing how few the conspirators were, put themselves at the head of some troops and released the Minister of Police and the Prefect from confinement. From that moment the government regained the control it ought never to have lost, and the three conspirators were arrested. At Paris the incident was hardly noticed. By ten o'clock in the morning order was everywhere restored.

According to the reports made to the Emperor, the conduct of the Prefect of the Seine, M. Frochot, was blameworthy, and later information confirmed this opinion.

The Minister for War took a different view of this conspiracy from the Minister of Police.

"Clarke," the Emperor remarked, "is convinced that this is a wide-spread conspiracy, and that it has other and more important leaders. Savary says the opposite. At first, the rumour of my death made everyone lose his head. The Minister for War, who parades his devotion to me, did not stop to put on his boots before running to the barracks to take the oath to the King of Rome and get Savary out of prison. Only Hulin showed any courage, and only Laborde any presence of mind. The behaviour of the prefect and the colonels is beyond understanding. What reliance," he added bitterly, "can one put on men whose early training does not confirm them in principles of honour and loyalty? I am disgusted at the feebleness and ingratitude of the prefect, and of the colonel of the Paris regiment, one of my old soldiers, whose fortune I have made."

These early particulars made the Emperor eager for the next despatch, to discover the result of the enquiries they were conducting.

"This revolt," he said, "cannot be the work of one man."

On the way to Pnevo [November 7] he was repeatedly asking me if I couldn't see the courier. The details that came in confirmed what the Duke of Rovigo had reported. General Clarke, however, continued to see behind this incident a widespread conspiracy; and it was his reports that occupied the Emperor's mind. The behaviour of those involved in the affair so exasperated him that he talked of it continually.

"Rabbe is a fool," he said to me. "A mess of print with a seal on it would take him in. But Frochot is a man of brains and quick intelligence. How was he tricked and dragged into it? He's an old Jacobin. The Republic must have tempted him again. He is used to revolutions—I don't suppose this one surprised him any more than the ten he's seen already. My death may have seemed quite probable to him; and he would consider how to keep his post before he thought of his duty. He must have taken twenty oaths of allegiance; and he forgot the one that bound him to my dynasty as he forgot the others. But to be the chief magistrate of Paris, and yet prepare a council chamber for the conspirators, without protest, in the Hôtel de Ville, in his own official quarters—not make a single enquiry, not take a single opposing step, not even make a gesture to uphold the authority of his lawful sovereign—he must be in the plot! Such credulity would be incredible in a man like Frochot. Cambacérès and Savary made a great mistake in not having him arrested. He is more of a traitor than Malet. Malet was always hatching plots; I have pardoned him four times already. With him, plotting is a vocation; my mercy weighed on him; he is a madman.[1]

"But Frochot—he sits on the Council of State, he is chief ad-

[1] In June, 1804, when Malet commanded the troops at Angoulême, the prefect requested that he should be cashiered. The First Consul was content to change his station, and sent him to Sables-d'Olonne.—On March 2, 1805, Malet was put on the retired list, on account of further brushes with the civil authorities of the Vendée. He appealed to the Emperor, who recalled him to active service on August 26.—On May 31, 1806, he was retired on account of financial irregularities, but this decree was never put into force and Malet continued to draw his active service pay.—For attempting a conspiracy against the Emperor in 1808 he was detained as a political prisoner at Sainte-Pélagie; and thence he was transferred, in June, 1810, to Doctor Dubuisson's private asylum.

ministrator of the principal Department of France, he is a man
on whom I have loaded honours. In him such baseness and
treachery are revolting! He did not have to fear starvation
if he lost his post. Now he has lost his honour. Does he
value that less than his post? Even if Malet had made him
prime minister, it wouldn't have saved him from the disgrace
of having betrayed his duty and his benefactor. I know that
one cannot always rely on men who turn the profession of arms
into a trade, a speculation, and will serve any man at all who
pays them with office for the dangers they run; but this man
is a leading magistrate, a man with a position, a man with
children to whom he should be a model of that loyalty to one's
sovereign which is the first duty of all! I cannot believe in
such baseness."

Plainly, the Emperor was cut to the heart.

"The French are like women," he added. "You must not
stay away from them too long. It's a fact; you can't tell what
schemers may get to them, or what may happen, if they go too
long without news of me. Yet go too long they will if the Russians have any common sense."

Judging by other remarks that the Emperor made to me (and
by what he said to Duroc and Berthier, who repeated it to me),
he had revised his opinion about the Minister of Police, and
understood, perhaps better than it was understood in Paris, how
Rovigo came to be surprised and carried off even though the
conspiracy had been conceived and executed only by Malet.
Clarke continued to suspect the existence of conspirators in all
ranks; and the name of Frochot, now compromised, gave some
weight in the Emperor's mind to this opinion also.

The Prince of Parma [Cambacérès] and the Duke of Rovigo
were fortunately of the opposite opinion. The latter continued
to represent Lahorie as a dupe, who knew nothing of the affair
until they came to fetch him from prison. The reports of the
Prefect of Police, and of several others, were to the same effect.

Although all the guilty were brought to trial and the affair was ended, the example of daring given by Malet and the behaviour of the Prefect of the Seine gave the Emperor much matter for reflection. He was particularly concerned about the inevitable effect of the incident in Europe. The demonstrable possibility of such an attempt, even though its outcome had also shown that it could not succeed, seemed to him in itself a serious blow to his authority, a source of trouble and further attempts on the part of a few hotheads in English pay. At Paris, he would have forgotten the matter in a day; at six hundred leagues' distance, and at a moment when the world might be for some time without news of him or of the army, the affair was bound to cause anxiety. Other intriguers might be tempted when they saw what one man, his plans laid in the solitude of his prison, could achieve within a quarter of an hour of leaving it, with no help but a false rumour, and in the heart of the capital, under a stable government and an alert administration. Such were the thoughts which crowded upon the Emperor's mind, and upon ours; and our circumstances were bound to give them added importance.

The news of grave events which arrived to beset the Emperor at Mikhaïlewska have interrupted my account of the military dispositions which he ordered. He had directed the Duke of Belluno to recapture Polotsk, and had announced his own intention of taking up a position at Smolensk. On the sixth the Emperor, as part of this plan, had moved Eugène off the route and sent him towards Dukhovtchina, so that he should later find himself in line; but Platow was following Prince Eugène, and Kutusof, as we learned at Smolensk, was marching parallel with us, by Ermakova, towards Yelnia. For several days the Emperor had discussed his plan of going into quarters at Smolensk; but on that day he announced openly that the army would do so at Witepsk and Orcha.

On the seventh, we were at Pnewo. The cold was becoming more and more intense, but everyone thought we were coming to the end of want, and so to the end of our worst misfortunes, when we reached the stores of Smolensk and the quarters that the Emperor promised. Every face looked brighter. The sight of a consignment of provisions on its way from Smolensk to Ney's rear-guard reminded us of happier days and happier outlooks; it lifted the hearts of the most discouraged. Everyone believed there was plenty at Smolensk, and that we were making harbour. The Emperor most of all flattered himself with this idea, and spoke of it several times. He already imagined his army in line.

The cold had been severe, and continued so, but the weather was clear and the sun shone. Yet all the way from Mikhaïlewska the sight of the road was made horrible by the bodies of the wounded who had been sent back, numbers of whom were found dead of cold or hunger, or abandoned by those charged with moving them. The road was also covered with stragglers, though on this day there was less disorder. Some of the soldiers rallied round their flags so as to share in the anticipated distributions of rations. The Emperor observed this, and it gave him a momentary consolation. Late in the day the weather became damper and it looked like a thaw, which made the way harder for the artillery and the transports. Luckily the frost set in again; for they would all have been bogged if the road had broken up. Meanwhile the Viceroy, marching towards Witepsk, was close pressed by Platow and his horde of Cossacks.

On the eighth, headquarters were at Beredikino. For a moment the Emperor thought of pushing forward as far as Smolensk himself; but the surface of the snow had been first melted in the thaw and then frozen when the frost set in again, and this made the road impracticable, particularly in the dark. The fear that by leaving he might draw swarms of stragglers

after him, and so cause disorder in the night at Smolensk, made
the Emperor decide to wait till the following day; and in this
he was well-advised, for even those on foot were hard put to
it to hold the road.

Nearly everybody travelled on foot. The Emperor followed
the march of the Guard in his carriage, accompanied by the
Prince of Neuchâtel; but he got down two or three times a day
and went on foot for a while, leaning sometimes on the Prince's
arm, sometimes on mine, sometimes on one of his aides-de-
camp. The road and the strips beside it were covered with
the bodies of wounded men who had died of cold and hunger
and want. No field of battle ever bore so fearful an aspect.
Yet, as I say, in spite of our misfortunes and these scenes of
horror, the sight of the spires of Smolensk, showing through
clear weather and lit with sunlight, had put heart even into
those most weighed down with misery.

It was on the ninth, about noon, that we came once more
within sight of Smolensk. The Emperor, who had already arranged in advance the dispositions of troops which the circumstances demanded, busied himself with the distribution of rations that was to be made to the army. Unfortunately the state
of the stores bore no relation to his hopes or to the general need;
but so few men had rejoined their units that we were able to
satisfy all who had done so. That was what really mattered,
for these brave men deserved every encouragement. Their
number, alas, was not very great. The Governor [General
Charpentier], who had known of our retreat only five days before, had done all he could to bake for the rear-guard and supply their other needs; and everything had been sent to them
as fast as it was made up. . . . He had few bakers, and the
rapid movement of the army had prevented his executives (who
in any case existed virtually in name alone) from making arrangements for baking in advance; thus we could not take full
advantage even of such resources as the town could have fur-

nished. Everyone thought of his own safety; and to march as quickly as possible seemed the great secret of escaping danger. Many officers, even those of high rank, quite destitute, set an example in this general rout, and, leaving their units, ran by themselves to the head of the column to get something to eat.

Our arrival and stay at Smolensk were notable for the fresh disasters which befell the Emperor and the army. For one may justly call disastrous an affair which, in addition to exposing our flank, deprived us of the reinforcements of fresh troops which should have restored the morale of our men and have checked an enemy as exhausted as ourselves. The Emperor must have been counting on Baraguey d'Hilliers's corps, which, come fresh from France, he had ordered to take up a position on the road to Yelnia. But the advance-guard of this army occupied a weak position at Ljachewo, under the command of General Augereau, who had made a bad survey of his ground and a worse disposition of his troops. He was surrounded [on November 9], attacked, and taken prisoner. Seeing that he had put out no guards, the enemy, who had had him under observation and were also kept informed by the peasantry, took advantage of this omission; and General Augereau, with more than two thousand men, surrendered to an advance-guard of the Russians, of which he should have taken more than half as prisoners if only he had remembered the name he bore.

This reverse was a disaster on more counts than one. Not only did it rob us of a needed reinforcement of fresh troops, and of the stores collected at that point, which would have been very valuable to us; but it also encouraged the enemy, who, despite our misfortunes and the privations our exhausted men had suffered since leaving Moscow, were not accustomed to such successes. The officers who had been on the spot spoke very bitterly of the affair and made no excuse for the generals. As for the Emperor, he laid upon this incident the responsibility for the continued retreat which he perceived was necessary, and for the abandoning of Smolensk, where, until a few days or perhaps even a few moments before, he had hoped to establish the main base of his advance-guard while he was in winter quarters.

From that moment he realized the impossibility of going into quarters at Witepsk and Orcha, as he spoke of doing up to forty-eight hours before. He learned also that the rear-guard under Marshal Ney had been hotly engaged by the Cossacks before Dorogobouje. Everything seemed to fall upon the Emperor at once, as though to crush him, during his halt at Smolensk. As the incidents I have just mentioned forbade his carrying out the plan of going into quarters there, he had to recall the Viceroy.

He did everything possible to reorganize the different units without delaying the march of the army as a whole. Many rations were distributed, and steps were taken for further distributions at Orcha and the other places which the Emperor thought were better stocked with provisions. He also busied himself with removing the little there was in the arsenal, as though the army had not already more equipment than the teams could draw, and as though these trophies, as he called whatever we abandoned, if they were left at Smolensk, would have more value for the enemy than what we strewed every day along the roads. Clinging still to the idea that he was going into quarters, the Emperor could not or would not show a trace of foresight. There is no doubt that we should have preserved much more undamaged if we had made the necessary sacrifices in time. But to two or three unfortunate horses we allotted guns and waggons that needed six; and by not abandoning one or two guns and waggons at the proper time, we lost four or five a few days later. We planned for the day only; and because we refused, as the saying is, to give the devil his due, we paid heavily in the end to the enemy.

It seemed as if the Emperor were expecting some miracle to alter the climate and end the ruin that was descending on us from every side. He gave his whole attention to the Guard, whom he hoped to save from the general disaster because they were still holding together. One of the generals commanding the artillery of this corps made so bold one day as to suggest the sacrifice of a few guns, in order not to exhaust the teams, already overdriven and reduced below the number needed. But he was not listened to. The generals and officers saw how desperate the situation was, but, just because they could see no way out of it, they did nothing to preserve for a few days longer what they knew must in a few more days be lost. Speaking generally, they were so tired of war, craved so much for rest, for the sight of a less hostile country, for an end to these far-flung expeditions, that most of them let themselves be blinded as to the present fruits and future consequences of our disasters, which—so they thought—would prove a useful lesson to the Emperor, and one that would cool his ambition.

This was the common view. One can imagine the effect of that temper upon the unavoidable difficulties of our predicament, and can judge how our troubles were increased by the general unwillingness to cope with them. One would have thought from the way many officers conducted themselves that la leçon, as they called it, could not be too severe. No one, seeing them so callous, would ever have guessed that the Emperor was learning his lesson at the price of Frenchmen's blood. The Emperor could see our sorry plight; he was living and marching in the midst of disorder and desolation; therefore even the most public-spirited held themselves excused from reasoning with him, or indeed from admitting that disaster was upon us.

Alas, the Emperor deluded himself; and our ruin followed on his misfortune. The leaders saw safety for the future in the very extremity of our reverses: the Emperor saw those reverses much smaller than they were. He still actually believed that he was coming to the end of his losses, that he would be able to halt and reorganize the army. This is amply proved by his fatal insistence that everything should be brought away and everything preserved, which only resulted in everything being lost. Fortune had so long showered him with favours that he could not believe she had now deserted him.

During this time I was employed night and day in reorganizing the Emperor's carriages. I had sent ahead orders for the forging of shoes with three calkins for all the horses. By means of a heavy payment I was even able to employ the workmen of the arsenal on this work during the night. By day they were working for the artillery. I stocked the carriages with all the provisions I could obtain for ready money. I had a great number of carts and carriages burnt—a measure I had been gradually carrying out for the last ten days, as the horses died off. In this way I spared the reserves. The Emperor found it very hard to consent to this; and seeing his reluctance, I no longer told him anything. I took everything upon myself, and I preserved only one carriage over and above the transports for food and wounded . . . only the carriage which carried MM. Beauvau, Mailly and Bausset. This last-named had the gout. I had set the example; everyone abandoned his lame or exhausted horses. In the end, after a stay of forty-eight hours, the carriages were lined up for the march in fairly good order.

During his stay in Smolensk the Emperor rode out each day, visiting the town and its surroundings as though he would have liked to preserve them also. He was already gravely concerned, and became more so after the Viceroy's setback. The state in which he saw the army in its march through the town convinced him, I think, that our plight was worse than he had been willing to admit to himself. However, he still took heart by thinking that the consequences would not be so gloomy as at that time they were expected to be. He did not doubt that he would be able to put the army into quarters as soon as he had joined the Volhynia and Dwina corps. He was expecting the arrival of the Polish Cossack levies which he had announced we should find near Smolensk. Was he misled in this respect, or did he promise this reinforcement to create an illusory hope in the minds of the rest? I do not know. The fact remains, however, that in Poland they were not busying themselves overmuch about these levies. Our communications had been intercepted for several days; we had no news from France, from Wilna, or even from the Dwina corps.

These circumstances were among the Emperor's chief cares; he showed, however, a firmness of character and an impassibility which sometimes irritated those who approached him, but were calculated to encourage those who were most downcast. All those who had money (and everyone had a certain amount) found supplies at Smolensk. Provisions had arrived there from France for the Emperor's household, together with rice and many other foodstuffs for the army. The Emperor's winemerchant, who had imported into Smolensk as a speculation a great quantity of wines, brandy and spirits, sold his entire stock for its weight in gold. We had already suffered so much that even the rank and file spent all they had to procure a bottle of brandy.

CHAPTER XI

ICE

THE Emperor left Smolensk on November 14, after ensuring a sufficient supply of flour for the Duke of Elchingen, who, acting as rear-guard, was due to arrive that same night. We halted at Korytnia [fifteen miles on], where we arrived quite early. The road was very hilly, and so difficult that we outstripped the carriages, which had left the day before. It was simply a sheet of ice; and the steep slopes, frequently found in that part of the country, were already littered with abandoned horses that had been unable to struggle to their feet. The leaders were so irresponsible, the riders and drivers of the waggons so tired, and their time so filled with marching and searching for food, that the artillery, like the cavalry, had not had a single horse shod for ice.

An hour after we arrived at Korytnia we learnt that, one league from where we were, the Cossacks had just attacked a small artillery park and the convoy of soldiers who were bringing back the trophies from Moscow.[1] Moreover, the Emperor's carriages, which we had passed, had just joined this park. The Cossacks had taken advantage of the moment when, the column having halted in order to double-up the teams for the ascent of one of those mountains of ice, there was a space between the front and rear of the column, so that the small detachments guarding it could not defend the whole of it. The Cossacks captured about ten horses and some of the Emperor's trans-

[1] Among the trophies lost was the cross of Ivan Veliki, which Napoleon had intended for the dome of the Invalides.—Castellane, *Journal*, I, 187.

ports. These were simply robbed of their contents, because the drivers in panic had upset them into a ravine. The waggon containing the maps was among them. The artillery lost half its teams; and most of the officers attached to headquarters, myself amongst them, lost their personal effects.

The loss of the maps was just the thing to throw the Emperor into a rage, yet he showed no displeasure—not even with his own servants. This incident made everyone more cautious, and served at least to bring back to the road, for some forty-eight hours, many of those who had straggled off after food. Our situation was such that one is forced, however, to question whether it was really worth while to rally-in wretches whom we could not feed!

During the night the Emperor sent for me, and spoke to me, as on an earlier occasion, about the necessity of his return to France. He again brought up all the questions he had already put to me concerning the army, the journey across Prussia, and the rest, and asked me if I had given thought to the plan. He was beginning to realize the disorganization of the army, but heartened himself by thinking that contact with the corps which we should find on the Beresina would quickly restore order; for those troops, which were well-organized, would act as a rear-guard and hold our position while he rallied the troops from Moscow. He talked to me again about those Polish Cossacks who should, he said, join us within a few days. The Emperor still flattered himself that he could get the situation in hand, and that he could even assume a commanding attitude as soon as he had control of the stores at Minsk.

"With every step I take, I shall find reinforcement," he told me; "while Kutusof, who will likewise be worn out with marching, will be getting further away from his reserves. He will be left in a countryside which we have exhausted. Ahead of us there are supplies in store. The Russians will starve to death back here."

Although he tried to convey a different impression to others, the Emperor was painfully disturbed. The lack of news from France caused him the greatest annoyance, and this he did not disguise from me. We were reduced to sending off little notes to Wilna every day or two by the hand of Poles, or by other people whom we did our best to bribe into reliability. Often we asked no more of them than to take a trifling note to some posting-station whence communications with Germany were still open. One day we paid a Jew two thousand five hundred francs to send a brief message through to the Archchancellor. M. Daru, who sent it off, took advantage of the opportunity to write a few lines at the same time to his wife. Only that note arrived. How? The Countess herself did not know. She had a letter from her husband, while the Empress had not a word from the Emperor. The Police and the Post Office were thrown into a state of agitation. M. Daru's letter, which, as one would expect, was very reassuring, first delighted his family and then created a sensation in Paris. Mme. Daru showed it round, and her husband's handwriting was too well known for any question to be raised about its authenticity. Guesses ran wild. Of the many despatches sent off by the hand of officers in disguise or natives of the country, only one or two reached their destination. As public affairs were mentioned only in cypher, the Emperor attached no importance to these letters except for the purpose of giving news to people in Paris and Wilna about the army and their relatives there; and they did not receive the news.

Since the Viceroy had rejoined us, we had marched in single column and by the same road. One can imagine the confusion wherever the way grew narrow. The zigzag road was a sheet of ice on which even men on foot could hardly stand upright. Every moment carts and waggons were capsized on the ice, and blocked the road. Everyone was in a hurry and no one troubled to maintain proper order. Sure of faulty obedience, and certain that any method they might establish would be but momentarily observed, the General Staff issued no instructions. As always, every freedom was allowed to the discretion of the commanding officers, except that orders issued by them could be countermanded at need. The officers saw the evils of the situation but did nothing to correct them, since, so they assumed, demoralization would immediately break out again.

How, indeed, could one exact service, or any test of endurance, from a man whom one had to let starve, in weather that froze his fingers if he left them exposed to the air? How make any dispositions whatever during an unceasing march, and when the staff officers have lost their horses and must go on foot to deliver the orders they carry? When all are crowded on to the same road, and flanked by Cossacks who hardly let them get ahead out of their sight? There remained not a single brigade of cavalry in a fit state to cover our movements. The exhausted, unshod horses could go no further unless men dragged them by the bridle. Without drawing upon the Guard, who were themselves much reduced, we had not sufficient cavalry to carry out a reconnaissance far enough or boldly enough to give us definite news of the enemy's position. Indeed we did not attempt it—not even though the Emperor had anticipated since the night before [November 13] that the enemy were moving into action against us.

We could not find a single peasant or man of any kind to act as guide. We had no means of information. Some detachments of Poles and of the Guard were sent out to scout, and returned after putting to the sword a few Cossacks whom they drove back upon a larger body, by which they were themselves obliged to retreat. They did not bring back a single Cossack to give us information about the troops in our neighbourhood. Like men in close confinement when they are allowed to take the air, we could make no sense of what was going on around us. The Emperor had remarked to us as early as Smolensk that the success of the Russians against Baraguey d'Hilliers would go to their heads, and that Kutusof would be forced out of his inaction. He was not mistaken; but the unity and soldierly conduct of the Guard reassured him as to the consequences of an engagement, of whatever kind it might be.

As we approached Krasnoë, we came into contact with Miloradovitch's army, which consisted of Ostermann-Tolstoï's and Ojarowski's divisions with the addition of some cavalry, and which had taken up its position near the village of Merlino on the left of the road. The Young Guard and the Dutch division of the Old Guard under the command of the Duke of Treviso were sent to oppose this force. They checked the Russians, and held them off so successfully that our progress along the road was not interrupted. The Emperor made for the place where this engagement happened, remaining there as long as things looked serious. M. Giroud, my aide-de-camp, was mortally wounded by a bullet that hit him in the upper part of his thigh.

At first the Emperor was inclined to believe that this attack was an offensive on the part of the whole enemy army. But Miloradovitch's indecision, and his withdrawal as soon as we took action, persuaded him that it was merely the skirmishing of an isolated body of troops, and was intended to harass and delay us whilst Kutusof was bringing the whole strength of his army against us. On first sighting the enemy, the Emperor had sent orders to Marshals Eckmühl and Elchingen to quicken their pace. He repeated these orders, and made up his mind to stop his retreat until he had more certain information about Kutusof's movements, and about the movements of our own troops still in the rear.

Reports about the enemy forces facing us indicated to the Emperor that they were considerable; reports reaching us from the lines of march proved that our communications were fre-

quently being cut by Russian contingents. We even knew from
information given by stragglers that villages on our left, at a
short distance from the road, were occupied by enemy infantry.
All these facts determined the Emperor to stay at Krasnoë on
the sixteenth, and prepare for a battle. Convinced that the only
way to drive the enemy off and prevent them from continually
harassing us—and also to rescue his own troops in the rear—
was by taking a vigorous offensive against the Russians and
thus proving to them that neither our courage nor our bayonets
had been frozen, the Emperor decided on a surprise-attack
by night.

His first intention was to put General Rapp in charge; and
he even gave him his instructions. Later, however, he changed
his mind. He entrusted the direction of the expedition to
General Roguet, who attacked Ojarowski's forces two hours
before daybreak on the sixteenth, killed or took prisoner most
of his infantry, and drove him as far as Lukino. This successful and daring action forced the enemy to withdraw; but the
Emperor, having gathered from prisoners that the whole Russian army was in the vicinity, decided to take the offensive, there
being no other means of safeguarding the Viceroy and the corps
that followed after him. The Emperor, who was in the plain
with the troops, was uneasy about Prince Eugène's failure to
arrive; his instructions had been to follow on behind us. But
he had only been able to set out from Smolensk late on the
fifteenth . . . and had made contact with Miloradovitch's
forces drawn up for battle on the sixteenth. Stragglers, thrown
back on to his vanguard by this enemy force, had been the first
to inform him of its existence.

The Emperor knew, from the sound of firing and from stragglers, of the attack directed against the Viceroy, whose delayed
arrival made him uneasy. He ordered General Durosnel, one
of his aides-de-camp, to take two battalions of light infantry
from his Guard, with two cannon, and go ahead of him so as

to help the Viceroy make his way through. General Durosnel, at the head of this body of troops commanded by General Boyer, had barely passed the Emperor's rear-guard emplacement when he came in contact with a horde of Cossacks, who made off at his approach. He was marching to the left of the road in order to carry out his manœuvres more easily. Halfway to Katowa he saw within cannon-range a strong line of cavalry drawn up for battle on the other side of the road. Following suit, he formed his men into a square, and fired a few cannon-shots to find out the intentions of this force, which replied to his fire but took no other action. General Durosnel, aware of the importance of the diversion he had been instructed to carry out, and full of confidence in the veterans he commanded, had no hesitation in continuing with his march and leaving this body of enemy cavalry behind him.

Having come within sight of the Russians, General Durosnel had barely time to fire a round from each of his cannon, and to form his men again into a square, when he was heavily attacked by cavalry and artillery fire. The cavalry vainly attempted to break up his formation; their charges were repulsed with as much coolness as bravery. The enemy, however, were continually being reinforced, and had spread over the whole countryside. It was thus impossible to delay a retreat without risking six hundred men belonging to the Guard, the only force left intact in the whole army. Durosnel therefore began to retreat in good order. Although vigorously attacked, and pursued for a league, he carried out his movement slowly, and in so orderly a manner that at last the enemy cavalry ceased their attacks. Cannon-fire cost him several men.

He rejoined the army just when General Latour-Maubourg was setting off with his cavalry regiment, under instructions to relieve him. The Emperor, perturbed at the thought that a part of his Guard was in action and cut off from the main body of the army—no reconnoitring party sent out had been able to break through to General Durosnel's contingent—was delighted at the safe return of this detachment. He was even more delighted at the arrival of the Viceroy, who had been helped to extricate himself by the diversion created by General Durosnel; and he invited him to supper, as well as the general, whom he praised several times.

This turn of events, which upset all the Emperor's calculations, and which, if the enemy had had even a little determination, might on the lowest estimate have endangered all our troops in the rear, would have overwhelmed any other general. But the Emperor was stronger than adversity, and became the more stubborn as danger seemed more imminent. Bracing himself against his bad fortune, he resolved to fight rather than abandon Marshals Eckmühl and Elchingen. He reiterated his earlier orders to quicken their pace. But was the road free? And if the orders reached them, would they arrive in time?

The Emperor had expected some sort of partial attack, and could not understand the Russian tactics.

"Kutusof would never make the mistake of following behind me along a devastated road if he had not some big project up his sleeve," the Emperor told us. "If Miloradovitch had any kind of force at hand, he wouldn't have given way before a few battalions of the Young Guard. . . . The distance between Junot [2] and the rear-guard," he added, "is so great that it is impossible to give any real help. If we stop and wait when there's nothing to eat, we risk everything—or rather lose everything, for we can't possibly gain our point in that way. How will we keep the troops alive, now we've halted them? We've been here twenty-four hours already, and everyone is dying of hunger. If I take the offensive against the Russians, they will withdraw. I shall have wasted my time, and they will have got ahead of us."

Notwithstanding these reflections, the Guard had been or-

[2] Junot, marching on Orcha, formed the advance-guard of the column.

dered to move back along the Smolensk road; strong batteries had been placed in position, and everything was prepared for a battle on the seventeenth. Although he had less than twenty thousand men, the Emperor had decided to come to grips with the enemy, and was full of confidence in his "old moustaches" whom he had doubtless kept in reserve for some such desperate venture as this. He had no doubts about his success, and believed, as in happier times, that his luck would hold.

On the seventeenth, however, he returned to his original plan. He ordered the Duke of Abrantès and the Viceroy to march on to Liadouï, whilst he arranged demonstrations which he hoped would make it possible for his marshals to get clear of the enemy. . . .

But, while the Emperor was defying adversity at Krasnoë, and while the Russians were profiting so little from their advantages, Marshal Elchingen, in command of the rear-guard, where there was fighting every day, had only arrived at Smolensk on the fifteenth. He found that Smolensk had been looted—according to his account by soldiers of the First Corps, and according to Marshal Eckmühl's account by stragglers. The fact is that the soldiers of the Third Corps, who counted on finding bread, found only disorder; shops practically empty, provisions scattered about the streets, the town full of stragglers who had just finished ransacking it, no one in authority, and no preparations made for feeding the rear-guard troops. In consequence of all this, no one wanted to remain there. The commissariat authorities had fled with the staff headquarters, and had even abandoned five or six thousand sick or wounded who, as we found out later, fell victims to the fury of the Russians when the Third Corps left.

Marshal Elchingen, who had been instructed to destroy the artillery abandoned at Smolensk and to blow up the ramparts, had now to find means of ensuring the subsistence of his troops as far as Orcha. This vital consideration, which inevitably prolonged his stay in Smolensk, could not in the circumstances be subordinated to any other. It must be borne in mind that his troops, obliged to fight every step of their way, had nothing to hope for from the places they would pass through; everyone else had been there before them. It should also be realized that the rear-guard had to march amidst the fires and general destruction which everywhere marked the track of our stragglers.

Such was the situation facing Marshal Elchingen. He had received the Emperor's various orders, and, in the evening, a last letter from Marshal Eckmühl, who advised him of what was happening on the road, and informed him that, in order not to jeopardize his own troops and give the enemy a chance of rallying, he proposed to speed up his march—and that he, Elchingen, would be well advised to do likewise. Marshal Elchingen, however, could not start before nightfall. Threatened on the one hand by the very real danger of his troops being demoralized through lack of food, and on the other of being attacked by superior enemy forces, he decided on the course of action most in keeping with his own daring and with the proved courage of his men.

"All the Cossacks and Russians in the world," he exclaimed when he received Marshal Eckmühl's last message, "shall not prevent me from rejoining the army."

He was as good as his word, and proved that the impossible itself is subservient to courage like his.

The various considerations which led the Emperor to believe that haste was necessary have been pointed out above, as well as the course of action he adopted on a basis of these considerations. He believed that, by forcing the enemy to withdraw from the road, he had done everything a general could do in so difficult a situation. Obsessed with the idea that Kutusof's object was to steal several marches on him, and that therefore the general good demanded that he should accelerate his own progress, he rejoined the Guard and his staff headquarters at Liadouï. . . .

The Emperor summoned me at four o'clock in the morning [November 18]. After repeating what he had already told us several nights before, and having reiterated the various considerations that led him to take his decisions, he expressed regret that he had allowed a gap of twenty-four hours between the departure of one regiment and another from Smolensk, and that he had not ordered Junot and a section of the Guard to start their march earlier, so as to cover Orcha. His announced intention was to speed up the pace of the retreat.

"Right now," said the Emperor, "I could be made a fool of in several ways."

The forces left in position to cover Krasnoë had orders to await the arrival of Marshal Eckmühl's column. It was assumed that, in view of the last orders sent to him, he would only march in conjunction with Marshal Elchingen. Communications had almost broken down; the despatch of orders and reports was next to impossible, or took place so slowly that they rarely arrived in time to be useful. Staff officers, having for the most part lost their horses, went on foot; and even those who had kept their horses were unable to make them travel on ice, and so arrived no sooner than the others. The frost was more severe than ever, and the road therefore more difficult. The country was more hilly; the steep descents had become impracticable. It is impossible to form any idea of the difficulties that the artillery and transport had to surmount on this march, or of the number of horses lost by the former. We had reached our destination [Liadouï] by a road that descended so steeply, that was so sunken, and a part of whose frozen surface had been so polished by the large number of horses and men who had slipped on it, that we were obliged like everyone else to sit down and let ourselves slide on our posteriors. The Emperor had to do likewise, for the many arms that were offered to him provided no adequate support. That fact will give some idea of the plight of soldiers with their rifles and equipment—of artillerymen and transports—but especially of the horseman, who risked being crushed by the weight of his faster-rolling mount.

At Liadouï there were inhabitants and some food supplies. Chickens and ducks ran about in the courtyards, to everyone's great astonishment. We had seen no such signs of plenty since crossing the Niemen; and every face cheered up, and everyone began to think that our privations were at last at an end. I mention these details in the course of describing our grave situation, because they bear on it, and because small things have a great influence on Frenchmen, whose spirits are quick to rise and fall. In the eyes of men accustomed since Moscow to find only uninhabited places, devastated houses, corpses instead of living men and women, it was a great event to come upon occupied houses with something to eat for supper. The modest resources of Liadouï, combined with what money would buy in its neighbourhood, enabled a good number of men to take the edge off their appetites—men who scorned every sort of danger, but who were reluctant to die of hunger, and wanted to live, if only to be able to face new perils.

Cossacks kept up perpetual raids along the road, which they constantly crossed between one division and another—or even, when there was a gap, between one regiment and another. Three determined men armed with rifles, however, were sufficient to keep them at a respectful distance. But wherever there was no shooting to fear, wherever transport waggons were moving along in disorder, or unarmed stragglers were making their way as best they could, the Cossacks improvised sudden attacks, killing and wounding, robbing all those whose lives they spared, and looting waggons and carriages when they came upon them.

It is not difficult to imagine the perturbation spread by such tactics, and their effect on the army's morale. What was worse, they made communication extremely difficult, not only between one corps and another, but between one division and another. The General Staff, as I have already explained, received no reports; its orders either did not arrive at their destination, or arrived too late to be of any use. Staff officers, who braved every sort of danger, were frequently captured. To make any progress at all, they had to join up with some detachment, halt when it halted, and go forward when another detachment came by. Then there was the ice! Officers who had kept their horses were unable to make them move. They dragged them along behind, finding that they made better progress on foot. To form a true idea of this tremendous drama, it is necessary to have been present when it happened, to have taken part in it. Without exaggeration, the simplest things became almost insurmountable difficulties. . . . As dangers multiplied and, at the same time, difficulties were augmented, all eyes turned towards Orcha, which the Emperor, like everyone else, considered to be an important base. He had ordered the advance-guard to reach it as soon as possible, and had given instructions for the bridge-head to be strongly occupied.

We made our way from Liadouï to Doubrowna. There on the following day [November 19], in the morning, just when we were about to set out, the Emperor learned that the First Corps had joined the troops he had left at Krasnoë . . . and that consequently this corps had passed through Krasnoë on the seventeenth, the day on which it was possible that Marshal Elchingen had just left Smolensk. We knew nothing definite about the Third Corps, of which the First had had no news since the sixteenth.[3] Not a single despatch officer had returned.

[3] Davout with the First Corps passed through Krasnoë on the seventeenth, in the evening, on his way to Liadouï, following behind Mortier. He bivouacked between the two towns. Ney with the Third Corps left the out-

Had any of them ever got through? The Emperor was lost in conjectures. Miloradovitch's remaining in his original position, and the departure of our own troops, made us realize all the dangers to which Marshal Elchingen was exposed.

The grave reproaches that the two marshals have levelled against one another, the severe judgment of headquarters and the whole army in regard to one of them, make it incumbent on me to report in this connection only the Emperor's own expressions, the Prince of Neuchâtel's private opinions, and details openly given to headquarters by trustworthy persons. The Emperor and the Prince of Neuchâtel said again and again that the two marshals ought to march in concert and support one another; that, as Marshal Elchingen made the progress of his retreat depend on the obstacles with which the enemy confronted him, Marshal Eckmühl should have modified his pace accordingly. But the two marshals did not like one another, and, having had a violent difference of opinion about the looting of Smolensk, they had ceased to co-operate.

The following details represent the facts of the case as recounted by the Emperor and the Prince of Neuchâtel at the time. The First Corps, aware of the dangers threatening the Viceroy, who was ahead of it, quickened its pace, keeping Marshal Elchingen informed of its movements but not bothering about whether he was able to follow. The harder the Russians pressed and attacked, the faster the First Corps marched, thus carrying out the orders which Marshal Eckmühl had received. Those orders he had passed on to Marshal Elchingen, assuming that the latter . . . would act on them, and hasten his pace also. No one expected a persistent attack, or was made anxious about the Third Corps by the wild shouts of the Cossacks. Marshal Eckmühl argued that any other policy would have vainly jeopardized the shattered regiments that still remained

skirts of Smolensk early on the seventeenth. Thus, at this time, there was a considerable interval between the two marshals.

with him. He could not have helped Marshal Elchingen, he said; for the First Corps would have been destroyed or taken prisoner before it could have got back to Marshal Elchingen or been overtaken by him. This version of the affair was given out during the day.

It is impossible to describe the unbridled rage and fury that everyone showed towards Marshal Eckmühl. Marshal Elchingen was the hero of the campaign—the general whom everyone felt anxious about. So universal and so warm was the interest in Ney's predicament that no limits were observed in speaking of Marshal Eckmühl, and scarcely any even when he came into the presence of the Emperor, or when anyone met him face to face. The Emperor and the chief-of-staff were the more eager to saddle him with responsibility for the tragic event they feared had come to pass, because thereby they might justify themselves for having left so large an interval between the departure of the two columns. . . .

The interval left between the departure of the various corps . . . proves the extent to which the Emperor deluded himself in regard to the army's situation and the dangers that threatened it. Did he flatter himself that he would once more bend Fortune to his use, and bring the cold within the compass of his will as he so often had brought victory? Things had come to such a pass that resignation was demanded by the force of circumstance. To have waited at Krasnoë would have jeopardized the army without serving any useful purpose; to return there, as was proposed by certain persons, when the First Corps was known to have arrived and the Third to have been abandoned to itself, would have been futile. Nevertheless, such a project was the expressed wish of many. Cooler heads saw, of course, how absurd that was; for Marshal Elchingen's fate was in fact already decided one way or the other, when, so far away from him, extravagant plans were being considered for his rescue. The General Staff said openly that, when he learnt what had happened, the Emperor ordered Marshal Eckmühl to go back and march at the head of the corps which he should have supported. Such an order, however, was given on the impulse of the moment, and with the certainty that it could not be carried out.

The Emperor hoped (at least, so he said) that Marshal Elchingen would have known or have found out that the pace of the retreat had been accelerated, and would accordingly have accelerated his own pace, even though the orders to this effect had not reached him. He added that Marshal Elchingen was known to be not far from Marshal Eckmühl's hindmost troops. But what was the point of such speculation? The Russian army was between him and us; and we were too far away to be able to help him, or for him to be able to make a sudden break through to us. The Emperor fixed all his hopes on Marshal Elchingen's rare courage and presence of mind. The army did likewise. Despite this legitimate confidence in his hero, the Emperor never ceased to lament his loss, which he regarded as virtually inevitable.

"He will attempt the impossible," he said, "and lose his life in some desperate attack. I'd give the three hundred millions in gold I've got in the Tuileries vaults to save him. If he is not killed, he'll escape with a few brave men. But the odds are heavily against him."

On the nineteenth, headquarters was established at Orcha, where the Emperor was relieved to find that his vanguard had arrived. Our troops had the bridge well in hand. We had relied on the local shops, but these served only to supply the needs of headquarters and the Guard. The countryside, however, provided further substantial resources, which, though certainly a boon to the army, were not an unmixed blessing; for large numbers of men, who hitherto had kept their ranks, left them when they found themselves amidst abundance. Of the many who went after food, but few returned. A deserter's

existence which held out to the men the hope of getting plenty
to eat, of being free, of having a roof over their heads instead
of bivouacking nearly always without rations, of obtaining rest
and warmth during the night instead of duties in the bitter cold,
—all these temptations were more than they could resist. Cossacks and armed peasants captured many of those stragglers
from day to day; for most of them had carelessly thrown away
their arms in order to get along more easily—and also to escape
being forced back into the ranks, where their lack of arms
made them useless.

But not even the pleasure of seeing an inhabited countryside with a few resources distracted attention from Marshal
Elchingen, who all this time was the object of common concern.
The Prince of Neuchâtel, as if he wanted to clear himself in
advance of any responsibility for whatever happened to Marshal Elchingen, showed everyone the orders given to Marshal
Eckmühl by the General Staff. He showed them to me. The
outburst of fury against Marshal Eckmühl was the more general
because the Emperor publicly charged him with being responsible for all the dangers that the Third Army Corps might have
to run. The fact is, of course, that the pace should have been
accelerated all along the line, and that Marshal Elchingen
should have left Smolensk on the sixteenth; but the Emperor
never could make up his mind when it was a question of ordering a retreat.

It should be pointed out, to the glory of Marshal Elchingen,
that the army was of one opinion about him. To overtake us
by way of the Krasnoë road was regarded as an impossible
task; but if anyone could do the impossible, then Ney was the
man. Every map was in use; everyone pored over them, trac-
ing the route that Ney would follow if courage could open a
way for him. "Once they've got rid of their artillery, the good
old infantry will come through anything with a leader like that.

He'll bring them back through Kiev rather than surrender"—
such was the general sentiment.

From the troopers to the Emperor, nobody doubted that if
he were still alive he would bring his corps in. There was but
one misgiving: that he might think we were waiting to second
his efforts the moment we heard his guns, and so might find
a glorious death in trying to cut a way through the enemy.
What finer tribute could be paid to a soldier than this universal
confidence that he would successfully carry out what most men
would hardly dare even to attempt?

After his arrival at Orcha on the nineteenth, the Emperor
had spent part of the day on the bridge. He had inspected the
environs as if there were still some chance that the town could
be held. Although there was no news of Marshal Elchingen,
we continued to hope. Every delay made our plight worse, and
so the retreat continued. The Viceroy was put in charge of the
rear-guard; and on the twentieth, in the afternoon, headquarters
were transferred to the manor-house of Baranouï, a short way
beyond Orcha and a quarter of a league off the road.

Here the Emperor learnt from a Polish civilian of the Moldavian army's march on Minsk. His informant, however, was
unable to tell him exactly when it had started or how far it had
progressed. All he knew was hearsay, picked up from someone
else.

"Tchitchagoff intends, no doubt, to join Tormasov," the Emperor said to me; "and they'll send an army to the Beresina—
or more likely to reinforce Kutusof here on the uplands. As
I've always thought, Kutusof is leaving us alone now in order
to head me off and attack me when this reinforcement has
joined him. We must hurry. Time has been lost since we left
Smolensk, although if my orders have been carried out I'll also
have my forces mustered on the Beresina. We must hurry to
get there, for that's where great things may happen."

The Viceroy, who had remained in Orcha, announced soon

after the Emperor's departure that Marshal Elchingen had crossed the Dnieper near Variski on the night of November 18-19, over barely formed ice; and that he had with him, besides his own army corps, four or five thousand stragglers and refugees from Moscow who had sought shelter within his squares. The Viceroy was given orders to move towards Marshal Elchingen and help him rejoin us. He had, in fact, already done so by sending back one of his divisions.

Never has a victory in the field caused such a sensation. The joy was general; everyone was drunk with delight, and went running to and fro to spread the news; it was impossible to resist telling everyone you met. It was a national triumph, and you shared it even with your grooms. Officers, soldiers, everyone was convinced now that we could snap our fingers at Fortune and the elements alike—that Frenchmen were invincible!

Here are the full details, as given later by the marshal himself:

In the afternoon of the eighteenth a thick mist prevented him from seeing an inch in front of him, and his advance-guard ran headlong into Russian batteries. There were three enemy corps with formidable artillery on both sides of the Krasnoë road and on the road itself. When he heard firing, he closed up with his advance-guard, which he overtook at five o'clock. Believing that we were waiting for him, and that the cannonade would be the signal for a general attack on our part, he renewed his own attack several times in the hope of breaking a way through the enemy. His troops fought with remarkable bravery despite a murderous fire from all quarters. After breaking through two ranks, Ney's men seemed doomed to die under the cannon-fire of a third, without being able to overcome all the obstacles that the Russians had prepared and now opposed to their valour.

Realizing that to break through was hopeless, he resumed

his original position, continuing to fight until ten o'clock in order to force the enemy to keep their forces concentrated at that point. Firing then ceased, and General Miloradovitch sent a second messenger [4] (this time a major) with a flag of truce, to propose that the marshal should surrender. He, however, had already laid his plans, and had sent out reconnaissances to explore the dictrict as soon as he had become convinced that we were no longer near enough to help him. The marshal was confirmed in his intentions by hearing from this Russian officer that the whole French army had left Krasnoë, and was already a long way off. He kept the major with him, and continued in absolute silence to prosecute the movement he had already begun for crossing the Dnieper, up and down which he had reconnoitred the evening before. Although at several places along its margin the ice was scarcely formed, few lives were lost. It was even possible to save the bulk of the horses.

When day broke, the Russians found only our spiked guns, and understood what one brave man can do with Frenchmen behind him. The marshal, having reached the other bank of the river, sent out small detachments to go to Orcha with word for the Emperor. Only one of these arrived, to give the Viceroy the first news of what had happened. Platow, coming from Smolensk by the right bank and flooding the country with his swarms of Cossacks, had learned of the marshal's crossing. He mustered all his men, surrounded the marshal, harassed him continuously on his march, and forced him to form squares at every moment to resist attacks from the enemy and to protect the stragglers, refugees and such wounded as he had been able to bring with him. The efforts of all the Don Cossacks were vain; Marshal Elchingen's six thousand brave men kept their formation, nor were they stopped even for a moment.

This daring retreat was freely compared with what was

---

[4] The first messenger had been sent on the same day, just when the fighting had begun.

called the "prudence" of Ney's colleague; and the comparison made all the more talk because Marshal Eckmühl was unpopular. Everyone, high and low, availed himself of the opportunity to throw stones at Davout, without considering whether the orders he had received, the instructions he had given Marshal Elchingen, the circumstances in which he had found himself, were not sufficient to justify the course he had taken.

Marshal Elchingen's return restored the Emperor's confidence in his Star—a confidence by now too inveterate to be good for him or us.

On the twenty-first, headquarters were at Kamienska. On his way there the Emperor received word a second time about the progress of the Moldavian army. He had it from Count Daru, who had been following at some distance behind the Emperor, and had kept himself occupied by helping the sick that encumbered the road or were crammed into the few remaining houses. He had [thus] met a Polish officer, who had asked him to carry the word to the Emperor until such time as he could confirm it himself—for at the moment his horse could go no farther. The Emperor peppered Count Daru with questions—as he did the Pole, later on—but there was nothing to be learned except that Admiral Tchitchagoff's Moldavian army had moved upon Borissow. This information roused the Emperor to anxious thought; and that evening he told us all about it.

"Shall we get there in time?" he said to me. "Will the Duke of Belluno take the offensive soon enough to divert Wittgenstein? If the Beresina crossings are closed to us, something may turn up—something unforeseen, some setback—so that we'll have to cut our way out with the cavalry of the Guard. How far could I get with them in five or six days, with their horses in the state they're in now?—how far, without letting the weakest fall by the wayside? With my Guard and the brave

men that turn up, it's always possible to break through.   I must
find out what my corps on the Dwina are up to—and Schwarzenberg.   Maret, with every means of information open to him,
has certainly warned them of the admiral's movements."

The Emperor then spoke to me about his journey to France
as of something already settled, and told me that I should accompany him; that he had no need of another captain of escort.

It was now behind the Beresina that the Emperor thought
he would be able to take up his position; the supplies in Minsk
were to provide the wherewithal to rally and feed the army.

"The Reggio and Belluno corps," he said to me, "will be
covering the retreat within a few days; the men from Moscow
will be stationed in the second line, and the stragglers will be
rallied."

There was still no news from France.   It was this privation
that the Emperor felt most.   He scarcely dared even to hope
that the Polish officers and men sent to Wilna had been able
to get through, and the Duke of Bassano thus enabled to send
reassuring news to France.   The Emperor realized all the unfortunate consequences that such a silence might have; and this
realization but added to the chagrin he was to feel over the
next piece of news that came in. . . .

On the twenty-second he stopped at Tolotchine, in a convent
of some kind.   It was there he found out that Minsk had been
evacuated, and that General Lambert, commanding Admiral
Tchitchagoff's advance-guard, had occupied the town on the sixteenth.   The Emperor was momentarily dismayed; to him this
news meant the loss of supplies—of all the resources he had
counted on, since leaving Smolensk, to rally and reorganize
the army.   Moreover, and worse than that loss, he now had to
face the disturbing certainty that the Moldavian army was not
moving to join forces with Kutusof and the main Russian army
on our flank, as he had hoped all along, but was massing instead
to cut off our retreat.

The Emperor's character, like steel by fire, was tempered anew by these reverses of circumstance and this vista of danger. He immediately made up his mind to quicken the retreat—if possible, to reach the Beresina before Kutusof arrived there—and to fight and vanquish whatever stood in his way. He adopted instantaneously the notion and the line of reasoning that would console him by putting his situation in the best light; he decided, in short, that Schwarzenberg and Reynier, fully informed as to what had happened, must already have moved, thus altering the whole state of affairs. In any case, so he thought, the concentration of all the forces he had in that district would inevitably occur at Borissow. He looked forward to that concentration as a great advantage from the point of view of safeguarding the army's retreat—which he now realized could not be stopped before Wilna. He was confident of finding the Borissow bridge well guarded. That was the main thing. Its defence had been arranged for some time; troops were available for the purpose, and, judging by what he was gracious enough to say to me as well as to the Prince of Neuchâtel, he had no misgivings about the matter.

That evening, when the Emperor had lain down, and had, as so often happened, kept Count Daru and Duroc to talk with him, he fell into a doze; and these gentlemen, waiting until he was well asleep before they withdrew, began chatting together. After a quarter of an hour the Emperor woke up and asked what they were saying.

"We were wishing that we had a balloon," M. Daru replied.

"What for?"

"To carry Your Majesty away."

"Good God!—things are bad enough now. You're afraid, then, of being taken prisoners of war?"

"No, not prisoners of war, because they won't let Your Majesty off so lightly as that."

"The situation is very grave; that's a fact. The issue is

growing more complicated. Just the same, if my leaders set a good example, I am still stronger than the enemy. I can very well afford to disregard all the Russians, if their troops are all that stand in the way."

It was on the next day [November 23] that the State Secretariat burnt its papers.[5] M. Daru had been asking to do this ever since we had left Ghjat, where the destruction of equipment began.

The Emperor sent for me in the small hours of the morning, and told me of the bad news he had received:

"This is beginning to be very serious," he said.

He asked me whether it was freezing enough for the rivers and lakes to be frozen hard, and whether the artillery could pass over the ice.

"I am inclined to think not, at least as far as the rivers are concerned," I replied.

"You don't know what you're talking about. Didn't Ney cross the Dnieper over the ice, after leaving his cannon behind, when it wasn't so cold as to-day? It's going to freeze, and we shall cross the Beresina marshes. Otherwise, we should have to break through the enemy, and then make a big detour. How many days of forced marches will it take to reach Vileika or Gloubokoje? The position is likely to turn critical if Kutusof has manœuvred skilfully; and if Wittgenstein is ready to support him, or has joined forces with the admiral. This damned sailor [Tchitchagoff] brings me nothing but bad luck. As for Kutusof—he knows nothing about war. He is brave enough when he comes to grips in a fight; but he knows nothing about strategy."

[5] What was called the State Secretariat's correspondence was very considerable; the mere administrative details of the army during the campaign amounted to a mass of papers. In addition, there were all the reports and projected decrees of the various French ministries—the portfolios, so-called—work that an auditor brought in each week. There were twenty-seven unreturned portfolios that had piled up.—Caulaincourt's note.

The Emperor told me what Daru and Duroc had said to him. "Their balloon would not be *de trop*," he added jokingly. "This is one time when only the brave can escape. If we can get across the Beresina, I can control the issue, because the two fresh corps that I shall find here, with my Guard, are adequate to defeat the Russians. If we cannot cross, we shall try what our pistols can do. Consult with Duroc about what we could take with us if we had to cut a way out 'cross country, without transport. We must be ready in advance to destroy everything so as to leave no trophies for the enemy. I would rather eat with my fingers for the rest of the campaign than leave the Russians a fork with my crest on it. So come to an understanding with Duroc about what belongs to his department—but keep it quiet. I have spoken only to him and to you. We should also make sure that my weapons and yours are in good condition, for we may have to fight."

The Emperor again went into great detail about his position and about the project of which he had spoken. I had a conversation later with Duroc, who told me what the Emperor had said to him and Daru. We agreed that henceforth everyone who fed in the Emperor's Mess should be responsible for his own cup, plate and cutlery if he wanted to keep them. The pretext we gave was that the canteen mules were giving out.

Although the cold was still severe enough, the weather was overcast and threatened a thaw, or snow at the least. The sick and wounded froze during the night near the bivouacs. Carelessness, and the difficulty of finding fodder and, above all, water, caused many of the horses to perish. To water them, it was necessary as a rule to go a fair distance, and to break the ice. Then there had to be a vessel of some sort to draw the water, since the banks were not everywhere fordable. We arrived in the night: where was there a river or a well? The surface of water was dirt-coloured; the frost had turned everything drab. The ice, which had been broken with difficulty in the evening, would be frozen hard again the next morning; fresh efforts had to be made; to break the ice at all, an axe or an iron rod was necessary—and there was a shortage of every sort of instrument. When he arrived in the evening, a driver, half-dead with cold, would be afraid of getting lost. He would try and find some means to light a fire, to shelter himself, and to get hold of something to eat. When he was not too much overcome, or if it were not too dark, he would try and do what he could for the horses. More often than not, however, when the weather was bad, he just left them where they stood; and we set out next morning without the wretched animals having been unharnessed.

M. Giroud, my aide-de-camp, who had been in my carriage since he was wounded at Krasnoë, died during the night [of the twenty-second]. He had been unconscious for two days.

From Tolotchine to Bobr, where we arrived on the twenty-third, the road was even more thickly covered with dead horses than on preceding marches. There were many human corpses, too; and at every bivouac one saw large numbers that had died of suffocation from the fumes of the fires, because they had dragged themselves too close when already frost-bitten and half-frozen. Others still moaned but could not drag themselves away, either because they were too weak or because their hands and feet were frozen. This horrible sight made a profound impression on everyone. It was impossible to convince a poor wretch numbed with cold that fire was fatal to him; that the only remedy was movement, dry friction, and, even better for the hands and feet, friction with snow. As the Emperor passed through that ill-starred multitude, there was not a murmur or a groan to be heard. How generous those Frenchmen were in their misfortune! They cursed the elements, but had not a word of reproach for *La Gloire*.

The Emperor was convinced that Kutusof's irresolution, and the time lost by Miloradovitch in waiting for Marshal Elchingen on the Krasnoë road, had put us several days ahead of the Russian main body; and that therefore we should have time to cross the Beresina. After what had happened at Minsk, that crossing had been a good deal on his mind.

It was at Losnitza, where we were the next day, the twenty-fourth, that we learnt of the skirmish [three days earlier] at Borissow. There the bridge-head, occupied by a Polish battalion, had been surprised and abandoned to a detachment of Cossacks. However, the gallant General Dombrowski . . . had forced a way back to the bridge-head with his division, and had held out valiantly for ten hours against three divisions of Russians. But, so we learned at the same time, the press of superior numbers had compelled him to cross back again at nightfall. His movement had been carried out with the best possible order; and he had taken up his position opposite the bridge-head, at Niemanitza.

This unexpected news, robbing us of our only means of retreat—of the sole properly constructed way, for a great stretch up and down, of crossing this river lined with steep banks and marshes—was the worst the Emperor could have received. The details given with it confirmed the news itself, and also certain other particulars implicit in it. There could no longer be any doubt, for instance, about the arrival of the Moldavian army, which the Emperor had so long believed was coming to reinforce Kutusof.

CHAPTER XII

THE BERESINA

IT looked as if we were fated in this cruel campaign to suffer
all the most infuriating reverses of which Fortune is capable. Everything best suited to upset the Emperor's plans
came then in quick succession. After having had to face the
loss of all the supplies on which he had counted to meet the
army's needs and to provide for its reorganization, he now
lost, when no other hope remained to him, the one assured
means of crossing the Beresina. Anyone else would have been
overwhelmed.

The Emperor rose superior to the mischances which had be-
fallen him. These reverses, instead of disheartening him,
brought out more than ever his characteristic energy; he showed
what sublime courage and a brave army are capable of, when
they have to contend against the worst that misfortune can do.
One thing is certain: the Emperor showed himself a match for
each emergency, and therefore fitted to prevent them all—if
only he could have presumed no further upon Fortune, Glory,
and Mankind. But hope, the merest inkling of success, elated
him more than the severest setback could depress him. The
indirect news, which he received almost at the same time as
the other, of successes contrived by the Prince of Schwarzenberg on the sixteenth and seventeenth, revived his spirits. He
had so often been loaded with Fortune's favours in the most
desperate of circumstances that he hoped, and was soon quite
confident, that the Austrians—whom his ministers must have
kept in touch with what was happening—would catch the in-

239

spiration of his genius; that they would take advantage of these
successes to come to our aid; and that their manœuvres would
extricate us and even give us a chance of snatching a victory
of sorts, in which he could show to advantage. Along with
such splendid talents, with a character so finely tempered, with
a soul strong enough to dominate all misfortune, he had as great
fondness as he had little need to indulge in self-deceit—the
refuge of the weak.

His confidence, his boundless optimism, was greater still
in the morning [November 25] when he received the Duke of
Reggio's report announcing the defeat of Tchitchagoff's advance-
guard. Under the command of General Pahlen, the Russians
had ventured as far as Niemanitza, and had lost, the marshal reported, a lot of prisoners and all the equipment they had been
foolish enough to bring to this side of Borissow.[1] A great deal
was made of this success, and we set out for Borissow at once.
Detachments were sent to points above and below, where they
were to reconnoitre the enemy's position and create diversions
at the crossings.

Marshal Reggio informed us of the return of General Corbineau, the head of his light cavalry. That general had just
carried out a careful reconnaissance of the Beresina's other
bank, and had been forced by recent events to swim across the
river.

These bits of information—but more especially the assurance that Kutusof was a long way behind us—put the Emperor
at his ease. Confident that he was three days ahead of the Russian commander-in-chief, he knew for certain that the issue was

[1] On November 23, Tchitchagoff started from Borissow in the direction
of Bobr. He believed that there was only Dombrowski's division in front
of him. His advance-guard, commanded by Count Pahlen, came in contact with Oudinot's corps near Losnitza, was thrown into confusion, and was
driven back to the right bank of the Beresina by the Fourth Cuirassiers,
who recaptured Borissow. It was found that the better part of the bridge
there had been destroyed.

in his hands, and that he was in a posture to face all dangers
and surmount all difficulties.

Here, in order to clear up certain circumstances that bear
on the disastrous crossing of the Beresina, it is necessary to
enlarge on the events referred to just above.

General Corbineau, in command of the Sixth Cavalry Brigade
of the Second Army Corps under the Duke of Reggio, had been
detailed off with the Bavarian division near Gloubokoje. On
the seventeenth, General Corbineau was ordered to make contact with the Moscow army, there having been no news of it
for three days. He reached Plechnitsie on the twentieth. M.
Tchernychev, with a thousand Cossacks, turned up there a short
while afterwards, but withdrew for a mile or so. (On his
march, quite by chance, M. Tchernychev had met and rescued
General Wintzingerode and M. Narishkin, whom two guardsmen were taking to France as prisoners of war.) On the twenty-
first the French brigade proceeded, with the intention of crossing the Beresina at Borissow.

On arriving at Zembin the general heard a cannonade, and
was attacked at the same time by Cossacks. However, his
rear-guard checked them sufficiently to let him keep moving.
Further on, peasants told him that the Borissow bridge-head
had been surprised, that the Polish general had not even defended the town, and that he had abandoned the bridge. This
gave the Moldavian army control of both banks of the Beresina,
safeguarded its communications with the Wittgenstein by the
only bridge in the district, and put the French brigade between
it and Tchernychev's Cossacks.

Hearing that General Tchernychev was coming from Lepel,
where he had been in communication with Count Wittgenstein, for whom he was probably acting as advance-guard,
General Corbineau realized how vitally important it was to inform the Duke of Reggio of what had happened. Consequently,

he made up his mind to take any risk in attempting to make
contact with the Duke, rather than to seek his own safety elsewhere. He halted at the first defile on the Borissow road, and
set watch on the roads from Minsk and Zembin that were occupied by Cossacks. By good luck the officers and patrols
whom he had sent out managed to get hold of a peasant coming from Borissow, who had crossed the Beresina near Wesselowo. Chance favoured General Corbineau's devotion. He
decided on his tactics then and there. That night he ordered
the guide to take him to the place where he had crossed the
river; and at midnight, on the twenty-first, he crossed at the
point where, though he did not know it at the time, he was
going six days hence to show the French army a means of escape. (It was the very spot where Charles XII had crossed
the Beresina, thus extricating what remained of his brave army
after his Ukrainian expedition.) The current and the floating
ice, difficult to avoid in the darkness, made him lose about
seventy men, even though his brigade was in compact formation and marching eight abreast.

General Corbineau had successfully surmounted one stiff obstacle; but Tchitchagoff's army, patrolling the river bank on
horseback, faced him with other dangers. Fortune was kinder
to him than he would have dared to hope. He avoided Plitsche,
where the Russians were, and moved upon Kostritza. A Cossack regiment had just left there when the French advance-
guard galloped in, at four in the morning of the twenty-second,
and took possession of its equipment and servants. Continuing his march with the same good luck, General Corbineau
came to a Russian nobleman's residence which had a good
bridge over the Natcha. It was the last obstacle he had to
overcome before reaching the Smolensk road, where, to his great
astonishment, he ran into the Second Corps a short distance
from Kroupki.

If the French army had taken the same road as he did, what

misfortune would have been avoided! How many lives would have been saved! But either the Duke of Reggio attached no particular importance to the details of the reports that General Corbineau made to him, and so did not pass them on to the Emperor, or else the Emperor did not consider it expedient to take General Corbineau's route. The fact is that, if we had taken it, we should have gained two marches. By screening our movement with a mere feint towards Borissow, our passage of the Beresina could have been kept from the admiral's notice altogether; and so all our losses would have been prevented. General Corbineau felt this so strongly that, not content with simply making a report to the marshal, he drew his attention once again, during the course of the twenty-third, to the advantages of the route he had taken. If the Emperor did have knowledge of all these circumstances, everything suggests that he must have been determined to carry out the general movement upon Borissow for the sake of putting Admiral Tchitchagoff wholly on the wrong scent. It is possible, of course, that Pahlen's defeat and other considerations led the Emperor to believe that a straightforward attack would enable him to get control of the Borissow bridge, and thus to cross the river more easily. On the whole, though, the probability is that he knew nothing of General Corbineau's suggestions at the time they were first made, since he never spoke of them, and even deplored the inconvenience of having to take the artillery and the baggage-train on such a long détour to reach Wesselowo.

The Emperor sent for General Corbineau on the twenty-third, but, as a result of one of those trifling occurrences which often have so much influence over great events, the general did not receive the order till the twenty-fifth. It is said that the Duke of Reggio's aide-de-camp, M. Cramayel, pocketed the order and forgot about it.

By the time General Corbineau saw the Emperor, to whom he gave an account of all the circumstances of his adventure—

and pointed out, moreover, that precious time was being lost by making a useless detour—the columns had already passed the road that ought to have been taken. The Emperor did not pause when this observation was first made. (He reverted to it later, and traced out General Corbineau's route on a map; but it was too late. He then spoke of it to me, as well as to the Prince of Neuchâtel, and took occasion to complain that he never was told about things in time.) After chatting for a few moments with General Corbineau, he sent him to Wesselowo to prepare whatever was necessary in the way of bridge construction. Without tools, without iron, with virtually no material—he had to pull down houses to get wood—his zeal, aided by the tireless energy of Colonel Chauveau of the artillery, triumphed over all difficulties. After having arranged everything and put all to work, he reported to the Emperor at Staroï-Borissow. There His Majesty had stopped for a few hours to give orders [eleven P.M., November 25]. He had reconnoitred Niemanitza, the banks of the Beresina, the country above and below Borissow, and its environs as well. The Emperor and I had even gone on foot to the end of the remaining quarter of the bridge.

The Emperor had hesitated about where to cross the river. He still had his heart set on Minsk; the more especially, since he hoped that the Prince of Schwarzenberg would have made his way there, and that, by means of a double manœuvre, the Russians would not have been given time either to remove or destroy the supplies. He therefore summoned the commissary officer who had been in charge there, so as to get exact information about the supplies likely to be available, the nature of the country, and recent events. He also made thorough enquiries about the route through Ukoloda; but the reports of General Corbineau, who arrived in person towards one o'clock, and further particulars from the Duke of Belluno about the extraordinary tactics of Wittgenstein, who restricted himself to following his movements, decided the Emperor. He sent General Corbineau back to hurry up the bridge construction, with orders to return immediately. . . . General Corbineau joined us again in the night, and the artillery, baggage and various army corps were directed to advance on to Wesselowo and Studianka. The last-named was a manor house, to which the Emperor proceeded with the Guard during the night. General Corbineau acted as guide.

The Emperor set off again two hours before daybreak [November 26] to join the Duke of Reggio at Wesselowo. He examined the banks of the Beresina, and placed strong artillery on the side we occupied, which dominated the other side across the whole stretch of marshland. This marshland bordered the river, and was a good five hundred yards wide. He had soundings taken in the ford. The river had subsided through freezing, and so there was no great depth except for a stretch of twenty or thirty feet, across which the horses had to swim to gain the other bank, which was rather steep. On our side the water only came up to the horses' bellies. A number of light cavalrymen—our fearless Poles—crossed and recrossed without difficulty, and drove away some Cossacks prowling on the other bank, who never fired a shot until they had been driven beyond the marshland. Later on there was a small engagement between the advance-guard of Dombrowski's division and a party of sharpshooters, infantry, hussars and Cossacks from Tchalitz's division, who were in the houses of the village of Brillowo, but who retired.

Meanwhile active work was being carried on to complete the trestles begun by General Corbineau; and material was collected to make two bridges—one for artillery and one for infantry. Threats of crossing were kept up all along the line. The army mustered in strength at Borissow, and then made in succession for Wesselowo. The Duke of Reggio's corps crossed the bridges before nightfall. General Dombrowski was wounded in a trifling engagement between his division and Tchalitz's, which had been attacked in the rear and driven out of Brillowo. The Third (Ney) and Fifth (Poniatowski) Army Corps crossed during the night on their way to support the Duke of Reggio, who, it was then thought, was going to be vigorously attacked by the admiral.

The Emperor was at the bridge all day. His presence encouraged the sappers and the pontoon-men, who showed real devotion by getting into the water every other minute to mend a matchwood bridge which broke down under every gun-carriage and half-company of men. The Emperor inspected the marshland along the other bank of the river, and in the afternoon took careful observations of this position. It was long past nightfall when he returned to Studianka, where he slept on the twenty-sixth.

He was back at the bridge at daylight. The crossing proceeded slowly. So as not to impede the troops and artillery, stragglers and camp-followers were stopped from slipping over the bridge, as they would readily have done in the intervals. Wesselowo was thronged with them. The Guard and the transport-waggons crossed on the twenty-seventh, in the daytime, and took up a position at Brillowo, on the other bank.

While all this was going on, the Duke of Belluno, who was covering our manœuvre, was getting into position at mid-day in front of Wesselowo with the Daendels and Girard divisions; Partouneaux's division, which he had left in front of Borissow, was to join him during the night. The inaction of the admiral, who had received orders from Kutusof to alter the direction of his march, baffled everyone. Nor was it any easier to understand the slow pace of Wittgenstein's pursuit. How had it come about that the admiral, who had been able to observe our tactics for thirty-six hours past, had not burnt or dismantled the Borissow bridge, and thus had that, at least, off his mind?

How was it that he had not made a quick sally with eighty or so of cannon, and knocked us to bits while we were crossing the river? Was he waiting for Wittgenstein? Had Kutusof joined forces with him? Was he manœuvring in our rear? We lost ourselves in conjecture; and, it must be admitted, there was ample ground for doing so.

Before sending the transport-waggons into the marshland, I had personally examined all the paths through it in the morning. If the cold, which had diminished during the three preceding days, had not become very much sharper again the day before, we should not have saved a single gun-carriage, as the soil was miry and trembled beneath one's feet. Although the path along which they were taken was constantly changed, the last ammunition waggons got bogged, because they cut or broke through the crust of hard frozen grass which served as a sort of bridge. The wheels had nothing to grip, and sank into the bottomless mud. It required all the perseverance, all the intelligence of which the men in charge of the convoys were capable, to deal with so awkward a situation. It can be said with truth that Fortune was never kinder to the Emperor than on these two days: had it not been for the intensity of the cold, he could not have saved a single cart.

The Emperor, who during the day had inspected Brillowo and the road leading thence to Borissow as well, returned to Wesselowo to view the Duke of Belluno's position. His Majesty had personally supervised the Guard's crossing of the Beresina, and did not return until a late hour to Brillowo—a miserable hamlet where headquarters had been established. It was ascertained from several marauders that Cossacks, from whom they had escaped, had appeared at Studianka in the afternoon and captured some stragglers. In the Emperor's opinion, these were Wittgenstein's advance-guard. Was he manœuvring in concert with the admiral to attack us on both sides? If so, it was too late for him to be successful. . . .

Since the condition of the cavalry made it impossible for us to send out strong reconnoitring parties, we could not ascertain the enemy's movements. Also, even though thus far our troops had crossed the Beresina without being troubled by a single rifle shot, and although everything suggested that the crossing would be completed with equal success, the Emperor's attention was fixed on Kamen. It was along this road that the enemy could stop our march and bar our way with obstacles far more difficult to surmount than the Beresina. The Emperor had just learnt from a peasant, and the report was verified by some officers who had travelled along the Kamen road, that it was constructed on a large number of bridges built over countless small streams which traversed it; that one of these bridges, over an impassable swamp, was more than a quarter of a league long. A light put to a bunch of straw would be sufficient to deprive us of this means of retreat.

On the twenty-eighth, in the morning,[2] the Duke of Reggio's advance-guard was attacked so vigorously by Admiral Tchitchagoff that the Third and Fifth Corps had to come to his support. Several hours passed with honours more or less even. The Duke of Reggio was wounded. The Emperor, who was present at the engagement, at once replaced him with Marshal Elchingen. A charge of cuirassiers, carried out by Doumerc's division, decided the affair in our favour. In a felled wood the Seventh Regiment, which had taken its place at the head of Berckheim's brigade, charged upon a column of infantry in close formation and dispersed it. The resulting disorder forced the Russians to retreat, leaving behind more than fifteen hundred prisoners, whom I saw. These prisoners were all soldiers from the Moldavian army.

This check to the admiral would have decided the hazardous operation of crossing the Beresina wholly in our favour, but for one of those events which no plans made by a human being

[2] At seven A.M. Battle of the Beresina.

THE DUCHESS OF VICENZA

Portrait by Gérard

From the collection of Mme. la Comtesse Gérard de Moustier

can take into account, as they are outside all reasonable probabilities. There can be no doubt that the rest of the army would
have crossed the river without difficulty, and so been saved, if
Partouneaux's division, which had remained at Borissow and
which was to join the Duke of Belluno during the night, had
not in the darkness mistaken the way where the roads from
Studianka and Wesselowo diverge. General Partouneaux and
a party of staff officers, thinking that they were on the right
road and that the Duke of Belluno was ahead of them, were
marching confidently at the head of the division so as to be
able to observe in advance the position it would take up, when
they found themselves in the midst of the Russians, and were
taken prisoner. The enemy, warned ahead of time of the mistake these officers were making—and the division after them—
had arranged matters in such a way that they would be allowed
to advance. The general of division was captured; the division
itself surrendered, acting under orders of Generals Le Camus
and Blanmont. These particulars were learnt afterwards: at
the time, what was a consequence of disastrous imprudence
was considered to be due to stupidity and cowardice.[3]

The arrival of this division's rear-guard battalion, which had
taken the right road, leaving Staroï-Borissow last, and had
caught up with the Duke of Belluno during the night, increased
the uneasiness to which the division's delay had already given
rise. This battalion had seen and heard nothing, and had found
the road free. Marshal Victor did not doubt but that the division had got lost during the night, and would join him at
daybreak. Everyone was constantly expecting to see it appear;
and uncertainty ceased only about nine o'clock when Wittgen-

[3] The Emperor was very hard on Partouneaux. In Bulletin 29, he said
of him: "Rumours are current that the general of division was not with his
troops, and had been marching on his own." Later on, however, Napoleon
forgave Partouneaux; for on July 14, 1813, while their father was still in
captivity, he decided that the general's three sons should be educated at the
State's expense.

stein's force, which had been drawn up facing the Duke of
Belluno since the evening before, was seen to be preparing for
an attack. Even then, the rear-guard battalion had arrived
without difficulty; no sounds of fighting had been heard; the
road, according to a reconnoitring party which had returned,
was still free. Thus, no one imagined that a division commanded by experienced generals could conceivably have surrendered without putting up a fight. Even supposing that General Partouneaux had been attacked by the main body of Wittgenstein's forces, there was nothing to prevent him from striking out, with his infantry and cavalry, for the river bank; that
route was still open. Was he still fighting? The battle that
was about to begin would show him that they were waiting for
him, and would serve him as a useful diversion. It was on
this supposition that, far from speeding up the passage of the
troops already delayed to await the missing division, reinforcements, including even a detachment from the Guard, were sent
back to support Marshal Belluno. He was vigorously attacked
about eleven o'clock while we were engaged in fighting Tchitchagoff.

The Emperor did not hear of the surrender of Partouneaux's
division until one o'clock. The notable success scored against
the admiral compensated somewhat for this misfortune, which
was kept as secret as possible at main headquarters, but which
was made known at the headquarters of the Duke of Belluno,
who at the time was severely pressed by Wittgenstein's army.
None spared himself in the effort to hold this position at least
until nightfall; but at last the marshal was compelled to cross
the Beresina in order to save his corps from total destruction.

It is impossible to conceive the appearance of the village of
Wesselowo and that bank of the Beresina after his withdrawal—
everywhere troops, stragglers, refugees, women and children.
The camp-followers, who were unwilling to abandon their waggons, had not been permitted to cross the river—the bridges,

and the paths through the fields, had been reserved since the evening before for the passage of the Duke of Belluno and the troops detailed to support him. The Emperor hoped up to the last moment that the position could be held until dark, in which case everything would have been saved. But when a retreat was decided on, the Wesselowo bank at once became a scene of horror, of indescribable carnage, especially when the Russians' repeated attacks on the last troops to cross the river had driven the crowd of non-combatants to the river's edge. Everyone then rushed the bridges, which were soon broken down, as much by the disorder as by the fugitives' weight. We Frenchmen, unhappy and helpless spectators of these scenes of horror and cruelty, were able from our side of the river to gauge roughly the number of the victims of Russian barbarism. Ten thousand lives were lost. This estimate of the number of unarmed stragglers, camp-followers, refugees, women and children is not exaggerated.

As may well be imagined, there was little inclination to spare General Partouneaux, to whose surrender this misfortune could largely be attributed. The Emperor and the General Staff, the marshals and officers, the whole army, were more than severe in their judgment on him. "His lack of foresight," everyone agreed, "is unpardonable. The surrender of his division without a fight is shameful." The word "cowardice" was used, and his surrender was compared with Marshal Elchingen's brave determination.

"When d'Assas faced certain death," the Emperor said, "he cried: *Follow me, men of Auvergne!* If generals lack the courage to put up a fight, they might at least allow their grenadiers to do so. A drummer could have saved his comrades from dishonour by sounding the charge. A canteen-woman could have saved the division by shouting, '*Sauve qui peut!*' instead of surrendering."

There is no doubt that, apart even from the very fair chance

we had of getting across the Beresina before the enemy started
to attack, this surrender had a powerful and unfortunate influence on the whole course of events; and that the Duke of
Belluno, with one division too few in his hands, was thereby
put at great disadvantage in defending his position.

While all this took place on what was now the farther bank
of the Beresina, the First and Fourth Corps were moving upon
Kamen. That, along with our success against the admiral, was
some consolation for the day's disasters; and the Emperor was
greatly comforted to feel sure that our progress, which could
so easily have been stopped by the burning of a few bridges,
would meet with no further impediment. . . . Whatever was
left of the artillery and the carriages was also going on towards
Kamen. But headquarters were maintained at Brillowo for
one day more, the twenty-eighth, so as to oversee the reorganization of the corps that had been hard hit, and to set a good example to the troops. Their morale had crumbled visibly under
the strain of the past few days.

On the following day, the twenty-ninth, the Emperor proceeded to Kamen, where General Lanskoï, sent there by the
admiral, had appeared about noon. He had surrounded a house
in which were the Duke of Reggio, General Legrand and other
wounded generals and officers, as well as two officers from the
Emperor's personal suite sent ahead to arrange accommodation.[4] All the servants were assembled, with a number of soldiers who had gone ahead of the main army; and this handful

[4] Caulaincourt is mistaken: cf. Fain, *Manuscrit de 1812*, II, 409; Castellane, *Journal*, II, 199; Denniée, *Itinéraire*, 163; Lejeune, *Souvenirs*, II, 441.
All agree that this episode took place at Plechnitsie (Plaszczenitzy), not
at Kamen. Caulaincourt is, therefore, confused in his recollection of some
of the events of the two days November 29-30.—The Duke of Reggio had
taken a bullet in his side on the twenty-eighth. Lanskoï's bombardment
wounded him again; a cannon-ball came through the roof, sending a splin-
ter into his thigh. Oudinot was wounded thirty-four times during his
military career.

of brave men sufficed to drive away the detachment of Cossacks. Finding that he was unable to capture the occupants of the house, Lanskoï bombarded it. Two persons close to the marshal were wounded. When our advance-guard arrived on the scene, the Russians decided to rest on their laurels for that day.

As the peasant had reported, and various officers confirmed, at a distance of half a league out of Brillowo, and for a stretch of about two leagues, the road is a causeway through a marsh. The way is so insecure that the greater part of it is constructed of wooden bridges, two of them nearly a quarter-league in length. Numerous others cross the little streams, which traverse the marsh here, there and everywhere. How could so easy a means of impeding our progress have been overlooked by the Russians? Six Cossacks with torches would have sufficed to cut us off from this means of retreat.

None of the deductions to be made from this strange lack of foresight on the part of the enemy escaped the Emperor. He was all the more infuriated by General Partouneaux's manifestation of that same lack, which, as he said, had cost us so dear, when he reflected how easy it would have been, but for this, to make the crossing of the Beresina one of the most perfect and illustrious military operations ever undertaken. He added that the Russian generals had not yet carried out a single genuinely military operation, not one useful manœuvre, without its having been worked out for them by their government. The Emperor's opinion of Wittgenstein, whom he had considered the most tenacious, and, during the Dwina campaign, the most capable of the Russian generals, steadily declined in consequence of his muddled tactics, his indecision and the deliberate slowness of his operations in order not to risk being isolated from the admiral. He had been saying ever since Polotsk that, given the circumstances in which we were placed, we might consider ourselves lucky in not having more capable adversaries. . . .

On the way from Brillowo to Kamen two of the Emperor's transport-mules, which had fallen behind the others, were stolen while their driver was some little way off. No one knew who had got them. I mention this insignificant fact because, in spite of the prevailing misery, it was the only incident of the kind that took place during the campaign. The respect in which the Emperor was held, the devotion to his person, was such that no one belonging to his suite, not even one of his servants, was ever insulted. Not one murmur against the Emperor was heard in the whole course of this disastrous retreat. Soldiers were dying by the roadside, but I never heard a single grumble; and my testimony in this respect is worth something, because after Wereia I always marched on foot, sometimes with the Emperor, sometimes in front of him, sometimes behind him, but always amongst groups of men, in uniform, without my riding coat and wearing my full-dress hat. Any discontent amongst the men would have manifested itself most readily, no doubt, in the presence of a general in full uniform. The individual behaviour of these unfortunate soldiers, who, lacking all the necessities of life, froze to death by the roadside, often astonished me, I admit; and I was not alone in admiring it.

From Kamen we proceeded to Plechnitsie, where the General Staff slept on the thirtieth. The Beresina had swept away a large number of our strays and stragglers, who had been looting everything and thus depriving the brave fellows who remained in the ranks of the supplies which they so badly needed. However, that was no gain, for, after the crossing, bands of irregulars formed in full view of everyone, with the object of recruiting still more stragglers. All that remained of the First Corps was its colour-guard and a few commissioned and non-commissioned officers surrounding their marshal. The Fourth was worse than weakened, and the Third, which had fought so valiantly against the Moldavian army, had been reduced by more than half its strength after that affair. The Poles were in no better case. Our cavalry, apart from the Guard, no longer existed except in the form of parties of stragglers, which, although the Cossacks and peasants attacked them savagely, overran the villages on our flanks. Hunger proved an irresistible force, and the need to live, to find shelter against the cold, made men indifferent to every sort of danger. The evil spread also to the Duke of Reggio's corps—now joined on to Marshal Elchingen's—and even to the Duke of Belluno's divisions, which formed the rear-guard.

Cavalry officers, who had been mustered into a company under the command of generals,[5] dispersed also in a few days, so wretched were they, and so tortured by hunger. Those who had a horse to feed were forced, if they did not want to lose it, to keep some distance away, as there were no supplies at all along the road. The Guard also lost more stragglers after Kamen; but this body of men—who of course grumbled a little, though always under their breath, and who got whatever supplies were going—still made an excellent impression by virtue of their general appearance, their vigour and their martial air. These veterans cheered up as soon as they caught a glimpse of the Emperor; and the battalion each day on guard-duty kept up an astonishing standard of smartness.

Thinking of the wonderful smartness of the Guard puts me in mind of the contrast between our men from Moscow and the troops from the Dwina [Victor and Oudinot], at the time when we joined forces with them. Our men, emaciated, bloodless, grimy as chimney-sweeps, enfeebled, were like spectres, although vigorous enough on the march and full of dash under fire. The others, less exhausted, better fed, less smoked by bivouac fires, seemed to us like men belonging to another race. They were alive, we were shadows. The contrast in the horses

[5] Napoleon had just formed what was called the *escadron sacré*, less to furnish himself with a personal bodyguard than to provide a centre for rallying the officers who had no longer any men under them

was even more striking. The artillery of those two corps was superb. The generals and officers were well mounted, had all their equipment, and had been enjoying all the good things that can be got on campaign. At Wesselowo the officers of the Emperor's General Staff—Duroc and myself, for instance—made more than one visit to the Duke of Reggio's kitchen, so great had been the privations to which all ranks in the army had been subjected. In the engagement against the Moldavian army, our worn-out fellows from Moscow were not behind their comrades as far as courage was concerned. In fact, as was said every day, our soldiers had more courage than strength.

When we reached Kamen [Plechnitsie?] the Emperor spoke again with me about his journey to France. He did not anticipate any further obstacles to prevent the army from reaching Wilna, where he considered that it would be as good as saved, and sure of a chance to recuperate. He hoped to come upon his despatches from Paris within forty-eight hours, and to get news of the troops which ought to be coming from Wilna to meet us. We were almost in communication with the Bavarians. The arrival of the Polish Cossacks, whom he took to be only a few marches away, was his chief concern. He continued to count on the Prince of Schwarzenberg's advance, which he hoped would divert the enemy's attention from our retreat, and give us a chance to take up a position in cantonments. He expected frequent attacks from Cossacks, but regarded them as unimportant, since our latest stragglers had organized themselves into powerful squads, under leaders, to repel them and to awe the peasants. It was common enough to see one of these small detachments of fifteen or twenty men chasing one hundred and fifty or two hundred Cossacks in front of them. The Emperor, then, considered himself to be out of reach of Wittgenstein and Kutusof; and the admiral could only follow along in our tracks—that is, unless he made a detour which would lose him two marches.

On December 1, headquarters were at Staïki. We had not hitherto had such a bad lodging. Staïki was nicknamed "Miserowo." The Emperor and the chief-of-staff each had a little niche seven or eight feet square. All the rest of the staff were crowded together in another room. It froze so hard that everyone sought shelter in this cubby-hole. We had to lie on our sides so as to save space. We were packed so tight together that a pin could not have been dropped between us.

Going out in the darkness, someone trod on the foot of M. de Bausset, who had been following us in a carriage ever since Moscow, suffering horribly from gout. The wretched cripple, suddenly awakened by the sharp pain that this clumsiness caused him, began to shout: "It's terrible!—it's murder!" Those who were awake shouted with laughter, which awoke the sleepers; and everyone—serious and lighthearted alike, the unfortunate sick man himself—paid tribute to this momentary nonsense with roars of laughter. I describe this scene to show how man is capable of accustoming himself to the most wretched circumstances; and how, just as the most trivial thing will distract him, so he can witness the greatest misfortunes almost unmoved.

After crossing the Beresina, our faces were less careworn. For the first time, Poland seemed delightful to everyone. Wilna had become a promised land, a safe port that would shelter us from all storms, and the end of all our troubles. The past seemed a dream; and the prospect of a better lot already made us forget, almost, the disasters that had come upon us. Weariness, the privations of the moment, the sight of poor devils dying every instant of cold and exhaustion—all this counted for little with the naturally gay and careless French soldier. Danger makes men egotists. Those who had survived were accustomed to seeing pain and destruction all around them. The strongest characters refused to succumb to misfortune, and tried by their calm to strengthen others who were weaker. We suffered terribly, of course; we had before us a constant spectacle

of fearful misery, of overwhelming distress; but the instinct
of self-preservation, the feeling of national pride, and the desire
to uphold national honour prevented us from taking full account
of this excess of adversity. Our spirits were exalted; and we
did not know, or rather did not wish to believe, all that subsequently transpired. Yesterday's dangers, then, like to-day's
and to-morrow's, meant no more to our imagination than risks
in a battle constantly renewed. Since we were all in it together,
we were generally gay, careless, even full of raillery, as one
is the day before, or the day after, or the very day of, a battle;
c'est la guerre. Unquestionably, despite our sufferings, our
headquarters were in as good a humour as were the Russian
headquarters.

We were approaching Wilna; we were in Poland, and still
no despatches had arrived. The Emperor could not understand
this delay, as we were very near the Bavarian Corps, then stationed at Vileika. This corps, under the command of General
Wrède, should have left the Gloubokoje district and advanced
on to Bunilowice after the Second Corps' retreat; but it had returned after the nineteeenth, and was defending Wilna. This
lack of letters from France, and especially the thought of the
probable effect there, as well as in Europe, of the absence of
all news about the army, was of greater concern to the Emperor
than anything else. He prepared a bulletin [the famous Bulletin 29] giving an account of the course events had taken, and
of our latest disasters. He said to me:

"I shall tell everything. It is better that these particulars
should be known through me than through private letters. Full
details now will mitigate the effect of the disasters which have
to be announced later to the nation."

Headquarters were established on the second at Selitche, almost as uncomfortable as the day before. But we found a store
of potatoes. It is impossible to describe the joy that everyone

felt at being able to eat his fill. The cold was so intense that bivouacking was no longer supportable. Bad luck for those who fell asleep by a camp-fire! Furthermore, disorganization was perceptibly gaining ground in the Guard. One constantly found men who, overcome by the cold, had been forced to drop out and had fallen to the ground, too weak or too numb to stand. Ought one to help them along—which practically meant carrying them? They begged one to let them alone. There were bivouacs all along the road—ought one to take them to a camp-fire? Once these poor wretches fell asleep, they were dead. If they resisted the craving for sleep, another passer-by would help them along a little farther, thus prolonging their agony for a short while but not saving them; for in this condition the drowsiness engendered by cold is irresistibly strong. Sleep comes inevitably; and to sleep is to die. I tried in vain to save a number of these unfortunates. The only words they uttered were to beg me, for the love of God, to go away and let them sleep. To hear them, one would have thought this sleep was their salvation. Unhappily, it was a poor wretch's last wish; but at least he ceased to suffer, without pain or agony. Gratitude, and even a smile, was imprinted on his discoloured lips. What I have related about the effects of extreme cold, and of this kind of death by freezing, is based on what I saw happen to thousands of individuals. The road was covered with their corpses.

The Emperor stopped for a little while at the crossing of the Villia, in the midst of a bodyguard and on an eminence overlooking a fairly wide reach of the road. I stood apart to watch the débris of our army file past. It was from here that I saw what stragglers had reported for several days past, and what we had refused to believe. Cossacks, tired of killing our stragglers, or of taking prisoners whom they were obliged to march to the rear, thus depriving themselves for a time of the chance of daily booty, were robbing everyone they came across.

They were taking their clothes, if they had decent ones, and
sending them away practically naked. I have seen cases in
which they gave in exchange inferior clothing which they had
taken from someone else, or from some poor wretch dead by
the roadside. Every one of these Cossacks had a pile of old
clothes—some under their saddles like pads, others over them
like cushions. They never had ridden such high horses before.
I spoke with some of the unfortunate stragglers whom I had
seen robbed quite near the bridge, and with others who had
been stripped farther away. They confirmed the particulars I
have given, and added that the Cossacks, when no superior officers were about, drove them along in front of them like a
herd of cattle.

On the third, we reached Molodetchna, where fourteen despatches from Paris were received all at once, as well as despatches from all along the line and the Duke of Bassano's news
about the Austrian advance. . . . He had no encouraging information to give about the levies of Polish cavalry. Cossacks
were out of the question. The Duchy was exhausted—particularly its funds; and the Emperor, whose object was to spend as
little as possible, was for this reason deprived of the Cossacks
on whom he had been counting, and whom he had daily been
expecting to meet.

Lithuania had no more resources than the Duchy. Laid waste
by war, it was barely able to fulfil its first quota of troops. We
lacked Lithuanian Cossacks, as we lacked Cossacks from the
Duchy, as we lacked all the other supports on which the Emperor had counted. Henceforth, it was clear that neither Wilna
nor even the Niemen would be the end of the army's retreat,
and therefore the end of our troubles.

On that same day, three Russian peasants threw the whole
transport section into a panic. However, when a number of
infantrymen rallied, they made off, after looting two carriages
belonging to generals. As for the Cossacks, they never ap-

peared where there were five or six bayonets near each other.

The Emperor was very busy reading his despatches from France, and everyone was glad to have news from home. In Paris there had been some uneasiness about the interruption of news from the army, but no conception of the extent of our disasters. The memory of the Emperor's exploits maintained confidence, and caused such a sense of security that the sensation produced by this long silence had been less marked, less disturbing, than there had been reason to fear.

The Emperor instructed me to send M. Anatole de Montesquiou, the Prince of Neuchâtel's aide-de-camp, to Paris to give word of him verbally to the Empress. His object was to prepare public opinion, by the details that this officer would give, for the bulletin on which he had been occupied since we crossed the Beresina.

The despatches from Paris revived the topic of the Malet affair. The Emperor always joked about the capture of the Minister and of the Prefect of Police. He appeared to be quite satisfied with the state of public opinion since this conspiracy, particularly during the interruption of news from the army. He was satisfied with all the details about the administration, with everything in general, and said as much to the Prince of Neuchâtel, who repeated his remarks to me that same evening.

The Emperor was occupied with the famous bulletin. He was still determined to hide none of his disasters, so as to impress them on everyone before his arrival. Then, he said, his presence would both calm and reassure public opinion. The more overwhelming our disasters were, and the more they were multiplied with every day that passed and every step we took, the more indispensable became his return to France. He summoned me one evening, and repeated to me what I had already heard from the Prince of Neuchâtel.

"In the existing state of affairs," he said to me, "I can only hold my grip on Europe from the Tuileries."

As usual, however, in spite of any remarks I might make to him, he let there be no doubt that the army was to take up its position at Wilna, and would have its winter quarters there. He counted on being able to set off in less than forty-eight hours; as soon, in fact, as he was in contact with the troops coming from Wilna, whereafter, in his opinion, the army would run no more serious risks. He was eager to start so as to forestall the news of our disasters. It is to be noted that, for the most part, nothing was known about them. Confidence in his genius, and the habit of seeing him triumph over even greater obstacles, were such that public opinion tended to minimize rather than exaggerate whatever news of our disasters was received. The Emperor was in a hurry to start. He thought that communications would be easier and surer at once rather than a few days later, because Russian partisans would not yet have had time to try attacks from the rear, as they certainly would do while the army was getting into position. He allowed me to make certain preliminary arrangements so that nothing should delay his departure when once it was decided upon.

The Emperor again asked me whether I thought he ought to give command of the army to the Viceroy or to the King of Naples. I said, as I had in previous conversations, that, with all due respect to Murat's courage, Prince Eugène was the more popular with the army and enjoyed more of its confidence. I added that the King of Naples, though a hero on the battlefield, was generally thought to possess neither the force of character, the sense of order nor the foresight necessary to save the remains of the army and reorganize it; that, without for a moment overlooking his services at Borodino and on other occasions, he had been accused of having an insatiable appetite for glory, of having instigated His Majesty to undertake the Moscow expedition, and of having lost the magnificent force of cavalry which started on the campaign. It was no longer a question of charging the enemy, I told him; the present need was to keep the army alive so as to reorganize it, and to hold the enemy in check.

The Emperor seemed to find my observations sound. He even subscribed to the opinion generally held about the King, but pointed out that his rank made it impossible for him to be put under the orders of the Viceroy. Thus he was obliged to give the preference to Murat, who would have left the army if the supreme command had been entrusted to Prince Eugène. He added that the Prince of Neuchâtel took the same view; that he was leaving him to see to everything, and that he, Berthier, preferred the King, whose rank, age, and reputation would be more imposing in the eyes of the marshals, and whose proved courage counted for something where the Russians were concerned. Certain other remarks which the Emperor had made formerly, and which I recollected because they cropped up again in the course of this conversation, gave me the idea (at least I fancied I could trace such a thought) that he would prefer to leave to his brother-in-law the honour of rallying the army, and that he did not care about his step-son having credit for this further achievement in the eyes of the army and of France. With all his greatness of character, this distrust of his relatives—and, in general, of everyone who had acquired personal renown—was entirely in keeping with the Emperor's general attitude.

He spoke to me again about the persons he would take with him. His choice was limited to myself, who was to start with him, to Duroc and Count Lobau, who were to follow after him, and to M. Wonsowicz, a Polish officer who had been through the whole campaign, a man of proved courage and devotion. It was arranged that the Emperor's other aides-de-camp and the officers of his suite should follow him in succession: each week the Prince of Neuchâtel was to send two of his orderly officers along to him. He was to have an escort only as far as Wilna. This would be provided by the Neapolitan cavalry, which was attached to Loison's division. Beyond Wilna he would travel under the name of the Duke of Vicenza.

I gave orders, therefore, to the post-stages, under the pretext of making sure that there were facilities for the use of despatch officers. Our troops soon disorganized these relays, however, and it was necessary to make other arrangements by sending ahead several transport detachments whose horses would serve our purpose. Our situation was such that the smallest accidents were liable to put obstacles, even insurmountable obstacles, in our way, unless steps were taken long in advance. For instance, we should not have been able to make use of our relays to get along the road, which was like a sheet of glass, if I had not kept under lock and key a sack of coal for the purpose of forging shoes for the horses which were to pull us.

We could do our smithing only at night because the supply-waggons were on the move for twelve or fifteen hours each day. The cold was so severe, even by the forge fire, that the farriers could only work in gloves—and then they had to rub their hands every minute or so to keep them from freezing. These particulars, quite insignificant in any other circumstances, give some idea of the causes of our failure, and of all that would have had to been foreseen in order to avoid it. Our failure, for the most part, was due rather to such unconsidered trifles than to exhaustion or the enemy's attacks.

The Emperor was well satisfied with the particulars transmitted to him by the Duke of Bassano regarding the tactics that he had just instructed Prince Schwarzenberg to carry out. Generally speaking, he was pleased with everything this minister had done and ordered whilst communications were interrupted. He did not, however, refer with the same satisfaction to what had been done in regard to raising the levies he had ordered in Poland. In this respect, he complained a great deal about M. de Pradt and about all his agents at Wilna and Warsaw. The promised Cossacks had not even been re-

cruited—a fact which upset the Emperor the more in that he
had been openly attributing all his defeats since Smolensk to
the lack of light cavalry. . . . The news from France, on the
other hand, was a real consolation. The Emperor spoke of this
with the utmost satisfaction, and with high praise for the Empress's conduct, for her prudence, and for the attachment that
she had shown to him.

"These difficult circumstances," he went on, "form her power
of judgment, and give her assurance and far-sightedness which
will win the nation's heart. She is just the woman I needed,
kind, good, loving as German women are. She doesn't busy
herself with intrigues. She has a sense of order, and concerns
herself only with me and her son."

On the fifth, headquarters were at Smorgoni. There a member of the Wilna government and Count van Hogendorp, aide-
de-camp to the Emperor and governor of the town, awaited him.
The Emperor interviewed them, and sent them off again at
once. He then sent for me to take the dictation of his final
orders:

Smorgoni, December 5, noon.

The Emperor leaves at ten o'clock to-night.

He is to be accompanied by two hundred men from his
Guard. Beyond the Smorgoni-Oschmiana relay station, as far
as Oschmiana, by the infantry regiment that halts for the night
fifteen miles from here; orders to this effect to be given by
General van Hogendorp.

One hundred and fifty good horses belonging to the Guard
to be sent to a point one league from Oschmiana. Staff officers from the infantry regiment and the squadron of lancers
from the Guard to be placed in relays between Smorgoni and
Oschmiana.

The Neapolitans, who are bivouacking to-night between
Wilna and Oschmiana, to arrange for one hundred horses to
be at Miedniki and one hundred at Rumsziki.

General van Hogendorp . . . to instruct the Duke of Bassano to wait upon the Emperor immediately at Smorgoni.

The Emperor to start with the Duke of Vicenza in His Majesty's carriage; M. Wonsowicz in front, a footman behind. . . .

The Master of Horse to notify the King of Naples, the Viceroy and the marshals to be at headquarters at seven o'clock.

The Master of Horse to get from the chief-of-staff an order to proceed to Paris with his secretary Rayneval,[6] his couriers and his servants.

The Emperor then repeated what he had already said in the morning . . . that the Prince of Schwarzenberg was on the move forward . . . that various regiments were arriving at Wilna and others on the Niemen; that the Wilna shops, and even the Kowno shops, were well supplied, and that the troopers, once they got hold of food and clothing, would soon rejoin the ranks. There could be no doubt, in his opinion, that the retreat would be over when there was no more privation.

Having tried on previous occasions to explain the real state of affairs to the Emperor, and what I foresaw would come to pass, I listened this time without making any reply.

"Why don't you answer? . . . What is your opinion, then?"

"I have grave doubts, Sire, as to whether the Niemen will be the end of disorder and as to whether the army will rally there. All the fresh troops ought to be sent to take up their positions wherever Your Majesty thinks we can really stop, since contact with our disorganized forces will spread disorder amongst them, and thus lose us everything."

"So you think that Wilna ought to be evacuated?"

"Unquestionably, Sire, and as soon as possible."

[6] The Emperor was going to travel under the name of Count F. J. M. Gérard de Rayneval, at that time first embassy secretary attached to the Duke of Vicenza.

"You make me laugh! The Russians are not in a fit state to proceed there now, and you know as well as I do that our stragglers don't give a f——— for the Cossacks."

The Emperor was convinced that more supplies could be got together in eight days at Wilna to resist the Russians than they would be able to collect in a month. In his mind's eye he saw Poland arming all her peasants to drive away the Cossacks, the French army tripling in size because it had food and clothing, and because its reinforcements were now within reach, whereas the Russians were leaving theirs farther and farther behind. The Emperor, as at Moscow, refused to take into account the fact that the climate favoured the Russians more than us. Already he saw our cantonments, even our advance-posts protected by the Poles, who were acclimatized and ready, with infantry as well as cavalry, to defend their country and their homes. He even saw our infantry, when once it had eaten its fill, less than two weeks hence, braving the cold and chasing away the Cossacks. The Emperor seemed to have no doubts about it all; and if I failed to alter his opinion by frankly expressing an opposite one, at least my doing so did not irritate him, since he discussed the situation for a long while with me.

The Prince of Neuchâtel was greatly upset at having to remain behind, although the Emperor, in accordance with his wishes, had made the King of Naples commander-in-chief. Berthier was consoled by the thought that he would be able to be of real service to the Emperor by remaining with the army, and that the presence of someone accustomed to being obeyed was necessary for the maintenance of good morale. His devotion and attachment to the Emperor were heartfelt. He, too, saw how many difficulties there would be in rallying the army, not because of any lack of fresh troops (he had enough at his disposal, and the Guard still formed a satisfactory basis for reorganization), but because the Emperor's departure, which otherwise he believed to be necessary, would provide a pretext for disorder, which might well complete the process of disorganization. At bottom, however, he was far from foreseeing what actually happened, although the troops from the Dwina and Belluno's men were going to pieces more every day.

The King of Naples, the Viceroy, the Marshals, the Dukes of Elchingen, Treviso, Istria and Danzig, the Prince of Eckmühl—all of them with the exception of the Duke of Belluno, who was in command of the rear-guard—arrived in turn. They constituted a sort of council to which the Emperor announced his determination to go to Paris. His manner was that of someone submitting a project for their opinion on it; and they were unanimous in urging him to go.

PART V
FLIGHT

CHAPTER XIII

BY SLEDGE TO WARSAW

WE set out at exactly ten o'clock in the evening. [December 5, 1812.] The Emperor and I were in his sleeping coach; the gallant Wonsowicz was on horseback, riding beside the carriage; and Roustam also was mounted, along with the outriders Fagalde and Amodru. One of them went ahead to order post-horses at Oschmiana. Duroc and Count Lobau followed in one calèche, Baron Fain and M. Constant in a second.[1] The necessary preparations had been so carefully made, the secret so well kept, that no one had the least suspicion of what was happening. With the exception of the Grand Marshal and Baron Fain, even those who set out on this journey did not know of it until seven-thirty, when the marshals were notified.

The Emperor reached Oschmiana about midnight. Loison's division and a detachment of the Neapolitan cavalry had taken up their position there during the afternoon. It was freezing hard. The troops were full of confidence, in the belief that they were covered by the main army; consequently the outposts were badly placed, and in addition badly manned. The main body of the division was quartered in the town, where everyone shut himself indoors to escape the cold, which was extreme. Shortly before the Emperor's arrival, a Russian commanding some irregular troops had taken advantage of this confidence

[1] If one could put any faith in the spurious memoirs of Constant (*Mémoires*, III, 472), one would have to believe that he travelled alone and arrived in Paris five or six days after the Emperor.

271

to carry out a raid through the town with Cossacks and hussars. The slaughter of a few sentinels and the capture of a few men were the only result of his expedition. A fusillade from every house soon forced the Russians to beat a hurried retreat, whereupon they took up a position overlooking the town, which they bombarded for some time. This was the state of affairs when the Emperor arrived. M. van Hogendorp, who carried the orders dictated by the Emperor, and even the ordinary courier, had barely preceded us, so that we had to wait for the horses and the Neapolitans.

The Emperor hesitated a moment in favour of waiting till daylight. The calèche following us had not yet arrived. We held a sort of council to decide also whether it would not be well to send a few squads of infantry to keep the road open, in case the Russians tried to occupy it. This precaution, however, would have delayed us, and might have informed the enemy of the Emperor's departure.[2] We therefore decided to put along the road a small advance-guard composed of the mounted Neapolitans. We sent two further advance-guards to follow them in echelon. The rest were divided, half going in front of us and half behind. The Emperor's saddle-horses, which had followed us from Smorgoni, were ordered to come on as far as Miedniki. The cold was increasing, and the horses of the escort could not keep their feet. Of all the detachments, there were not fifteen men still with us when we reached the relay, and hardly eight, including the general and some officers, as we approached Wilna.

At a league's distance from Miedniki and at the break of day we met the Duke of Bassano, who took my place beside the Emperor. Since His Majesty did not wish to enter the town,

---

[2] Cf. Bourgoing, *Souvenirs*, 178. One should bear in mind that for this period the *Souvenirs militaires du Baron de Bourgoing* are especially valuable because the author had before him an unpublished account, prepared by Wonsowicz himself, from which to draw his history of the Emperor's journey.

I went ahead in M. Bassano's carriage to carry the orders to the government and make further arrangements for our journey. It was well that I went to Wilna myself; for M. van Hogendorp, who had just arrived, had so far been able to get nothing prepared. He had had to awaken people who had just got home from a ball at M. Bassano's. They danced while others froze to death. The inhabitants of Wilna had no conception of our situation, of what had already happened, or of what was to come. I mustered a dozen men for the escort. There were no post-horses. I had to take M. Bassano's for the second relay. No one had any suspicion that the Emperor was so near.

The Emperor stopped to change horses in the suburbs of the town. I arrived there at almost the same time, and we set out immediately. In Wilna I had bought fur-lined boots for all the travellers of our party; and they thanked me for them more than once when we met later in Paris, for they would certainly have arrived there with a frost-bitten limb or two if it had not been for this precaution. Duroc and Count Lobau arrived as we were leaving. The Neapolitans, who were still acting as escort, had their hands or feet frost-bitten. I found the commanding officer with both his hands pressed against the stove. He expected to relieve the acute pain, and I had great difficulty in making him realize that he was risking the loss of his hands, and in making him go out and rub them with snow—a treatment which so increased his sufferings that he was not able to keep it up.

M. Wonsowicz, who had no more lead-horses and was tired besides, took the footman's seat of the Emperor's carriage. We reached Kowno two hours before dawn [December 7]. The courier had had a fire lit in a kind of tavern, kept by an Italian scullion who had set himself up there since the passage of the army. The meal seemed superb because it was hot. Good bread, fowl, a table and chairs, a table-cloth—all these were novelties to us. Only the Emperor had been well served throughout the retreat: that is to say he had always had white bread, linen, his Chambertin, good oil, beef or mutton, rice, and beans or lentils, his favourite vegetables. The Grand Marshall and M. Lobau rejoined us here.

I do not remember that I ever suffered so much from cold as on the journey from Wilna to Kowno. The thermometer had gone to twenty below. Although the Emperor was dressed in thick wool and covered with a good rug, with his legs in fur boots and then in a bag made of a bear's skin, yet he complained of the cold to such an extent that I had to cover him with half my own bear-skin rug. Breath froze on the lips, and formed small icicles under the nose, on the eyebrows, and round the eyelids. All the clothwork of the carriage, and particularly the hood, where our breath rose, was frozen hard and white. When we reached Kowno the Emperor was shivering as with the ague.

At Rumsiszki we found a regiment on the line of march. On the way from Wilna to Kowno the Emperor again raised the problem whether he should take, as he had first intended, the direct route through Königsberg. Would it be prudent, with the possibility that some incident would lead to his recognition, to cross the whole breadth of Prussia? We had a commandant in every town, but apart from the regiments on the line of march we had no troops.

On the other hand there was so much snow that we might be seriously delayed if we followed a less frequented road, on which there were no post-horses. These considerations made us hesitate to take the road through the Duchy of Warsaw, which from other points of view was the safer. If we were not to be delayed, however, it was necessary to make up our minds, so that we could order the horses. After weighing again the advantages and disadvantages of each arrangement, we came to a decision. I say we, because the Emperor refused to judge the question and insisted that I alone should decide—which, I confess, seemed to me a heavy responsibility, and worried me considerably. I took a chance, and sent [word] forward along the road to Königsberg, but left myself free to change direction at Mariampol if I heard that the roads through the Duchy were passable.

Fagalde was sent in advance as far as Gumbinnen [on the road to Königsberg]. It was not without some difficulty that we climbed the almost perpendicular slope which one must surmount on leaving Kowno for Mariampol. We were forced to get out and walk. As the horses were falling or losing their foothold at every moment, the carriage was several times on the point of running backwards and tumbling over the precipice. We heaved at the wheels, and at last reached Mariampol. I held a consultation with the master of the posting-house, an honest fellow full of zeal and good feeling. He assured me that the roads were passable, and that if we gave him two hours' start he would undertake to arrange relays of horses for us as far as Warsaw, going by Augustowo. The desire to meet his despatches from France en route made the Emperor incline a little toward the road by Königsberg; but he left the final choice to me. I did not hesitate. I sent instructions to Fagalde to rejoin us at Posen; and I sent the post-master along the road to Warsaw with instructions to order horses in my name as far forward as Pultusk, where he was to wait for us. He had seen the Emperor before, and so recognized him when we first arrived; he promised me, however, not to mention his name, and he kept to his word. The Emperor spoke to him, which delighted him.

We set out an hour behind him, and found peasants' horses everywhere; but, as our carriage was on wheels and there was no time to fit runners on it, we were unable to get through the snow, which was piled up everywhere to a considerable height. The couriers' sleighs, on the other hand, flew over the surface.

Chance led me to discover a covered sledge at the first relay station. This was a piece of good fortune, in view of the Emperor's impatience to reach his journey's end. The gentleman who owned the sledge was glad to let me have it for a few gold pieces. The Emperor and I took our places in it. We left the carriage in charge of the footman, who had gallantly stuck by it, seated on the flunkey's step. The Emperor hardly gave us time to transfer our rugs and arms; for lack of space in the sledge, he was even forced to abandon the toilet equipment which was so useful to him.[3] The seats were uncomfortable, we were poorly supported against the jolts of the road, and the air was close; the Emperor, for the sake of arriving sooner, had sacrificed everything which makes a long journey endurable. Henceforward we travelled much more easily; we even made time. The Grand Marshal, who had again caught up with us at Mariampol, now fell behind us in the first mile we covered beyond the town. Thereafter we never saw again either a carriage or a man of all that had left Smorgoni with the Emperor.

The Emperor had become very cheerful as soon as we entered the Duchy,[4] and had been talking incessantly about the army and about Paris. He had no doubt that the army would remain at Wilna, and did not in the least recognize the extent of his losses.

"Wilna is well stocked with food, and will put everything to rights again," he said to me. "There are more supplies than it will take to stop the enemy. The Russians will be at least

[3] "The berline [mounted on sleigh-runners] was harnessed without delay, and the Emperor took his seat in it, together with the Duke of Vicenza and Count Wonsowicz. The Mameluke [Roustam] was put on the driver's seat. . . . General Lefebvre-Desnouettes alone was able to follow, in a little sleigh which he had promptly obtained."—Bourgoing, *Souvenirs*, 194.

[4] The Emperor had entered the Duchy of Warsaw by crossing the Niemen at Kowno.

as tired as we are, and suffer just as much from the cold; they are certain to go into cantonments. Nothing will be seen of them but Cossacks. The orders and recommendations I left with M. Bassano will anticipate everything that can come up. Maret is confident of Schwarzenberg's sense of honour, and says he will hold his position and defend the Duchy. M. Bassano has written to him, as well as to Vienna and Berlin."

The Emperor was anxious only about the effect that our reverses had had upon those two courts. He felt, though, that his return to Paris would restore his political ascendancy.

"Our disasters," he said, "will make a great sensation in France; but my arrival will counter-balance their bad effects."

He planned to take advantage of his passage through Warsaw to bring the Poles to life.

"If they really want to be a nation, they'll rise in a body against their enemies," he added. "And if they do, I shall take up arms to defend them. Later on I should be able to grant Austria those concessions she has so much at heart; then we could proclaim the re-establishment of Poland. Austria has a greater interest in that than I have, because she lies nearer to the Colossus of Russia. If the Poles don't do as they should, that will simplify things for France and for everyone else; for peace with Russia will then be easy."

He chose to believe, or at least tried to make me think so, that all the cabinets of Europe, even those most wounded in pride by the power of France, were anxious that the Cossacks should not be allowed to cross the Niemen.

"The Russians should be viewed by everyone as a scourge," he said further. "The war against Russia is a war which is wholly in the interests—if those interests are rightly judged— of Old Europe and of civilization. The Austrian Emperor and M. Metternich realize this so well that they often said as much to me at Dresden. Emperor Francis understands perfectly the weak and shifty character of Tsar Alexander, and mistrusts him, having already been deceived by his protestations and tricked by his promises. The Viennese government understands perfectly that, apart from Russian contact with Austria over a long frontier, and all the divergent interests arising from such a situation, Russia's designs upon Turkey made her doubly dangerous. The reverses that France has just suffered will put an end to all jealousies and quiet all the anxieties that may have sprung from her power or influence. Europe should think of only one enemy. And that enemy is the Russian Colossus."

I answered the Emperor frankly.

"As a matter of fact, it is Your Majesty they fear. It is Your Majesty who is the cause of everyone's anxiety and prevents them from seeing other dangers. The governments are afraid there is going to be a World State. Your dynasty is already spreading everywhere, and the other dynasties are afraid they will see it established in their own countries. Even now all the German interests are being hurt by the system of taxation adopted three years ago. And the political inquisition set up by certain tactless representatives offends national opinion, wounds everyone's self-respect, and runs counter to all their habits of thought. All these causes and considerations, which are perhaps partly hidden from Your Majesty, make their hatred of you a national force. And what has stirred up the people, even more than it has the governments, is the military régime imposed upon Germany under the administration of the Prince of Eckmühl." [5]

The Emperor was so far from checking my frankness that he listened and replied not only without anger but with sly good-humour. From the way in which he received and discussed several of my remarks, one would have thought they did not touch him at any point. He smiled at the things which

[5] Since January 1, 1810, Davout had been in command of the Army of Germany which, after November 1, 1811, was called the Army of Observation of the Elbe.

came closest to him, and kept up the air of taking them in good part and of wishing to encourage me to say all I had on my mind. At the things which doubtless seemed to him rather strongly expressed, he tried to tweak my ear; but he could not find it under my fur cap, and so my neck or my cheek received the pinch—a kindly rather than an irritable one. He was in such a good mood that he admitted the truth of some of the points I brought forward. Others he refuted. Concerning still others he remarked that particular interests might here and there have been disturbed by police measures, or by combinations of circumstances which had nothing to do with the end he had in view. The people, however, were too enlightened, he said, not to see, from the very administrative system of the countries he had merged together, that our laws, under which they now lived, offered real guarantees to every citizen against all arbitrary action. He insisted that our administration was based upon principles that were broadly conceived, noble, adapted to the ideas of the century, and suited to the real needs of the people. He went on to say:

"I could treat them like conquered countries, but I administer them like Departments of France. It is wrong of them to complain. It is the checks on trade that irk them. But those depend on considerations of a higher order, to which the interests of France must also yield. Only peace with England can end those inconveniences and their complaints. They need only be patient. Two years of persevering effort will bring about the fall of the English government. England will be forced to conclude a peace consistent with the commercial rights of all nations. Then they will forget the inconveniences they complain of; while the consequent prosperity, and the state of affairs that will then be established, will for the most part provide means for the prompt repair of all their losses."

The Emperor complained that in these days everyone obstinately refused to look beyond the little circle of his own difficulties. Even the most capable men held to this narrow range of vision. Whereas it needed no more than a little good-will to realize all the advantages they were on the point of enjoying as a result of a larger view. All the sacrifices had been made; it needed only patience to gather in the harvest. It was not given to everybody to judge the new road he had pointed out. The System he had been forced to adopt against England could be judged, together with everything that followed from it, only after the passage of some years. It ran counter to too many habits, and damaged too many petty interests, not to stir up discontent in a lot of people. And it was of these malcontents that the forces of stupidity and blind hate were now taking advantage.

He added that the Continental System was nonetheless a great conception, and was destined to win the voluntary consent of every people; for it was as much to the interest of individuals as it was to the interest of the Continent as a whole. Prohibition against prohibitioners was common justice. Moreover, in his desire to establish on the Continent industries that would make it independent of England, he had had no choice of means; he had adopted the sole method which would really hit England's prosperity. It was a great undertaking; and only he could carry it out. If the present opportunity were allowed to pass, another would not come; for the enterprise had needed just that combination of circumstances which had in fact obtained in Europe during the last few years. He already had proof that he had not been mistaken, and could cite in support of his plea the flourishing condition of industry, not only in the original territory of France but also in Germany—and that, too, even though the wars were still going on.

The Emperor inferred from this that the Continental System had built up the industries of France and Germany. It would therefore, he said, be a source of wealth which would replace the foreign trade which we were at present missing. The benefit would be still more perceptible a little later. In less than three years the Rhineland, Germany, the very countries which were most hotly opposed to the prohibitions, would do justice to his foresight and his achievements. To have taught the French and the Germans that they could themselves earn the money which English industries had previously drawn out of the country, was a great victory over the London government. This result alone would immortalize his reign, through the internal prosperity it would bring to France and Germany.

The Emperor concluded from this that what I referred to as the colossus of the power of France was, at that time, a state of affairs wholly advantageous to Europe, since it was the only way to check the excessive pretensions of the English. England, he added, by the very fact that she weighed less heavily than he upon the chancelleries of Europe, weighed all the more heavily upon the people. For she seized for herself alone all the benefits of industrial development. As an island, she doubtless excited less jealousy and anxiety in the minds of governments that had no coast-lines. Her maritime ascendancy seemed for this reason less burdensome to the governments of Europe than the ascendancy of France. Her situation precluded the danger of territorial disputes with them. But her exclusive commercial policy was nonetheless damaging to individual interests. This fact was not willingly recognized at the present time because the various governments found it convenient to go to London for subsidies when they wanted them; and it mattered little to them if the cash they received had come from the pockets of their own subjects—or rather, had been earned at the expense of these subjects, whose industries would never be able to develop so long as the English monopoly continued.

The Emperor admitted that the annexation of Hamburg and of Lübeck,[6] towns whose independence was useful to commerce,

[6] The decree of the Senate dated December 13, 1810, in addition to regularizing the annexation of Holland, had joined with France the Hanseatic

must have alarmed the traders as well as the governments of Europe because these changes were thought to indicate a policy which would be continued.

But he justified these measures of expediency by the necessity of confronting England, along that coast, with our own rigid system of prohibition of imports. He added that, as he was in conflict with the actual trade of the towns, he must win over the sentiments of all thinking persons in the population. Constitutional government and our code of laws would bring about that change. Being unable to maintain an army of twenty-five thousand men in the new Departments, he had instituted governmental reforms to ensure us the confidence of the inhabitants. This step, he added further, which was wholly advantageous to the greatest number and in the true interest of the landowners, already counter-balanced the opposition of the maritime trading interests, which could not be expected to become friendly so long as they could not resume their activities and find outlets for their capital.

The Emperor's opinion was that, far from giving way on some points, he ought to strengthen every measure that might force England to make an earlier peace. He thought it better to suffer severely all at once than to suffer over a long time. Since the English tried every means to evade the prohibition of imports, in order to support their industries and uphold their credit, it was his duty to do all he could to triumph over their cunning, and force his enemy to yield.

"It is a battle of giants," he went on to say. "The seaport merchants are caught between the two champions. How could anyone help being jostled in the fight? But this fight to the death is in the interests even of the men who grumble. They will be the first to gather the fruits. The English have driven me, forced me, to every step I have taken. If they had not

towns and a large strip of territory extending as far as Lübeck. These annexations had been divided into ten Departments of France.

broken the Treaty of Amiens, if they had made peace after
Austerlitz, or after Tilsit, I would have stayed quietly at home.
Fear for my commercial capital would have kept me in check.
I should have undertaken nothing outside France, for it would
not have been to my advantage. I should have grown rusty and
easy-going. Nothing could be more delightful. I am no enemy
to the pleasures of life. I am no Don Quixote, with a craving
for adventures. I am a reasonable being, who does no more
than he thinks will profit him. The only difference between
me and other rulers is that difficulties can stop them. But I
like to overcome difficulties whenever it is clear to me that the
end in view is a great and noble one, worthy of myself and
of the people over whom I rule.

"If the English had let me," he repeated, "I would have lived
in peace. It is in their own interests alone that they have carried on the fight, and refused offers of peace; for if they had
acted in the interests of Europe they would have accepted them.
Holding Malta in the Mediterranean, and being in a position
to protect other points necessary for the safety of their trade
and the victualling of their fleet, what other claim could they
advance? What further security could they want? But it is
their monopoly they want to keep. They need an enormous
volume of trade if their customs-houses are to pay the interest
on their public debt. If the English were acting in good faith,
they would not so consistently have refused to negotiate. They
are afraid they would have to explain themselves, and they dare
not admit their designs. If we negotiated, they would have to
put their cards on the table. And then the world would see
which side had been acting in good faith.

"They say—and you are the first to say it, Caulaincourt—
that I abuse my power. I admit it, but I do it for the good of
the Continent at large. Now England thoroughly abuses her
strength, the power that comes from standing isolated among
the tempests. And she does so for her own good alone. The

good of that Europe which seems to envelop her with goodwill counts for nothing with the merchants of London. They would sacrifice every State in Europe, even the whole world, to further one of their speculations. If their debt were not so large they might be more reasonable. It is the necessity of paying this, of maintaining their credit, that drives them on. Some day they will certainly have to do something about that debt. Meanwhile they sacrifice the world to it. The world will realize that, in time; men's eyes will be opened; but it will be too late. If I triumph over them, Europe will bless me. If I fall, the English will soon drop their mask. The world will see that they have thought of nothing but themselves; that they have sacrificed the peace of a continent to their momentary interests.

"The Continent cannot—or rather, should not—complain of measures that aim at closing it, for the moment, against English trade. The annexations that have provoked such an outcry are temporary measures"; so he told me in confidence. "They are designed to inconvenience the English, to wreck their trade, to break off their trade relations. They are pledges which I hold in exchange for our colonies, or those of the Dutch, or certain claims which the English must give up for the general good."

Since peace could last and could promise a future for everyone only if it were general, it was wrong, according to the Emperor, to complain of all his efforts to achieve it. Clearsighted people and real politicians well knew what was his aim.

The Emperor asked me several times during the journey if I thought that Russia would make peace. He added that it would be wise of the Tsar Alexander to conclude it while he was enjoying some measure of success. I replied that I still doubted if he would negotiate so long as we were within his territory, and that the reverses we had suffered would not in the least incline him towards peace.

"So you think he is very proud?"

"I think he is obstinate. He may well be a little proud of having to some extent foreseen what has happened, and of having refused to listen to any proposals while we were at Moscow."

The Emperor took up the point:

"The burning of the Russian towns, the burning of Moscow, was merely stupid," he said. "Why use fire, if he relied so much on the winter? He has arms and soldiers for fighting. It is madness to spend so much money on them for nothing. One should not begin by harming oneself more than if one were beaten by the enemy. Kutusof's retreat was inept as it could be: it's the winter that has been our undoing. We are victims of the climate. The fine weather tricked me. If I had set out a fortnight sooner, my army would be at Witepsk; [7] and I should be laughing at the Russians and your prophet Alexander. He would be regretting that he did not negotiate. All our disasters hinge on that fortnight, and on the failure to carry out my orders for the levies of Polish Cossacks.

"Those prophetic proclamations of his were all nonsense. If they had wanted to draw us on into the interior they should have retired in the first place and not have endangered Bagration's army by spreading their forces over a line which, being too near the frontier, had to be too long. They should not have spent so much money building card-castles along the Dwina. They should not have collected so many stores there. They have been planning from one day to the next without settled scheme. They have never been able to fight to any purpose. But for the cowardice and stupidity of Partouneaux, the Russians would not have captured a single waggon from me at the crossing of the Beresina; and we should have cut off part of

[7] Napoleon was to return to this line of reasoning at St. Helena. On September 29, 1817, he said to Gourgaud: "My great mistake was in staying too long in that city [Moscow]. But for that, my undertaking would have been successful in the end."—Gourgaud, *Sainte-Hélène, Journal inédit de 1815 à 1818*, edited by Grouchy and Antoine Guillois, II, 337.

their advance-guard, taken eighteen hundred prisoners, and, with an army of wretches who had nothing left but their lives, we should have won a battle against the pick of their infantry, which has fought against the Turks. Actually, though, when the wreck of our army was surrounded by three of theirs, what did they do? They picked off the wretches who were dying of cold or whom hunger forced to break away from their units!"

On another occasion the Emperor remarked to me that if the Russians had really intended to draw him into the interior, they would not have marched to attack him at Witepsk; that from the beginning they should have harassed our flanks more. He said they should have waged only this guerilla warfare, intercepting our despatches, our smaller detachments, the officers who came out to join us, and the raiding parties. He regarded it as a serious fault to have given battle so near to Moscow.

"Everything turned out badly," the Emperor said to me on another occasion, "because I stayed too long at Moscow. If I had left four days after I occupied it, as I thought of doing when I saw the town in flames, the Russians would have been lost. The Tsar would have been only too glad to accept the generous peace which I should then have offered from Witepsk. Even from Wilna, if the cold hadn't robbed me of my army, I should have dictated the terms of peace; and your precious Alexander would have signed them, if only to be rid of the military guardianship of his boyars. It was they who thrust Kutusof upon him. And what has Kutusof done? He risked losing his army on the Moskowa, and brought about the burning of Moscow. During the retreat when he had nothing to fight against but lifeless troops, nothing but walking ghosts, what did he attempt? He and Wittgenstein permitted the crushing of the admiral.

"All the other Russian generals were worth more than that old dowager Kutusof. Tolly did at least spare the army: he did not fight with a capital at his back. Even Wittgenstein, who had just committed so many blunders so as not to put himself under the orders of the admiral or Kutusof, was far superior to him. If the King of Naples plays me no foolish tricks, if he supervises the generals and stays at first with the vanguard so as to encourage the younger troops, who will be a little scared, things will soon be righted again. The Russians will halt, and the Cossacks will keep their distance as soon as they see us show our teeth. If the Poles support me and the Russians don't make peace during the winter, you will see what has happened to them by July.

"Everything has conspired to cause my failure. I was not well served in Warsaw. The Abbé de Pradt was afraid: he played the busy-body instead of the *grand seigneur*. He looked after his own interests, and chattered in drawing-rooms and newspapers. But in public affairs—nothing. He roused no enthusiasm in the Poles. The levies were not made; I got nothing from all the resources I should have been able to rely on. Bassano bungled things in Poland as he did in Turkey and in Sweden. I was wrong to be angry with Talleyrand. The boudoir intrigues of the Duchess [8] irritated me against him; and now my affairs have miscarried. He would have given a much more definite direction to Polish effort. As it is, the Poles have immortalized themselves in our ranks, as individuals, but they have done nothing for their country. Everyone lauded this Abbé de Pradt to me. He has intelligence, but he's a muddler."

On another occasion the Emperor said to me, speaking of the Tsar Alexander:

"He is an intelligent prince, and full of good intentions. He is more capable than all his ministers. If he were less distrust-

[8] The Emperor was referring here to the Duchess of Bassano, as is proved by a later passage. She had indeed done everything possible to prevent Talleyrand from being appointed to the Embassy at Warsaw.

ful of his own powers he would be better than all his generals. He needs only decisiveness to be very capable indeed; but he is not master in his own house. He is continually hampered by a thousand petty considerations on account of his family, and of individuals, too. Although he takes a close interest in the army and gives a good deal of attention to it—perhaps more than I do, to questions of detail—yet he is deceived about these very things. Distance, custom, the opposition of the nobility to recruiting, and the interest that ill-paid commanders have in drawing pay and rations, all combine to keep the army from being up to strength. They had been working ceaselessly for three years to bring it up to strength; and as a result they had less than half the number of men under arms that they were supposed to have had before the day of battle came. You must admit you thought yourself that the army was much stronger than it was. I always thought you overestimated them, but you never would believe me.

"That Cossack at Ghjat was right when he said that the Russian generals valued their comfort and didn't know how to fight properly. One must do justice to the Cossacks. It is they who have achieved all the Russian successes in this campaign. They are certainly the best light troops in existence. That army might go a long way if the Russian soldiers had someone else to lead them."

At various times the Emperor discussed with me the sacrifices that peace would involve, and what the Russians would probably demand on behalf of the Duke of Oldenburg.

"They will want to re-establish him in his possessions," he said. "Alexander takes the matter very much to heart because of the dowager Empress."

Since he had asked my opinion, I put it to him that I found it difficult to suppose the Russians would not try to profit by the occasion, to the extent of obtaining the evacuation of Danzig and the other positions in the North which we had used as starting-points against them. I said that if we were obliged to abandon the Niemen, as I expected we should be, their demands would surely include the surrender of our fortified positions on the Oder. At this the Emperor cried out in protest that he would then lose all the advantages he had so far obtained against the English; that the main issue still was to force them to make peace, for without that there could be no lasting tranquillity. I replied that it might be possible to maintain the customs-organization in the ports and along the coast without turning them into French citadels.

"And the Russians?" he asked. "What attitude will they take with regard to England?"

"Your Majesty is in a better position to pronounce on that question than I," I replied. "But certainly you will not persuade them to put themselves in the same position that they were in before. I doubt if even the Tsar could do that."

"Then peace is impossible," the Emperor replied sharply, "if it is not to be general. One must not deceive oneself."

The conversation later turned on the situation in France and on the uneasy state of Europe, which I attributed to the invasions that had taken place. I suggested to the Emperor that a system of more modified power within more restricted limits would bind our allies to us, and even those States which would remain outside the system. I pointed out to him that from the Duke of Gotha to the Emperor of Austria, all the governments were frightened by the expansion of our political system; that they saw it as a step towards a universal monarchy, for which the war with England seemed to them a pretext.

The Emperor listened to me attentively, joked about my moderation, and repeated to me what he had said on other occasions about his intentions and his motives. He tried to prove to me that he was far from having in view those ends with which he was credited. He was working against the English alone;

since their trade had ramifications everywhere, he had to pursue them everywhere. He said it was the intrigues of the English, what he called *fides Punica,* which had continually forced him to extend his sphere of operations. He spoke of how needful it would always be for him to maintain a considerable army, as long as the struggle with the English continued, because their government was always working to stir up Europe against him—and so forth.

I spoke of the impression produced, even in France, by these frequent annexations of provinces and by these changes of allies which disturbed the loyalties of the people. I told the Emperor that instead of looking on these things as advantages, people were disturbed by them, and were made anxious about the future. And I added the following reflections on these points. These amazing extensions of power were, I thought, destructive to the feeling of stability, and actually prevented that feeling of confidence through which institutions acquire their sanctity. Even those who flattered him felt that while his genius might make these new structures last for his lifetime, they would never last beyond it. People did not dare to tell him so, but they thought so; and this opinion was all the more strongly held for being suppressed. It was felt that he was creating great difficulties for his son. He was arming Europe in advance against the King of Rome, and even against his family; and it was a pity, when founding a new dynasty, to give room for a growing expectation of some change. No one would be able to support the burden of that colossus which the course of events and the vigour of his rule were now setting in motion. These diverse nations would never make Frenchmen; the Rhinelanders already were finding it hard to persuade themselves that they had become French.

The Emperor admitted with absolute frankness the justice of my remarks. He did, however, rebut several of them:

"I shall create institutions," he said, "to strengthen the organization I have set up. No one can foretell what sacrifices I might not make—and even gladly—to secure such a state of affairs in Europe as would guarantee a lasting peace to all people, and which would guarantee to the French, and to the Germans, domestic prosperity such as the English enjoy. They are a worthy people, the Germans," he added. "They must be repaid for the sacrifices they have made. I am not clinging to Hamburg, or to any other place in particular. I am not one of those narrow-minded men who see things from only one point of view and are obstinate on a question. There will be many ways of arranging things as soon as the English make up their minds to peace, and agree to concede to others those rights and privileges which Heaven never intended for them alone. We can never make peace with the English unless we have compensations to offer them, because among them the ministry have a responsibility toward the people about which they must be set at rest. They cannot take so decisive a step as making peace with France unless they can say to the nation: 'We have made a certain sacrifice for such and such reasons; but here are the compensations made to us, and the advantages we have gained.' There is a delicate and difficult relationship between the country and the ministry, and still more so, therefore, between the ministry and myself. Without this English peace, however, all others are merely truces. The English are playing for too high stakes to give way lightly. They know very well that I shall take advantage of a peace to establish a navy—that I shall not allow ourselves to be robbed again of our commercial capital during a state of peace. They know that a navy in my hands could do them considerable damage. If they were sure I should live only three or four years more, they would make peace to-morrow; for the difficulty of the question lies in the navy that I shall have—that I shall build up within a few years."

He added further that he had greater need of peace than

anyone, and frankly desired it. How could anyone doubt that?
He did not live under canvas for his own pleasure. It was
the English who would not decide upon peace and who, according to him, might not be in a position to decide upon it,
being afraid of the future. The English ministry included some
clever men, who could not have overlooked any of the major
considerations of which he spoke. He was well aware that
the institutions of France were incomplete. He did not disguise
from himself that peace alone would put him in a position to
give them their full development. And who could doubt that
he desired peace, when only peace could consolidate this
achievement? In the forefront of those institutions he put the
Senate, which by no means enjoyed the independence it must
have if it were to command respect enough to influence the
opinion of the country. He told me that he would raise it to
the status of a Chamber of Peers.

The Emperor pointed out that the failure of this campaign
was an obstacle to everything. There had to be a buffer state
as an outpost against irruptions from the North, and to exercise
a moderating influence on the ambitions of other powers.
Europe owed its misfortunes to the weakness of the Bourbons
in allowing a partition of Poland. The Emperor of Austria
and the King of Prussia fully realized the mistake that had been
made. They had, quite openly, entered the war against Russia solely because they were the people most interested in the
creation of this barrier. The Austrians expected through these
arrangements to obtain a redistribution of territory which
would give them necessary outlets for their trade. The King
of Prussia flattered himself perhaps that the new state would
come under his rule.

The Emperor added further that the silence maintained by
the Russians towards the Austrians when the latter attempted
mediation, before the opening of the campaign, had left the

Emperor Francis in no doubt as to the ambitious intentions of the Tsar Alexander. Francis had told him so several times at Dresden. The Russian government snatched with both hands, from friends as much as from enemies. Everything looked good to them. After Tilsit they had profited at the expense of their allies the Prussians; after the war against Austria they had accepted a portion of Galicia. No delicate scruples ever hindered the Tsar from rounding off his territory.

The Emperor put forward the reflection that the Tsar, with his gentle methods and air of moderation, had done more for the interests of Russia than the ambitious Catherine whom they idolized; and that Finland was of far greater importance to an empire whose capital was at Petersburg than the uninhabited Crimea and all that which Catherine had conquered from the Turks.

The Emperor kept reverting to the idea that the Austrians desired the restoration of Poland, and that they were by no means set on retaining what remained to them of Galicia, adding that, at the Peace of Vienna, they would gladly have surrendered their millions of Galicians for a part of Illyria, no matter what, or for a few fragments of territory on the Inn. This arrangement could be made, therefore, whenever he wished.[9] His father-in-law had urged it upon him at Dresden, and indeed had probably come there in the hope of concluding the matter. He, however, had wished to be sure of the attitude of the Lithuanians, and to see for himself whether the Poles were capable of becoming and remaining an independent country. The result of this policy was that he had not yet set all the Poles free; and events were proving him right. He would soon be able to see whether they were as worthy of independence nationally as they were individually; for adversity steels a

[9] This was precisely the prize promised to the Austrians in the Treaty of Paris, March 14, 1812, as compensation for Galicia in the event of the restoration of Poland.

gallant spirit more than prosperity. He intended to speak
to that effect at Warsaw. He would tell the Poles all our misfortunes, and even all the dangers in which they stood. But
he would tell them also all that he hoped for, if they, as a
nation, would second him.

I pointed out to the Emperor that the lack of unity and zeal
of which he complained on the part of the Poles was surely
due to his leaving them in too great uncertainty about their
future. In practice there was no limit to the sacrifices asked
of them; the unfortunate Duchy, after furnishing supplies for
everything over a long period, seemed now to be exhausted,
and even the richest no longer had a penny to their names. I
reminded him that I had always appreciated the advantages
of this restoration, for it would form a buffer state; and held
that this motive was sufficient, as I had had the honour of telling
him in other circumstances, to justify the war against Russia.
But for several years, I, like many others, and even like some
of the Poles, . . . had seen in his references to Poland and
in the measures he had taken, only a method of arriving,
through that restoration, at a different goal. In fact, Poland
had become a military and political stepping-stone.

Moreover, I pointed out to him jokingly that everything he
told me about his conversations at Dresden with the Emperor
Francis, about his refusal to give up Illyria to the Austrians,
and indeed about all that had passed between M. Bassano and
M. Metternich, showed me that he wanted to hold over Austria
his power of giving or refusing, according to circumstances.
He wished always to be able to make use of the Poles, I told
him; to stimulate them with hopes, but not to make any undertaking so definite as to inconvenience his further plans or prevent him from adapting his course of action to future events.
I added that when Poland was once restored, the Poles would
show scant eagerness to supply us with troops to fight in Spain.
In fact it was perfectly plain that if he really had been guided

by those broad European considerations that demand a buffer state, he would at once have indemnified the Austrians for the loss of their Polish interests and proclaimed the restoration of Poland.

The Emperor replied with a smile:

"You make the same political calculations as the English." Then he added sharply: "But how was I to make peace with the Russians if they would not cede Lithuania? I could not bind myself to be at war all my life for this object. I certainly did want a restored Poland, but not a Poland whose king would tremble before the Russians and after a couple of years put himself under their protection. Under an elected king, the state could not maintain itself. It would be out of tune with the rest of Europe. Under a hereditary monarch the jealousy of the great houses would again have brought about its dismemberment. Do you suppose, for instance, that the Lithuanians would have reconciled themselves to a Poniatowski? The condition of the Court at Petersburg, and the protection of the ruler of a great empire, would always have suited them far better than the petty court of Mme. Tyszkiewicz at Warsaw.[10]

"Poland must be made into a powerful state by the addition of further provinces. It must have Danzig, and a coast-line, so that the country may have an outlet for its produce. And it must have a foreign king. A Pole would create too much jealousy. To name this king in advance would have cooled the zeal of the Poles, for they are none too sure themselves what they want. The Czartoriskis, the Poniatowskis, the Potockis, and a host of others, are full of pretensions. Murat would have suited them, but he has so little sense! Jerome, of whom I had thought, has no other quality but vanity; I've had nothing but blunders from him. He left the army because he would not serve under Davout, as though he did not owe his throne to the Battle of Auerstädt. His behaviour in the Duchy when he

[10] Constance Poniatowska, niece of King Stanislas.

passed through was regrettable. My family have never backed me up. My brothers are as full of pretensions as though they could say "The King, our father . . ."

Breaking off suddenly, the Emperor asked me:

"Whom would you have made king?"

I replied that as I had never made any kings, I was not prepared to answer him offhand.

The Emperor laughed, and said the choice was very difficult. I replied that I thought, even more definitely than he, that to establish his own dynasty on that throne would create yet another cause of anxiety in Europe; that it seemed to me very difficult even to hope for such a thing in the present state of affairs; that in any circumstances a member of his family on the throne of Poland would have been yet another obstacle to peace with the English, although in itself the creation of this buffer state would have suited their policy.

"In that regard you are quite right," the Emperor said.

The conversation gradually turned to past events, to Prussia and the Peace of Tilsit. I told the Emperor that, instead of destroying Prussia, it seemed to me he should have reconstructed it—even perhaps under the name of the Kingdom of Poland, if he thought it useful to revive that power. I said that he had there broken down the very buffer state which it was so useful to have in the centre of Europe; and that in his place I should freely have pardoned the Prussians, and reorganized their power on a larger scale and without the intervention of the Russians, in order to bring them within my system of alliances—a result which would certainly have followed from making Prussia Polish.

"The policy of the Prussians has always been so tortuous," said the Emperor, "and they have always shown such bad faith towards everyone, and have been so clumsy, that no government was genuinely interested in them. I hesitated for a moment whether to declare that the house of Brandenburg should no longer reign; but I had used the Prussians so severely that some consolation had to be left to them. And then Alexander took so much interest in the fate of that family that I gave in to his requests. I made a serious mistake; for I left the King enough power to keep him mindful of the power he has lost."

I replied that to change the ruling house, if he mistrusted it, was undoubtedly preferable to depriving Europe of a State whose power would continue indispensable to him, even if he insisted on taking that power out of the hands of the house of Brandenburg. The Emperor answered that it would have been difficult to make the Tsar Alexander take that view, though more on account of the King than on account of the country; and at that time his main and absolutely necessary object had been to close the Continent against the English. It was to achieve this that he had made the concession.

The Emperor complained yet again of his brothers. I pointed out that it was difficult not to desire complete independence from the moment that one became a king. Moreover, it was often necessary for their popularity in their own countries that they should resist the Emperor's demands. As my frankness did not seem unpalatable, I said that his intention was indeed to create kingdoms, but that in fact he only allotted his kings extended prefectures in place of independent States; and that, his kings being mere proconsuls, their position did not match with their title and the condition of their affairs. The Emperor smiled as though he found my remarks correct.

Probably the conversation did not displease him; he reverted to it five or six times during the journey, and I needed no urging to repeat the same views. The Emperor nearly always tried to bring me to his own opinion. He put patience and detailed care into the endeavour, discussing and reasoning as though I were some foreign power whom it would be to his advantage to persuade. Though his reasoning brought me to share his view on one or two points, in the main I held to my own. I

noticed that he passed lightly over points which he did not wish
to explain.   Then if I came back to them, he would say:

"You see things as a young man; you don't understand."

He also said at times, when my opinion was too much at
variance with his:

"You don't understand anything about public affairs."

Often he would not agree that things were as I represented
them.   In answer to the remarks which most directly attacked
his ambition and his passion for war, he smiled, joked, and
tried to get hold of my ear and pinch it—an action which my
fur bonnet always made difficult.   He would give me several
friendly taps on the neck, and say jokingly:

"They're wrong! I'm not ambitious. Long nights, fatigue,
war—I'm too old for all that. I like my bed and my rest as
well as anyone; but I want to finish my work. In this world
there are only two alternatives: command or obey. The attitude of all the governments towards France showed me that she
could count on nothing but her own power: which means, on
force. So I've been obliged to make her powerful, and to
maintain large armies. I did not pick a quarrel with the Austrians, when they grew alarmed about the fate of England and
forced me to leave Boulogne and fight the battle of Austerlitz.
I had not been threatening the Prussians, when they forced me
to go and dethrone them at Jena. But in any case, what is this
power they talk about? Nothing! The power of the whole
Continent is nothing so long as the flag does not protect trade.
The passports of the Duke of Gotha are respected at Paris as
they are at Weimar, but the Austrians cannot send out a felucca
loaded with Hungarian wine without the permission of the
Court of St. James.

"I have more foresight than the other rulers," the Emperor
added. "I want to take advantage of this opportunity to wind
up the old quarrel between England and the Continent. Similar
circumstances will never occur again. What seems to offend

no one but me to-day will offend the other rulers before long. Emotion and habits of thought are against me. The ministries are blinded by prejudice and favouritism. After a few years of harmful peace the nations and their rulers would realize their need. I am the only one who can see it now because the others are determined to shut their eyes to it. The power of the English, as it is at present, rests only upon the monopoly they exercise over other nations, and can be maintained only by that. Why should they alone reap the benefits which millions of others could reap as well? The proof that they exploit for themselves what should belong to others lies in the fact that they live only by their customs-houses, by their trading, and that their population cannot consume all that pays tax to them. Why should what others consume pay dues to London?

"If I were so weak as to give way on certain points in order to make an improper peace, the Continent would blame me for it within four years. There would be no time to change it then. All our wealth would be at sea; and the English—who would have taken advantage of the truce to fill their coffers and get their breath—would confiscate it all if we showed the least sign of provocation before certain governments had been roused by the howling of their merchants. Then ten years of war, of trouble and misfortune, with three or four coalitions formed and broken up, might not take us even so far as the point we have reached to-day. But posterity sums up without favour and will judge between Rome and Carthage. The verdict will be for the French. They are fighting now, whatever the world may say, only for the general good. It is therefore just that the flags of the Continent should stand in line with ours. The French are fighting for the most sacred rights of nations: the English are only defending their self-assumed privileges."

Returning later to this subject, the Emperor remarked to me that the more he studied the government of England the more innately vigorous it seemed to him. It had all the advantages possible to an oligarchy. It was strong in wealth and influence; it ruled the country with the support of the public opinion which it created itself through its many connections. He considered, moreover, that it drew added force even from the opposition— which, according to him, grew weaker every day because it only served to show the strength of its adversaries. According to the Emperor the ranks of the opposition would be still further thinned; for men starting on a career would for their own advantage take the side of power, which is also the side of Fortune. He was of opinion that, if the war continued, the English would fall within two years into a kind of bankruptcy, by reducing the rates of interest. And if peace were made, this bankruptcy would come within ten years unless the new conditions, which would follow on the great changes now about to take place in the New World, should offer the English an enormous outlet for their trade.

"In English affairs," he said, "everything depends on an imaginary factor. Their credit rests upon confidence, since they have nothing on which to secure it; although I admit the government has something even better, since all individual fortunes are wrapped up with those of the State. The system of continual borrowing, which continually links the present with the past, does in some degree compel confidence in the future. By involving everyone's fortunes in the fortunes of the State, their government has gained something better than the actual security it lacked; for by that means it has created an unlimited security in the shape of individual self-interest. That," the Emperor added emphatically, "is why we must have perseverance. The time is not far off when the ministry will not be able to raise loans so easily—or at least not such big ones. Then they will not be able to grant their subsidies, which have a great influence on the Continent. For, apart from France, the States of the Continent possess nothing but worthless paper;

only at London and Paris is there any money or any credit. At this moment, English affairs are at a crisis. Their trade is damaged. Doubtless the Russians, by opening their ports to them, are delaying the effect of the depression; but since the cause continues the evil hour is only postponed. The English have, it is true, considerable resources yet; but since with them everything depends upon confidence, the least thing may paralyze, endanger, and even destroy their whole system, in spite of the fact that there are among them some very capable men and citizens moved by a true love of their country."

The Emperor returned continually to the subject of England, which occupied his mind above everything else, and during one of our conversations he said to me:

"The people of Europe are blind to their real dangers. They pay heed to nothing but the inconvenience they feel on account of the war at sea. One might think that all the politics and all the interests of this unhappy Continent are bounded by the price of a cask of sugar. It is pitiable: yet that is how things stand. They protest only against the French, and refuse to see anything but the French armies—as though the English also were not present on every side, and more threatening by far. Heligoland, Gibraltar, Tarifa, Malta—aren't all those English citadels? Don't they threaten the trade of all the powers much more than Danzig threatens the trade of Russia? Yet if I gave the people of Europe their head, they would deliver themselves into the hands of the English. Next day they would let the English have Corfu—yes, and Madeira—just as they have already given them the Cape. Yet from the rocks of Malta the English already control Turkey, and consequently the Black Sea and Russia also. At Gibraltar they hold the entrance to the Mediterranean. If they could seize Corfu they would have a foothold in Greece, and be masters even of the gulf. [The Adriatic.]

"The situation leaps to the eye; yet the Austrians will not, any more than the Russians, admit the dangers that threaten them.

Jealousy of France is stronger than reason. They refuse to
exercise any foresight. But for me, the European governments
would grant the English to-morrow the supremacy they desire.
When all trade protection is subject to the whims of the London government—when we are forced to eat no sugar but of
their selling, and to wear only stockings and cloth of their manu-
facture—then Petersburg, Vienna, and Berlin will grasp the
fact that the English have a monopoly. Until then they will
shut their eyes to it, for fear of recognizing that I am defending the interests of all of us alike. The fact is plain to people
of goodwill. But where is there any goodwill? The blindness
of European politics is pitiable."

The same trend of conversation led us on another occasion
to discuss the outlets that the English had secured for their
trade; and the outlets they were seeking, and would secure, in
the Spanish colonies brought us finally to the war in the Peninsula.

"Doubtless it would have been better," the Emperor said to
me, "to have wound up the war in Spain before embarking on
this Russian expedition—though there is much room for discussion on the point. As for the war in Spain itself, it is now
a matter only of guerilla contests. On the day the English are
driven out of the Peninsula, there will be nothing left of the
war but isolated bodies of rebels; and one cannot hope to clear
a country of those in a month or two.

"Since the opposition to the new régime comes from the
lower classes, only time and the conduct of the upper classes—
assisted by a strong and cautious government which has the
support of a national gendarmerie and, at the same time, of
the presence of some French troops—will calm the storm. Their
hatred will wear out when they see that we bring them only
wiser laws; a code more liberal, and better suited to the times
in which we live, than the ancient customs and the Inquisition

by which the country used to be governed. At present the Spaniards are fighting because they still believe that we want to
make Frenchmen of them. Everything will settle down as soon
as we can persuade them that it is to our interest that they
should continue to be Spaniards. But for the disasters in Russia the time would be drawing near when the French troops
would not need to occupy more than a few fortified points in
certain provinces. If the peasants saw no more French troops
about the countryside, if they were governed only by their own
governors and controlled only by Spanish police, confidence
would be established, and this would lead to a spread of peace
and reconciliation."

According to the Emperor the presence of the English army
was the greatest obstacle to the pacification of Spain; but he
would rather see it in that country than be threatened with it,
at any moment, in Brittany or Italy, or anywhere, in fact, where
the coast was accessible. As it was, he knew where to look for
the English; whereas if they were not occupied there he would
be forced to prepare for them, and hold himself ready for defence against them, at every point. And that would use up
many more troops, give him much more anxiety, and possibly
do him much more damage.

"If thirty thousand English landed in Belgium," he said to
me, "or in the Pas-de-Calais, and requisitioned supplies from
three hundred villages—if they were to go and burn the château
of Caulaincourt—they would do us much more harm than by
forcing me to maintain an army in Spain. You would make
a much worse outcry, my good Master of Horse! You would
complain much more loudly than you do when you say that I
aim at universal monarchy! The English are playing into my
hands. If the ministry were in my pay, they could not act in
a way more favourable to me. You must take good care not
to repeat the ideas I express to you; for if the idea entered
their heads to make expeditions against my coasts, now at one

point and now at another—to re-embark as soon as forces were collected to fight them, and go at once to threaten some other point—the situation would be insupportable.

"As it is," he added, "the war in Spain costs me no more than any other war, or any other compulsory defence against the English. So long as peace is not made with that power, there is not much difference in cost between the present state of affairs in Spain and an ordinary state of war with England. In view of the great length of Spain's coast-line, and with the situation as it now stands, we must limit ourselves to keeping the English under observation—unless, indeed, they should march into the interior, or unless a highly favourable opportunity should arise for giving battle; for if we forced them to re-embark at one point, they would disembark again at another, since they would always be sure of finding auxiliaries.

"The marshals and generals who have been left to look after themselves in Spain might have done better; but they will not come to an agreement. There has never been any unity in their operations. They detest each other to such an extent that they would be in despair if one thought he had made a movement that might reflect some glory on another. Accordingly there is nothing to be done except hold the country and try to pacify it, until I can myself put some vigour into the operations there. Soult has ability: but no one will take orders. Every general wants to be independent, so as to play the viceroy in his own province. In Wellington," he added, "my generals have encountered an opponent superior to some of them. Moreover, they have made childish mistakes. Marmont shows a really high quality of judgment and logic in discussing war, but is not even moderately able in action. In fact, our momentary reverses in that war, which delight the city of London, have little effect on the general course of affairs—and cannot indeed have any real importance, since I can change the face of affairs whenever I please.

"Events at present," he said, "are giving Wellington a reputation; but in war men may lose in a day what they have spent years in building up. As to the outlet for English trade which the war has created in the Spanish colonies, I admit that that is certainly unfortunate; for within two years those outlets may counter-balance our prohibition of imports on the Continent."

The Emperor saw, in the separation of these colonies from their mother country,[11] an important development which would change the politics of the world, which would give new strength to America, and in less than ten years would threaten the power of the English—which would be a compensation. He did not question that Mexico, and all the major Spanish possessions overseas, would declare their independence and form one or two nations under a form of government which would force them, in their own interests, to become auxiliaries of the United States.

"It marks a new era," he said. "It will lead to the independence of all other colonies."

The changes that would arise from this development he regarded as the most important of the century, since they would shift the balance of commercial interests and, in consequence, alter the policy of the different governments.

"All the colonies," he said, "will follow the example of the United States. You grow tired of waiting for orders from five thousand miles away; tired of obeying a government which seems foreign to you because it is remote, and because of necessity it subordinates you to its own local interest, which it cannot sacrifice to yours. As soon as colonies feel strong enough to resist, they want to shake off the yoke of those who created them. One's country is where one lives; a man does

[11] Mexico in September, 1810, Venezuela, New Granada, Chile, and the Argentine, in 1810 or 1811, had all gone into more or less open revolt against the dominion of Spain. Paraguay had declared its independence in 1811.

not take long to forget that he or his father was born under another sky. Ambition achieves what self-interest has begun. They want to have a standing of their own; and then the yoke is soon thrown off."

I spoke to the Emperor of the moral effect which the resistance of the Spanish nation was having on people in general, and suggested to him that he was mistaken in attaching no importance to the example they were setting. I reminded him of the remark of the Tsar Alexander, which had struck me and which I had repeated to him on my return: "You have beaten the Spanish armies but you have not subdued the nation. The nation will raise other armies. The Spaniards, without any government, are setting a noble example to other nations. They are teaching the sovereigns what can be accomplished by perseverance in a just cause."

The Emperor treated as a joke what he called "the maxims of the prophet of the North." He added, however:

"Although he made many mistakes—or, at least, allowed his generals to make them—the Tsar Alexander is the only one [among the rulers] who has shown good judgment, and made a sound estimate of his position and of the course of events. That prince has more intelligence than men think; and he has good judgment. His misfortune lies in being so poorly seconded."

Returning to affairs in Spain, the Emperor said:

"It is easy to pronounce judgment upon what is past; and easy to exalt as heroism what pertains to causes that are in truth hardly honourable. The heroism with which, in their hatred of France, they now credit the Spaniards, arises simply out of the barbarous condition of that half-savage population and out of the superstitions to which the mistakes of our generals have given new vigour. It is out of laziness, not out of heroism, that the Spanish peasant prefers the dangers of a smuggler's life, or a highwayman's, to the labours of cultivating the soil. The Spanish peasants have seized the opportunity of taking up this nomadic, smuggler's existence which is so well suited to their taste and to the relief of their extreme poverty. There's nothing patriotic about that."

The Emperor cited, in support of his dictum, that armies of fifty thousand Spaniards gave ground and took to flight before much smaller forces, because the Spaniards would only go into danger where there was hope of booty.

"The Romans and the Spartans," he added, "had other aims. They faced death for other motives. The land of their fathers meant something to them; but the wretched Spaniard is only moved by the attractions of booty. Anything is better than the miserable existence he leads in his own village. It is nothing but bias that has pompously ascribed nobility to a course of action whose objects have never been honourable, although the result may be useful at the moment to the cause they think the Spaniards are defending. The Spaniard of to-day is still the same as in the time of the Romans; like a savage, he hates the foreigner—or, rather, whatever is unfamiliar to him. He hates anything that tends to bring him out of his state of barbarism. The Spanish peasantry have even less share in the civilization of Europe than the Russians.

"It is true," he went on, "that the proximity of the Spanish Bourbons to my own dynasty, which sits on the throne of Louis XVI, seemed to me a state of affairs which was likely to prove inconvenient. I often discussed it with Talleyrand, as I did so many other questions which are involved in the broader interests of the world. For a long time, however, I did not think that it bore directly upon the affairs of the moment; for it seemed to me very clear that the obstinate stupidity of the King, controlled as he was by Godoy, the 'Prince of Peace,' would keep the country from any development that might cause me anxiety. Accordingly I had no other intention than to make Spain useful to me against the English. The weakness of the King—

combined with the interests of his favourite, who would wish, I thought, not to be in bad odour with the French—suited my policy too well for me to have any thought of other arrangements.   And then suddenly, roused no doubt by the mutterings of Castilian pride which had been wounded by some proposal, or by some clumsiness on the part of our diplomatic representatives, the King felt the moment favourable to regain the respect of the Spaniards by calling them out against me, to whom he was thought to have sold himself.   The fool!   At the moment when his favour was disappearing in a general outcry against him, he thought to save himself by rousing the nation in the very direction of its discontent; and in trying to save himself he lost Spain.   And Murat, in his turn, lost Spain for me by trying to save the favourite.   For in the Madrid rebellion the nation was angry only against Godoy; they only looked upon us as enemies because Murat tried to save him and by this tactlessness gave the nation ground for believing what ill will whispered against us: that we were partners with Godoy, or he with us."

The Emperor discussed Godoy's insolent proclamation to the Spaniards—the proclamation of October 3, 1806.[12]

"The behaviour of the favourite," he said to me, "seemed a little suspicious even before Jena.   It would have seemed thoroughly suspicious if my ambassador had been a capable man and had kept me informed of what was happening in Spain; but I was not well served.   Amazed to find then an opposition to which I was not accustomed in that cabinet, I was on my guard.   This change of policy even made me wish to arrange the differences which had arisen with Prussia, although otherwise I should have made haste to pick up the gauntlet

[12] In this proclamation Godoy, the "Prince of Peace," summoned the Spaniards to arms without, however, telling them what enemy threatened them.   Cf. Geoffroy de Grandmaison, *l'Espagne et Napoléon*, Paris, 1908, I, 67.—Godoy's proclamation was not posted in Madrid until October 15, the day after the battle of Jena.

which the Prussian court threw down at such an ill-judged moment. I could see there was some discontent among the Spaniards but I thought only their vanity was wounded, which I could have soothed at a later date; and I confess I was a long way from thinking that I should receive a declaration of war from the favourite. I though him better advised."

The Emperor added that he had been amazed at receiving, after Jena, this strange proclamation, by which he was not misled for a moment. He went on:

"Not being able to disguise from myself the intentions of this new enemy, I disguised my attitude from him. Although the success I had just gained stood me in as good stead as I could have wished, and although, being more subtle in politics than Godoy, I had myself provided him, for the moment, with the means to explain everything to me so as to think me satisfied, yet I promised myself to take a startling revenge upon him at the first opportunity, or, at the least, to put the Spanish court in such a position that it could not prove an embarrassment to me on any future occasion.

"This behaviour opened my eyes," the Emperor remarked to me more than once; and he added: "The 'Prince of Peace' might have caused me some grey hairs on the day before Jena, but on the day after I was master of the circumstances. For a moment I thought the Spaniards more decided than they seemed and my ambassador their dupe; but that anxiety didn't last. Godoy was more fatal to Spain on the one occasion when he showed some energy than by all his weakness, and the dishonour with which publicly, and for years, he had stamped his master. He did not stop to realize that when a man in his position draws his sword against a sovereign ruler, he must conquer or die; for though kings may forgive each other their injuries, they have not and should not have the same indulgence towards subjects. He should have seen that there could be no possible pardon for a man, who, like himself, had no roots in the land; neither reason nor policy would allow of it. He made a sacrifice of Spain in order to continue the favourite; and the Spanish sacrificed themselves in order to be revenged on him and on those whom they wrongly believed were his supporters. In a state of revolution, rumour and popular hatred can strike roots. Once the first gun is fired, there are no more explanations; passions rise and men who cannot agree kill each other."

[Here the Emperor reviewed the story of the intrigues, French, Spanish and Portuguese, which led to the removal of the Bourbons from the Peninsula, and to the placing of Joseph Bonaparte on the Spanish throne. The Emperor's argument was that he never had wished to deal with the quarrelling Bourbons—Charles IV and Marie-Louise, and their son Ferdinand— at Bayonne in 1808, nor thereafter to compel the abdication of their rights.]

". . . There were three courses I might have followed in this affair. I chose the one which was indicated to me by my concern for the well-being of Spain and our own interests. Of the others, the second would have made me accessory to a crime, and the last accessory to the humiliation of a nation which was trying to throw off the disgrace of the previous reign. I could not hesitate over the choice; and it was these considerations that prevented me from sending those princes back to Spain, as my own interests advised. Ferdinand would soon have exhausted the enthusiasm of the nation; and his father's return would have humiliated him so badly that he would certainly have turned to me and called me to his aid within six months. But C—— and M——[13] thought it would be best to take advantage of the moment when everything was ripe, and the change all the easier to bring about, because the Bourbons had suc-

[13] Only these initials appear in the manuscript. It is safe, however, to read them as Champagny and Maret, of whom the first was then Minister of the Interior and the second Secretary of State.

ceeded in discrediting themselves at Bayonne—even in the eyes of those Spaniards who were most devoted to their cause. Murat told me fairy-tales, which also led me into error. I thought to cut short the misfortunes of the country: I was mistaken. If I had followed my own instinct, I should have sent those princes home. To-day, Spain would have been at my feet.

"I was misled—or rather, the course of events defied all human foresight. Could one have foreseen that Murat would commit nothing but stupidities, and Dupont an act of cowardice? [The surrender at Baylen, July 22, 1808.] The Spanish will one day regret the loss of the constitution I gave them. It would have given the country new life. It was Dupont's greed, his grasping spirit, his desire to preserve at all costs his ill-gotten fortune, which led to the Spanish revolt.

"The surrender at Baylen ruined everything. In order to save his waggons of booty, Dupont committed his soldiers, his own countrymen, to the disgrace of a surrender which is without parallel—and to the disgrace, so damaging in its effect on the Spanish people, of giving proof of the acts of sacrilege and church-robbery that their general had tolerated in order to cover his own depredations. When Dupont stipulated that the soldiers' packs should be examined and his own waggons go untouched, he wrote his own shame into the pages of history forever. These are the Caudine Forks of our history. The sight of the stolen objects was the signal for the rising; and the ring-leaders made use of them to incite the superstitious people to vengeance."

Returning to the affairs of Spain in general, the Emperor said that intelligent people, those who knew something of him, would never suspect him of having wished to debase the sovereign authority.

"I look at these things from a higher standpoint," he went on. "I am too conscious of my strength to stoop to such intrigues, so far beneath my character. I proceed more frankly. It would be a more reasonable reproach, perhaps, to say that

I shape my policy as a torrent shapes its course. While you were at Petersburg, you must have heard the details of the revolt from the Russian envoy to Madrid, and from Tchernychev, who came to Bayonne; for the Emperor Alexander, who for a long while refused to recognize King Joseph, did in time come to realize that I had nothing to do with those intrigues."

The Emperor discussed M. Talleyrand:

"He boasts that the disfavour in which he thinks himself held arises from his supposed opposition to the war in Spain. In truth, he didn't urge me to it at the moment when it began, for I was myself far from seeing the events which afterwards took place and which brought it about; but no one was more convinced than he that the co-operation of Spain and Portugal and even the partial occupation of those States by our troops was the only way of forcing the London government to make peace. He was so strongly of this opinion that that was his object in negotiating with Isquierdo the treaty Duroc signed at Fontaine-bleau. Talleyrand was the moving spirit of those negotiations, although he held no office. This method of forcing the English to make peace—peace with the object of securing the evacuation of those States—seemed to him imperative.

"He brought great energy to bear on the situation, too, when the departure of the Court of Lisbon for Brazil altered all our plans. It was he who sent Isquierdo to Madrid. If it were not that he had a great interest in the success of that journey, I should have suspected him of contributing to the anxiety that came upon the King when his agent arrived at Madrid.

"Talleyrand, realizing later that he had been mistaken in the hopes of fortune and influence that he had built upon these treaties, and realizing that I was doing without him, thought himself tricked. Being a clever man, he has since attempted nothing but to justify himself in the eyes of the public for the part he is known to have taken in this affair; and he has constituted himself the apostle of discontent.

"He forgets that he also conceived the idea, previously, of deposing the dynasty in Spain as we had done in Etruria. I am far from reproaching him for that. He has good judgment. He is the most capable minister I have ever had. Talleyrand was too well-informed about public affairs, and too good a politician, to admit that the Bourbons could return to Madrid when there were no longer Bourbons at Paris or Naples. Time might perhaps have brought about this change without violence; the interests of France, and even those of Spain if rightly understood, pointed in that direction. There was never anything settled on the point: an infinite range of conjecture, as on all the more far-reaching political questions—and that was all.

"Talleyrand saw and pointed out to me all that intelligent people were thinking and that policy demanded. In a difficult position, in a war against a section of Europe, could the French take the risk of having a hostile dynasty on their flank? Talleyrand, who is among those who have done most to establish my own dynasty, was too much concerned in its maintenance, too clever, too far-seeing, not to advise everything which would tend to its preservation and to the preservation of tranquillity in France. He sided against that war only because he was not made a minister with plenary powers, as he had hoped. Forgetting then that it was French blood which was being spilt in Spain, he began, like a bad citizen, to preach against the affair more loudly as he saw it taking a bad turn. With him, as with many people, one would need to be always successful. I knew what he was up to—and I made him feel that I did—because his ill will began with the defeat of Dupont. Like a coward, he threw stones at me when he thought I was beaten.

"Everything that has been done against the Bourbons has been done under his ministry and at his suggestion. It was he who kept preaching to me about how necessary it was to take

all political influence away from them. It was he who persuaded me to have the Duke of Enghien arrested, to whom I
did not give a thought until the prefect Shée and the English
intrigues of Drake [at Munich] drew the attention of the police
upon him. At the time I was far from attaching the least importance to his stay on the banks of the Rhine, and consequently
I was far from having any settled intentions with regard to
him. It was either Moncey or Shée who then told me that he
often came to Strasbourg. I had not known of it. Berthier
and Cambacérès were doubtful about having him arrested, on
account of the court of Baden. Talleyrand insisted: and so did
Murat and Fouché.[14]

"Taken in by the revolutionaries, and urged on by them,
Murat, alarmed by Fouché and Rœderer, saw no safety for
himself or for me, as soon as he heard of the Duke's arrival
in Paris, except in his execution. To listen to him, one would
have thought the government was threatened and the Commandant of Paris in danger. He's a brave man on the battle field,
Murat, but he has no head. He likes only intriguers, and is
always taken in by them. All the men who had taken part in
the Revolution—the generals, the men bred in republican ideas
—were disturbed by my advance to power. The royalists, intriguing still and clumsy, spread the rumour, without giving
much thought to it, that I was going to play the rôle of Monk.
I was not steady in my seat. To hear Murat, Fouché and the
rest, one would have thought that public opinion was drifting
out of my control; that in this uncertainty no party supported
me; that the weak royalist party regarded me as only a tran-
sitional figure. No party, moreover, could achieve anything.
The nation then would be against me; the revolutionaries were

[14] In the Council held on March 9, 1802, at which were present the three
Consuls, the Chief Justice, Talleyrand, and Fouché, "the two leaders of
the opposing parties were M. Talleyrand and M. Cambacérès. M. Talleyrand advised the utmost rigour against the Prince."—Pasquier, *Mémoires*,
I, 178.

afraid of me, but still more afraid of the Bourbons. They scared Murat, and made him lose his head.

"For my own part, they made no great impression on me. I protected them because it is the duty of the government to protect everyone, without distinction. I myself looked at things from a higher standpoint than the rest, and was no more inclined than usual to seek support among the parties; but I felt that France needed a government which would embody the results of her sacrifices and the glory she had won—a government whose concern it would be to create confidence and security for all the nation's interests, within and without the country. I felt that I was the Strong Man, designed by my nature to preside over these great destinies. I was not so foolish as to work for others when I felt myself the only man equal to the demands of the French people. I had read my history; and I was no more eager to put France at the mercy of vengeful émigrés than I was to raise to power men who would show no gratitude—not when I knew myself competent to keep everything in hand.

"So I took a stand. I prepared everything for the reorganization of a monarchy. It is the only form of government suitable for France, and the only one which can keep the European monarchs quiet. They needed me; experience had proved to me that I was not mistaken there. As for the Duke of Enghien, I believed him of no great importance at the time I sent Ordener to arrest him. I thought they would take Dumouriez as well, which was of more concern to me; for his name lent the air of a major conspiracy to the plot. I was within my rights, because the Bourbon Prince was conspiring against me, as were Georges Cadoudal and the others. All these intrigues were interconnected.

"They caught Enghien fifteen miles beyond my frontier, *flagrante delicto*, while the assassins hired by his family, urged on by him and by the English minister at Stuttgart, were arrested in France, sword in hand. You ought to know this,

Caulaincourt. Weren't you instructed to effect a reconciliation between ourselves and Baden over the violation of the territory?"

I answered yes, and that some charitably minded people had even attributed the Prince's arrest to me.

"That is notoriously untrue," replied the Emperor. "The chief of the gendarmes even denounced you at the time as having secretly warned the Prince that Ordener intended to arrest him, and as being the cause of his having tried to shoot Ordener and nearly killing him. I didn't believe a word of it."

The Emperor added that, having given orders for the Prince to be brought to Paris, he was rather undecided as to what policy he should adopt. However, Murat, urged on by the revolutionaries, had so impressed upon him that all would be lost if he did not make an example, that, without giving his positive consent, he had sent orders that the prince should be tried by a military commission. This, he reflected, was only a legitimate precaution on his part. The Prince asked to see him, and even wrote asking for an audience, but he only learned this after sentence had been carried out.

"This haste on the part of Murat," the Emperor continued, "was the reason why the police had no time to question Enghien, and therefore missed some important intelligence concerning other branches of the conspiracy. Berthier and Cambacérès would have preferred that he not be arrested at all, and above all that he not come to Paris, since they felt that, directly he was there, the situation would become awkward and even embarrassing for me, faced as I was by the nation whom I must leave in no doubt as to my intentions. Their common sense told them that I should have to show severity, and at the same time they veered towards leniency. Talleyrand, more politic than they, was quite properly in favour of the arrest. No account was taken then of what effect the execution would have upon the people; nothing was seen but some conspirators who wanted to assassinate the First Magistrate of France, and so deserved the same fate.

"Although there was a good deal of gossip in Paris about the whole business, I should do the same thing should a similar case arise.[15]

"All the same, it is possible that I might have shown mercy had Murat let me know of the Prince's request. Enghien certainly would not have perished if I had received it, even though the law was mandatory that condemned him, no motive being strong enough to authorize his conspiracies on our frontier and his hiring sixty ruffians to have me murdered. It is not I who have dethroned the Bourbons; they really have no one but themselves to blame. Instead of chasing them out and ill-treating their friends, I have offered them pensions and paid off their servants. They have answered my kindness by arming assassins. Blood calls for blood. However, I have always rejected the proposals made to me. At a million a head I could have found people who struck with greater precision than their conspirators; but such methods were beneath me. Had I known of a plot against their lives, I should have had them warned. I showed mercy to Polignac and Rivière because they were conspirators by nature, and because public morals had been sufficiently avenged by the execution of mere assassins.

"It is not I, it is not even the leaders of the Revolution, whom the Bourbons should blame for their expulsion; Coblentz was the cause of the King's death. There are documents in the archives which leave no doubt on that score. They disclose

[15] It is known that even in his testament (April 15, 1821) Napoleon maintained this statement. "I had the Duke of Enghien arrested and sentenced because it was necessary to the security of the French people, in the interest of whose honour it was done. . . . If a similar circumstance arose, I should do the same thing again."—After these phrases, quoted by Montholon, there is an added note by the latter: "This passage was written in between two lines after he had heard read, from an English review, an article in which the Dukes of Vicenza and Rovigo were outrageously attacked."—Montholon, *Récits de la captivité*, II, 510.

plots compromising to none but the principal émigrés. No doubt the execution of the King was a great crime. That calamity was none of my work—the Bourbons have no right to conspire against my life on account of it. If I were not occupying the throne it would be occupied by another; for the nation did not want them in any case."

The Emperor returned to M. Talleyrand.

"He is your friend," he told me, adding: "He is a born intriguer, and quite immoral, but he's very witty and certainly the most capable of all the ministers I have had. We were on very cool terms for a long time, but I am no longer angry with him. He would still be minister if he had wished to be. I thought before the campaign of sending him to Warsaw, where he would have been very useful to me; but monetary intrigues on his part, and bedroom intrigues on the part of Mme. Bassano, prevented this. The Duchess, seeing in his entry into politics the probable removal of her husband from the office of Secretary for Foreign Affairs—husband and wife both clung to that, above everything—she did all she could to get M. Talleyrand out of the way. Having started an intrigue with one of her friends, they contrived to make me so annoyed with M. Talleyrand that I was on the point of having him arrested. I found out the truth too late, from the police.

"It was this intrigue," added the Emperor, "which led to the Abbé de Pradt's nomination, of whom Savary and Duroc were so loud in their praises—as Maret was, too, who thought him a prodigy of nature because he had the gift of gab and wrote articles for the papers. Choosing him lost me my campaign. . . . Talleyrand would have done more there, through the medium of Mme. Tyszkiewicz's salon, than Maret and the Abbé de Pradt with their fret and gossiping and all their dealings with Poland from which, thanks to them, I got nothing I could turn to any account in the Russian business, even though that was really Poland's affair."

On another occasion the Emperor, in repeating to me what he had already said about M. Talleyrand, added that it was his inveterate longing for grandeur which had lost him the ministry; that he had wanted to be a great dignitary, a prince, and, above all, Archchancellor of State; but that he, the Emperor, had never wished it, partly because the office of Secretary for Foreign Affairs could not be occupied by two people, and partly because it would have been distasteful in the extreme to the Duke of Bassano, who was accustomed to his own manner of working and did his job perfectly.

"He understood me, which is the privilege of very few people," added the Emperor. "As for Talleyrand, he has always regretted his loss of the ministry because to him it represented a means of getting money, of which he and those around him are always in need. I would, however, give him back the office if he would consent to separate from his wife. It isn't fitting that the diplomatic corps should associate with that b——. I have no desire that my affairs should be put up for auction by her."

I observed that M. Talleyrand was not on sufficiently good terms with his wife to warrant any suspicion of his confiding in her, or the belief that he would be susceptible to the least influence from her. He would, I said, fall into disrepute if he were to leave her now to enter into politics; that such a condition made the whole thing impossible—which was unfortunate, since choosing him would appear to all the cabinets to indicate moderation, and would even seem to be a preparatory step towards peace. Something of that sort was necessary at this juncture to satisfy public opinion in Europe and in France. I added, furthermore, that I failed to understand the importance which he laid on Mme. Talleyrand's removal, since she had already done the honours of her husband's house and had even been received at Court several times.

To this the Emperor replied with spirit that Talleyrand

would have to change some of the company he kept; besides, that he would have to get rid of his m—— and his ——; and he told me that I had no idea of what went on in that house. When Talleyrand was minister the salon was an auction-room with his supposed friends as the brokers; and he wanted no more scandal of that sort. Talleyrand had believed, moreover, that he could not do without him and that he would, in consequence, make him Archchancellor and leave him to look after everything; whereas in such an arrangement the Minister for Foreign Affairs would have been merely a head clerk—and Talleyrand had probably forgotten that the Emperor did not want two authorities in the State; that it was the Emperor who was governing. . . .

I pointed out to the Emperor that the general esteem did not seem to me to have grown with his power during the past two or three years; indeed, that in my view we were declining even as we expanded. I paid tribute to the noble qualities of M. Bassano; and this seemed to please the Emperor. But I pointed out to him that amongst the general public his minister was more blamed for having been a supporter of this war, and generally for not opposing His Majesty's warlike zeal, than for the Turkish peace and the Russo-Swedish alliance, because everyone knew that the Emperor ruled singlehanded, and that his ministers were neither accustomed nor able to settle problems out of hand, to dispose of millions, or to despatch, on their own authority, agents with the power to do so. M. Bassano, being his sole confidant, had had plenty of other resources at his disposal. To my expressions of doubt regarding this assertion, the Emperor replied to me peevishly:

"When I tell you a thing, you've got to believe it."

The conversation was interrupted by our arrival at a stage, where supper had been ordered. The Emperor seemed displeased with me. He was tired, and his displeasure was height-

ened by the fact that he could not shave, as he wished to do,
because Roustam had not arrived. He lay down as usual, on
the long couch which is generally to be found in Polish houses,
and rested there for an hour. Supper restored his good humour.
That evening we were very well entertained. Was it in my
honour? Or had the postmaster, as he approached the end of
his course, been less afraid of indiscretion? I cannot tell. The
fact remains that we were in an excellent house, enjoyed an
excellent supper, and that the masters of the posting-house did
the honours with much care and discretion, if they really did
know that this was the Emperor.

Every morning between eight and nine o'clock, when coffee
could be obtained at a stage, the Emperor drank a cup with
milk, sometimes without emerging from the sledge. At night,
between five and nine, according to the particular stage, the
courier ordered supper for us. We rested then for an hour,
sometimes an hour and a half when the meal was slow in coming, so that M. Wonsowicz and the courier could also have time
to eat. On arrival the Emperor sometimes made his toilet. He
bathed his eyes, and stretched out on a couch—for after we
left his carriage he could no longer sleep en route. I took
advantage of this time to make hasty notes of our conversations,
at least of the matters which seemed to me to have some interest.

On [December 10], two hours before dawn, we reached
Pultusk, where I dispensed with the services of our worthy postmaster, whom the Emperor suitably rewarded. While the
horses were being changed, the Emperor, feeling chilled, entered the local postmaster's house, he being away from home.
His young wife made haste to light a fire and to prepare the
coffee and soup which we asked for, as we had suffered severely
from cold during that night. A Polish servant-girl, half dressed,
poked and blew the flames as well as she could, and nearly
scorched her eyes out over the poorest fire that ever was made.
The Emperor inquired what this poor girl earned. It was so

little that he remarked that the sum would hardly pay for his woolens. He bade me give her a few napoleons and tell her they were for her dowry. The poor child could not believe her eyes, and it was not, I think, until after our departure that she realized her joy and her small fortune.

The Emperor remarked that, in that class, it was possible to make many people happy with very little money.

"I am impatient, Caulaincourt," he added, "for the day of a general peace, so as to get some rest and be able to act the good man. We shall spend four months in every year travelling without our own frontiers. I shall go by short stages with my horses. I shall see the cottage firesides of our fair France. I wish to visit the Departments which lack proper communications, to build roads and canals, to help commerce and encourage industry. There is an enormous amount to be done in France; there are Departments where everything has to be built up from the beginning. I have already busied myself with many improvements, and through the Ministry of the Interior I have collected very valuable information. In ten years' time I shall be blessed as wholeheartedly as I am hated to-day. In some seaports commerce is selfish to the point of injustice, constantly anxious to profit, heedless if others lose. Whatever happens, it is I who have created industry in France. A few more years of perseverance, a few more bivouacs, and Marseilles and Bordeaux will soon be gathering in the millions they have failed to win."

The soup and coffee were slow in coming, and the Emperor, numbed by the cold and the growing heat of the fire, fell asleep. I seized the opportunity to make notes. When he awoke, his sorry meal was soon swallowed and we clambered into our sledge again.

Although the snow was knee-deep, the Emperor visited the defences of Sierock and Prago. We shook the snow off as best we could before re-entering our cage, for such was exactly the shape of the ancient box in which we were. It was so cold, and we were so pleased at having found this means of progress, in spite of the depth of snow everywhere, that the Emperor's vanity did not assert itself until we reached the gates of Warsaw. On reaching the bridge over the Vistula, we could not repress a humble reflection on the modest equipage of the King over Kings. The aged box, which had once been red, had been mounted on a sled, and had four large windows—or rather panes of glass set in worm-eaten sash-frames, which did not close properly. The joints of this wreck, three-quarters rotten, gaped on all sides and gave free access to the wind and snow. I had to be sweeping out the interior of our domicile constantly, to keep us from getting soaked through by snow melting on the seats.

CHAPTER XIV

WARSAW TO DRESDEN

IN spite of all these vexations the Emperor continued very cheerful. He seemed delighted to find himself at Warsaw, and was very curious to see whether he would be recognized. I think he would not have been sorry to have met someone who guessed his identity, for he traversed the city on foot and we did not take our seats on our humble sledge until we had crossed the main square. It was so cold that no one who could keep warm within doors set foot abroad, and the Emperor's green velvet cloak with gold braid only attracted the attention of a few humble passers-by, more eager to regain their own firesides than curious about the names and quality of the travellers, whose costume, however, engaged their attention. They turned to glance, but did not stop. Anyhow, it would have been difficult to recognize the Emperor, for the fur cap he wore covered half his face.

At eleven o'clock we alighted at the Hôtel de Saxe,[1] where Amodru had arrived only a few moments previously. I at once sent to the director-general of posts to order the Duke of

[1] Caulaincourt is mistaken in this. Chambray, Bourgoing, Countess Potocka and de Pradt (*Histoire de l'ambassade dans le grand-duché de Varsovie en 1812*, 209) agree in saying that the Emperor put up at the Hôtel d'Angleterre, and not the Hôtel de Saxe.—The Abbé de Pradt, whose hatred and dishonesty render his narrative so suspect, cannot, however, have had any inducement to be other than truthful when he described the Emperor's apartment in the following terms: "He was in a low-ceilinged little room, freezing cold, with the shutters half-drawn to prevent his being recognized. A wretched Polish maidservant was on her knees puffing at a fire of green wood which rebelled at her efforts, sputtering out more damp into the chimney than heat into the room."

Vicenza's horses for Glogau, for it was always I who was the distinguished traveller, and the Emperor simply my secretary, under the name of M. Rayneval.

Having established the Emperor in front of a poor fire in a room on the ground floor at the end of the courtyard, I made my way to the ambassador's residence, which was near at hand in the Saxony Palace. On entering the house I encountered M. Rumigny, one of the secretaries of the legation, who had been with me at St. Petersburg, and whom I was delighted to meet again. He announced me to the ambassador, who was not a little astonished to see me, especially dressed as I was,[2] but who was even more amazed, believing neither his ears nor his eyes, when I said that the Emperor was at the Hôtel de Saxe and was asking for him.

"The Emperor!" he repeated again and again in astonishment.

When he had somewhat recovered from his surprise, he said:

"How does he come to be here, Your Grace? How is the Emperor?"

These were M. de Pradt's first questions.

"The Emperor is on his way to Paris; we have left the army at Smorgoni; by now it must be in position at Wilna."

"The Emperor would have been more comfortable here than at the hotel."

"He wishes to remain incognito; we are starting again at once."

"Will you not take something, if only a plate of soup, Your Grace?"

"I am taking luncheon with the Emperor at the hotel. But

[2] M. de Pradt, who has travestied this interview of December 10 into a caricature, in his *Histoire de l'ambassade*, 207, says: "The doors of my room were flung open and gave entrance to a tall man who stalked in, supported by one of my embassy secretaries. 'Let us go; come, follow me!' said this phantom. His head was enveloped in a silken shawl, his face lost to sight in the depths of the fur in which he seemed buried, his gait hampered by fur-lined top-boots. It was a kind of ghost-scene."

send a bottle of Burgundy there. His Majesty prefers that wine; and as he has been unable to obtain any on the road, he will be very glad to find a good glass."

"Is the Emperor's health good? What state is the army in?"

"The army is in a dire plight, overwhelmed by misery, hunger and cold. Only the Guard still looks like a body of troops."

"M. Bassano writes of nothing but successes. . . ."

"Actually we have beaten the Russians everywhere, even at the crossing of the Beresina, where we took sixteen hundred prisoners, as I counted myself."

"M. Bassano said six thousand."

"The fact remains that we beat the Russians, who ought to have beaten us."

"Why make out that we have taken six thousand prisoners?—and why, in such grave circumstances, when it is essential that he should know the truth, write to an ambassador as if he were the editor of the *Moniteur?*"

"The number of prisoners is of little matter, as we cannot keep them."

"What is to hinder us?"

"How are we to feed prisoners when our own men are littering the roadside, dying of hunger?"

"Have we suffered heavy losses?"

"Too heavy," I answered, with a deep sigh. "These disastrous results are well worthy of those who urged this war. What folly!"

"Not everyone urged it. Not everyone has deceived the Emperor as to what would happen. But what does it matter? Your Grace will have justice done you now, for it is well known that you did your best to prevent it. As for me, I have not hesitated to displease the Emperor by exposing the true facts of the situation and the state of Poland. I continually write to the Duke of Bassano; but he only replies by sending accounts

of victories which deceive nobody here. This country is ruined.
It has been crushed."

I stopped the conversation by leaving the ambassador to
change his clothes, and returned to the Emperor. He was all
the more impatient to see M. de Pradt because, being dissatisfied
with him, he was anxious to show his displeasure. Ever since
leaving Sierock the Emperor had grown more excited as the
moment of meeting the ambassador drew nearer, and he repeated again and again what he had already said about him.
For this reason he did not alight at his ambassador's house,
which I had suggested as more comfortable and convenient for
seeing various members of the Polish government whom he
wished to interview.

"I refuse to stay with a man whom I am going to dismiss,"
he said. "He has given me too much cause for complaint."

I shall omit what the Emperor added to this speech, and so
often repeated in the access of his ill-humour. He blamed
M. de Pradt for meanness, for lack of tact, for misdirecting the
zeal of our adherents.

"He has ruined all my plans with his indolence," said the
Emperor. "He is a chatterbox, and nothing more. I have often
wished Talleyrand here."

The ambassador arrived just when these last words were
uttered. The Emperor received him coldly. M. de Pradt came
forward eagerly, and asked how His Majesty was. His words
had the ring of genuine interest; but this seemed to be even
less in his favour. The Emperor would rather have been
blamed, even criticized and found fault with by any other man,
and was ill-disposed to tolerate this man-to-man air of interest
on the part of one against whom he was deeply incensed. Perceiving the effect he had produced, M. de Pradt became colder
and more reserved. These preliminaries showed me clearly
that I should be doing the ambassador a service by leaving him
with no witness, and so giving him an opportunity of private

conversation with the Emperor; and I left the room. But the Emperor by the same token desired the presence of a third party to increase M. de Pradt's discomfiture, and he bade me remain. When I explained, however, that certain orders had to be given for the continuation of our journey, and that I had to buy him an extra cloak, he let me go, bidding me send for Count Stanislas Potocki, as well as the Minister of Finance. He added that I was to get everything ready for a speedy departure, and to return immediately. I bought the cloak for the Emperor, who suffered severely from the cold at nighttime, although I covered him with half my own cloak, thereby almost freezing myself.

I hurried up the dinner and returned to the room adjoining the Emperor's, to send off a courier to Wilna and an outrider to precede us to Posen. As the door between the two rooms closed imperfectly, I could not help hearing the Emperor heaping on his ambassador all the reproaches he had already enumerated in his conversations with me. He concluded by saying that neither his tone, his conduct, nor anything about him, had been French. He reproached him with making plans for a campaign, with acting the soldier when he knew nothing about military matters, and added that he ought to confine himself to politics and saying his Mass. He had been sent to Warsaw to represent France honourably, and not make petty economies and lay plans for a fortune for himself, which would have been assured him had he performed his duty as he ought. But as it was, he had achieved nothing but blunders.

M. de Pradt tried to justify himself, protesting his devotion, his zeal, his regret for any errors he had committed, his desire to do better. He defended and justified Poland for not having done all the Emperor desired for the success of the Russian expedition. He enumerated the sacrifices she had made, the forces she had raised, which he placed as high as eighty thousand men. He declared that everyone was ruined, that not a crown-piece could be found in the whole country, that financial

THE CHATEAU AND THE PARK OF CAULAINCOURT (1843)

Watercolor by Comte E. de Montesquiou

From the collection of Comte Bernard de Kergorlay

help would have to be given if anything at all was to be done. The more M. de Pradt justified himself, the angrier the Emperor became. He blamed him for the incalculable consequences that must ensue from his neglect to call up the levies, and added that, from the ambassador's own words, it was plain that he was courting foolish popularity; that a clever man like himself ought to have seen, and made the Poles understand, that to prolong the struggle by withholding the means of bringing it to a speedy end would merely injure themselves.

The Emperor called me in; he seemed bored to death with the ambassador's presence. His gestures, the way he shrugged his shoulders, showed his mood so clearly that I really shared the embarrassment of his victim, who was in an agony of mortification. I felt I should be doing them both a kindness by going out for a moment, and returning an instant later to inform His Majesty that dinner was served. But he had again started his tale of reproaches and went on, now with vehemence, now with cold disdain, until, seeing a card on the mantelpiece, he stopped suddenly in the middle of a sentence, snatched it up, wrote a few words on it, and handed it to me.[3]

All this time M. de Pradt was trying to get in a few words in self-defence, casting blame on all the French authorities, of whom he complained bitterly, as well as of the generals, and so forth. It seemed to me that, on some grounds, his remarks were not without reason.

This criticism of the military aspect annoyed the Emperor still more; he would not even permit any comments on the

[3] This paper, as it transpires later, was an order to instruct Maret to arrange the immediate replacement of M. de Pradt. The latter had observed the incident; at a later period Vitrolles, who enjoyed his confidence, was to write: "While the Archbishop was carrying on his impertinent discourse, Bonaparte took up a pencil as though to write some urgent order, and passed over to M. de Caulaincourt a paper on which he had scribbled, 'Délivrez-moi de ce faquin.' The Master of Horse left the room as though to carry out the order, and shortly afterwards called the Archbishop and sent him away, I know not on what pretext."—Vitrolles, *Mémoires*, I, 195.

operations undertaken by Prince Schwarzenberg. As for the tactics of the troops in the Duchy of Poland, of which the Emperor actually approved no more than did the ambassador, he told him sharply that he would not allow a priest to pass any judgment on the matter. The Emperor spoke of the defence of the Duchy, which he considered would be a simple matter if the levies were raised, although the ambassador held that the country was unprotected and in great peril. The Emperor always argued on the hypothesis that the army would remain at Wilna, and that Schwarzenberg would do what was expected of him. He anticipated holding and defending the Duchy by Polish levies, and by a general mobilization. He even wished to cover his army quarters by a screen of those Polish Cossacks of which he was never tired of talking, though, for lack of money, they had not yet even been collected into depôts.

The discussion had by now taken a turn for the better and was no longer disagreeably personal, and M. de Pradt, zealous in military controversies, adopted a rather dogmatic tone in refuting, with some reason as it seemed to me, what the Emperor laid down in the tone of a master who expects silence rather than disagreement. The ambassador even seemed to allow himself more freedom in his observations than would have been permissible in private conversation. He saw safety only in what we no longer possessed—well-organized and well-paid armies; and he asserted that without money not a horse nor a man could be hoped for in the Duchy.

"Then what do the Poles want?" the Emperor demanded sharply. "It is for them we are fighting, for them that I have lavished my treasure. If they mean to do nothing for their own cause, it is useless for them to work up such a passion for the restoration of their independence."

"They want to be Prussian," answered the ambassador.

"Why not Russian?" rejoined the Emperor indignantly.

He turned his back on M. de Pradt, telling him to return in half an hour with the ministers who had been summoned.

When M. de Pradt had gone the Emperor launched into a long and violent tirade against him, accusing him of being afraid of the Russians; of having, throughout the campaign, frightened rather than reassured the Poles; and of having ruined all his plans in Poland.

"Carry out at once the order I gave you," he said sharply, referring to what he had written on the card which he had handed to me in M. de Pradt's presence. It said: "Send Maret word that fear of the Russians has made the Archbishop of Malines lose his head—that he is to dismiss him and put someone else in charge."

I had thrust the card in my pocket. At the moment I continued pacing up and down with the Emperor, without answering or executing his orders.

Noticing his silence, I reminded him that dinner had been growing cold for some time, but he paid little attention to this, directing me again to carry out the order. After a moment I pointed out to him that this change would produce a bad effect on the Council at Warsaw.

"If M. de Pradt," I said, "has, as Your Majesty thinks, played up to the members of the Council, he will be all the more acceptable to them at a moment of difficulty. No harm will be done by leaving him here for some time. He will do his best to remedy his errors, and circumstances will stimulate his zeal. He will even do better than a new man could do. If you dismiss him, he will say it is for having protected the interests of the Duchy, and that will have a bad effect."

The Emperor then enumerated the different orders which the Duke of Bassano had given M. de Pradt concerning levies. He went into lengthy details as to the means placed at the disposal of the ambassador and the Duchy, and concluded by saying:

"You shall write from Posen. Now let us dine, so that I can see the ministers and then start off."

To keep the Emperor from going back on his decision, I threw the card in the fire in his presence. Preoccupied by affairs, anxious to see the ministers and be on the road again, His Majesty did not remain long at table, although the cup of coffee we had snatched at Pultusk had refreshed us but little.

"Business nourishes me," said the Emperor, "and I have a surfeit from discontent. This priest has annoyed me. What impudence! He complains of everyone, criticizes everything. What has *he* ever done to entitle him to blame others? He is losing this campaign for me."

The Emperor also received Count Taillis, lieutenant-general in command at Warsaw, who had nothing to say in praise of the ambassador's behaviour in the moment of crisis.

The Emperor accorded a good reception to the ministers who accompanied M. de Pradt. These gentlemen spoke of the dangers His Majesty had run, and their happiness in seeing him in such good health. His mere presence was to them a guarantee of better days to come . . . and so forth, and so on. The Emperor brushed aside the idea that he had ever run any risks. He laughingly observed that rest and quiet were the lot of none but sluggard monarchs, adding that he thrived on fatigue. He told them that the army was still strong in numbers, with more than one hundred and fifty thousand men, which was hardly the truth. The Russians, according to him, were not holding out; they had been beaten in every direction, even at the Beresina. These Russians were no longer the men of Eylau and Friedland. Before three months had elapsed he would have as strong an army as he had when he opened the campaign. His arsenals were full, he had all the essentials in equipment and troops to make a splendid army. From his private study in the Tuileries he could impose his will on Vienna and Berlin better than from army headquarters. "I carry more weight

when I am on my throne in the Tuileries than when I am leading my army," he said. He spoke of Marengo and Essling,
battles that had been almost lost yet which, a couple of hours
later, had placed Austria at his disposal.[4]

I went into the other room to make certain that everything
was ready. The sledges were drawn up before the door. I
paid the hotel-keeper, gave a few directions, and made notes of
the strange conversation I had just heard. After dinner, while
the Emperor was at his toilet, I had jotted down particulars of
what I had said to the ambassador and of his conversation with
the Emperor. As soon as I was able to pay attention to what was
being said now, I heard the Emperor attributing his reverses
solely to the climate, and admitting that he had possibly stayed
too long at Moscow because, having sent Lauriston to Russian
headquarters, he had hoped to be able to conclude a peace. He
said that Wilna would be held, but agreed that the Russians had
shown strength of character, and that they loved the Tsar
Alexander. The burning of Moscow, he acknowledged, had
upset his plans. He emphasized the fact that it was the Russians who had set fire to their own capital. He spoke of the
need for showing strength of mind on our side, adding that even
grave reverses might lead to astounding successes. He talked
with eagerness of the levies to be raised, especially of the indispensable Polish Cossacks.

The ministers emphasized the distress of their country. The
Emperor did not seem to pay attention to this. M. de Pradt
supported them generously when they asked for money. The
Emperor granted some millions from the Courland assessment
and from an issue of copper coinage, and concluded by announcing the imminent arrival of the diplomatic corps from

[4] See Countess Potocka's account (*Mémoires*, 332) of the interview between Napoleon and Potocki. Her concluding remarks are: "The fascination that this extraordinary man exercised over all who heard him was so
powerful that my father-in-law, who had been in the depths of gloom when
he left us, returned full of hope."

Wilna. He then started to talk of his journey, and then I entered the room. The ministers urged the Emperor to rest for a few hours while relays were being organized along the road. They enquired whether he would take the Silesia route by Glogau.

"Yes, by Prussia," answered the Emperor.

This crossing of Prussian territory, short though it was, worried him. He told them, questioning me as he did so, that I had given all the necessary instructions for relays, and that he was about to start at once. He then dismissed the ministers very graciously, amid their renewed expressions of devotion, in which they were all joined by M. de Pradt, who seemed to have forgotten the rebukes administered before dinner.

We mounted our sledge without further delay [about seven P.M., December 10], and once again the Emperor gave vent to his spleen against M. de Pradt. He passed the most bitter comments on the Archbishop's terror when the Russians had nearly reached the Duchy, and on the bad example given by his behaviour on that occasion. He spoke of his breeding and his manners, which were out of keeping, His Majesty said, with the education he had received, with the company in which he must have mixed, particularly with the religious calling he had chosen. The Emperor kept on alleging that M. de Pradt had lost him Poland and ruined his campaign. It had been a mistake to pay heed to foolish intrigues and not send Talleyrand, who would have served him well, as he had previously done at Finckenstein [April-May, 1807].

The most difficult part of our journey had certainly been accomplished, but we had still to cross the little strip of Prussian territory after Glogau; and this worried the Emperor more than all the rest of his journey. We travelled at great speed, but when a shaft of our sledge broke we were obliged to stop at Kutno to have it mended, which delayed us more than two hours.

The sub-prefect recognized the Emperor, and gave him the best reception that lay in his power. His wife and sister, two pretty Polish girls, were thrilled with excitement at having His Majesty under their roof, and were delighted beyond measure at seeing him in good health. No physiognomy is so expressive as the Polish. The Emperor appreciated the warmth of his reception, but had so much business on hand that there was no opportunity for chatting with the ladies or the sub-prefect, and he employed his time in dictating orders for the Duke of Bassano and for Warsaw. He instructed his minister to hurry on the levies and the arming of the Duchy, informing Maret of what he had granted the Poles and ordering him to send a fresh courier to Vienna and to Prince Schwarzenberg. He also issued orders to Lauriston, who was to go to Warsaw, instructing him to remain there, to assume command of the entire army, to arm Modlin and Sierock. To General du Taillis, whom he had seen at Warsaw, he confirmed in writing the orders he had given him verbally: that he was to keep all the troops passing through the city, and to organize and arm the National Guard.

The Emperor grew impatient with my slow writing, my fingers being still numb with cold, and decided to write himself while I made drafts of what he had already dictated. But his own fingers were stiff, his handwriting was at the best illegible, and after writing two letters which he could not even read himself he was obliged to dictate fresh ones to me. Dinner put a stop to this correspondence. I preserved the two historic letters written in the Emperor's own hand, and sent off the despatches while he dined. By this time the sledge was repaired. His Majesty barely took time to eat; I managed to snatch a piece of bread with which to make my meal as we went on our way. The Emperor was deeply touched by the reception he had met with at Kutno, and instructed me to tell Duroc, when we arrived in Paris, to send a gift to the sub-prefect's wife.

During the journey from Warsaw to Kutno, the Emperor had spoken of England, of the difficulty of forcing her to make peace unless some financial crisis or internal embarrassment forced the hands of the cabinet. At the moment he seemed to regret that his idea for the restoration of Poland had embroiled him with Russia. He agreed that she was of great importance in the Continental System.

"Rumiantsof," he went on, "was aware how advantageous this alliance would be to me. He was no genius, but he was a man of sound judgment, with a thorough understanding of the European situation as it developed after Tilsit, and as we envisaged it at Erfurt. He also realized so fully the advantages we should draw from the alliance in France's relation to England, that he would not even believe in hostilities until we had crossed the Niemen. He always doubted my real intention of attacking Russia. He thought my object was to make them shut their eyes to what had happened, and that my hostile demonstrations were only to force Russia not to receive neutrals and to consider herself fortunate that I stopped at threats.

"I could not permit this admission of pretended neutrals," the Emperor continued, "as it furnished the English with a means of eluding the Continental blockade. But I would have passed it over, and we should have reached an understanding if I had been able to entertain any hope of persuading the Tsar Alexander to organize a great expedition on India. At the point we had reached in our struggle with England, whose cabinet was staking its all, this would have been the only way of alarming the London merchants. The nation would have forced the government to treat for peace. But after Erfurt I felt suspicion in the air. For my part, affairs in Spain were more or less spoiling my other projects. Alexander and Rumiantsof did not incline so much as I had expected to the partition of Turkey, and thus all my plans made at Tilsit had to be modified. I may be obliged to look at things from another angle. By some means or other we must get out of the rut we are in, find some means of forcing England to make peace, weaken Russia, solve the problem of Europe by creating a great buffer state. It would be a splendid and noble thing to rob England of any hope of forming a new coalition, by sapping the strength of the only great power which could still be her ally."

The Emperor told me that he had long thought that Constantinople was coveted by Russia. In the hope of an expedition, or at least a demonstration, against India, he had planned another expedition by sea (possibly independent of the land operation), to which he would have been able to furnish a strong contingent if he could have persuaded the Russians to allow a French corps to march through their country. But from what he knew, and from what the Tsar and Rumiantsof had told him, this would have been difficult to negotiate.

The Emperor appears to have planned his expedition against India in the following manner. He had obtained from the navy all the necessary information. It seemed to him that the main obstacle was the impossibility of carrying sufficient water for twenty-five or thirty thousand men for such a long voyage. Otherwise he had found no insuperable difficulty. He would have directed the expedition against Surat—a landing to be made at some point on the Mahratta coast, where the people were natural enemies of the English and ready at any moment to take up arms against them. The expeditionary force would have been thirty thousand strong. They would put in at only one port, Mauritius, to water and take on board provisions and leave their sick. These latter would have been replaced by two or three thousand negroes for whom the colonists would be paid in ready money.

France, the Empress, and the King of Rome were subjects of daily conversation. His Majesty never wearied of exclaiming how glad he would be to see them again, and expressed the most tender affection for them. The Empress he praised constantly, talking of his home life with a feeling and a simplicity that did one good to hear. Of France and the French he spoke with an enthusiasm which was consoling after so many sacrifices.

"I make myself out to be worse than I really am," he said to me laughingly; "for I have observed that the French are always ready to eat out of one's hand. They lack seriousness; consequently, that quality impresses them most. I am supposed to be severe, even hard! So much the better! It saves me from having to be so! My firmness passes for insensibility; and it is partly to this impression that we owe the existing state of good order, although the Revolution is so recent, and although we have a generation among us reared in disorder and with no conception of morality or religion. So I do not complain of my reputation. Believe me, Caulaincourt, I'm only human! Whatever some people may say, I have a tender heart—but it is the heart of a sovereign. The tears of a duchess move me to no pity whatsoever, but I am touched by the woes of peoples. I want to see them happy; and the French shall be so. If I live ten years, there will be contentment everywhere. Don't you suppose I enjoy giving pleasure? It does me good to see a happy face; but I am compelled to defend myself against this natural disposition, lest advantage be taken of it. I found that out more than once with Josephine, who was always begging me for things, and could even cry me into granting what I ought to have refused her."

The Emperor often asked me if I too should not be delighted to see my loved ones again. This good and natural manifestation of His Majesty's real feelings refreshed me more than I can say. I should have liked the ears of all Europe to hear his words, and every echo to repeat them. I am positive that I lost not one syllable of this conversation, which I would gladly have prolonged indefinitely.

The Emperor was most anxious to meet his couriers in order to get the eagerly awaited letters from France—the first we had received since Smorgoni. He accordingly hastened our journey as much as he could. At Posen we would regain the road the army had taken on its way to Königsberg.

Meanwhile the Emperor reviewed his cabinet. He praised Archchancellor Cambacérès as a man of prudent counsel and a great lawyer. His equitable and singularly clear judgment had thrown much light upon several articles in the Code, notably those presenting the greatest difficulties. Alluding to the death of the King, "Only fear," he said, "prevented him from voting his acquittal." [5] Cambacérès, he added, was far from being a revolutionary. He was a man worthy of confidence and incapable of abusing it; he had always made the best use of the trust given him; his high repute was most justly acquired.

The Emperor cited the Duke of Rovigo as a man entirely devoted to him, a man of strong character and independent viewpoint. He had a kind heart, he said; he was thoroughly good-natured, even obliging. He would often have been duped if the Emperor had not stopped him. But he was too self-interested, and this displeased His Majesty, who had decided to deprive him of the gaming monopoly, for he was incessantly asking for money, although he had already been given large sums, and his fortune, since he became a minister, had risen to five or six millions. As for the rest, the public was unjust in its opinion of him. It was held up against him that he had been present at the execution of the Duke of Enghien.

"But," he added, "he had received orders to attend the execution, and, being commandant of the picked gendarmerie, it

[5] In the Convention, Cambacérès voted "Yes" on the question of the guilt of Louis XVI, but on the question of the application of the death penalty he voted for a reprieve until the cessation of hostilities.

was his duty to be there. Anybody else would have obeyed orders exactly as he did. He was a much better man, much less of an inquisitor than Fouché. It is now the fashion to laugh at Savary. It was, indeed, ridiculous that a divisional general, Minister of Police, should be taken from his bed and whisked off to gaol by a madman just escaped from a lunatic asylum. This [Malet] incident very naturally made all Paris roar with laughter; and ridicule is more fatal to those in authority than their mistakes."

Turning later to the Duke of Otranto [Fouché], he said:

"The man is merely a schemer. He is prodigiously clever and facile with the pen. He is a thief, and steals anything he can lay hands on. He must be worth millions. He was a great revolutionary, a man of blood. He thinks he can atone for his misdeeds, or anyhow cause them to be forgotten, by playing up to the relatives of his victims and making himself out to be the protector of the Faubourg Saint-Germain. He is a man whom it may be useful to employ, for he is still the fugleman of many revolutionaries and is, besides, exceedingly capable. But I can no longer place any confidence in him."

The Duke of Gaeta, who appeared next in this review, was, His Majesty said, a good financier, a man of method and probity, who had rendered great services in his sphere. M. Barbé-Marbois, whom he named next, was a schemer with the appearance of a Quaker and a deceptive resemblance to an honest man.

"I was duped by him for a long time," he said, "for he professed a certain rigour in his principles and a severity of judgment on other people, and on events, which made me think he would be no more indulgent to himself. He is discontented with everything, fondling power, detesting it and belittling it. He is, at heart, an unprincipled man, full of envy and fault-finding, devoid of capacity. Thinking him a man of talents, I placed great confidence in him for some time, only to discover too late that I was mistaken. I paid dearly for the error. He is safe in the Court of Accounts; he cannot make blunders there, and he is obliged to carry out his new functions with the probity for which he is renowned."

Upon my observing that he had the reputation of being virtuous and unimpeachably honest:

"Oh, he is honest enough," replied the Emperor. "As for being virtuous, that is simply a part he plays; at heart he is a rascal."

Of M. Fontanes the Emperor said:

"He is too much of a sycophant. He has great talent. He serves me with zeal and for the moment is directing public instruction very competently. The Revolution has made us too full of the Greeks and Romans; we must give our children monarchical ideas, and that is quite in accordance with Fontanes's opinions; or so he proclaims, at least. If I allowed him, he would go too far in that direction. He is a man of parts, but his head is small. If I had not checked him, he would have given us an education of Louis XV's style. He thought it would please me, but I stopped him. One day I said to him: 'Monsieur de Fontanes, at least leave us the Republic of Letters!' [6] Those words put him back on the right road.

"I am not afraid of energetic men; I know how to use and guide them. Besides, I can do nothing which is opposed to equality; and youth, like the nation, clings to equality. If you have talent I can push you forward; if you have merit I can protect you. This is recognized, and it is very useful to me. Fontanes would have reared marquises for me. Their only place is on the comic stage—though the taste of to-day has really dethroned them there, since Molé quit the scene and

[6] In 1806 Fontanes, at that time president of the Legislature, had inserted in the *Mercure de France* the advance notice of a book he had written in support of absolute monarchy. It was this that drew the reply from Napoleon quoted here.

Fleury broke down. I need councillors of state, prefects, officers, engineers, professors. Therefore the scope of our instruction must be broadened, to season these young heads full of Greek and Roman ideas. It is important to give a monarchic turn to the vitality of those traditions; for that is history. I shall give my first attention to education; it will be my first care as soon as peace is established, for it is the safeguard of the future. I want all instruction to be public—even my son's, in part. I have a great plan in that connection."

To my great regret this conversation was interrupted by our arrival in the early hours of the morning [December 12] at the Hôtel de Saxe, at Posen.

"Give me my despatches," were the Emperor's first words.

In accordance with my orders the director of posts had kept the two which came through.[7] The Emperor's impatience was such that he would have ripped open the cases if he had had a knife at hand. Numb with cold, my fingers were not quick enough for him in working the combinations of the padlocks. At last I handed him the Empress's letter, and one from Mme. Montesquiou enclosing the report on the King of Rome. This was the first news since leaving Wilna, for luck had been against us; we had met no courier between that town and Mariampol. The Emperor had never ceased to speculate on the impression that would be caused by the total lack of news of the army, so it can easily be imagined with what eagerness he read the despatches from the Archchancellor and the other ministers. I could not tear the envelopes open quickly enough to keep pace with his impatience. He scanned the pages rather than read them, to obtain a general idea of their contents. After this hasty review he settled down to perusing carefully those despatches which had struck him as being the most important.

[7] At Posen the Emperor regained the line of communication between France and the army, which he had left at Mariampol.

He did me the honour of reading aloud the letters from the Empress and Mme. Montesquiou.

"Haven't I got an excellent wife?" he said.

The particulars that the Empress gave him about his son, all of which were confirmed by the governess, delighted His Majesty. Notwithstanding that he was so preoccupied with affairs, in this moment he was just a good husband, indeed the best of husbands, and the fondest of fathers. I cannot describe my pleasure in contemplating him at such moments. His joy, his happiness, glowing in every feature, went to my heart.

He made me read the Archchancellor's letters, as well as communications from the Ministers of Police and War. I took advantage of the momentary freedom afforded me, while the Emperor was going through his correspondence, to give orders for the continuation of our journey. The travelling carriage had been unable to catch up with us, and, as the Emperor had given me no time to take money out of it when we parted from it, all my funds were exhausted. I had the director of couriers fetch me some money. I notified the general in command in Glogau that I should be arriving, and that he was to have the city gates ready [to open], and supper prepared. I then employed the two hours left before our departure in putting my notes in order, and completing the particulars I had taken of our last conversation since leaving Warsaw.

The Emperor took an hour's rest. He lunched, and we then took to the road again. We were now meeting the bearers of news, and the further we proceeded the shorter we made the intervals between receiving despatches. In this manner we were able to receive in one day's journey our friends' letters covering three or four days. Every letter received was a source of fresh happiness to the Emperor. He made me read most of his despatches, except those in the post [censorship] packet. Only once did he give me a few extracts from this to read, saying, as he did so:

"What imprudence!   What fools men are!   I have not sufficient opinion of Mankind to be malicious, as they say I am,
or eager for revenge!"

The Emperor's observation was very just.   The imprudence
and impudence expressed in some of these intercepted letters
afforded opportunities for incontestable proof that His Majesty
was neither malicious nor vindictive; for in the circumstances
he might justly have been severe, whereas when I reached Paris
I saw the two persons who had given occasion to these observations, and they had not been in the slightest degree molested
or reprimanded.   One of them occupied a position at Court.

The Emperor was highly satisfied with the particulars he
received as to the situation in Paris and in France.   Everyone
was so accustomed to seeing him triumph over difficulties, and
even extract some advantage from events which seemed the
most contrary to his interest, that public confidence had been
but little shaken by the long silence of which people complained.
This interruption in communications had not produced exactly
the effect that he had anticipated.

"In the actual circumstances," the Emperor said, "this sense
of security is rather a pity, for, when it comes, the army bulletin
will upset confidence.[8]   A certain disquiet would have been
preferable; it would have prepared the ground for bad news."

Speaking of the Minister of War [Clarke], he called him a
typical courtier, the most conceited man he had ever met:

"The greatest happiness that could befall him would be if
he could persuade everyone that his grandfather had come out
of the Ark.   He is an honest man, of mediocre talents, without
character, and so addicted to flattering that one never can tell
how much reliance to place on any opinion he may express.
He does not know me yet," added the Emperor.   "He imagines

[8] Bulletin 29, dated from Molodetchna, December 3, and sent direct from
Smorgoni to Paris, appeared in the *Moniteur Universel* of December 16,
1812.

I am like Louis XV, and that he has to get round me and be agreeable to me. If I kept mistresses he would be their most devoted servant. He considers the Malet affair a great conspiracy with many ramifications. He would like to have many Jacobins arrested—and even some public figures. But I think Pasquier and Savary are right in judging that that insolent attempt was simply hatched in the minds of a few idiots. It was quite right not to arrest any prominent men, for rigorous action causes irritation. If there are any guilty parties at large they will not escape the police, and it would not do to have the government betraying unwarranted suspicion. In the eyes of Europe as of France, it is preferable that this conspiracy should appear as nothing more formidable than a madman's escapade. Savary anticipated my wishes perfectly by adopting this attitude."

On our arrival at Glogau that evening the general in command was not a little surprised to discover that the Master of Horse was none other than the Emperor himself. His Majesty went closely into the state of the place and the condition of the country, issued various orders, and barely took time to sup, so anxious was he to be on the way once more. We set off in the carriage offered by the general and accepted by the Emperor, who was very tired from being unable to lie at full length in the sledge.

Certain as I was that the snow would prevent us going far on wheels, I took the precaution of having our faithful sledge follow us; and it was as well that I did so, for, being unable to proceed in the carriage at more than a walking pace, we had not left Glogau far behind when we transferred into our less comfortable conveyance. Half frozen in this modest vehicle, which we should have done well not to leave, the Emperor was unable to sleep, and began to talk of the army, of which, owing to the rapidity of our movements, we could have no news.

He longed to get into Saxony. He did not like having to cross Prussian territory, and this led to the following conversation.

"If we are stopped, Caulaincourt, what will they do to us? Do you think I shall be recognized, that it will be known that I am here? You are popular enough in Germany, Caulaincourt; you speak the language; you protected the postmasters and took all my gendarmes to furnish them with escorts. They would never allow you to be arrested or ill-treated."

"I do not suppose they will have very grateful memories of a protection that did not hinder their being pillaged."

"Bah! They may have suffered for twenty-four hours, but you had their horses given back to them. Berthier never stopped talking of your claims on their behalf. Have you ever been in Silesia?"

"Only with Your Majesty."

"Then you are not known here?"

"No, Sire."

"I did not reach Glogau until after the gates had been closed for the night. Unless the general or the courier have been chattering in front of the postilion, it is impossible that anyone should know I am in Prussia."

"That is true; and no one would imagine that it was the Emperor travelling in this sorry vehicle. As to the Master of Horse, he is not of sufficient importance for the Prussians to compromise themselves by arresting him. Your Majesty's journey has been so speedy that no one on the road so much as knows about it. Some sort of plan would have to be arranged before any attempt could be made on us; even a spiteful and determined man must get three or four kindred spirits to help him."

"If the Prussians were to stop us, what would they do to us?"

"If it was the result of a definite plan, not knowing what to do with us they would kill us. So we must defend ourselves to the utmost extremity. We may be lucky; there are four of us."

"But if they take you alive, what will they do to you, my good Duke of Vicenza?" said the Emperor jokingly.

"If they take me it will be because of my secretary, in which event I shall be in a bad way."

"If we are stopped," rejoined the Emperor briskly, "we shall be made prisoners of war, like Francis I. Prussia will get back the millions she has paid, and will ask for millions more."

"If they dared strike such a blow, Sire, we should not get off so cheaply as that."

"I think you are right. They fear me too much; they would want to keep me."

"That is highly probable."

"For fear I should escape, or that some terrible reprisals would be undertaken, the Prussians would hand me over to the English."

"Possibly!"

"Can you picture to yourself, Caulaincourt, the figure you would cut in an iron cage, in the main square of London?"

"If it meant sharing your fate, Sire, I should not complain."

"It is not a question of complaining, but of something that may happen at any moment, and of the figure you would cut in that cage, shut up like a wretched negro left to be eaten by flies after being smeared with honey," rejoined the Emperor, with a laugh.

And there he was for a quarter of an hour, laughing at this foolish notion, and the idea of that man in the cage.

Never had I seen the Emperor laugh so heartily, and his gaiety was so infectious that it was some time before we could speak a word without finding some fresh source of amusement.

It was with considerable relief that the Emperor reflected that nothing could be known of his departure and that the

Prussians, even if they did learn about it, would not dare take any action against him while their troops were in the midst of ours and we were as strong as they imagined us to be.

"But a secret assassination, an ambuscade would be easy," said His Majesty, thus betraying his lively desire to be across this strip of Prussian territory, which gave him food for such serious as well as amusing reflections.

This thought so preoccupied him that he asked if our pistols were in good order, at the same time making sure his own was ready to hand. I had inspected them at Posen, so we firmly made up our minds to give a warm reception to the first person who interfered with us. Any inquisitive fellow who had thrust his head in at our door that night would have fared ill.

The change of relays interrupted our conversation. As the Emperor had not wished the courier from Glogau to be more than an hour ahead of us, and as he had travelled slower than we had, he was only a short distance in front, and the relay horses were not ready. The Emperor could think of nothing but this delay. Accustomed to having everyone at his beck and call, he could not understand that it should take more than the half hour, which was all the advance-notice the courier could give, to have his horses ready. We were at a Prussian posting-house, and what I attributed to nothing but the habitual slowness of Prussian postmasters seemed to him intentional delay. I had satisfied myself as to the real causes of this delay, but had not succeeded in arousing the postmaster from his imperturbable nonchalance; nor had I been able to urge on the postilions who, according to their wont, harnessed their horses as slowly as possible so as to leave them time to feed. I spent my time going to and fro between the stables and the sledge where the Emperor sat, shivering with cold. To while away the time he asked for some tea, which can be had at any posting-house in Germany. Two cups warmed him up a little, but they did not seem to allay his impatience, which increased every instant. He asked if our escort had followed us. Of the six gendarmes we had taken from Glogau only the two were left who sat at the back of the sledge, and they were half-dead with cold. At last, after waiting for an hour, we took the road again.

We passed one of the most painful nights on the whole journey. The change of vehicle had frozen us. For my own part, it was thirty-six hours before I was warm again.

"I thought," said the Emperor laughingly, as soon as we were on the move again, "that the curtain was rising on the first act of the cage play. How was it possible to take two hours to harness four horses, or even six, which were waiting in the stables?"

But ill fortune dogged our steps. Our sledge broke down, and this made our progress slow. However, we reached Buntzlau [9] where we had to stop to have it mended. We took advantage of this delay to have our breakfast. The Emperor chatted with the inn-keeper, a worthy German. I acted as interpreter. His Majesty asked him as to the state of the country, taxation, the administration, and what they thought of the war. Taking us for simple travellers, the inn-keeper replied to all his questions with the utmost candour. The less his replies were made to please the Emperor, the more the latter plied him with questions, often observing to me with a smile:

"He is right: he has more common sense than many a man at the head of affairs. He isn't merely a courtier."

The kindliness and sincerity of this inn-keeper delighted the Emperor. His place was taken by a seller of glass beads who forced her way into the Emperor's room. The confiding nature of this woman, who did not know in the least who we were, yet wanted to let him have the whole of her stock on trust, without receiving any money or even giving any indication of

[9] On the Bober, in Silesia; the morning of December 13.—The whole of this account furnishes hitherto unknown details as to the Emperor's journey.

why she placed this confidence in us, amused him very much. He bought some necklaces, rings, et cetera, and said to me:

"I will take them to Marie Louise as a souvenir of my journey. It is only fair, Caulaincourt, that we should divide them between us. You must give some to the lady of your heart. Never had man such a long tête-à-tête with his sovereign as you have had. This journey will be a historic memory for your family. The Emperor will never forget all the care you have devoted to him."

He was so good as to give me half of what he purchased, instructing me to pack up the other half for the Empress. He then threw himself on a hard bed, telling me to let him know as soon as the sledge was ready. While the Emperor rested I hurried up the repairs to the sledge, and occupied myself with the continuation of my notes, from the time we left Posen.

All the Emperor's remarks showed that his mind was continually occupied with the army, and that he persisted in believing it could be rallied at Wilna. His opinion did not change. He made all his arrangements and based all his plans on this presumption.

"The bad effect of our disasters will be balanced in Europe by my return to Paris," he said.

The consolation afforded by reflections such as these made our journey a happy one. The nearer we got to France, where all his hopes were centred, the less did the Emperor seem preoccupied and careworn.

"Schwarzenberg is a man of honour," he said. "He will keep his corps in readiness. He has no wish to become a traitor at the first moment Fortune turns her back on us. The Prussians will model their conduct on that of the Austrians. I shall be at the Tuileries before anyone knows of my disaster or dares to betray me. My cohorts make an army of more than a hundred thousand men, well-disciplined soldiers led by war-trained officers. I have the money and arms to form excellent cadres, and before three months have passed I shall have conscripts and five hundred thousand men under arms on the banks of the Rhine. The cavalry will take the longest to collect and form, but in the coffers of the Tuileries I have the wherewithal to do everything."

The further we went, the more snow we found. The gales that had been blowing continuously for some days had caused such drifts in several places that the difficulties of the road made our progress too slow even for the liking of our phlegmatic Saxon postilions and horses.

The Emperor often spoke of the effect that would be produced by his return.

"The nation needs me," he said. "If it responds to my attentions all will soon be put right."

The news from Paris did not make him forget the army. He was more certain than ever than it would hold Wilna, and based all his calculations on this hypothesis. For my own part, I reckoned aloud the days it would occupy in its retreat, as far as the Vistula at least, without arousing the Emperor's annoyance.

"You see the black side of everything; you are not encouraging," was his remark.

What I had observed in the Duchy of Poland left me with no doubts as to the abandoning of Wilna.

"If there are no Polish Cossacks there can be no rest for your army," I said to the Emperor, who agreed that this shortage of cavalry somewhat changed the situation.

He would not, however, admit of the necessity for evacuating Wilna. He enumerated his forces, from the Prince of Schwarzenberg's corps to that of the Duke of Taranto, and was no doubt justified in thinking that numerically he had more men than were necessary to stop the Russians, provided that every one of them had done his duty. He thought that the sense of discouragement in the army had been allayed as soon as they got into touch with the stores at Wilna, and he tried to persuade himself that the levies were already raised, or at least were being collected while we were on our way to Paris. To hear him, one might have imagined that no more need be done but march them from the barracks to the frontier. Not admitting the need for the evacuation of Lithuania, he also refused to admit the existence of those almost insurmountable obstacles which the near approach of the enemy and the fear of invasion would place in the way of raising the levies.

Thus the Emperor journeyed on towards his capital, cherishing illusions such as these and in no way put out with me for not sharing in them. As was natural, our conversation continually reverted to the army, to politics, to the administration, to men we knew, to various institutions, to what he would do to better these, and to his son. He asked me once more who could be entrusted with his education; and added that France, so rich in talent, was yet poor in superior men, when it came to making a choice like that.

"Are you not hard put to it, Caulaincourt, to name a single one?—to make a choice, even from amongst all the people we have discussed?" ". . . Fontanes," he said, "is too much the man of letters. Since he is head of the University, that choice would be pleasing—the more so because he directs public instruction in the right spirit. Though distinguished for his great gift of eloquence, he is not gifted with great ideas; with the broad grasp of politics and administration that constitutes the statesman. Besides, he has extolled me so highly that the public would not fail to say that I was setting my most confirmed flatterer to be preceptor for my son."

He asked me to look about for a tutor. He passed in review nearly all the men in official positions or at Court, even those of little prominence. The way he spoke of several confirmed in me more than ever the belief that, in general, he had but a

poor opinion of Mankind. It seems to me that this explains
the absence of any animosity towards various persons who had
done him real injury; he had every reason to heap reproaches
on them, but he contented himself with dismissing them at once
and not saying a word. He seemed to place great value on
the delicacy of mind and honourable sentiments inculcated by
good training in early years.

"It corrects the most vicious traits in a man's character," I
have heard him say more than once. "The man who has not
been well brought up has a certain uncouthness, a basis of
egotism that makes it difficult to rely upon him. Self-interest
is his only criterion. He lacks a sense of restraint, and this
makes him prone to do anything."

He mentioned several notable men whom he employed in
very responsible situations, adding that he did not trust them,
that they were capable of betraying him at the first opportunity
when they considered it in their interest to do so, although they
owed everything to him. According to the Emperor, the bind-
ing nature of an oath, fidelity in the execution of the functions
or service in which one is employed, the sense of honour that
makes it impossible to betray the man one serves, meant nothing
to these men: religion and fidelity were sentiments wholly lacking in their natures.

"Even patriotism," he went on, "is a word that conveys nothing to them if it is not consonant with their own interests. . . .
When certain people meet with the slightest disappointment,
such as the refusal of a post they have requested for some rascal
who happens to be a relation, they turn against me; some are
even ready to plot against me if I put a stop to their pecula-
tions and open pillage."

In this connection the Emperor mentioned certain names so
prominent that I dare not commit them to writing. I have no
wish to tarnish the glory of these names, which will go down
in history.

"But these men," the Emperor added, "are heroes nonetheless."

He concluded these reflections by observing that some people were wrong in complaining that he did not fill up all the appointments in his gift. Not wishing to exclude any who might claim preferment by right of their eminent services, he chose rather to leave the whole question to be solved by time, which would settle many things.

"By then," he said, "the children will be well educated and will make their start in life at a period of peace and calm; they will not have their fortunes to make, and I will give them the recompense earned by the good services of their fathers."

This conversation led the Emperor to speak of various episodes in his life. It was with pleasure that he recalled some of the incidents of his youthful days—his success at the military academy—his family, which had met with so little favour from Fortune, though of distinguished rank in Corsica. He spoke of various affairs of gallantry, of the preference that some society women had shown him above that granted to comrades who were at that time more conspicuous than himself.[10]

"The reading of history," he said, "very soon made me feel

[10] Later, in reviewing these traits of the Emperor, Caulaincourt wrote: ". . . He often referred, and with a certain air of affectation, to the fine company he had kept in his youth. He loved to talk about his successes with women. In short, if this great and astonishing character had a flaw, it was through the conceit of past achievements; as though so much glory and such genius had need of antecedents." ". . . It is incorrectly thought that he had many mistresses. His head was turned sometimes, no doubt; but for him love was seldom a necessity, or perhaps even a pleasure. He lived too much in the public eye to give himself over to private distractions which, in reality, amused him little and lasted but a moment. He was, however, actually in love with Mme. D[uchâtel] for a few days. As a pastime, and to break with the Empress Josephine, he devoted himself between the divorce and the Archduchess's arrival to Mme. Gaz[zani] and Mme. Mat[his]. During the last years of the Empress Josephine's sway he had Mlle. George and several other women—though more out of curiosity than to avenge the jealous scenes which these infidelities provoked. Mlle. Wal[ewska] gave in to him at Warsaw. He had a child from that

that I was capable of achieving as much as the men who are placed in the highest ranks of our annals, though I had no goal before me, and though my hopes went no further than my promotion to general. All my attention was fixed upon the great art of warfare, and on increasing my knowledge of that branch in which I believed my destiny to lie. I was not long in discovering that the knowledge I had set out to acquire, and had hitherto regarded as the end I needed to attain, was very far short of the distance to which my abilities might carry me. So I redoubled my application; what seemed to present difficulty to others to me appeared to be simple."

Of a serious nature, and inspired with a thoughtful turn of mind by love of his profession, the future Emperor sought in every direction for knowledge, and for the development of the ideas and views germinating in his head, principally by conversing with those of his senior officers and comrades in whom he had remarked some superiority of intellect. The Revolution marched forward with giant strides; its ideas began to seethe in his young head as in many others. The corps in which he served was, by its composition and instructional training, peculiarly susceptible to new impressions and notions. He watched the progress of the Revolution with enthusiasm, though

affair, and felt more sentimental attachment for it than for all the rest. But none of these passing fancies ever occupied him enough to divert him for a moment from affairs of State.

"His haste to recount his successes was so great that one would have thought he pursued them merely to make them public. The Empress was always his first confidant. Woe to the beauty who had surrendered, unless she were the Venus de' Medici's equal; for not the least items escaped either his appraisal or the pleasure he took in going over them with several people, in whose presence he enjoyed the retailing of his *bonne fortune*. Josephine had, on the very night, full particulars of the conquest of Mme. D[uchâtel]. The morning after the first rendezvous the Emperor also told me all about it, without omitting a thing that would have flattered or hurt the lady's self-esteem. That grenadier at the Boulogne encampment was not far wrong, when he replied to one of his comrades who asked him if the Little Corporal had any children: 'F—! Don't you know that all his loves are in his own head?' "

he condemned not only its excesses, but also its mistakes, with more severity than one would have expected from one of his age. Although he was without any experience himself, the conduct of the Court seemed to him ill-chosen, perfidious and, above all, weak. He was no Republican; he wanted a constitutional monarchy; he would have defended the King if the King had wished to be defended, although Louis and his Court did not appear to be acting in good faith. Like so many even among the ardent royalists, the young Corsican wished to have the way of promotion opened to merit, to have advancement possible without distinction of class, without the necessity of being the relation or friend of someone in high places or of invoking the patronage of a lady entitled to demand favours. He was quite unable to understand how the Princes of the Blood and the nobility could take refuge outside France while abandoning the King to danger. He was disgusted at the way the émigrés wandered about Europe exhibiting their incapacity and immorality, instead of putting themselves at the head of a party in France or forming one that would rally the waverers to their side.

The Emperor would have ranged himself on the side of the émigrés, he said, if they had raised their standard in France and chosen prudent leaders to unite the ranks.

"The French," he went on, "never forgive cowardice; and it is cowardice to fly from danger and go begging foreigners for help against one's country when there is such a noble cause to fight for at home. One should never wash dirty linen in public."

He had always been sorry for the King. All his concern was for him; he would have liked to have been able to defend him when his life was threatened.

"His death," said the Emperor, "seemed to me a disgrace to the nation, though, so far as that goes, the nation was innocent of the crime, for it was Coblentz that killed him. As for the King's judges," he went on, "with many of them it was fear rather than hatred or spite that inspired their sentence. What I have already done at Saint-Denis,[11] and what I count upon doing at the Madeleine, will prove that I have always considered his death a crime, and that I thought so before I became a sovereign myself. Since I have worn a crown I have shown clearly enough that I mean to close the doors against revolution. The sovereigns of Europe are indebted to me for stemming the torrent of revolutionary spirit that threatened their thrones; but to prevent the evil breaking out again it is useless to rake up the memory of wrongs done at a time of general upheaval. People must be induced to forget, or remember only in order to prevent a recurrence. I am far from being an advocate of the Convention; but if anyone is to be called to account for the evils done at that time, it is not the men of the Convention, who were carried away by the frenzy of the moment, but the Revolution which had been brought about by the Court itself. As a matter of strict justice the reckoning for our past misfortunes should be laid to the Princes and men of the Court who caused the Revolution. The Montmorencys, the Lameths, the d'Aiguillons, the Talleyrands, the Lafayettes, the Rochefoucaulds, Monsieur (the King's brother), and many others were the real malefactors.

"These men," he went on, "ought to have laid down their lives on the steps of the throne instead of attacking it. Speaking generally, the nobility ought to have fought to the death instead of saving themselves by flight abroad, which was nothing but a convenient way of escaping danger by professing a false devotion. As for the others, those called revolutionaries, they belonged to a lower class which naturally wanted to raise

[11] Napoleon had undertaken the restoration of the basilica in 1805. After the violation of the royal tombs during the Revolution, the church, robbed of the lead on its roof, had served as a storehouse for wheat and flour.

itself. They looked after themselves, and circumstances proved stronger than they were. Those who carried on intrigues abroad did more to bring about the death of the King than the Convention. To be perfectly just, it is impossible to say who is to blame for that death which is now known as the Cause of Sovereigns. The two million individuals who clamoured for it in the addresses they sent up to the Convention were more guilty than many of those who were frightened into voting for it by the knives of the Paris Jacobins. My government has always acted on the principle that what happened prior to its establishment did not take place, always making an exception of services rendered. That is the principle to adopt in order to avert reaction, to quench all hatred and stifle revenge. The greatest seigneurs of the Old Régime, the leaders of the Emigration, those whose families have perished by the axe of the Revolution, dine with the Duke of Otranto and even have relations with him and Merlin, not to speak of other revolutionaries. My government has brought about this fusion. Incomplete though they are, the institutions guarantee the existing state of affairs and are made for the benefit of the sovereign as much as of the people.

"I am, however, designing a monument which, without wounding the living, will honour the names of the dead, and will keep alive in the minds of our children sufficient memories of the unhappy times we have passed through so that they shall know that kings are not to be killed, and that monarchs are not to be buried like private individuals."

The Emperor then asked me if I shared the general opinion that the Madeleine was meant for a temple to *La Gloire*.

"You are the first," he told me, "to know all my ideas for this scheme. I have raised too many monuments to the immortal glory of the French for there to be any need thus to consecrate the Madeleine. I am not a pagan monarch. I have given enough proof of that, for none of the Kings of France, not even the most pious of them, did as much for religion as I have done. The re-establishment of the Church is due to me; only power and a will like mine could have brought this about. Although I am not always in political agreement with the Pope, I venerate him from a religious point of view. I respect his character. I have great projects. Give me a year of peace, and the development of my plans will amaze ——, as it will these upstarts who date everything from their own time and dislike to hear their predecessors mentioned. I will exhibit the glory of ancient France beside that of modern France —her old civilization with her new—her sciences and arts, which are the oldest in Europe, along with her present-day marvels; in a word, I will exhibit her kings along with her Emperor. All her illustrious men, of all ranks, of all conditions and all ages, belong to the fair France of to-day. They must mingle and speak to our children, calling forth their admiration as much as that of the rest of the world.

"I want no idols made of me, nor even any outdoor statues. It was to my great disgust, and without consulting me, that Denon had my statue made for the column in the Place Vendôme. Indeed, it is very likely that I shall change this arrangement, although the publicity already given to the plan may make it inconvenient to make any alterations. They can do what they like after I am dead. If France attains to the summit of glory and prosperity that I purpose for her, they may decree a statue in my honour if they feel like it. If I succumb in the carrying out of my enterprises, it is better that there should be nothing left exposed to the criticism of the world. I want no homage in the form of flattery, nor, as happened to Louis XV, a statue subjected to public ridicule.[12] A

---

[12] It had been said about the equestrian statue of Louis XV, with its pedestal adorned with female figures representing the cardinal virtues: "The Virtues go on foot, Vice on horseback."

nation, like history itself, rarely takes account of anything but success."

The Emperor went on to say it would be impossible to raise a Temple of Glory in a Christian country. Having achieved more than all the other generals or statesmen, and being Emperor, people would not be slow to say, and perhaps with some degree of justification, that he had raised a fane in his own honour—that he was the real object of worship within it, under the conventional name of Glory. He repeated his words that that Glory was the heritage of all Frenchmen, that he would immortalize its memories in every monument, every establishment of public utility which he had created or was yet to create. It was upon reminders such as these that he rested his imperishable fame. Had he announced, in advance, the project of raising an expiatory monument to all the victims of the Revolution, especially to the most distinguished, he would have awakened unhappy memories and given offence to many men who, when the Revolution was finished, rendered eminent services to France, and to whom—it ought never to be forgotten— France owed the honour and glory of having resisted the power of all Europe. Her legal codes and her good administration were partly their work.

"It is to the energy shown by several of their number that France owes the conclusion of the Reign of Terror," he said. "By hurting the feelings of some of these men I should likewise wound the self-respect of their families and connections. Ultimately this would wound the susceptibility of the nation. Time brings things to pass imperceptibly; the great art is to act opportunely. As the monument of the Madeleine will take some years to complete, I have time to make such preparations as shall ensure that its inauguration will fulfil my purpose without giving offence to anyone. From now on we shall enjoy peace. Our internal situation thus permitting me to complete our institutions, the great changes that I plan and that I shall then put into execution will distract public attention. The Senate will become a Chamber of Peers, but in a truly national spirit. All things being so bound up together and simultaneously intermingled, no one will feel that his sensibilities have been wounded."

The Emperor envisaged the peerage in the following manner. He had drawn the families of the old aristocracy into his service so that names that were famous in history, appearing side by side in our ranks with those associated with our modern glory—taking the same chances with them and encountering the same dangers—should no longer be objects of jealousy with the old campaigners. His purpose had been to identify the youth of the old families with the glory and great deeds of modern days, and thus bind the new and old names together by means of a personal pride in the most recent events. He wished to place them in such a situation that he might with justice mend the fortunes of several who had fallen on hard times. It was contrary to his wishes for a Montmorency to be poor when Ney was rich. It was not right that the nephew of Cambacérès, if he should come into the title and fortune of his uncle, should splash a d'Aguesseau or a Molé with the mud from his carriage wheels. . . .

But time was necessary for him to make the fortunes of those who had the right to a peerage and were not wealthy enough to keep up the position. He spoke of men of the old stamp and of the new stamp. All the notabilities would be admitted to the peerage. It was for this purpose that he would retain his "extraordinary domain" [13] and devote the annual revenue from it to increase the capital: for he did not intend this Chamber of Peers to be a charge on the State. The peer-

---

[13] The "extraordinary domain," created by the Senatus Consultus of January 30, 1810, consisted of the portable and fixed valuables acquired by conquest and treaty. The Emperor disposed of the revenues according to his sovereign will, either on the army, or for the encouragement and reward of eminent civil or military services rendered to the State.

age would carry no privileges outside the Chamber nor would noble rank give any, the social distinction being nothing but a question of title and thus in no way offensive to national ideas. The law must be the same for all. Otherwise the idea of a peerage would so shock public opinion that it would rather bring down on its recipients a torrent of public hatred than confer on them the distinction of holding a title. The door of promotion to all posts and functions being open to merit, no matter what a man's extraction or condition of life, the nation would be less offended by his creation of titles. There could be no question of the need for instituting this distinction, yet no act of his had made him more enemies.

As the career lay open for any soldier to become a general, a baron, a duke and then a marshal; or for the son of any peasant, schoolmaster, lawyer or local mayor to become councillor of state, minister and duke, this peerage would, in time, cease to offend any susceptibilities, as it would afford a means of rewarding everyone impartially.

It was his intention to summon to the peerage all the chief men of note, so that the French people, whom he had been the first to proclaim as a great nation, should feel itself honoured in the selection of its most distinguished men, who would, moreover, have sufficient means to be independent; for those who are governed have no guarantee of safety if their representatives lack the first element of independence, especially in a country like France where property must necessarily be the first condition for any form of eminence.

He went on to say that many people thought him violent and despotic because he had an adamantine will; yet at the Council of State, when the Code was being discussed, he had been the most moderate of all those present. It was to him that France owed the Code which would be her eternal glory, the envy of all other peoples and the object of admiration to posterity. He might have let things remain in the chaos in which they had been left by the Old Régime and the Revolution, and ruled the country as he pleased. As it was, no one could deny that France was governed by law.

"That is sufficient answer to make," he said, "to those who construe my firmness of will as despotism."

The Emperor cited several examples of officials and magistrates being dismissed and censured for having been drawn into taking measures or making arbitrary decisions through a mistaken zeal or ill-considered notions of government. He said once again that his principle of government, his own tendency and that of his Council of State, was to uphold, so far as justice allowed, the weak against the strong, and, as a corollary of this, the private individual against the authorities, who, having power on their side, were prone to encroach and carry off things with a high hand. As a broad principle, he exhorted his ministers to be vigilant—to prevent evil rather than be obliged to punish it. The people who observed and were in a position to judge of his government realized perfectly well that the repute in which his strength of will was held served him more than his reputation for severity.

"Everything goes to prove this," he went on. "It is said that I love power. Well, has anyone, in any department, cause for complaint? Never have the prisons been so empty. Does anyone complain of a prefect without obtaining justice? Forty-five out of every fifty complaints are decided against the prefects. The government is strong, my hand is steady, and the officials are sensible that I shall not slacken the reins. So much the better for the people, for while this system traces out a definite path for each to follow, my watchfulness inspires the authorities with vigilance; officials fulfil their duties; all citizens and all forms of property are equally well-protected. The roads have never been safer. Thanks to me there are no more squabbles, no more petty spites, no more parties. Such things are no longer known in France. I have never wished to be anyone's man, I have never sought support from public opinion nor from any class of men. I rely on myself, on the results of what I have successively created in the interests of France, on my institutions, on the moral effect of a government that is not swayed by outside opinions.

"Whether as First Consul or as Emperor, I have been the people's king; I have governed for the nation and in its interests, without allowing myself to be turned aside by the outcries or the private interests of certain people. This is well known throughout France, and the French people love me. I say the French people, and by that I mean the nation, for I have never shown undue favour to the class that some folk understand by the word 'people'—the dregs of the populace. Nor have I shown favour to the landed gentry, for if the unenlightenment and miseries of the former make them very prone to creating disorders, so do the pretensions of the latter render them quite as dangerous to those in authority. Constantly restive against any sort of power that does not emanate from themselves, if they dared they would be in a continuous state of revolt. Are they not always preaching, in every salon of the undisciplined Faubourg Saint-Germain, the revolt that they dare not raise? It is the same now as in the days of the League. The leaders of the Vendée fought better for their own privileges than for the rights of the Crown. The unfortunate people is always the dupe. It was the pretensions of the petty squires, even more than those of the greater gentry, that kept that war going. An aristocracy is necessary for France, but it must be on a different basis from that of the old one, which has become incompatible with the new régime.

"Woe to the sovereign who delivers himself into the hands of the Faubourg Saint-Germain, for it has not changed its nature! Into whatever excesses the Revolution may have been swept, the populace has generally been found to have bowels of mercy. The Faubourg Saint-Germain has none. It wants to reconquer an influence which it imagines belongs to it by right. In its opinion, kings are its own choice, the people are its vassals. Kings must govern by its authority and in its interests, and the people must obey. That is the limit to which the *grands seigneurs* would permit the king to go, if the good old times were ever to return. At one time the Faubourg thought I was its Messiah and would have taken me up. I am still acceptable in their eyes for lack of a better and because they hope my son will prove more manageable than myself. Not daring to rise in revolt, they have submitted without being converted. It matters little to me. As the children of this old aristocracy grow up they will form fresh ideas, they will see that what I offer them is more suitable to the present age than that which their fathers want to restore. The small country landowners, too, will find it advantageous to submit, and my institutions will do the rest. Some of them, perceiving that I want to be a protector to all classes, have withdrawn apart. They will come back, for above all else they like power and the Court. If they keep up their attitude they may find it too late. At the moment these folk are almost ready to make common cause with such hare-brained visionaries as Lafayette and Tracy, who cry out against despotism as though the very fact that they can protest, intrigue, and criticize at their ease were not proof enough that no such thing as despotism exists in France.

"The Legion of Honour," he said, "is the finest of my institutions. It is, with all due deference to poor Moreau and his dreams, one of the greatest conceptions of modern times and as well suited to the needs of the Throne as to those of the people. It establishes a fraternity of honour between the civil and the military, between the marshal and the private, between the peasant and the duke.

"I am the only man alive who knows the French thoroughly, as well as the needs of the peoples and of European society.

The Old Régime was full of excellent things which now need only to be adapted to modern conditions. Those people who think that they have a right to interpose themselves between the people and the Emperor do as much harm as the Jacobins, who desired no government of any sort, or at best an authority so split up that it was tantamount to none at all, our habits and failings being what they are. If I had accepted the beliefs of the Jacobins I should have founded a government on the lines of that established in the United States; but I knew France too well not to see that such a thing would be impossible. The lessons we have learned from the Directory have shown this clearly enough. Others, such as Lannes, who had no fixed ideas, would have liked liberty for themselves and their friends, but none for those who held opposite views. The security of the Consul or President would have depended on the loyalty of the Guard. Pretorian guards are greedy, insatiable, and are a heavier drag on the people than on the sovereign. I did not consider that method of governing suitable. Relying on the support of partisans, one becomes a despot despite oneself; and this form of power was repugnant to me. I threw off that yoke soon after I was named First Consul. My eyes were opened to the embezzlement carried on by the Guard. It is impossible to give any idea of what was going on. Being unable to obtain any accounts, I dismissed the chiefs who tried to hamper me by forming round me a ring of apparently devoted men, as though one could govern France by such means."

Reverting to the subject of the Senate, the Emperor said that it was composed of nothing but spent torches or dark lanterns which would lead the country on the wrong road, even if it overcame its greater difficulties. The greater part of the Senators would, if the occasion arose, imitate Frochot, who liked the Emperor, if the Duke of Bassano was to be believed, but who had nonetheless shown not the slightest objection to having a room in his house prepared as the council chamber for the government that was to be set up by Malet and Lahorie. What Frochot wanted was to remain Prefect of the Seine. (The continual changes of government since the Revolution have made men too familiar with such a state of things. This is an evil which only time will cure.)

"Not only does Frochot owe everything to me; he has also sworn fidelity. Yet, when he believed that I was dead, he was faithless to my son and to his oath—and still thought himself an honest man thereafter. If he had promised you a hundred millions he would have paid you on the appointed day. Nothing would make him fail his given word, yet he broke his oath without the slightest scruple. Such are the men and the notions begotten by the times we live in. Who is to be trusted?"

My remarks directed the conversation to various things that had caused discontent in France, notably conscription, into which the needs of continual warfare had swept all those who compose the classes liable to service. The Emperor replied:

"I agree that conscription is a law that bears harshly upon families, on account of the frequent calls which circumstances have caused me to make; but it is national, because it allows of neither privilege nor exception. In times of peace it will even become popular, for the French love the career of arms, and as the door to promotion is open to ability and courage, an honourable career will thereby be opened to many young men. In this, as in so many things, the appreciation of principles of equality gives strength to the government and ensures success to the levies. If I granted exemption to one single conscript, if there were a single privilege granted to anyone, no matter whom, not one man would obey the order to march.

"The notions of equality that made the Revolution are to-day an integral part of the government's strength. It is because no one anticipates or suspects any preferential treatment and because it has no interest in showing favouritism that the government inspires no distrust. Public confidence in the justice of its dealings gives it as much authority as the exercise of its power. That is the secret of my success. It is said that I love war, but as its charges are laid upon all alike, as I show no preference for anyone and reward all alike if they show courage, everyone submits to it. To inspire people with supreme confidence in my sense of justice—to convince them that I favour no man's interest above that of his neighbour—there lies the grand secret of how to govern the French. That is my all-powerful lever."

The Emperor made another remark to the effect that a Frenchman is a fault-finder by nature.

"Society in the salons," he said, "is always in a state of hostility against the government. Everything is criticized and nothing praised. Although society men and women are in general courtiers, and the greater numbers of them frankly flatterers, even in their chattering they are nonetheless inimical to the government in power. There was a great outcry because I happened to banish from Paris for a few months certain persons who would have had to be arrested a fortnight later if I had not sent them out of the country in time and had not in that way brought their intrigues to naught. That is what they call my tyranny. I am said to be a tyrant because I will not allow a few schemers and fools to get themselves talked about as conspirators; their plots make me laugh, and I would let them come to a head if it did not mean that I should have to exercise severity; whereas it is my desire to be firm, not harsh. Under the Old Régime no one at Versailles was willing to obey. This sort of privilege ruined and discredited the Court. Mistresses and favourites were all intriguing to make or unmake ministers, for they knew that the sovereign was weak; this was actually conspiring against his authority.

"Did it not reach the point of risking our fame just for the sake of ruining such-and-such a general or minister, without a thought of the blood that this treasonable behaviour would cost France and the consequences that a defeat might bring upon the country? Robbery was carried on with impunity in those days, if one had a certain amount of credit and the support of a few men in office. The entire Court, even the Princes of the Blood, were interested in business enterprises or took allowances from contractors. Money was made out of everything. The streets of Paris were badly swept and even worse lighted because the Princes, notably the Count of Artois and the highest of the nobility, accepted commissions or pensions from the scavenging and lighting contractors. I have the proof of it in my possession.

"Such an abuse as this," he continued, "is unknown in my government. There are no gratuities, so far as I am aware. Men are paid good salaries, they are paid regularly, and it is well known that I should show no mercy on swindlers, still less to officials who did business on their own account. Never has the Treasury been in such good order. It has been necessary to make examples. Sometimes the delinquents have been men who were connected with prominent personages; but I have stopped for no considerations of that sort. Feeling myself strong enough to do what was right, I have gone on to my goal allowing nothing to turn me aside, paying no heed to the outcries of various cliques.

"Who makes an outcry in France? A few salons; a few people who have soon forgotten their debt to me for the position or fortune they now enjoy; others whom I have brought back from exile and restored to their property, which they would never have recovered but for me; a few obscure lordlings who are discontented at no longer being sprinkled with holy water on Sundays; a number of self-centred shopkeepers who are under a cloud at the moment because they can find no scope for speculation; some army contractors, veritable bloodsuckers whose ill-gotten gains I have made them disgorge. These are the people who cry out against me. The great mass of the nation is just: the nation sees that I am striving for its good fame, its happiness, its future.

"What can I personally wish for? Born of a distinguished class, though of an unlucky family, I now occupy the greatest throne in the world. I have given law to the whole of Europe. To make the fortunes of those who have served France well, I have furnished millions without touching the State revenues. In my privy purse, and in the 'extraordinary domain,' I possess all the money and treasure that a man could possibly desire; but I have no need of money for myself. No one is less occupied than I in personal affairs.

"That France should prosper under my government is the object of my desires, of my ambition, of my entire attention. It is I who have re-established order, regulated finance, paid the country's debts. I am becoming too heavy and stout not to like rest or have need of it—not to feel a great weariness of the constant movement and activity demanded by warfare. As with all men, my physical condition affects my mental state. You tell me, and everyone likes to believe it, that I love glory and war, that I envisage what you call universal monarchy. But this universal empire is a dream, and I have awakened from it. If, once upon a time, I might have been carried away by this warlike passion, it would, like all passions, have misled me for but a moment."

The conversation reverted to the subject of England.

"If it were possible to have a three or four years' truce," he said, "Europe would feel soon enough the unparalleled and hostile sway of that power's commerce, and the intolerable burden her monopoly imposes. Before long we should see the petitions of Germany asking to have back the prohibitive System that is followed to-day with such repugnance, and demanding vengeance on this foreign government that proves such an enemy of any kind of industry—on this colossus of commerce that cannot exist save at others' expense, and can only meet the interest on its debts, pay its subsidies and confront its own cost by the monopoly it enforces against other nations. But by then it will be too late. Europe will never again be situated so favourably as to-day. The period of quiet will only render these sacrifices more painful. The capital that has been amassed as a result of peace will be put in jeopardy and, to avoid losing it all, we shall have to resign ourselves to our painful lot. I seized the only available instant. I acted as a wise and far-seeing policy dictated. Had I done otherwise, I should have earned the undying reproaches of posterity and history."

The Emperor insisted at some length on the possible advantages of the situation created by the events that had ranged the United States against England.[14] He had no doubt that the actual struggle would end to the advantage of the former. He considered this to be the real turning-point of their political emancipation and their development as a great power. He talked of the respective methods of aggression and defence, as well as of the endeavours that England might make; but he came to the conclusion that reverses at some points, where they might be caught unawares, would simply arouse the Americans and temper the national spirit.

"The English," he said, "will end by subscribing to all that the Americans desire, and the American government, placed in the hands of able statesmen, will gain increased strength. It will profit by the opportunity to make the nation give it the means of organizing and maintaining a larger army, of forming the nucleus of a permanent force, and will obtain more facilities for assembling and forming a militia. If the Americans are wise they will build forts, even strong fortresses, at

[14] The United States declared war against England on June 18, 1812. The cause of this war was the refusal of the English Cabinet to abolish the Order in Council which made it necessary for all neutral vessels to call in at London or Malta for permission to navigate.

certain important points, and this will be of the utmost service to them in the future. This juncture," he said, "will give the United States an anti-English turn that will strengthen our French system, and in the future that country will be England's most powerful adversary. Before thirty years have passed it will make her tremble."

This conversation, from my record of which I have suppressed many details of less importance than the points I have noted, brought us to Görlitz. From that town I sent Amodru in advance to warn Baron Serra, our minister at Dresden, of our approach. I told him that the Emperor would sup and sleep at his house, and that he was to inform the King of Saxony that His Majesty would go to see him incognito. The snow had drifted to such depths in the valleys that our progress was slow. When, at last, we reached the posting-house of Bautzen, we were kept waiting so long for fresh horses that I had to alight from the sledge and go in person to ascertain the reason of the delay. This was occasioned by nothing more than the habitual dilatoriness of the postmaster, and the prevalent bad habit of giving the horses their feed just when the traveller arrived. In vain did I urge the postmaster to hasten matters. There was nothing to be done but exercise patience and get warm while waiting. The Emperor took the opportunity to snatch a nap for three-quarters of an hour; for my part, I made notes of the interesting conversations I had just had with His Majesty.

CHAPTER XV

DRESDEN TO PARIS

WE did not reach Dresden until midnight. [December 13-14.] Our postilion, who had assured me that he knew where the French minister lived, spent so long driving us up and down the town without finding it that at last I grew impatient and ordered him to stop and make enquiries. But everyone was asleep. The whole place was in darkness and we had to go on a long way before we could see a lighted window. The postilion knocked at the door and rang the bell for some time before a man, wearing a nightcap, put his head out of the window and asked what we wanted. Upon our asking him to direct us to the French minister's house, the doctor (for such he was, as I subsequently learned) shut his window with a bang, evidently considering that he was under no obligation to expose himself to the cold by talking to people in good health. So we had to resume our exploration of the town for some considerable time in search of a constable. Luckily we met a Saxon who proved more obliging than the doctor. He conducted us to M. Serra's door, and there we found everything ready, as though he had been waiting for us.

The Emperor started work at once. He dictated to me despatches to the King of Naples and the Prince of Neuchâtel, several orders for Warsaw and a despatch for Vienna. When he had finished his correspondence the Emperor left us the task of sending it off. He supped and went to bed, telling me to wake him when the King of Saxony arrived—for that sovereign did not want His Majesty to be put to the trouble of going to the Palace. While he took his rest M. Serra helped me send off the despatches.

The Emperor had been asleep for an hour when the King of Saxony appeared [three A.M.], accompanied by Counts Loss and Marcolini. He insisted on His Majesty's receiving him in bed; consequently I had the honour of taking the King immediately to his apartment. The two sovereigns were together for three-quarters of an hour.

Instructions had already been given for the continuation of our journey through Saxony. Our sledge was not in a fit state to proceed farther,[1] so the King lent the Emperor his berline fitted with runners. After I had had the honour of accompanying the King to his carriage the Emperor told me that he would start at five o'clock, and bid me awake him at half-past four, in time to sign his letters before taking his seat in the carriage. At his orders I wrote to Baron Saint-Aignan, his minister at Weimar, instructing him to prepare his carriage and have it ready at Erfurt. For two relays we were drawn by horses from the Court, and near Leipzig we passed the couriers who had been sent on to have horses ready for us in my name. So we were obliged to stay in that town to let them get ahead of us. Dusk was falling. While supper was being prepared the Emperor had the curiosity to stroll about the square and in the gardens outside the city. We stayed outdoors for a couple of hours; the cold was much less intense than in Poland.

During the journey that we had just made the Emperor talked again about the Tsar Alexander, Erfurt, the Duke of Abrantès, the peerage and the hatred in which the nobility were held. What I am about to record is the gist of several conversations in the course of which he repeated the same things. He spoke in praise of Count Daru.

---

[1] When I returned to Dresden in 1813 I was assured that an Englishman had bought it as a historical relic, and that everyone had come to look at it, when the Allies were in occupation.—Caulaincourt's note.

"He works like a horse," he said; "he is a man of rare capacity, my best administrator. He has never asked me for anything. He administered Prussia and the conquered territories with a tact and delicacy of feeling of which he alone has given the example. In an enemy country he lived at his own expense, not even benefiting by the advantages enjoyed by others, and which he was entitled to claim. I took care to recompense him for his disinterestedness."

The Emperor returned to the subject of Tilsit. There he had found the Tsar Alexander an ideologist full of ill-digested notions as to his situation, but actuated by excellent intentions, though he lacked experience. The emotions which estranged him from his wife [2] had filled him with false ideas, even as to the need experienced by nations and great States for an heir to the dynasties which ruled over them. These notions had apparently carried him to the length of admitting advantages in an elective monarchy that placed merit on the throne—whereas hereditary succession commonly placed there an incapable, ill-trained fool. The Tsar Alexander felt no regret at his Empress's having borne him no children. In general, he substituted all the virtues of good nature for those resulting from clear reason. He was a conscientious private individual, not a prince. In his childlessness he saw only one responsibility the less, and a responsibility which by his love of what was right seemed to him a serious burden. He was apparently imbued with the idea that monarchs ought to govern for the people, and are instituted for the people.

"That is also my maxim," added the Emperor, dwelling on this principle as if he suspected me of doubting it, and wished to convince me. "Instead of enjoying it, the Tsar appeared to me to be weary of sovereign power and a monarch's life, with

[2] An allusion to Alexander's passion for Marie-Antovna Narishkin. According to the Grand Duke Nicolas Mikhailowitch (*l'Empereur Alexandre I*er, I, 48, 56), the affair lasted from 1804 until 1818.

its round of exacting duties for the man who regards the happiness of his people as a sacred trust held by him from Providence. Alexander is very religious. He is too liberal in his views and too democratic for his Russians. He will be the victim of this: that nation needs a strong hand. He would be more suited to the Parisians, he is just the sort of king the French would like. Gallant to women, flattering with men, even with those towards whom he ought to show his displeasure (for he knows better than anyone else how to hide his feelings), his fine bearing and extreme courtesy are very pleasing. Your good Frenchman loves flattery. He does not like my serious mien, and my firmness often proves irksome to him.

"Our conversations at Tilsit, his relations with you, and what passed at Erfurt have all combined to form the Tsar's opinions. He is clever. Nothing escapes him and his memory serves him perfectly. Since that time his own reflections and the course of events have furnished him with the experience that he previously lacked. He came to Erfurt quite a different man from what he appeared to be at Tilsit. I noticed at Erfurt that he was defiant and unspeakably obstinate. He wanted to treat with me as between equals. As a matter of fact, circumstances were in his favour and he took advantage of them. He might have obtained much more, but fortunately he only paid attention to the effect that would be produced in Russia by the hope of getting Wallachia and Moldavia; he did not insist upon the evacuation of the forts on the Oder and of part of Prussia. More fortunately still, Austria exhibited some ill-humour and distrust. If the man she sent to Erfurt had been enabled to explain openly the views held by his Court, and to show some interest in Prussia, it would have made some impression on Alexander. I should have been placed in a very awkward situation: but even Prussia only sent an incapable fellow, and no one profited by the occasion.

"Anyhow, I was prepared for whatever might happen. I

still had my troops at hand; the sacrifice in Spain was three-quarters made; I should have crushed Austria before anyone could have stopped me. The Russians had not got over their defeat and were in no condition to make war. One might even have done me a service by forcing me to leave Spain; though it would have been disagreeable, after the reverses we had met with there, and especially to have left the English in the field. Threatened by Austria, I should have evacuated a great part of Prussia and retained only a fort on the Oder, as security for the assessments. It is probable that such an arrangement would have caused many changes. We should not be here now. Other combinations would have been necessary in order to establish a buffer-state. With Prussia liberated, restored and re-established, all political combinations would have been modified. Perhaps things would have been better and more advanced, for I should have been obliged to pay more attention to my war in Spain; I should have induced Russia to maintain the alliance and carry out the Continental System against England.

"Thus it is that the most insignificant incidents can change the fate of the world, just as the mistakes of our enemies often serve them to better purpose than the talents of their generals and lead us into even greater errors ourselves. I was wrong in not remaining at Witepsk to organize the country, or in not leaving Moscow a week after I entered the city. The reverses I have met with are due solely to that. I thought that I should be able to make peace, and that the Russians were anxious for it. I was deceived and I deceived myself. Then, Maret and the Abbé de Pradt have not turned Poland to account. I expected to find it in arms, and it was asleep. Maret beguiled the Poles, the archbishop discouraged them. I could not have made a worse choice or entrusted my affairs to a less capable man. I have been deceived by his cleverness. He knows how to argue and flatter, but he is incapable of showing

action. The most insignificant of my secretaries would have
done better.

"Men of his stamp, belonging to the Old Régime, are usually
worth more than that. They are not liked in the army or the
Court; yet look at Narbonne! Never did leader inspire more
zeal in his men; despite his age he undergoes fatigues and
privations like a young man. Yet he is upheld solely by a
sense of honour. You men of the old army do not like these
new adherents; in general, you do not like the émigrés. Every
time I admit one, whether to the Court or to the army, I find
grumbling and sulking. The bolder spirits take umbrage; it is
not so long since they were even ready to rear like a horse annoyed by the bad hands of a poor rider."

I maintained that the opposition of which he spoke was well-
founded so far as some people were concerned, for they but
little merited the personal benevolence he showed towards
them; though so far as M. Narbonne was concerned, he was
universally liked and appreciated.

"This even applies to you, Caulaincourt," he said. "Although you have risen from the ranks like the rest, though you
are a soldier and your success the fruit of your own labours, as
is the case with all my generals—yet your birth and your position as a nobleman arouse jealousy. I have had to uphold you,
and on more than one occasion have been obliged to defend
you. You are an object of envy; I have often received accusa-
tions against you; they tried to discredit you in my eyes after
Moreau's trial, because you continued to see him, even after
the days of the army of the Rhine.[3] It was but a pretext; your
real fault, in the eyes of those zealous souls, lies in the fact
that you are of noble birth. I was not taken in. These preju-
dices are shared by many honest men. Having brought about
your downfall they would have attacked Duroc and Lauriston.

[3] As Colonel of the Second Carabineers, Caulaincourt had made the campaign of 1800 in the army of the Rhine, under the command of Moreau.

The men who are so proud of bearing a title to-day, not so long ago were bitter against those who had one. Junot alone does not share this weakness. He considers himself more a marquis, more of a great nobleman than the Beauvaus; but Lannes and Bessières and Lefèbvre were eaten up with resentment. If I did the slightest thing for a man of noble birth, even if his claim to a title extended to no further than his father's purchase of it, they talked to me as though I were acting against my own interests; but I saw through them. Fortunately I have never had a favourite, but if I had singled out any particular person, if I had favoured anyone of noble birth with my confidence, it would have made some men actually ill. By consolidating all interests, by mingling all classes and fortunes, time will exhaust these jealousies."

The Emperor spoke well of various persons, especially of Marshal Bessières, upon whose attachment he relied. He praised his integrity, and his effective administration of the Guard.

"I was obliged to take it from Lannes," he said. "The itch to amass a fortune, and the advice he took from some knaves who made him their dupe, would have ruined him had I not removed him from that administration. No man," he repeated, "has ever been or still is [4] more attached to me than Lannes is at heart. More than once he has given me proofs of this by exposing himself in perilous circumstances, but he loves me as a man loves his mistress and wants to manage me, or at least influence me, in order to obtain what he wants. Having been often refused, for his demands are in favour of schemers, he loses his temper; and being passionate by nature, he is then capable of anything. More than once, in such moments, he has done me a wrong which might have proved serious to anyone

[4] Lannes had died May 31, 1809. The Emperor's use of the present tense, as recorded by Caulaincourt, must be the result of an error on the part of whoever copied the MS.

else, if he had to do with a sovereign of a different nature from mine, or one who held the human race in greater esteem."

After mentioning several acts which had led him to forbid Lannes for a time to appear at the Tuileries, the Emperor went on to say that this marshal had a strain of opposition and censoriousness in his character which blinded him and outweighed his attachment to his person. He was indiscreet and immoderate. To support this assertion he told me of a certain person to whom the marshal had boasted of what he had said to the Tsar of Russia, shortly before the last war with Austria. At the time of the Erfurt interview the Emperor had accredited Lannes to meet the Tsar, and as he travelled in the carriage with that monarch, he told him that the Emperor Napoleon meant to deceive him, that his ambition knew no bounds, that he breathed only war as the means of reaching the end he had in view, and that he, the Tsar, should know better than to trust him. Lannes even bragged of having added various intimate details and cited facts to enlighten the Tsar, as he called it, and prevent his becoming the Emperor's dupe.

"I heard this in confidence," said His Majesty; "and it explained Alexander's conduct and his distrust at Erfurt. I did not mention the matter to the marshal; it would have compromised the man who reported it to me, and I might have had further occasion for his services. Nothing I could have said to the marshal would have changed him. Had he found himself unmasked he would have become an irreconcilable enemy, whereas he subsequently behaved like an honest fellow. Besides, in other circumstance he had made a rampart of his body in my defence and he died a hero's death, though his conduct had been that of a traitor; for his mission to the Tsar was simply a matter of courtesy and he had not been called upon to express any opinion on me or my affairs. He was not proof against flattering remarks or the confidence that Alexander pretended to place in him; still less was he able to forget an old grudge he had against me—I do not know on what score—for he was as violent in his feelings as he was impetuous on the field of battle. In his latter years he had an admirable coolness and had become as distinguished a general as he was audacious as a leader. He was one of my best generals, perhaps the most efficient on the battle-field. Men are like that, Caulaincourt," said the Emperor. "I am condemned for holding them in slight esteem. Am I wrong? Should I ever grant pardon, should I ever forget, if I expected them to be better than they can be or than they really are?"

I return once more to the inn at Leipzig where, by the time we returned, the stove had become red-hot to warm us. Our dinner or supper, whichever you like to call it, was not yet ready, so the Emperor stretched himself on some chairs which I had placed together near the fire, and I seized the opportunity to continue my notes. At last supper was served. Extremely impatient to be on the road again, His Majesty cut the meal as short as he could.

Just as he was going downstairs a young Frenchman, who said he was a staff officer and was staying at the hotel, presented himself to the Emperor for the purpose of giving an account, as he said, of a secret mission on which he had been sent by the general of the staff. I was habitually so close to the Emperor at any time he was likely to be accosted, that I found myself between him and this officer, who was so eager that he jostled us. A crowd had collected, attracted by the splendid appearance of the King of Saxony's sledge. The Emperor was hurrying to reach this vehicle and for the moment paid no attention to the man, but, struck by his manner rather than by his insistence, His Majesty paused. Then, guessing that it was probably a spy—or worse—posing as an officer, he promptly dismissed him. The whole bearing and appearance of this officer appeared to me suspicious. As we left the town I looked behind the carriage, for I had a presentiment that he was following us.

There he was, in fact, seated beside our courier, telling him that he had been ordered to accompany us. I ordered him to get down, but it was not easy to make him obey.

Beyond Lutzen there was so little snow in certain parts of the road that the runners of the berline broke. After leaving Auerstädt we had to abandon the King's fine sledge; and we entered Vigenov at daybreak [December 15] in the courier's modest calèche. The postmaster, who knew me, came to chat while the relay was being put to, and I believe he recognized the Emperor, although he gave no sign of having done so. His Majesty partook of coffee without alighting from the carriage. At Erfurt we found Baron Saint-Aignan at the posthouse. The Emperor breakfasted with him, spoke of affairs and issued various orders to him and to the commandant of the place. After an hour we started again, in a landau that M. Saint-Aignan had caused to be fitted up so that the Emperor could lie at full length in it. His Majesty was delighted with this, and several times said that a good carriage, at the end of a long journey, gave greater pleasure than a comfortable bed after three months under canvas. He made me get rid of the Saxon gendarme who had been on the seat behind us since we had left Dresden, and we took a French one in his place.

When we reached Eisenach the horses were not ready, although it was more than two hours since they had been ordered. Tired of waiting in the carriage, after half an hour the Emperor alighted and entered the posting house to warm himself and chat with the postmistress, a very pretty young woman. Her husband made us the deepest of bows, but without putting himself to the trouble of getting us on our way. Seeing that the horses he said he had requisitioned from the inhabitants did not appear, and that my repeated demands evoked nothing but *Gleich* (immediately), it was clear that nightfall would find us in the difficult defiles of mountain and forest, so I left the Emperor and went out to make enquiries.

All I could learn was that the horses ought to arrive. My mind was filled with the idea that perhaps it was known that the traveller was none other than the Emperor; that they were deliberately delaying us until nightfall with the intention of setting an ambuscade. I was surprised, moreover, that a posthouse which I knew to be so well supplied with relays should have to requisition horses when they had been warned in advance of our coming. As we had met no travellers on the road, I was anxious to speak to someone and assure myself that there really were no posthorses. I went into the courtyard to find out why the horses requisitioned in the town had not come, and talked to a postilion as my eyes wandered round looking for the stables. I enquired whether the postmaster had no horses. He stealthily pointed with his finger to the stables, which were closed. I tapped on the door softly, saying in German *Mach auf* (Open!). Mistaking my voice for one of his fellows', a postilion opened the door immediately. I found ten excellent horses which were being reserved, no doubt, for some better occasion.

All the postilions ran up as soon as they saw me in the stable. I ordered them to harness the horses and put them to the carriage. At this they tried to make off, but I stopped three of them and called to the gendarme, whom I saw beneath the archway, to hold the others. Warned by one of the postilions, the postmaster hastened up and forbade his horses to be used. Upon this a great turmoil ensued. When I saw that the best reasons in the world failed to move him and that the postilions dared not disobey, I grabbed him by the collar and forced him into a corner of the stable, ordering him to have the horses put to instantly. He resisted, and I saw that the noise of our struggle had already attracted a small crowd. Also, the gendarme was having trouble detaining the postilions, who were trying to make their escape. I drew my sword, presented the point to the postmaster, and told him that if anyone came in from outside or made a movement, or if the horses were not harnessed in five minutes' time, I would run him through. Thanks to the sword point, which made him realize that I was a man of my word, this argument proved as irresistible to him as to his postilions. The horses were harnessed in the twinkling of an eye. One of the postmaster's friends, who called himself a counsellor of the Duke, appeared on the scene and at the beginning of the discussion was inclined to take his part, but I told him so curtly to mind his own business that he went off without another word. The postmaster's wife appeared when she saw their horses being led out. Learning what had happened, she ran weeping to the Emperor and stammered in broken French that her husband was being ill-treated. The Emperor came up just as the last horses were being led across the courtyard. I followed them with the postmaster, to whom the Emperor handed over his loving wife, telling them that they had done wrong to treat travellers in such a manner.

The Emperor did not know what to make of the postmaster's behaviour. The delay had startled him, and we remained on the alert all night. [December 15-16.] Never, I think, was I so glad to see daybreak, for never had the Emperor been in any situation that worried me more. It was bitter cold. We travelled rapidly, despite the bad Westphalian roads. A clumsy postilion managed to snap the carriage pole, but a couple of straps sufficed to mend it and we lost no more than half an hour. The Emperor stopped at Hanau and sent for M. d'Albini, minister of the Prince Bishop, to whom he talked while at his breakfast. This gentleman was not a little surprised to see His Majesty, especially with such a modest suite.

A league before reaching the Rhine we met M. Anatole Montesquiou, whom I had despatched from Molodetchna. He was on his way back from Paris, where he had stayed but a few hours. The news he had carried thither would have prepared the public for the bulletin. He brought word of the Empress, and was, I assume, very agreeably surprised to meet the Emperor and thus have his journeying brought to so speedy a conclusion. His Majesty asked him about the Empress and his son, and then started him off for Paris at once with news of us. But we met him again on the banks of the Rhine which, by reason of the floating ice, had to be crossed by boat. Thereafter he followed us.

When we had reached the farther side the Emperor went on foot to the posthouse, while his carriage was being ferried over and disembarked. I never remember seeing the Emperor so light-hearted. Setting foot once more on French soil made him forget all his weariness, and perhaps even his misfortunes, for a moment. When he reached the posting-house the post-master recognized him. Marshal Valmy, for whom he sent and to whom he talked while the horses were being harnessed, could not believe his own eyes. We were on the road again before seven o'clock. Fagalde, who had been sent by way of Gumbinnen and had rejoined us at Glogau, had acted as courier,[5] together with Amodru, since we had left Dresden. They continued their duties now that we were in France.

Fresh despatches from Paris led the conversation to the Malet affair and elicited from the Emperor several observations that . . . seemed to me worth recording.

"Observe," said the Emperor, "how the Revolution and the confirmed habit of changing governments have destroyed all idea of order and stability. There is still much for me to do towards re-establishing the social order. . . . When my death was announced, not one of those soldiers or officials gave a

[5] The meaning of the word "courier," as it is used here, has become a little obscured. In the days of stage-coaches it was applied to the man who went ahead to prepare the changes of horses and see to the travellers' accommodation.

single thought to my son. The idea of the King of Rome did
not even occur to Frochot. It seemed to him simpler to have a
fresh revolution than to maintain the established order of things.
But when I get to Paris everyone will boast of his own devotion
to me, and Frochot with the rest of them, if I admit him to my
presence. An example must be made, for fidelity is perhaps a
more sacred duty in a magistrate than in a soldier, who has
only to obey the orders he receives without questioning them.
Errors committed by magistrates are serious matters; for they
are expected to set an example. How blind men are, even where
their own interests are concerned! . . . France needs me for
another ten years. If I were to die there would be general
chaos; every throne would collapse if my son's collapsed; for
I perceive that all I have done still is very unstable."

"Our institutions and organizations are not completed," I
said. "All the powerful interests of the country must be enlisted for the preservation of the existing—"

"You need a peerage," the Emperor interrupted briskly; "an
aristocracy adapted to the time we live in; but with the fickleness
of this nation and the pretensions of the generals it will be a
good ten years before those new institutions will exercise sufficient influence. If there were more talent among the army
commanders, they would be like Caesar's lieutenants and divide
the world among themselves; but none has the genius necessary
to accomplish a revolution so great as this, though it might save
you in the event of my dying. . . . If I were to die, the danger
would lie in the weakness of the Regency and the intrigues of
the generals who want all the interest, all the places, and especially all the money. You would not pull through, particularly
if you failed to take immediate steps to decrease the numbers
of the Guard. Observe that I, myself, have not put all arms
of that service under the same commander. A very firm will
is needed to keep the Guard in hand.

"Malet is a lunatic. He must be, if he believed he could

overturn a government just by suspending the activities of the police and hoodwinking some senior officers and a prefect for a matter of three hours, when there was an army of two hundred thousand men abroad and he had not one accomplice in high office nor in the provinces. He is a man who wanted to get himself shot by getting himself talked about, but his action has proved conclusively what I had partly suspected—that no great faith can be put in mankind. The men of the Old Régime were unruly and factious. They rose in revolt when they dared, but they would not permit an underling to rebel and they were faithful to their oath. The notions of monarchy and hereditary titles—the desire to preserve the existing order of things—these belong to a new language which is to be learned by the rising generation; but they will never be in the dictionary of the men of to-day. They have already forgotten the misfortunes of the Revolution.

"Clarke boasts of his devotion, of what he did and the orders he gave, possibly after the event; but he did not even put on his boots to go to the nearest barracks and make sure of the troops. . . . He saw Jacobins everywhere. We will see who is right. To ensure that the thing shall be unravelled I have not even changed the Minister of Police; for he is more concerned than anyone else in repairing the harm brought about by his lack of foresight.

"Savary clings to his ministry and the salary. He is afraid of losing his post, although, so far as that goes, he no longer needs it, as I have given him plenty of money. He has at least five or six millions. Whether as aide-de-camp or as cabinet minister, he was always asking me for money, and this displeased me. Not that he was alone in this, for never did Ney or Oudinot or many another open or finish a campaign without coming to me for cash. Savary had no fortune; he has children and an extravagant wife. I must, however, do him the justice to say that he serves me with zeal. He has a fine appearance, and this is essential in Paris. His squabbles with Maret weary me. He is always at odds with him. I do not like this bickering; they are jealous of each other. Savary thinks that I prefer Maret to himself. Do you know who put them against one another?"

"I do not know at all."

"Probably their wives: they would embroil empires. My other ministers never bother me on that score. They understand one another and do not weary me with their petty jealousies or dislikes. Sometimes I have wanted to get Cambacérès married, but, when all is said and done, it would have been a nuisance. Women have pretensions, and the wives of functionaries have always been a nuisance at Court. One does not know where to rank them, nor what precedence to give them when there are foreign ladies present.

"Poor Savary is not treated well by the Paris correspondents. Everyone ridicules him. It is always a stroke of luck for many conspirators when a Minister of Police gets the worst of it, though another comes to take his place. Savary's fall appears certain, and it seems as if everyone wants the honour of dealing him the first blow."

"That is one reason, Sire, why you should stand up for him and keep him, for, as you say, he will now do better than another. If there has been no conspiracy, if Malet is the sole author of this folly, Savary is justified."

"You are right, but I can scarcely believe it is so. Savary is the dupe of some conspirators who have blinded his eyes, or this would have slipped out to Pasquier, who is a good observer. We shall know all about it—tell me, in how many hours?"

"In forty-four hours, Sire."

"I say in thirty-six."

Upon this the Emperor made me relight the candle; and he set to work reckoning alternately by the map and the road-book how many hours it would take us. After disputing about minutes, as if it lay in my power to prolong our journey, he then spoke of his anticipated joy at seeing the Empress and his son, and then began to tease at my ear and joke about the eight hours that he was obliged to add to his calculations—which he spent a couple of hours in going over again. Each stage, each quarter of a stage, each quarter of an hour, each minute, was reckoned up. Our inevitable halts, our moments of rest, all were curtailed; the difficulties and delays of the road were whittled down to a minimum. The Emperor forgot Malet, the police, all his troubles. By daylight his expression showed me that he was already dreaming of the Tuileries, where I was as anxious to see him safely installed as he was to be there. He seemed so confident and happy that for me, also, this was one of the pleasantest moments of our journey.

The following day the Emperor supped at Verdun. [December 17.] Having resumed a wheeled carriage at Erfurt, we had to stop twice a day to grease the axles, and we took advantage of this forced delay to eat. After leaving Dresden the Emperor spoke of nothing but Paris, of the Empress's surprise at seeing him, of how everyone would be astonished. From Frankfort onwards he calculated the hour of his arrival in Paris and at each stage confirmed his certainty of reaching there before midnight, if nothing delayed us. The more frequently he met the couriers, the more avid he was for details. He was more satisfied than he had expected to be with the attitude of public opinion, and with its reception of the news of our retreat from Moscow, coupled with the interruption of all communications, but he was much concerned with the effect the bulletin would have caused, and was surprised at getting no news of it, especially as M. Montesquiou, who preceded his messenger, had rejoined us. Judging by private correspondence, every family was too occupied with its own stake in Russia to pay great attention to public affairs. It was not thought that there could have been a battle; the Russians were supposed to be in no condition to fight. This opinion made any disquietude less lively. Our disasters were entirely ignored. As we subsequently learned, it had not been possible to publish the famous bulletin which depicted them so tragically until the sixteenth, two days later than the Emperor thought.

This delay annoyed the Emperor, who would have liked the publication to have preceded his arrival by some days. He had travelled more rapidly than he realized. Habitually so calm and impassive, His Majesty was now agitated by so many diverse emotions, regrets and hopes, he had such happiness before him and had left such misery behind, that he could not hide his feelings. After talking for some considerable time about the various things that filled his mind, he returned for the third time to our adventure at Eisenach. He could not understand the behaviour of the postmaster, who had been warned a long time in advance, and knew that the horses were for a distinguished traveller. The place, the hour, everything rendered his conduct suspicious. The Emperor ordered me to write to Baron Saint-Aignan, instructing him to obtain precise information regarding the motives for the man's behaviour, and to complain to the government if necessary. He was to make his report at once.

"As it is a personal matter," added the Emperor, "I do not wish the postmaster to be arrested now, nor to be dismissed. But it would be satisfactory to know there was no intrigue at the back of it."

The conversation returned to affairs in general. What the Emperor had said to me about the King of Naples's schemes [for a United Italy] gave me a chance to speak of Rome and the Pope. I deprecated the latter's captivity,[6] which, I told him, created a bad effect everywhere, even though Christendom no

---

[6] Pius VII, arrested at Rome on July 6, 1809, had been held prisoner at Savone for three years and then transferred to Fontainebleau in June, 1812.

longer drew the sword to back up the thunders of the Vatican.
The Emperor agreed that it was an unpleasant business. He
said:

"In removing the Pope from Rome for the time being, I had
thought to get him away from some bad advice. I should
perhaps have done better to leave him there; my government is
strong enough in Italy to make even the priests feel it. To this
coup d'état, nonetheless, I owe the tranquillity that that country
has enjoyed for the past year. The English have not stopped
pouring money in there, to start at least partial insurrections;
and they have miscarried. Not even the most timid consciences,
if their owners wished to be fair-minded, could find anything
more than a political difference in my disputes with the Pope.
The Church has me to thank for the re-establishment of the
True Faith in France—perhaps for its survival in Europe—and
I am surely as good a Catholic as Charles V was, who also
carried off a Pope without becoming a heretic in consequence.

"If I had followed the advice of several very enlightened men
at the moment when I restored religion, I should not have made
myself dependent upon Rome. They suggested alternatives to
me. I might have done like the Tsars; have created a sort of
Patriarch, and made myself head of the Church, or at least its
protector, as the King of Prussia is of Protestantism. (Speaking of that, everybody is Protestant now, since no one goes to
confession any more.) The other alternative was to form a
permanent council or committee of bishops for the administration of matters spiritual—in fact, a Gallican Church. That
would have changed no usages, and so would have offended
none of the devout; for no one would have known the nature
of my accountings with Rome.

". . . Now," the Emperor added, "it is indispensable to
establish the Pope in France, and to bring the cardinals there,
so as to have the Sacred College under one's influence. This
preference belongs to France; her papist population forms the

largest clientele the Pope has. He would then find himself in the midst of his flock. Where should I be now if the Pope had died, and this sensible, moderate successor to the Chief Apostle had been replaced by an Austrian or an Italian, angry and ultramontane—as would inevitably have been the case?

". . . The clergy," he said, "is a power that never is quiet. Against you unless it is for you, it serves none free of charge. You cannot be under obligations to it, wherefore you must be its master. . . . Before it can be the auxiliary of government, it has to be its friend; and to secure that, the clergy must have its rights clearly defined. With me its pretensions can come to nothing; but after me they could cause disorder. God has given me the strength to undertake great things, and to delight in them. I must not leave them incomplete. The clergy must be restricted to reconciling us with heaven—to consoling our women and us, when we grow old—and must surrender to us the power of this world: *Roi dans le temple, sujet à la porte.*"

The army and Poland furnished inexhaustible topics of conversation. Two army couriers, with news of the happenings during the sixty hours that succeeded our departure, reached us one after the other. The King of Naples and Berthier reported that the rout continued; the intensity of the cold had caused many to desert the colours, even many of the Guard; but there was nothing to prepare us for the events that were to follow—nothing even that might have made us foresee them.[7] The Emperor was well aware that his departure would have increased the disorder to some extent, and that it would affect the

[7] The final disasters were in progress while this conversation took place. As Caulaincourt has noted, the thermometer was falling when the Emperor started from Smorgoni on December 5. Two days later it had reached 34° F. below zero. The King of Naples then kept himself as warm as he could in Wilna, and left the troops to do likewise. Wilna was evacuated in panic on the tenth; Murat and the generals rode on ahead; and two miles beyond the town what remained of the artillery and supply-waggons was abandoned in a great dump. None even paused to set fire to it, though the enemy was off guard; only the Treasury funds were salvaged on horse-

Guard more than the other corps, but as Wilna was the goal that everyone was striving for, it mattered little to him whether the men reached there singly or with their units. As the issue of rations and clothing were only to be made to men with the colours, he appeared certain of being able to rally the army. His despatches confirmed him more than ever in the opinion that the army would hold Wilna. It was in vain that I combated this view. He jested and laughed at my arguments, which he called misgivings.

"You see everything in its worst light," he said.

Nothing but the actual outcome of events was able to undeceive him. At that moment he was more than ever filled with hopes. To find himself back in France seemed to signalize the return of his good fortune. He had a presentiment that his Star was again in the ascendant, and, certain of being able to control events, he could think no more about the disasters which, forty hours previously, he had been able to face as clearly as I did.

Towards Harville we overtook Fagalde, one of the grooms, who had not been able to get beyond Mars-le-Tour. At Saint-Jean the front axle-tree of our carriage broke, some five hundred paces from the posthouse. The Emperor took his place beside me in a little open cabriolet which had served for the courier who had followed us. We had to give up our heavy cloaks, as there was no room for them. Since leaving Fulda we had noticed a great difference in the temperature. It was in this *croquant* that we drove into Meaux. Only Amodru had

back. Kowno was pillaged on the twelfth. On the fourteenth, four days before Napoleon reached Paris, all that was left of the Grand Army had crossed the Niemen into East Prussia. Berthier fell ill of exhaustion, and of chagrin at having seconded the King of Naples's appointment. The rout continued. On January 16, 1813, at Posen, Murat left the army without a commander and fled in disguise to Naples. When orders had had time to come through from Napoleon, Prince Eugène rallied the remnant of the six hundred thousand that had entered Russia the preceding June. Of the survivors, a thousand men of the Guard eventually reached Paris in formation.

remained with us; and he still had the energy to ride ahead of us and order horses, though we were driving as though the devil were behind us.

The Emperor had been recognized at Mayence; the postilions told everyone who he was, but the postmasters would only believe it when they saw him for themselves. As for the postilions, they whirled us onward like men certain in advance of the napoleon that I was to give to each. It is impossible to convey any idea of the eagerness exhibited by the stable hands and postmaster, immediately on our arrival at the beginning of a stage, when they heard from the men who had brought us that it was the Emperor himself and not merely the Master of Horse, as our advance-courier had announced. From Metz onward we thought we had come into spring; the ice had given place to horrible mud. At Meaux the postmaster gave us his own chaise that closed properly and took us right to the Tuileries. Since leaving Claye poor Amodru, overcome by drowsiness rather than by fatigue, kept swaying in the saddle, and I had to encourage him every moment. At the sound of my voice he would wake up with renewed energy. At last the moment arrived when he was to ride ahead into the courtyard and hand us out at the Tuileries.

Without being told to do so, and before the mounted sentinels had time to challenge him, the postilion drove at a gallop through the Arc de Triomphe.[8]

"That's a good sign," the Emperor said to me.

Safe and sound, he got out at the main gateway just as the clock was striking the quarter before midnight. [December 18, 1812.] I had unbuttoned my overcoat far enough to show the braid of my uniform. The sentries, taking us for despatch officers, let us pass; and so we got through to the door of the

[8] Right of way through the Arc de Triomphe was reserved for the Emperor's carriage.

open gallery that overlooks the Gardens. The porter, who had gone to bed, came out with a lamp in his hand, and dressed only in his shirt, to see who was knocking. Our faces looked so strange to him that he called his wife. I had to repeat my name three or four times over before I could persuade them to open the door. Nor was it without difficulty and a lot of blinking—she stuck the lamp right into my face—that either of them knew who I was. Then she unlocked, while he was calling one of the regular footmen. The Empress had just retired. I asked to be shown into the quarters of her ladies-in-waiting, ostensibly to give her word that the Emperor would follow me, as our custom was. All this time the porter and the rest of them were looking over the Emperor from head to foot. "It's the Emperor!" one of them shouted. I cannot tell you how pleased they were. They could scarcely contain themselves.

The two ladies-in-waiting on the Empress came out of her apartment at the very moment when I came into theirs. My two-weeks' beard, the state of my clothes, my fur-lined boots,—all this, I imagine, struck them as unfavourably as it had the porter; for I had to repeat the good news of the Emperor's arrival over and over before I could stop their fleeing from the ghost they thought they saw. Finally the Emperor's name reassured them, and helped them to recognize me. One of them announced me to the Empress. Meanwhile the Emperor, who had scarcely been able to hide his impatience, brought my errand to an end by coming into the Empress's apartment and saying to me:

"Good-night, Caulaincourt. You need some rest, too."

I went immediately to the Archchancellor's, as the Emperor had instructed me to do. The Prince had little thought that the despatch he sent off by the evening post would reach its destination so quickly. If I had not come by the post-chaise—if a footman in the palace livery had not come with me, and the postilion's uniform had not been my passport—I should have had trouble again in being admitted at the Archchancellor's. I could have got nowhere on my looks. The Court footman had more or less to stand sponsor for me, for the Prince's servants looked me over and did not know for sure what to make of this figure that none of them recognized or would announce. M. Jaubert, of the Bank, and a number of others who were in the Prince's salon, stood as though petrified at this apparition. Everyone looked at me without saying a word. None knew what to make either of my arrival or of this figure that seemed not to fit the name which had been announced. After the first impression produced by my attire and my beard, the same thought came to them all:

"Where is the Emperor? What's the news? Can something have happened to him?"

That was what everybody said, without being able to utter a word. The terrible bulletin had come out; none had awakened that morning with pleasant impressions. They felt glum. None knew the Emperor was in Paris; why was the Master of Horse there? Why had he left the Emperor? The hour, the pale lamp-light, the uncertainties they had been through, the melancholy details they had learned and those for which they were waiting,—all this filled their minds with gloom and inclined them to sad forebodings. Such was the state of those in the salon, while I stood there waiting for the footman to return from announcing me in the Prince's study. That dumb show cannot be described. All stared at me without the power to speak: they seemed to be holding their breath. Each tried to read his own sentence in my glance—and the expression of all their faces betrayed more fear than hope. I had spoken to M. Jaubert; when his first astonishment had worn off, he exclaimed:

"And the Emperor, Your Grace—?"

He could not finish his question. Each repeated those words with an air of dismay:

"And the Emperor? Where is he?"

"In Paris," I answered.

At that all their faces brightened up, and I went in to see the Prince. He greeted me with the same exclamation, which I broke in upon to give him reassurance. I conveyed the Emperor's orders, chatted a few minutes, and enjoined upon him to have the cannon announce the Emperor's return at dawn. He was also to advise the ministers and the Court that levee would be held at eleven o'clock, and so on.

On reaching my quarters I ordered that a page be sent to Madame Mère and to each of the Princesses at eight in the morning, to announce the Emperor's arrival to them. I wrote the Lord Chamberlain concerning the palace staff. . . .

On the morrow [December 19] the Emperor ordered me to take over the portfolio of Foreign Affairs during the Duke of Bassano's absence, and to bring him certain parts of the Viennese correspondence, together with the latest treaties with Austria and Prussia. I was wearied from the fourteen nights I had spent on the qui vive, without a wink of sleep, and in a measure depressed by the sense of the responsibilities that such a journey, made under such circumstances, had heaped upon me. Apart from that, moreover, I had been heavily preoccupied lest something happen to the Emperor, who had entrusted himself to my care and good faith. All these recent impressions had induced such a state of nervous exhaustion that I needed some repose. I therefore requested the Emperor to excuse me from this task, and to turn it over to M. de la Besnardière. He acceded.

At eleven o'clock I was at the Tuileries for the levee. The ministers and many of the Household officials (the chamberlains in particular) were at hand. They crowded around and made much of me, as though I had been a favourite—as though I were a man with influence, who had just spent fourteen nights and as many days tête-à-tête with Authority.

The dreadful bulletin had appeared in the *Moniteur* on the sixteenth. We had had word of that from the last despatch we met along the way. It had produced so strong an impression, even upon the most subservient, that they too sought to read from my expression some news of their dear ones. None dared to ask me for it. The bulletin alone had arrived; not one private letter had been given out. I had the satisfaction of setting many peoples' minds at rest. But there were, alas, many whom I saddened—even though, after Malo-Jaroslawetz, the army had been so disordered and strung out that the General Staff was unable to give reports about many officers, even of the highest rank. They, unhorsed and in total want, had had to seek their subsistence by following the gangs that ranged along the flanks of the column, now towards the head and now towards the rear. The most resolute were reduced to this cruel necessity; for a whole handful of gold, even before the Beresina, would not have procured a crust of bread. . . .

I return to the attendance chamber, before concluding what relates to the campaign and the Emperor's journey. As I was saying, the bulletin had produced so woeful a sensation that none dared question me. The lone servant [Roustam] who had accompanied us was sleeping, and had been forbidden besides to tell anything in his conversation. The Emperor spoke out as frankly about our reverses as the bulletin had done. As yet, however, no news could be had of the army's arrival at Wilna; and consequently he, like everyone else, knew nothing of the worst disasters. His legs were a little bloated, his eyes were puffy, and he had the hue of one whose skin has been tanned by the cold. Otherwise he appeared in good health. He was so happy to find himself in Paris that he did not need to compose his countenance in order to appear satisfied and not at all downcast. He worked the whole day and even part of the night, sending out orders and imparting to all branches of administration the impulse he wished them to have. He seemed to me well content with the state of opinion and of public spirit since the printing of the bulletin. His arrival had calmed many fears and allayed the greatest anxieties— though unhappily without drying the tears of families that had losses to weep for.

The Emperor spoke of his disasters, of the mistake he had made by staying at Moscow, as a stranger might have done.

"The venture failed by a week's time," he said. "Everything in the world depends on that. The right moment, timeliness, those are everything."

In receiving MM. Decrès and Cessac, his first words were:

"Well, well, gentlemen, Fortune dazzled me. I let myself be carried away, instead of following the plan I had made and that I spoke of to you, Monsieur Cessac. I have been to Moscow. I thought to sign peace there. I stayed there too long. I had thought to gain in a year what only two campaigns could achieve. I have made a great blunder; but I shall have the means to retrieve it."

From the very first the complexion of Paris had looked cheering to him. His return had produced a tremendous effect. The Emperor sensed as much; and after the second day he felt reassured about the consequences that his losses might entail. The losses at Wilna did not alter his opinion.

"The terrible bulletin has had its effect," he said to me; "but I see that my presence is giving even more pleasure than our disasters give pain. There is more affliction than discouragement. This state of mind will communicate itself to Vienna; and all will be retrieved within three months."

If I have omitted many things from the details here given of the conversations I had with the Emperor during our long tête-à-tête, I can at least guarantee the accuracy, for the most part down even to the very words, of what I do record. Neither conscience nor memory has played me false. I had long been in the habit of telling the Emperor candidly what I thought, without fear of offending him; and I owe it to him to declare that, during this journey, he more often requested me to speak out boldly than to mind what I was saying. He encouraged me especially by the frankness of his discourse and of his confidences. He proved to me what I had already believed: that he did not always love the plain truth, but that he esteemed those who spoke it plainly.

Under other circumstances, if the conversation touched on a matter he would not discuss, he broke it off somehow or other. If he were at home he would leave or dismiss you, or would interrupt with an order foreign to the subject at hand. Sometimes, too, he would say: "You know nothing about that."

In the sledge, on the contrary, he always prompted. Did he feel himself hurt?—he joked about it. More than anything, he showed the need of unburdening himself. If certain topics were too displeasing to him, he would change the subject momentarily. But that day or the next he would revert to the same question. I venture to assert that during this journey the Emperor was kind enough to hear me without taking offence; and I say once again that I was able to convince myself, from the nature and frankness of his conversation, that one could lay many claims to his confidence who could lay none to his favour.

Use this map as a visual help to reading. Lay the book flat, unfold the map, turn back to the page in which you are reading.

THE RUSSIAN CAMPAIGN

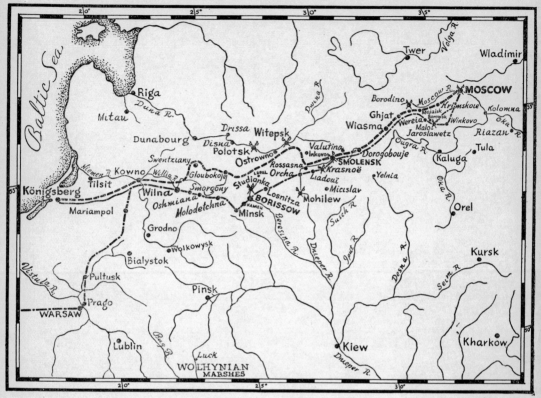

MARCH TO MOSCOW ------   RETREAT ━━━━━   BATTLES ✗

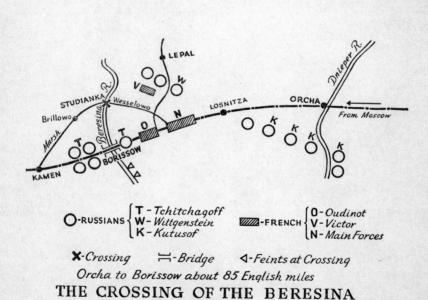

O - RUSSIANS { T - Tchitchagoff   W - Wittgenstein   K - Kutusof }   ▨ - FRENCH { O - Oudinot   V - Victor   N - Main Forces }

✗ - Crossing   ⊨ - Bridge   ◁ - Feints at Crossing

Orcha to Borissow about 85 English miles

THE CROSSING OF THE BERESINA

THE CROSSING OF THE BEREZINA

BIOGRAPHICAL NOTES

BIOGRAPHICAL NOTES

ON THE MOST IMPORTANT MEN ASSOCIATED WITH NAPOLEON

ABRANTÈS, Duke of. *See* JUNOT.

BASSANO, Duke of. *See* MARET.

BEAUHARNAIS, Prince Eugène de, VICEROY OF ITALY: born in Paris, 1781. Son of Josephine, and step-son of Napoleon. Resented his mother's second marriage; aide-de-camp to Napoleon in Italy and Egypt; with his sister, Hortense, helped to reconcile Napoleon and Josephine in 1799. Granted two hundred thousand francs yearly, and title of Prince, after the Empire was established; Viceroy of Italy, with large administrative powers, after Napoleon became King there in 1805; married Princess Amelia Augusta of Bavaria the same year, by Napoleon's arrangement; Grand Duke of Frankfort, 1810. Commanded the Fifth Corps in the Russian campaign, and distinguished himself at Borodino and Malo-Jaroslawetz.—Eugène, despite the favouritism shown in his rapid advancement, was one of Napoleon's ablest officers, civil or military. He rallied what was left of the Grand Army in February, 1813, following Murat's abdication of command. After Napoleon's downfall Eugène retired to live in Munich, under the titles of Duke of Leuchtenberg and Prince of Eichstädt. He died in 1824.

BELLUNO, Duke of. *See* VICTOR.

BERTHIER, Louis-Alexandre, PRINCE OF NEUCHÂTEL; chief-of-staff: born at Versailles, 1753. Son of an officer of the Engineers Corps. Entered the army at seventeen, after instruction by his father;

went to America with Rochambeau in 1780, and returned a colonel. Protected the aunts of Louis XVI in 1791, and aided their escape; served in the Vendée, 1793-95; general of division, Army of Italy, the year following. Thereafter Napoleon's chief-of-staff in every campaign until Fontainebleau; a marshal of the original creation; Prince of Wagram, 1809; married the King of Bavaria's niece.—With Marmont and Murat, Berthier made up the chosen three whom Napoleon met at the siege of Toulon and took to Italy with him in 1796. He abandoned the Emperor before the first abdication. The manner of Berthier's death, on June 1, 1815, is uncertain. He had gone to Bamberg at the start of the Hundred Days; and there he either was assassinated by secret agents, or threw himself from his window when he saw Cossacks on their way into France.

BESSIÈRES, Jean-Baptiste, DUKE OF ISTRIA: born near Cahors, 1768. Served first in the Constitutional Guard of Louis XVI; captain in the Italian campaign of 1796; went to Styria with Napoleon in command of the Guides, from which the Consular, later the Imperial, Guard was built up. Brilliant service with the cavalry at Marengo; general of division, 1802; marshal, 1804; at Wagram, his horse was killed under him. Replaced Bernadotte as head of the Army of the North; commanded the Guard Cavalry at Borodino and during the retreat from Russia.—Bessières was put in command of the fifteen thousand cavalry that Napoleon was able to muster in the spring of 1813. Three days after the campaign opened, he was killed by a musket-ball while reconnoitring the terrain at Posema-Rippach.

CAMBACÉRÈS, Jean-Jacques-Regis de, PRINCE OF PARMA: born at Montpellier, 1753. Descended from a well-known family, *noblesse de la robe*. Accepted the ideas of the Revolution in 1789, after progress towards the magistracy of his province; deputy to the Convention, 1792; voted the King guilty, but suggested withholding sentence; President of the Committee of Public Safety, 1795; Second Consul in 1799. Adviser in the drafting of the Napoleonic Code; helped the First Consul obtain appointment for life; disapproved of the Duke of Enghien's execution. Appointed Vicechancellor, prince of the Empire, and President of the Senate in perpetuity.—Cambacérès was renowned as much as anything else for his fine table, which Napoleon took advantage of for diplomatic purposes. After the second abdication the Duke of Parma was exiled, but afterwards regained his civil rights and lived in retirement until his death in 1824.

DAVOUT, Louis-Nicolas, PRINCE OF ECKMÜHL: born at Annoux (Yonne), 1770. Son of a nobleman. Entered the army as sub-lieutenant at eighteen; already a brigadier at the Revolution, he embraced its ideas but was removed from the active list; reinstated under the Directory; on the Rhine, 1794-97; Egypt; held command in the Consular Guard, 1801; created marshal at Napoleon's accession, and later Duke of Auerstädt for his defeat of the main Prussian Army in the battle of that name.—Davout was the strictest disciplinarian amongst the Imperial marshals, to which fact, and to the consequent employment of his corps for arduous duties, he owed his general unpopularity. After the first abdication he retired to private life. He reorganised the army for the Hundred Days, held Paris with the reserves during Waterloo, and thereafter threatened to make a campaign of his own unless the Allies signed a general amnesty. He was deprived of his titles after the amnesty was violated, but later he regained them, was admitted to the Chamber of Peers, and died in Paris in 1823.

DUROC, Géraud-Christophe-Michel, DUKE OF FRIULI: born at Pont à Mousson, 1772. Son of an army officer. Gazetted second-lieutenant of artillery, 1793; aide-de-camp to Napoleon, 1796; Italy; seriously wounded in Egypt; first aide-de-camp, 1798, and brigadier two years later. Grand Marshal of the Palace, in charge of the Household administration and of the Emperor's personal safety. Employed as diplomatist in forming the Confederation of the Rhine; Senator after the Russian campaign.—Duroc was mortally wounded at the battle of Bautzen, May 21, 1813, and died two days later in a near-by farmhouse. Napoleon bought the farm and erected a monument there. The Grand Marshal was buried in the Invalides.

ECKMÜHL, Prince of. *See* DAVOUT.

ELCHINGEN, Duke of. *See* NEY.

FRIULI, Duke of. *See* Duroc.

ISTRIA, Duke of. *See* Bessières.

JUNOT, Andoche, Duke of Abrantes: born at Bussy-le-Grand (Côte d'Or), 1771. A law student at the outbreak of the Revolution; joined a volunteer battalion; served Bonaparte as secretary during the siege of Toulon, and as aide-de-camp in Italy; gravely wounded at Lonato. Brigadier in Egypt; wounded again, in a duel on his commander's behalf; was left in Egypt to recover, and fell into British hands on his way home. General of division and Commandant of Paris; Grand Cross of the Legion of Honour when his associates became marshals. Ambassador to Lisbon; deserted his post to serve with distinction at Austerlitz; created duke for his brilliant but vain effort to seize the Portuguese fleet in 1807. Governor of Portugal; his weak administration compelled the French evacuation of that country; served under Masséna in Spain, 1810-11; seriously wounded again. Corps-commander in the Russian campaign; Governor of Illyria thereafter.—Junot is thought to have suffered from nervous instability consequent upon his first wound. His uncertain temper and his extravagance made him difficult to employ in peace-time; he was always bitterly resentful over not being made a marshal; and he was one of the few reputed lovers of Pauline Bonaparte who procured no advancement in that way. His growing derangement during the Russian campaign made a scapegoat of him, and put an end to his days of active service. On July 29, 1813, in a seizure of insanity, he threw himself from a window at Montbard.

MARET, Hugues-Bernard, Duke of Bassano: born at Dijon, 1763. An advocate and publicist. Helped to publish the debates of the First National Assembly in the *Moniteur universel;* served in Ministry for Foreign Affairs, 1792; appointed ambassador to Naples; captured by the Austrians and held prisoner for thirty months. Secretary to Napoleon, 1799, and editor of the *Moniteur;* created count, 1807, and duke, 1809. Minister for Foreign Affairs, 1811; served at Wilna as link with the home offices during the Russian campaign; again private secretary to Napoleon, 1814-15.—Maret was replaced by Caulaincourt as Secretary for Foreign Affairs, when the events of 1813 began to take shape. (The Grand Ecuyer was thought to be more devoted to the cause of peace, and more personally acceptable to the Tsar Alexander.) Following the second Bourbon restoration the Duke of Bassano retired to Grätz, where for five years he was engaged in literary work. He was made a Peer of France upon his return there in 1820, and he died in Paris in 1839.

MORTIER, Edouard-Adolphe-Casimir-Joseph, DUKE OF TREVISO: born at Château Cambrésis, 1768. Entered the army as sub-lieutenant, 1791; served in the Netherlands, and on the Meuse and Rhine, 1792-3; promoted to brigadier and the general of division for service against the Second Coalition, 1799. Commanded the French occupation of Hanover, and was made a marshal of the original creation, 1804; corps-commander in the Ulm campaign, and at Friedland; was created duke, and led two campaigns in the Peninsula, 1808-9. Led the Young Guard in Russia, and again in 1813; rejoined Napoleon after the return from Elba; was given the high command, but fell ill at the opening of the Waterloo campaign.—Mortier, after his readmission to the Chamber of Peers in 1819, served the Bourbons as ambassador to St. Petersburg, as Minister of War and as President of the Council. Along with eleven others, while in attendance upon Louis-Philippe, he was killed by a bomb-thrower's attempt to assassinate the King in Paris, July 28, 1839.

MURAT, Joachim, KING OF NAPLES: born at La Bastide-Fortunière (Lot), 1757. Younger son of an innkeeper. Obtained a bursary to study for the priesthood at Cahors, and later at Toulouse; after dissipating his allowance, he joined the cavalry; dismissed for insubordination, 1790. After various abortive efforts at a military career, he met Bonaparte in Paris, 1795; obtained the guns for the "whiff of grapeshot"; Italy, 1796; general of division, 1799, following the battle of the Pyramids; returned to France with Bonaparte; led the grenadiers into the Council of Five Hundred at Saint-Cloud, thus implementing Napoleon's coup d'état. Commandant of the Consular Guard thereafter; married Caroline Bonaparte, 1800; Governor of the Cisalpine Republic; Duke of Berg and Cleves, 1806; commanded the cavalry at Jena, Eylau, Friedland; general-in-chief in Spain, 1808, whereafter he expected to be made king there.   Became Joachim Napoleon, King of Naples, after Joseph Bonaparte's transfer to the Spanish throne; took Capri from the British.   Commanded the cavalry in Russia; was left the high command after the Emperor returned to Paris; fled to Naples in disguise, February, 1813, after his mismanagement had destroyed the remnant of the Grand Army. Made the second campaign of 1813 with Napoleon, but concluded a separate peace after Leipzig; joined the allies by treaty in 1814, in an effort to keep his throne.—Murat, who introduced shock-tactics into cavalry warfare, was one of the greatest leaders of all time in that branch.   He had a photographic eye for the contour of terrain; blunders such as that of the sunken road at Waterloo were unknown under his generalship.   In other capacities, however, he was worse than useless to Napoleon after the coup d'état.   He thought himself a statesman; he seized the occasion of the return from Elba to lead Neapolitan forces against the north of Italy, which he hoped to make into a united kingdom; and thus he provided the overt act which set the allies in motion and compelled Napoleon, who had refused his services, to undertake the Belgian campaign.   After Murat's troops had been scattered by the Austrians at Tolentino, King Joachim attempted to regain Naples, but was captured, tried by court-martial and shot, October 13, 1815.

NAPLES, King of.   *See* MURAT.

NEUCHÂTEL, Prince of.   *See* BERTHIER.

NEY, Michel, DUKE OF ELCHINGEN: born at Saarlouis, 1762.   Son of a cooper.   Enlisted in a hussar regiment at Metz, 1788; first commission, 1792; general of division, 1799.   Begged Napoleon to make himself Emperor, 1803; marshal of the original creation; commanded the Grand Army at Elchingen, where his victory insured the Austrians' surrender at Ulm, and whence his title, 1808; Jena, Eylau, Friedland; with Napoleon to Spain; Peninsular War, 1808-11.   In 1812, commanded the centre at Borodino, and was created Prince of the Moskowa that evening; in charge of the rear-guard at start and end of the retreat from Moscow.   Corps-commander in the campaign of 1813; protested devotion to the Bourbons upon Napoleon's return from Elba; was sent to bring the returning exile back to Paris "in an iron cage," but let his men go over in a body to the Imperial recruits at Grenoble; received a command on the eve of Waterloo, where he led the last charge of the Old Guard.—Ney, who received the epithet "bravest of the brave" from Napoleon himself, appears, like many others who made that campaign, to have been a little "touched" after his return from Russia. His conduct at Waterloo was most erratic. There, in the midst of the action, he beat fieldpieces with the flat of his sword. On August 5, following—his spirit broken—he allowed himself to be arrested, and demanded that his trial for treason be conducted before the Chamber of Peers. Despite the general amnesty which Davout had exacted, the younger Bourbons were determined to make an example of Ney, who had made them ridiculous at Grenoble. (Two of them were to have got credit there for Napoleon's capture, after Ney had done the work.) The Marshal-Prince of the Moskowa, sentenced to death by a body which included even a few of his former brothers-in-arms, was shot in the Luxembourg Gardens, December 7, 1815.

OUDINOT, Charles-Nicholas, DUKE OF REGGIO: born at Bar-le-duc, 1767. Son of a bourgeois family. Entered the army at seventeen, but withdrew three years later with rank of sergeant because none but a noble could go higher. Elected lieutenant-colonel, volunteers of the Meuse, 1792; brigadier, 1794; general of division and chief-of-staff, 1799; Grand Cross of the Legion of Honour when his associates were made marshals; divisional commander of grenadiers at Hollabrünn, Austerlitz, Ostrolenka, Friedland. Governor of Erfurt and count of the Empire, 1808; marshal, 1809, and Duke the year following; administrator of Holland, 1810-12; corps-commander in Russia; defeated at Gross Beeren, and afterwards superseded by Ney, in the last Napoleonic drive on Berlin.—After Fontainebleau, Oudinot stood by the Bourbon government. Louis XVIII made him a peer, and he died governor of the Invalides, September 13, 1847.

PARMA, Duke of. *See* CAMBACÉRÈS.

PONIATOWSKI, Prince Joseph: born in Warsaw, 1762. Nephew of the last King of Poland. Entered the Austrian service at sixteen;

returned to Poland and fought against the Russians in 1792; later commander-in-chief and Minister of War for the Grand Duchy of Warsaw. Organized the Polish forces for the campaign of 1812, and commanded the Fifth Corps of the Grand Army; refused all offers to desert Napoleon thereafter; made the campaign of 1813, in command of the Polish contingent.—Poniatowski had been unwilling to accept French honours, since he did not wish his countrymen to think him forgetful of their cause. Against his wishes, however, Napoleon created him a marshal of the Empire, October 16, 1813. Two days later Poniatowski, wounded in three places, was drowned while trying to swim the Elster. The Emperor, retreating from Leipzig, had left him and the Polish remnant to hold back the entire allied advance, and had blown up the bridges without waiting for him.

REGGIO, Duke of. *See* OUDINOT.

ROVIGO, Duke of. *See* SAVARY.

SAVARY, Anne-Jean-Marie, DUKE OF ROVIGO: born at Marcq in the Ardennes, 1774. Attended the College of St.-Louis at Metz; entered the army, 1790; squadron-leader, 1797; Egypt; attracted the First Consul's notice at Marengo, and thereafter was put in charge of the Consular gendarmerie. Commanded the troops at Vincennes at the Duke of Enghien's execution; general of division, 1805; ambassador to St. Petersburg, 1807, and soon after to Madrid; succeeded Fouché as Minister of Police, 1810, and as such attended to the exiling of Mme. de Staël and the destruction of her works.—Savary was Caulaincourt's predecessor at St. Petersburg. He was recalled from Russia, partly of his own motion, because the post required someone with a better knowledge of the great world. Later, he was one of the few who stayed with Napoleon at Fontainebleau, and, following the second abdication, he attempted to follow him to St. Helena. However, he was sent back from Plymouth, afterwards regained his civil rights, and died in Paris in June, 1833.

TREVISO, Duke of. *See* MORTIER.

VICEROY, the, of Italy. *See* BEAUHARNAIS.

VICTOR (né Perrin), Claude, DUKE OF BELLUNO: born at La Marche in the Vosges, 1764. Son of a process-server. Joined the army at seventeen; brigadier, 1793; was noticed by Bonaparte at Toulon; general of division, 1797; made both Italian campaigns, and commanded the vanguard in the second; distinction at Marengo. Captured in the Prussian campaign, and exchanged for Blücher at Friedland; marshal of the later creation, and Governor of Berlin after Tilsit; corps-commander in Spain with some success, but was defeated by Wellington at Talavera. Commanded the Ninth Corps in Russia, and bore the brunt at the Beresina crossing.—Victor was one of the first to go over to the Bourbons, and so was made chairman of the military commission appointed to try Ney and other recidivist officers after the Hundred Days. In 1821 he served the Bourbons as Minister of War, and in 1823 he went into Spain as second-in-command of their Peninsular expedition. Habits acquired during the great days in the Peninsula were too strong for him, however; he had to be recalled on suspicion of complicity in fraudulent contracts. Victor lived until March 1, 1841.

INDEX

INDEX

415